The Great
Victorian Sacrilege

The Great Victorian Sacrilege
Preachers, Politics and The Passion, 1879–1884

ALAN NIELSEN

McFarland & Company, Inc., Publishers
Jefferson, North Carolina, and London

> The present work is a reprint of the library bound edition of The Great Victorian Sacrilege: Preachers, Politics, and The Passion, 1879–1884, first published in 1991 by McFarland.

LIBRARY OF CONGRESS CATALOGUING-IN-PUBLICATION DATA

Nielsen, Alan, 1946–
   The great Victorian sacrilege : preachers, politics, and The Passion, 1879–1884 / Alan Nielsen.
      p.   cm.
   Includes bibliographical references and index.

   ISBN 978-0-7864-7387-8
   softcover : acid free paper ∞

   1. Morse, Salmi, 1826–1884. Passion. 2. Morse, Salmi, 1826–1884—Censorship. 3. Jesus Christ in fiction, drama, poetry, etc. 4. Theater—Censorship—United States—History—19th century. 5. Christianity and the arts—United States—History—19th century. 6. Politics and literature—United States—History—19th century. 7. Christian drama, American—History and criticism. 8. Passion-plays—History and criticism. I. Title.
PS2434.M43P336 2013
792.9′5′0973—dc20   90-53514

BRITISH LIBRARY CATALOGUING DATA ARE AVAILABLE

© 1991 Alan Nielsen. All rights reserved

No part of this book may be reproduced or transmitted in any form or by any means, electronic or mechanical, including photocopying or recording, or by any information storage and retrieval system, without permission in writing from the publisher.

On the cover: icon of Jesus (iStockphoto/Thinkstock) with *Passion* playwright Salmi Morse's head (Wikipedia commons); engraved stone (Hemera/Thinkstock)

Manufactured in the United States of America

McFarland & Company, Inc., Publishers
   Box 611, Jefferson, North Carolina 28640
   www.mcfarlandpub.com

Table of Contents

Acknowledgments vi

Preface... vii

Part One: The Passion *in San Francisco, 1879*

    Prologue: The Most Despised Human Being
    in America 3

    1. A "Wicked, Unchristian Pastime" 8
    2. Don Quixote, Munchausen, and Salmi Morse 29
    3. "A Miracle Play in Ten Acts" 50
    4. Preachers, the Press, and Politics as Usual 70
    5. *The Passion* Premieres 92
    6. "It Is the Cross Strangled by the Cross" 106

Part Two: The Passion *in New York, 1880–1884*

    7. "The Grandest Thing I Ever Listened To" ...
    "A National Disaster"........................... 125
    8. *The Mirror's* War on Mr. Abbey 146
    9. The Shrine of the Holy Passion 172
    10. *The Passion* Plays New York at Last 192
    11. The Aftermath: "Alas, Poor Yorick!"............. 208
    12. The Resurrection and Redemption of
    The Passion 222

Notes 239

Bibliography 281

Index 289

Acknowledgments

This work's completion has depended upon the kindnesses and assistance of many individuals and organizations, to whom I extend my gratitude. Among the libraries and collections consulted were the Library of Congress in Washington, D.C.; the California Historical Society, San Francisco; the San Francisco Archives and the newspaper room at the San Francisco Public Library; the Bancroft Library, University of California at Berkeley; the Billy Rose Theatre Collection of the New York Public Library at Lincoln Center, as well as that system's Main Branch Library and Newspaper Annex; the Municipal Archives of the City of New York; the New York Historical Society; the Mina Rees Library at the City University of New York; the Museum of Modern Art Film Study Center; and the Wilson Library and the Law Library at the University of Minnesota, Minneapolis.

For permissions to reproduce photographs, I would like to thank the Billy Rose Theatre Collection; the San Francisco Archives; the Bancroft Library; and the International Museum of Photography at George Eastman House, Rochester, New York.

Among the many individuals, librarians and friends who have helped along the way, I would especially like to thank Messrs. Edwin Wilson, Stanley Kauffmann and Daniel Gerould, whose critical suggestions for an earlier version of this book were of inestimable value; Ms. Judy Sheldon, formerly Principal Reference Librarian of the California Historical Society; Ms. Wendy Littlefield and Ms. Bobbie Bell, who, knowing of my research, returned from lunch at MOMA one day with a circular listing a silent-film Passion play — would that be of any interest?; Mr. Charles Silver of the MOMA Film Study Center; Mr. Robert Tuggle, Archivist, Metropolitan Opera Archives; Mr. Danny Geoly of the Eaves-Brooks Costume Company; and finally Mr. Ron Sandberg of the Dramatists Guild, and Mr. Lionel S. Sobel of the *Entertainment Law Reporter* (Santa Monica, Calif.), both of whom submitted patiently to telephone pleas from a theatre historian at sea in the intricacies of the law.

Most of all, I would like to acknowledge the assistance and support of my family, and of Mr. Charles E. Wagner, who not only helped in research, but without whose generosity I could not have completed this book.

Thank you all.

Preface

> [If] there is any principle of the Constitution that more imperatively calls for attachment than any other it is the principle of free thought—not free thought for those who agree with us but freedom for the thought we hate.
> —Justice Oliver Wendell Holmes
> *United States v. Schwimmer* (1929)

To paraphrase Justice Holmes, if there is, sixty years later, any principle of the Constitution still more problematic than any other, it is that very same principle of "freedom for the thought we hate." And for no area of American society has that freedom been more at risk than for the arts. The freedom for dramatists, filmmakers, composers, photographers and other artists to express their ideas without fear is being challenged not only by citizens and religious leaders, but increasingly by legislators determined to protect America's moral fiber by force of law.

It is a story as old as the nation itself, a story as yet without an end. And an important early struggle to vouchsafe that principle of free expression on behalf of the American stage is the subject of this volume.

I first came upon the story of Salmi Morse and *The Passion* quite by accident. While researching another project several years ago, I had occasion to consult the 1931 autobiography of the popular actor Jefferson De Angelis. De Angelis as a boy had seen the San Francisco production of Morse's drama, the first Passion play of the American professional stage; his brief, sympathetic description of it and of the incredible events that followed piqued my curiosity.

Some time later I returned to the subject. As luck would have it, the first account I read at that time was by the Victorian drama critic William Winter, and there I found a very different tale—even a different protagonist. Whereas De Angelis had presented Morse as a misunderstood genius, Winter's Morse was a misfit Jew who never seemed able to accept the fact that his play was utterly worthless. So it went through other tellings by other writer/historians—all of them relating the major events, but none really looking into the matter with much depth or seriousness. For most, it was simply a comical anecdote, an aberrant episode in the biographies of David Belasco or James O'Neill, lacking further historical significance and without contemporary resonance.

It was only when my own growing interest prompted further research that the true significance of Salmi Morse and *The Passion* began to emerge. For, whereas all of the earlier accounts examine the San Francisco events, with varying degrees of accuracy, none follows the story in detail through the New York years to its tragic conclusion. And it is in New York, where Morse fought on alone for his play in the courts, that the true import of Salmi Morse's four-year legal battle with Victorian society lies. Morse did far more than simply pen America's first professionally staged Passion play, and that is the improbable story that the following pages attempt to tell.

Ironically, during the three years it has taken to research and write this book, eerie echoes of *The Passion*'s troubles have appeared with growing frequency in the pages of my daily newspaper. Religious groups protest the film *The Last Temptation of Christ*; Iran's religious leader condemns British novelist Salman Rushdie to death for writing *The Satanic Verses*, a novel deemed offensive to Islam; the photographs of Robert Mapplethorpe and Andres Serrano are condemned as "immoral" in the houses of the United States Congress, and Senator Jesse Helms masterminds legislation forbidding the National Endowment for the Arts to fund creative projects it finds morally offensive; church and community leaders in Springfield, Missouri, attempt to suppress a local university's production of *The Normal Heart*, a play about AIDS, because they claim it "promotes homosexuality" — all of these controversies have replayed the very same art-vs.-religion battles that raged around *The Passion* one hundred years ago. Have we learned nothing? Isn't freedom for "the thought that we hate" especially vital in an age of special-interest politics? (Or has it always been that the majority of the artists who survive in any given historical era are those who know which special-interest groups *not* to offend?)

The story of *The Passion* and its suppression by the state has never been so timely. It touches upon American religious history, constitutional history, political and social history, theatre and even film history. And only by understanding the fuller contexts in which this controversy unfolded can we perhaps draw parallels to the social/political climate of today, when moralists once again claim the right to control artistic expression and suppress unpopular ideas, if not by outright censorship then by economic strangulation.

Alan Nielsen
November 1990

Part One:
The Passion in San Francisco, 1879

Prologue:
The Most Despised Human Being in America

On a cold, grey morning in late February 1884, Michael Grubey was gathering driftwood along the westernmost shore of Manhattan, beneath the high bluffs of Riverside Park near West 88th Street. This far north in 1884 the island was still relatively uninhabited, despite the building boom that had been steadily inching the city northward beyond its original boundary at Wall Street; only recently the *New York Herald* had noted, "There are many persons still living who can remember Canal street as out of town . . . and there are at present residents of Fourteenth street who were once regarded with amazement by their friends, for establishing their homes in such a remote locality."[1] But the new row houses were as yet rare commodities on West 88th, and the desolate shoreline made for excellent driftwood hunting, for those seeking fuel to help fight the February chill. One could walk along the tracks of the Hudson River Railroad at the foot of the bluffs, where, skirting the rocky shallows, the line took a northward path out of the city, parallel to the Hudson (at that point also known as the North River).

It was about 9:30 a.m. and a slight morning fog still clung to the water. As Grubey reached 88th Street, he glanced out into the river and saw what he thought was a large piece of timber, floating among the rocks a few yards offshore. A second look, and he knew that it wasn't timber: it was the body of a man, floating face up, feet toward shore, mouth open.

Dropping his load of driftwood, the excited Grubey ran hurriedly back along the tracks until he found John Nevins, a flagman for the Hudson River line. Nevins returned to the site, where he waded out to the body and secured it with a rope to a large boulder on the shore. Grubey, meanwhile, summoned a police officer, Tom O'Connor, and then went to call for a dead-wagon. Patrolman O'Connor piloted a rowboat out to the corpse and lifted it from the water; then, after going through the pockets, he rowed to 90th Street, where the dead-wagon was waiting to take the body to the city morgue.

O'Connor later told a reporter that the man's underclothes were still relatively dry, meaning that the body had probably been in the water no more than an hour or so. And a gentleman's black silk hat (containing a tract entitled "God Loves You"), found lying on the railroad track at 93rd Street, suggested that as the site from which the man jumped—or fell—or was pushed?—into the icy water.

The contents of the dead man's pockets were a pitiful lot—42 cents, some counterfeit Hebrew sheckels, a signet ring and some personal papers —but they were enough for the police to make a positive identification. The victim was a 57-year-old Jew by the name of Salmi Morse.

The police could have identified Morse even without such papers, however, for he had been for the past several years a familiar figure in the precinct houses and police courts of New York City. Salmi Morse's troubles with the law were familiar to virtually every man and woman in New York as well, since his trials had been splashily recounted in the pages of every city newspaper—had, in fact, been covered by journals all across the United States.

It can be stated without hyperbole that Salmi Morse had been for a brief time the most despised human being in America.

Yet Morse was not a mass murderer nor a corrupt politician nor even, as we would see it today, a lawbreaker.

Salmi Morse was a playwright.

His "crime" had been to write and produce America's first professionally staged biblical Passion drama, a pious and wholly reverent pageant depicting the last days on Earth—the Crucifixion, Resurrection and Ascension—of Jesus Christ. Its initial production in San Francisco in 1879 touched off what would grow to be one of the greatest moral/religious backlashes in the history of the American stage. It was an incredible saga of censorship and moral bigotry that spanned the next four years, during which time the merest rumor of the play's revival evoked immediate and vehement opposition from preachers, politicians and the press. Laws were passed banning its production. One city authority after another ruled against it. Morse was denounced by editors and ministers throughout the nation. What was worse, even the theatrical establishment actively lobbied for the play's suppression.

And, as in most such controversies, the success of the opposition has determined how the event has been remembered. Subsequent historians have dismissed the play as a minor theatrical curiosity and labeled the production a "fiasco," "disastrous," a "catastrophe." On the other hand, there are the writings of those who, having seen it, never forgot the experience. David Belasco defended *The Passion* as "holy" and "superb"; the playwright James A. Herne wrote, "I have never heard or read anything anywhere which so ennobled and dignified religion as did that play"; and the actor

Prologue: Most Despised Human Being in America 5

Salmi Morse, c. 1880. The eccentric Jewish author penned America's first professionally produced Passion play, thus setting off one of the greatest moral/legal controversies in American theatre history. His defense of the play was one of the first known instances of a playwright claiming that a play was a form of "speech" protected by the First Amendment. (Courtesy Billy Rose Theatre Collection, The New York Public Library)

Jefferson De Angelis recalled, some fifty years afterwards, "I still regard [it] as one of the greatest productions in American theatrical history."[2]

What was this controversy that could evoke such divided opinions? And why does it warrant a closer look now? From our vantage point late in the twentieth century, the deity having been portrayed onstage as everything from a Depression-era black man to a white-faced clown to a rock-and-roll superstar, the furor raised a hundred years ago over Salmi Morse's reverent, straightforward presentation seems laughably quaint and easily dismissed. But Victorian Americans saw Morse's *Passion* as anything but reverent. To them, it was a case of the church being desecrated by the stage, an outrage that must be remedied by the secular law. The story has the disconcerting feel of contemporaneity, with lawmakers deciding in favor of government censorship of the arts, with ministers decrying the "immorality" of an artist's work, with well-meaning citizens forcing the removal of that work from the public marketplace. The voices are joltingly familiar.

But Morse, too, believed in the law—enough to entrust the fate of himself and his play to the courts, time and time again. By all accounts, Morse would not have been anyone's ideal choice as martyr to the cause of freedom of speech. He was a mediocre talent at best, and except for the events surrounding *The Passion* (and the fact that several future notables were involved in the San Francisco production), he would have been as lost to us today as so many lesser playwrights of his time. As it is, even now Morse is relegated to footnote status in the biographies of others.

Yet in an age when scandals by the dozens centered on the supposed sinfulness of actors and actresses, the case of Salmi Morse was unique. Not only was the charge of "moral degeneracy" here leveled almost exclusively against a playwright (as opposed to only the actors in his play), but the "immoral" behavior for which he was accused was the very *act* of writing a play—and, paradoxically, a play of the utmost moral purity.[3]

The story of America's first professional Passion drama, then, does more than merely reflect the tenuous position in society still held by the theatre one hundred years ago. It also provides an instructive look at how Victorian America dealt with some troubling artistic/constitutional issues that continue to perplex us today: freedom of expression vs. the "public good"; the legislation of morality; censorship; the call for "moral" art; the complex and often conflicting applications of the First Amendment. And at the heart of the saga, the age-old antagonism between the church and the stage.

In all, it represents issues that we, in our modern, enlightened society, still have not resolved. In a 1987 editorial the *New York Times* rebuffed Robert Bork, the ultraconservative Reagan nominee to the Supreme Court. After duly noting the candidate's restrictive views on freedom of speech, the *Times* confidently asked its readers the rhetorical question, "What kind of ... country would this be if artistic expression were held to lack Bill of Rights safeguards?"[4] The succeeding two years have shown us just how fragile those safeguards can be: the moral/legal threats to the film *The Last Temptation of Christ*, the novel *The Satanic Verses* and the photographs of Robert Mapplethorpe seem to indicate that First Amendment protection for art that offends is still not sacrosanct in the eyes of our government.

As Salmi Morse's saga shows us, the very *idea* of First Amendment protection for artistic expression on the stage is only a twentieth-century development.

And its acceptance has been anything but easy.

1
A "Wicked, Unchristian Pastime"

I

The story of *The Passion*'s suppression is the story of collusion among an unusual triumvirate: the pulpit, politicians and the press. The ministers, powerless to legislate *The Passion* out of existence themselves, had to convince the lawmakers that it was their civic imperative to do so. The medium through which this was accomplished was the press. But the reasons why each of these disparate forces should take up the same cause with such righteous vengeance are far more complex than the simple protection of public morality.

Protestant ministers of the time were fighting to hold on to some degree of social and political control in a society heady with the advancements of industrialization and scientific inquiry; at the same time, they were also feeling threatened by a soaring Catholic immigration rate. Elected public officials feared, as they always do, the political consequences of defying "public sentiment." And the press happily exploited the controversy as a means of increasing circulation.

This is not to imply that the moral outrage expressed by so many was not sincerely felt. After all, the myth of America as a moral nation built on the teachings of Christianity was already firmly established by the late nineteenth century, and any poll of the general populace would surely have revealed the vast majority claiming themselves to be "Christians." But it is equally clear that there were other, more self-serving motivations at play in the suppression of *The Passion*. And as in any other social phenomenon, the specifics of this Victorian tempest can only be fully appreciated by putting them into some historical perspective.

The church/stage conflict triggered by *The Passion* can be traced back two hundred years, to the very founding of the American colonies. Viewed as the enemy — first by the religious, who argued that the stage was a tool of Satan designed to tempt away the faithful, then by American patriots, who saw the theatre as both a distraction and a too-potent symbol of the hated British — the hapless acting companies attempting to find a home in

1. A "Wicked, Unchristian Pastime"

the New World found themselves instead hounded and harassed from colony to colony. Finally, during the Revolutionary War, they were banned outright by the Continental Congress. The restrictions imposed on the earliest theatrical managers in America were thus from the beginning both religious *and* political in nature; and when the moral idealism of the former was wedded to the legal powers of the latter—as was the case in every one of the first American colonies—it represented an antitheatrical bias that has affected attitudes toward the stage in this country down to the present day.

In order to better understand how the suppression of *The Passion* fit into this tradition of moral/legal controls on theatre in America, it is important to reexamine the historical relationships in this country between the Theatre and the Church, and the Theatre and the Law.

II

The Theatre and the Church

In the beginning, to speak of the church was, in effect, to speak of the law. Even those colonial settlements not associated with a specific religious sect—such as Jamestown, founded in 1607 purely as a money-making venture—eventually professed fealty to some organized religion. Thus Jamestown, as a Royal colony, came to support the Church of England. In fact, by 1758, with the formal establishment of Anglicanism in Georgia, the Church of England was the officially recognized religion throughout the colonial South.[1]

To the north, the Dutch colony of New Amsterdam originally recognized the Dutch Reformed Church, but when the British took control in 1664 and renamed it New York, that colony, too, officially embraced the Church of England. Maryland had been chartered as a refuge for Catholics; William Penn's "holy experiment," Pennsylvania, was in the hands of the Quakers; and New England had been controlled by the Puritans since its founding in 1620. Providence, Rhode Island, was begun when Roger Williams was banished from Massachusetts in 1636—but while it was Williams's stated goal to found the first colony embracing complete religious freedom of conscience, he himself was such an ultra-Puritan purist that he, too, as one historian put it, "attempted to exercise a moral influence over social affairs" in Providence.[2]

So, in the broadest sense, the first American colonies were indeed, as many modern ministers would have it, founded on the Word of God. The problem was that they were not the *same* "Word of God." Even worse, the legal establishment of these different official religions led to political consequences that were decidedly undemocratic — in some cases downright unchristian.

In Virginia it was a crime to support or maintain any religion other than the Church of England. By law, tax monies were allocated to Anglican churches and parents were required to baptize their children in that faith, while other believers — especially Quakers — were ordered imprisoned "till they should abjure the country." Similar imprisonment awaited them should they return, and if they were foolish enough to visit the Old Dominion a third time, they were to be put to death.[3] For their part, the Quakers in Pennsylvania were somewhat less violent in their attitudes toward non-Quakers in their midst. Nevertheless, they, too, expected all visitors to observe the Friends' standards of morality and virtue. This meant that when those standards of morality were violated by a nonbeliever, it was the Quakers who took the necessary (and legally sanctioned) disciplinary action.[4]

Of course, the apotheosis of religious/legal partnerships was found in Puritan New England, where any nonconformity, theological or social, was dealt with swiftly and severely by the civil authorities, whose punishments, it was believed, had been sanctioned by the Almighty Himself. Following this reasoning, when the colony expelled Anne Hutchinson and she was subsequently slaughtered by Indians, the Puritans could see the bloody deed as "divine confirmation of the community's sentence."[5] It goes without saying that the Puritans, too, decreed harsh penalties for members of any faith other than their own. As Gore Vidal once oversimplified it, the Puritans left Europe "not because they were persecuted for their beliefs but because they were forbidden to persecute others for their beliefs."[6]

Yet perhaps no other religious group in our history has had as far-reaching an effect on the American imagination as have the Puritans. Across the decades, moral reformers of every stripe have harkened back to this band of New England dissidents to support the claim that America was founded on religious freedom and Christian — or, more precisely, on *Protestant* Christian — principles. Glorification of the "Puritan ethic" has never lost its vogue. Today's conservative fundamentalists still stoutly aver, as does Jerry Falwell in *Listen, America!* (1980), that "the foundation of our government, our laws, our statutes, our civilization, the structures of our homes, our states, and our churches have come from the Word of God."[7] This "Sunday-school picture of the pilgrims getting off the boats all dressed up for Thanksgiving" is, Perry Deane Young points out, "such a neat and tidy image, we seem to have adopted it as a metaphor for the settling of the whole country rather than of one tiny region of the North by a very unusual group of immigrants."[8] But such is the romance of the ascetic Puritan image.

In sum, it might be said, in the simplest terms, that by the latter half

1. A "Wicked, Unchristian Pastime"

of the seventeenth century, North America was a checkerboard of isolated colonies, theologically diverse and spiritually divided. There was, it seemed, only one important area in which all of the various Protestant sects were agreed: they all hated Catholics.

A religious body holding power in any given colony maintained its power chiefly by outlawing every other religious body. It did this by passing legislation that turned its own moral prejudices into law. The concept was simple, the ramifications profound. As the legal writer David H. Flaherty succinctly puts it: "The essential contribution of the moral law to the secular law was the equation of sin with crime." That phrase is worth reading again: "The equation of sin with crime." It was a philosophical concept that had been growing since the Middle Ages, and by the seventeenth century, Flaherty notes, the idea had taken root deeply enough that, for many religious theorists, "it was not possible for the divine and secular laws to contradict one another." The moral law, what Calvin called "the law of God," could thus become the basis for the civil law itself.[9]

Unfortunately for the theatre, this meant that the church's rabid hatred of the stage would find its way into colonial lawbooks everywhere. This equation provided inarguable logic for seventeenth-century American clergymen, who could keep their parishioners out of the playhouse by preaching that the theatre was criminal because it was immoral. Moreover, this argument worked just as well in reverse: theatre *must* be immoral— after all, it was against the law.

Religious condemnation of the stage did not simply spring into being in America for no reason, of course. Colonial Protestants had been nurtured in this prejudice long before they embarked from Europe's shores in the 1600s. Attacks on the theatre in England had been ongoing since 1575, from polemicists such as John Northbrooke (*A Treatise wherein Dicing, Daucing, Vaine Plaies or Enterludes ... are reproved*, 1579); Stephen Gossen (*Plays Confuted in Five Actions*, 1582); Phillip Stubbes (*Anatomy of the Abuses in England in Shakspere's Youth*, 1583); and William Perkins (*The Whole Treatise of the Cases of Conscience*, 1608), among others. The culmination of these broadsides had come in 1633, with *Histriomastix*, by William Prynne, which Jonas Barish in *The Antitheatrical Prejudice* (1981) calls "a gargantuan encyclopedia of antitheatrical lore which scourges every form of theater in the most ferocious terms." Prynne's "catalogue of horrors" demonstrates the Puritans' astonishingly wide array of "criminal" sins:

> ... effeminate mixt Dancing, Dicing, Stage-playes, lascivious Pictures, wanton Fashions, Face-painting, health-drinking, Long haire, Love-locks, Periwigs, womens curling, pouldring and cutting of their haire, Bone-fires, New-yeares-gifts, May-games, amorous Pastoralls,

> lascivious effeminate Musicke, excessive laughter, luxurious disorderly Christmas-keeping, Mummeries,... [all] wicked, unchristian pastimes.[10]

Prynne seems, in Barish's opinion, fearful of anything "that might suggest active or interested sexuality."

A far more important element in Prynne's attacks, however — one which stretches even further that early Puritan equation of "sin" with "crime" — is the fact that not only are plays and players sinful, but so are those who watch them. Playgoers themselves, says Prynne, are "*Adulterers, Adulteresses, Whoremasters, Whores, Bawdes, Panders, Ruffians, Roarers, Drunkards, Prodigals, Cheaters, idle, infamous, base, prophane, and godlesse persons, who hate all grace, all goodnesse, and make a mocke of piety*"[11] [his emphasis]. No wonder his God-fearing readers feared the stage! To see a sin — or even to imagine it — is to participate in it. Such a view makes theatre, in effect, doubly sinful.

Barish points out that Prynne's "overloaded and hyperthyroid" diatribe was in no way unique, but merely raised "to fever pitch themes already familiar in pulpit and pamphlet for over a generation."[12] The climax of this moral backlash in England had resulted in the closing of the theatres in 1642, and it is important to bear in mind that this was also the period during which the Great Migration to America was at its peak. Those thousands of Puritans leaving an England in which the theatres had already been closed were all the more predisposed to keep the immoral stage from ever gaining entrance into their pristine New World.

It should also be noted that the Puritans' restrictive world view conformed as well to the religious sentiments of every other major religious sect in power in colonial America — including the Anglicans. Flaherty finds that "there is hardly a specified moral offense in New England that did not have its counterpart in the criminal code of Virginia in the seventeenth century," and he quotes Crane Brinton's observation that "Puritanism as a moral ideal and as a way of life is broader than any theology."[13] It is not surprising, therefore, to find moralistic prejudice against the theatre also manifested in every colony, regardless of its religious ethic. Nor is it insignificant that the first recorded proceeding undertaken against a theatrical performance in America occurred not in strict, conservative Puritan Massachusetts, but in the more liberal Anglican Virginia (which had no laws banning the theatre). When William Darby, Cornelius Watkinson and Phillip Howard were arrested for presenting some sort of dramatic entertainment in Accomac County, Virginia, in 1665 — the first documented theatrical event in America — the charge sworn out against them by their offended neighbor John Martin was "indecent conduct."[14]

III

So long as power in the respective colonies resided with the church, the legal suppression of the stage was accomplished with little or no opposition. Indeed, since the entire community was theoretically of the same mind, specific antitheatre laws were not even felt to be necessary — in some colonies, at least — until the spectre of an actual theatrical performance, no matter hcw crude, reared its sinful head. Then the magistrates were quick to act. This explains how Massachusetts could manage to successfully discourage the drama without having to actually suppress it by law until as late as 1749.[15]

In many other colonies, however, the authorities took no chances: antitheatre legislation was included in their earliest bodies of laws, even though the threat of such an "impropriety" was, to say the least, remote. William Penn, in his original Great Law — adopted by the Pennsylvania Assembly in 1682, the year of the colony's founding — wrote wide-ranging provisions banning "rude and riotous sports," including "stage-plays, masques, [and] revels."[16] North and South Carolina and Georgia had similar measures in their legal codes. Of the original thirteen colonies, only Virginia and Maryland passed no laws regulating the stage.[17]

All of this interest and fear in regard to the theatre seems excessive, considering the primitive conditions of colonial life in the 1600s. After all, how many colonists really had time to think about a neighborhood playhouse, when basic survival demanded all of their time and energy? Yet the laws were there, and remained in place long after the church had lost its power to make public policy; and as a result, the attitude that decreed the stage to be somehow morally suspect would never quite be excised from the American subconscious.

If evidence is extremely sketchy as to whether or not there was much theatrical activity attempted during this early period, it is generally accepted that no true, full-time professional acting company successfully toured the colonies until the Hallam troupe, in the mid–1700s.[18] By then, several factors were coming into play that would lead to a change in the political fortunes of the established churches, and ultimately result in their official removal from the civil affairs of the state.

The most important of these factors was the gradual secularization of colonial society. The trend away from separate religion-based communities toward a network of trade-based states could be seen even before the end of the 1600s. Ship-building and whaling were well-established in New England, while Virginia, Maryland and Carolina had grown dependent on the plantation system. The inevitable result of this subtle but fundamental shift was the rise of a new merchant middle class, whose view of society was determined more by economics than by religion. Concurrent with the emergence of this American bourgeoisie came the rise in popularity of newer, more intellectual philosophical creeds, such as deism, rationalism, and especially the American Enlightenment.

But there were counterdevelopments taking place in the religious life of the country as well, trends which, while they also contributed to the erosion of power in the monolithic established Protestant churches, nonetheless, in the long run, reinforced and perpetuated many of the old moral prejudices—including those against the stage. One of these developments was the loss of religious exclusivity long enjoyed by the old colony-supported faiths. During the latter 1600s, an influx of immigrants brought European Baptists, Presbyterians, Lutherans and Catholics, among others, into the respective citadels of the Congregationalists, Quakers and Anglicans. The scope of this influx can be seen in Daniel R. Ernst's observation that "in 1650, only four colonies had two or more denominations; by 1750 *all* colonies had at least three denominations, while New Jersey, Pennsylvania, and South Carolina had seven and New York had eight."[19] Not surprisingly, these new outsider religions gradually began agitating for a little influence of their own.

Actually, their chance to claim a part of the pastoral pie came as early as the late 1720s, when the worldwide revivalist movement known as the Great Awakening reached the shores of America from Europe. Beginning with localized revivals in New Jersey and Pennsylvania, the Awakening's cry for moral regeneration quickly spread. Over the next fifteen years, this extraordinary prairie fire of religious fervor swept the colonies, fueled by the evangelistic tour of the English Anglican priest George Whitefield, from 1739 to 1741. Significantly, the groups who immediately grasped—and turned to their own advantage—the importance of this grassroots fundamentalist movement were not the established powers, who all but ignored it, but the so-called "dissident sects"—most notably the Baptists, Calvinists and Presbyterians—whose Protestant evangelical leaders took control of the tent meetings being held at the edge of town. The result was, in effect, a religious revolution. In the South, especially, according to Leigh Eric Schmidt, "by the 1770s the Baptists had taken over [many counties], shifting the locus of political and religious authority from the gentry's courthouse and their [Anglican] parish church to the Baptist meetinghouse."[20]

Over the next century and a half, there would be a gradual but complete turnaround in the dominant religions in America, with the long-legally established colonial churches—Congregationalist, Anglican, Quaker—declining, and the sects that had never had state support—Baptist, Methodist, Catholic, etc.—usurping the throne. It is ironic to note that the faiths that have come to dominate twentieth-century American society and politics (and that now enjoy their own political protections), owe their current positions of power and influence to the separation of church and state that decreed the *dis*establishment of their old religious overlords.

This shift in ecclesiastical power did not mean an end to religious opposition to the theatre, however. The rising order was just as prohibitive — in some cases more so — than the old.[21] For they were fighting an America that was, despite their preachments, becoming increasingly industrialized and democratized. The new fundamentalists were determined to hold back the tide of change with every possible means — especially the law. The petitions and letter-writing campaigns organized in every colonial city to protest appearances by a now-growing number of itinerant acting companies well attest to the continuing animosity toward the stage maintained by local moral forces, and reveal a still-held belief that it should be within religion's power to affect civil legislation, when its members perceive that certain freedoms have gone too far. New Yorkers mounted such antitheatre campaigns in 1753, '58, '61 and '66. Likewise, Quakers and their supporters in Philadelphia led protests in 1752, '54, '59, '66, '67, '70 and '72.[22] These actions were not always successful in preventing the scheduled performances from taking place, but the point is that moral objections to the stage did not die out as society became more secular.

It is possible that religionists continued battling the theatre because the stage was an enemy that could still be defeated. For the church was finding far less success in other, more important arenas. Despite the residual power wielded by organized religion in the eighteenth century, the secular influence of the Enlightenment on the colonial intelligentsia was having greater impact on the evolving structure of our federal government. Inspired by Locke and other European humanists, colonial leaders such as Jefferson, Madison and Paine began arguing *against* the granting of legal powers to the church. Jefferson forcefully wrote of the "natural," as opposed to "God-given," rights of man. Indeed, in much of his work, he carefully referred to a "Creator," rather than to "God," and denounced "that religious slavery under which a people have been willing to remain." "The legitimate powers of government extend to such acts only as are injurious to others," he wrote. "But it does me no injury for my neighbor to say there are twenty gods, or no God. It neither picks my pocket nor breaks my leg."[23] His philosophy ultimately led him to pen Virginia's "Act for Establishing Religious Freedom" (1779), in which it was decreed that "no man shall be compelled to frequent or support any religious worship, place or ministry whatsoever,... nor shall [he] otherwise suffer on account of his religious opinions or belief." Denouncing "the impious presumption of legislators and rulers, civil as well as ecclesiastical," who had "assumed dominion over the faith of others," Jefferson declared that our civil rights have no dependence on our religious opinions, more than our opinions in physics or geometry;... therefore, the proscribing any citizen as unworthy the public confidence ... unless he profess or renounce this or that religious opinion, is depriving him injuriously of those privileges and advantages to which in common with his fellow citizens he has a natural right....[24]

This was the complete antithesis of the foundation on which every colony in America had been operating in the 1600s.

The final separation of church and state came with the new Constitution, which should have left little doubt as to the role that organized religion was to play in the new United States of America, as envisioned by its Congress: the document contained not one single reference to God, and Article VI specifically stated that "no religious Test shall ever be required as a Qualification to any Office or public Trust under the United States." Full separation of theologian from lawmaker, however, had to wait for the First Amendment, ratified in 1791: "Congress shall make no law respecting an establishment of religion, or prohibiting the free exercise thereof."[25]

The movement toward disestablishment had actually begun as early as 1777, when New York had stopped giving state support to the Anglican Church. But in other states the old religious/legal partnership died more slowly. It took, in fact, *another forty years* after the ratification of the Bill of Rights for the separation of church and state to be fully completed in the United States. Nor should it come as any surprise that the last such church/state union to be dissolved was the Congregational Church in Massachusetts, which stopped receiving tax monies only in 1833.[26]

IV

The Theatre and the Law

Despite the decline in influence of the established churches around the time of the Revolution, and despite the Enlightenment values that so determined the course of Revolutionary American political theory, hostility toward the theatre remained strong in many colonies, and opponents of the stage remained determined to legislate its progress. But, as befit the economic and social upheavals that preceded the war and unseated the church, the objections against the boards underwent a significant change: the cry became less and less "sin" and more and more "dissipation." If those arguing the former willingly aligned themselves with those who argued the latter, it only made the outcry that much louder. The rebel New York Sons of Liberty, for example, countenanced the Chapel Street Riot in 1766, in which the Chapel Street Theatre was torn apart board by board by an

1. A "Wicked, Unchristian Pastime" 17

angry mob. They excused the rioting with the observation that, at a time when money was so badly needed for the payment of debts, the theatre was an "unnecessary extravagance." Ten years later, with the political/economic crises in the colonies nearing the breaking point, such sentiments were being expressed on the official governmental level. In Charleston, South Carolina, in 1774, a grand jury considered a resolution denouncing the stage as "unfit for the present low Estate of the Province."[27]

It must be admitted that the theatre itself had been responsible for much of this nonsectarian resentment. Opponents were not without cause in charging the stage with fostering immoral behavior: it is abundantly clear that the galleries in many colonial auditoriums were, in Hugh F. Rankin's words, "the province of the less genteel element . . . and, eventually, a market place where women of easy virtue solicited their customers."[28] Nor is it hard to see why many citizens found fault with the plays themselves, for, according to the diary of Moreau de St. Mery, a Frenchman visiting postwar Philadelphia, plays were frequently bawdy, with "such words as Goddamn, Bastard, Rascal, Son of a Bitch. Women turn their backs to the performance during these interludes."[29]

In a calculated bid to upgrade their image, colonial theatre owners had turned for patronage and support to the wealthier classes, who both had the money for playgoing and were less inclined to be swayed by church prohibitions. But with the onset of hard times in the mid-1770s, that reliance began to prove counterproductive. The Gentlemen and their Ladies came to represent for many a sort of American aristocracy—exactly what the rebels were trying to rid themselves of—among whose most visible symbols was the opulent, extravagant playhouse. Thus the newer charge, of "dissipation."

The stage had always been seen by many colonists as a British affectation, anyway. Moreover, it certainly didn't help to have the Crown's armies, whose numbers swelled ominously during the 1760s and early '70s, ignoring public sentiment and staging amateur theatricals wherever they were quartered. Typical was a regiment based in Albany that produced *The Beaux' Stratagem* and *The Recruiting Officer* in 1760—almost a decade before any other theatre was allowed in that city.[30]

In increasingly troubled times, it was a new kind of prejudice that began to express itself, a prejudice the champions of the stage were ill-prepared to meet. David Douglass, who succeeded the elder Hallam, changed the name of the troupe from the London Company to the American Company,[31] and even added patriotic songs to the repertoire, but such steps were not enough. Generations-old religious hatred now joined with economic resentment of a perceived upper-class luxury, to create an antitheatrical sentiment that could be subscribed to by pietist and patriot alike.

On October 20, 1774, fifty-three members of the First Continental

Congress, meeting in Philadelphia to find a way of forcing England to "redress" the colonies' grievances, signed a petition calling for "a non-importation, non-consumption, and non-exportation agreement." The eighth of its fourteen provisions read, in total:

> Eighth, We will, in our several stations, encourage frugality, oeconomy, and industry, and promote agriculture, arts and the manufactures of this country, especially that of wool; and will discountenance and discourage every species of extravagance and dissipation, especially all horse-racing, and all kinds of gaming, cock fighting, exhibitions of shews, plays and other expensive diversions and entertainments; and on the death of any relation or friend, none of us, or any of our families will go into any further mourning-dress, than a black crape or ribbon on the arm or hat, for gentlemen, and a black ribbon or necklace for ladies, and we will discontinue the giving of gloves and scarves at funerals.[32]

What the moralists had been unable to accomplish for religious reasons — the colony-wide closing of the theatres — Congress had now presented them for its own mundane political ends.

V

Why the church should so zealously oppose the theatre is, perhaps, understandable; why the *state* should collaborate in its banishment for so many years, especially after religion had lost its singular power to dictate laws, requires more explanation than a simple bowing to a few petitions. A large part of that explanation has to do with control. Given the excesses exhibited by certain of the rowdier patrons of colonial theatres, and given the violent zeal demonstrated by certain members of God's Army, it simply became easier for secular law-enforcement officials, who had no strong *legal* interest in banning theatres, to maintain law and order by enforcing those proscriptions already in place, proscriptions based on earlier *moral* arguments. As Flaherty writes,

> The motivations for the enactment of moral regulations did not remain uncontaminated by baser considerations.... [M]any moral offenses were punished not simply because they were immoral but because they caused social problems and disturbances as well.... The prosecution of moral offenders allegedly helped to avert various social and economic ills.[33]

Thus, the many "public nuisance" ordinances and "Sunday Blue Laws" — many aimed specifically at restricting theatrical performances — passed originally for the protection of community morals, were allowed to remain on the books for so many years for the sake of civil control.

1. A "Wicked, Unchristian Pastime"

In the case of the ban enacted by the First Continental Congress in 1774, it is interesting to note that the clause in question banned all "shews, plays, and other expensive diversions and entertainments," and yet at the same time promised to promote all native "arts." Patricians such as Jefferson constantly championed "the arts" in America, whose object, said Jefferson, "is to improve the taste of my countrymen, to increase their reputation, to reconcile to them the respect of the world, and to procure them its praise."[34] But the "arts" in question were invariably those endeavors that could be enjoyed by a gentleman dilettante: painting, poetry, music, architecture. Although Douglass, following a long-held practice in the English theatre, had allowed gentlemen to perform in selected vanity productions, the theatre was by far too complex and collaborative a medium to become practicable for even the most talented amateur. Add to this the long-held prejudice against actors ("the very offals of society," huffed the Reverend Timothy Dwight of Yale; the stage was "the sure path to shame and disgrace, and the common landing-place of the clever reprobate"[35]), and it is not difficult to understand why no one at the time considered the professional theatre a legitimate art but only a crass, commercial enterprise. It also helps explain why, during the entire Revolutionary War period, when some of the best-educated, most sophisticated political thinkers this country has ever produced were arguing the far-reaching principles of the Constitution, including the First Amendment, the theatre was not considered important or vital enough to warrant the same protections as the press or public speech. (Or, for that matter, religion.)

But then, suppression of the stage did not have nearly the immediacy that suppression of the press had at that particular moment. Indeed, government suppression of newspapers and censorship of books had been a sore issue in America almost from the start. The first public burning of a book took place in Boston in 1650; Boston authorities also had the honor of suppressing the first attempt at a colonial newspaper, some forty years later.[36] Over the years, and through many subsequent, similar episodes, resentment toward government and religious censorship of ideas gradually gained popular momentum. Whereas the 16-year-old Benjamin Franklin in 1722 had been taking a chance in promoting in the pages of his elder brother's newspaper the concept of freedom of press, speech and thought, almost seventy years later—in 1791, when it was incorporated into law as the First Amendment—this tenet of free speech had bloomed into a "fundamental right." Of course, it was, for many of the amendment's Framers, in their own self-interest to argue freedom of speech as a fundamental right: their own free speaking had put their very lives in jeopardy from the Crown.

Yet for those same Framers, the thinking seems to have been that only public speeches, political tracts and newspapers held any ideas of worth.

Even then, the amendment guaranteeing their protection almost never made it into the Constitution: why bother to write a law protecting "fundamental" rights? You might as well put into law, the argument went, that a citizen "has the right to go to bed when he feels like it and to wear his hat when he feels like it."[37] But James Madison, among others, countered that "the great rights," such as freedom of speech and of the press, had to be free of *any* kind of intervention — whether from government or, when necessary, from the tyranny of "shifting popular tides." "In this new America," Nat Hentoff has written, "Madison reemphasized [that] the greatest danger to liberty is to be found 'in the body of the people, operating by the majority against the minority.' The minority, even of one, must have its liberty protected."[38]

The theatre, of course, had already been the victim of such majority censorship for over a hundred years. But at that time, the minority in question was perceived to be the press, public speakers, and pamphleteers. Plays — or, for that matter, novels — would not be routinely defended under the First Amendment until the twentieth century, although Salmi Morse, as we shall see, would be among the first to try and claim such protection for a stage work.[39]

VI

What makes the First Amendment's implied position with regard to the theatre so ironic is the fact that the plays being written during the Revolution — and there were many — were, almost without exception, being written to express political points of view. From 1773 to 1783, at least thirteen propaganda plays and dialogues, what Norman Philbrick calls "alarms and excursions in dramatic form," were published in America.[40] *A Dialogue Between a Southern Delegate and His Spouse on His Return from the Grand Continental Congress* (Anonymous, 1774), *Americans Roused in a Cure for the Spleen* (Anonymous, 1775), General Burgoyne's notorious *The Blockade* (performed in Boston in 1775) and *The Battle of Brooklyn* (Anonymous, 1776) all defended the pro–British attitudes of the Tories. Mrs. Mercy Otis Warren's *The Adulator* (1773), on the other hand, as well as her second effort, *The Group* (1775), attacked real-life Massachusetts Tories for working against the colonists' cause. While it is possible that neither of her plays was performed (the title page of *The Group* reads, "As lately acted"), both were widely circulated in printed form. Hugh Brackenridge's 1776 verse play *The Battle of Bunkers Hill*, and *Bunker-Hill or, The Death of General Warren* by John Daly Burk (1797) both celebrated the important battle of 1775 (Brackenridge's play within one year of the battle itself!), while *The Fall of British Tyranny or, American Liberty Triumphant*

(1776, attributed to John Leacock) may have been both the earliest American chronicle play and the first to portray George Washington on stage.[41] All of these pro-patriot plays glorified, like Burk's *Bunker-Hill*, such blatantly political concepts as "freedom," "sacred rights," "pure republic," "proud democracy," "equal laws," while denouncing the evils of "tyrants," "despotism," "thrones," "bondage," and "lawless power." Whether or not these various works were actually staged, intellectuals and writers were using the dramatic form to debate the major social and political issues of the day.

Why, then, was the theatre perceived to be nothing but an "expensive diversion," an "extravagance and dissipation" to be cavalierly closed by law of Congress?

To begin with, the practice of theatre was conveniently separated from the writing of plays, thus allowing colonists to make a very fine distinction between the "Stage" and the "Drama." No one—not even those who plied it as their trade—was able to successfully defend the "Stage" as a forum for thought, for the examination of current social questions, or personal expression, or simply for political propaganda.[42] If anyone did take such a stand, his voice was lost in the overwhelming flood of pulpit rhetoric and editorial posturing that limited the issue to questions of morality and or public welfare. Therefore, to even its staunchest supporters, the theatre was at best a school for teaching morals, at worst a purveyor of harmless entertainment. The notion of the "Stage" as a form of speech whose freedom should also be protected simply never became an integral part of the debate. It was an easy thing, then, intellectually, to justify the banning of the "Stage."

But the "Drama"—published volumes of classic plays—was to be found in the libraries of a majority of the Revolution's leaders, many of whom considered a knowledge of dramatic literature essential to a well-rounded gentleman's education. Thomas Jefferson, when asked in 1771 to recommend a list of books for a basic library, included plays by Shakespeare, Steele, Congreve, Addison and Molière, as well as works by the Greek and Roman playwrights.[43]

Then, too, colonial colleges and universities helped foster this intellectual separation by using the dramatic form, under the guise of "college dialogues," to hone the oratorical skills of future lawyers, preachers and politicians. While most of these dialogues were just that—specially composed two- or three-character debates in dramatic form—many of the presentations were more ambitious, not only turning to the "Drama" for models, but even, in some instances, for the material itself. Theatrical standards, from *Tamerlane* (Nicholas Rowe's 1702 adaptation of Marlowe) and *The Rival Queens* to popular works such as *Cato* and *The Drummer*, are to be found in the "dialogues" presented by various colonial colleges during the eighteenth century.[44]

However, it should also be noted that most college officials were quick to condemn any "dialogue" that crossed over the boundaries into "theatre," as evidenced by a Yale faculty memorandum from 1756 that chastised some students for enacting a "play" at "the house of William Lyon": "whereas this practice is of a very pernicious nature, tending to corrupt the morals of the seminary of religion and learning, and of mankind in general, and to the mispence of precious time and money,...." etc.[45] What was instructive as a "dialogue" was *de*structive as a "play."

Even more telling is the fact that from the very first the Hallam/Douglass troupe had been staging many of those same works recommended in Jefferson's basic library. Shakespeare's *Merchant of Venice* had been Hallam's inaugural production in America, on September 5, 1752. The company also offered *Henry IV*, *Hamlet*, *The Merry Wives of Windsor*, *Richard III*, *King Lear*, *Romeo and Juliet* and *Othello*. Congreve's *Love for Love*, Steele's *The Conscious Lovers*, Addison's *Cato* and *The Drummer*, *The Beggar's Opera* by Gay, as well as Farquhar's *The Recruiting Officer* and *The Beaux' Stratagem* — all are found in the American Company's repertoire, along with the more vulgar popular farces and artificial comedies that provided easy fodder for pulpit and editorial page. In fact, the only names from Jefferson's list not represented were Molière and the Greek and Roman dramatists.

Still, it is clear that such a compartmentalizing attitude toward the theatre was common, and sometimes led to moral stands that could only be called hypocritical. The Massachusetts lawyer and Revolutionary patriot Josiah Quincy wrote in his *Journal*, May 11, 1773:

> Went to the playhouse [in New York City]... I was ... much gratified upon the whole, and I believe if I had staid in town a month, I should go to the theatre every acting night. But as a citizen and friend to the morals and happiness of society, I should strive hard against the admission, and much more the establishment of a play-house in any state of which I was a member.[46]

This double standard could also explain why that incurable theatre-lover and -patron, George Washington, who was a delegate to the First Continental Congress, could have subscribed without argument to the Congressional act that closed his beloved playhouses for the duration.[47]

It might be argued that the 1774 Congressional act was merely a "catch-all" provision, the kind of legislation often passed during wartime in order to deal with minor problems by temporarily putting them aside altogether. Witness that the act also prohibited other "extravagances," including such inconsequential items as funeral wear. In that case, any antitheatre sentiments should not be given too much importance.

The only problem with such a view is that it ignores how those most

1. A "Wicked, Unchristian Pastime"

concerned at the time reacted to the closing of the theatres. Douglass took it seriously enough to leave the country with his company, to weather the war in the English West Indies. Moreover, as the law proved insufficient to stop all theatre activity in the colonies, Congress did not hesitate to pass two *more* provisions outlawing theatre during the course of the war.[48] Clearly, antitheatre sentiment was not of minor import among colonial representatives.

A still better indication that Congress was serious about suppressing the stage is the fact that no other art form was included in its condemnation. Neither musicians nor popular authors nor poets nor visual artists were suppressed during the war years; only stage performers—and cockfighters—were forbidden access to the public.

This is no small distinction, for the other arts, especially music, had developed relatively unhindered in the colonies, and had always enjoyed wide popularity. Music had not only been tolerated but encouraged by the Puritans. Massachusetts may have had the dubious honor of seeing the first book burned in America, but it was also the site of the first book *printed* in America; and that very first book was a volume of music: *The Bay Psalm Book* (1640).[49]

Despite the grumblings of a few church conservatives who objected to music performed by "sinful men," by the end of the seventeenth century musicians enjoyed a position in America that actors could only envy. Francis Hopkinson is a case in point. One of the first native American composers, Hopkinson moved among a group of gentlemen amateurs active in the musical life of Philadelphia in the mid-1700s. It will also be remembered that he was one of the original signers of the Declaration of Independence (written by an amateur violinist). This would certainly indicate that musicians were not considered the "offals of society."

In fact, the degree of colonial interest in music was high enough to warrant more than 370 tunebooks being published before 1811.[50] Public concerts of Baroque masterworks began to be heard as early as 1726.[51] In the very decades that Bach, Handel, Vivaldi, Scarlatti, Haydn and Mozart were writing in Europe, their music was being performed professionally in the American colonies. "Whatever cultural lag America may have suffered in other respects," writes Julian Mates, "as far as the orchestra was concerned there was none at all." As proof, he points out that Handel's *Messiah* was heard in New York in 1770, one year before it was performed in the composer's native Germany.[52]

Painters, while they did not enjoy the same high public recognition as composers, nonetheless moved in comparable social circles. As opposed to actors, who were universally shunned during this period, or musicians and poets, who were respected and even emulated by amateur talents, painters seemed to be alien beings, objects of a kind of admiring bewilderment.

Their status as "artists" somehow put them beyond the rules applied to everyone else. Benjamin West, John Singleton Copley and other American artists living or studying in Europe when the war broke out, spent those years safely painting in London. Copley even sent for his wife and family when hostilities began. Yet, after the war, Americans surprisingly overlooked what must have seemed to many cowardice. According to the historian Page Smith:

> Regardless of the fact that West and Copley resided in England, Americans claimed them as their own and constantly put them forward as evidence that the United States excelled in art as well as politics. The editor of the *Massachusetts Centinel* [sic] declared: "While we boast a *Washington*, as the great master of the art of war—a *Franklin* the chief of Philosophers—an *Adams*, and an infinitude of others, as statesmen and politicians whose abilities have been acknowledged throughout the civilized world; America may pride herself in giving birth to the most celebrated Artists of the present age."[53]

Needless to say, America was not quite so forgiving of the actors of the old American Company, when they decided to return from the West Indies shortly after the war.

VII

Many chroniclers begin the history of the American theatre after the Revolutionary War, and indeed that period could be viewed as the true beginning rather than a building on what had gone before. That is not to negate the struggles of the prewar pioneers nor to underestimate what progress they did make; rather, it is to admit how effective were the campaigns of the church in the seventeenth and eighteenth centuries, and how destructive the Congressional resolution of 1774.

When Lewis Hallam, Jr., and several actors from the old Hallam/Douglass troupe ventured back to the newly formed United States of America in 1785, the situation here was not all that different from that which had greeted Hallam's father thirty years before. As far as the stage was concerned, it was almost as if the country had reverted to the days of the seventeenth-century religious colonies: the wartime laws banishing theatre, passed by most states in emulation of the 1774 Continental Congress, were still in effect; Massachusetts had the year before extended its Act of 1750 for another fifteen years; Pennsylvania would replace its 1779 law in '86 with a similarly harsh "Act for the Prevention of Vice and Immorality and Unlawful Gaming and to Restrain Disorderly Sports and Dissipation." The New York City Common Council was still "discountenancing" plays, and where theatre was not banned outright by law, it was severely limited by other legal means. The city of Charleston, for example, in 1786 was imposing a 100-pound tax on all amusements taking place within the city limits.[54]

If Hallam had hoped that the Revolution might have brought about a significant change in attitudes in this country, he must have been initially disappointed. The mere resurfacing of his company in Philadelphia that summer of 1785 was enough to set the tireless Pennsylvania Assembly debating for the umpteenth time the status of the theatre in that state. In New York, Albany, Charleston, Richmond—anywhere a touring company advertised, there were immediate protests to and resolutions from city councils.[55]

This is only to state the obvious: that long-held prejudices are not easily changed, especially when those prejudices are tied in with one's most basic religious beliefs. But America was fortunate in its formative years to have had leaders whose world views, differing so radically from those of the colonial leaders of a century before, led them to infuse the new nation's laws with a concept of freedom that was both liberating and restricting at the same time. The very notion that *everyone* must be allowed his or her freedom has been, down to the present day, a fragile thing; it is still maddening to those who want to believe they have a monopoly on the nation's moral agenda.

It was fortunate, too, for the theatre that the ideas of men like Jefferson and Madison helped mold the conception of "America" on the popular level. For the gradual, general realization that America was indeed an independent nation and not merely an extension of England was found to have a profound effect on the way in which many citizens viewed their native culture. It would be that awakening sense of nationalism that would finally allow Americans not only to accept but in time to promote an "American theatre." As courts grew less willing to enforce civil laws controlling such religious concerns as adultery, fornication and blasphemy, so public sentiment grew less tolerant of moralists' efforts to completely ban the stage. In the years immediately following the Revolution, therefore, one by one local statutes restricting stage performances slowly began to fall. The last holdout was—again—Massachusetts, whose legislature finally bowed to public pressure and repealed its 1750 statute in 1793, one year after the ratification of the Bill of Rights.[56] Within another year, the Federal Street Theatre had opened in Boston, and the professional stage, for better or worse, had at last come to Puritan New England.

With the lifting of legal restrictions, major theatres and resident acting companies wasted no time in laying claim to the four chief "circuits"— Philadelphia, New York, Charleston and Boston—and soon the stage was firmly established all along the eastern seaboard. By 1815, not only prominent American actors but visiting English stage stars as well were beginning to tour extensively.[57]

But it was in the first half of the nineteenth century, when cities were being choked with a flood of new immigrants, and westward expansion was the national cry, that the American theatre found its greatest audience: the common man. As the theatre historian Robert C. Toll points out, this new audience changed forever how the American stage would define itself:

> [O]ver the years, common people reshaped stage performances to suit their own tastes. While this process produced actors and plays that average Americans understood, enjoyed, and identified with, it alienated the social and cultural elite. Critics warned against "the depraved taste of a corrupt multitude...." Some theater managers did try to create an American theater on an artistic par with Europe's best, but they usually found themselves facing financial bankruptcy even when they won critical accolades.[58]

Toll dubs this general popularization of drama "the first step in the development of show business in America."

This is all true, but there was one other important difference between the theatre in America and that in Europe, another factor that also helps explain why theatre managers in this country *had* to turn to that mass audience in order to survive: the matter of state support of the arts. As we have seen, unlike the tradition of national theatres found in Europe, the legal precedent in America had been to suppress, rather than support, the stage. The attitude inculcated in the collective government consciousness had decreed from the beginning that the theatre was not an art but an "economic venture," a "commercial" theatre, a business; thus, it can be argued that the "first step" toward "show business" in America actually occurred long before Mr. Toll's common man plunked down his twenty-five cents for a ticket to see *Metamora*.

VIII

Finally, just as the theatre grew in the 1800s, so did the church. Before the Revolution, the established Protestant churches had predicted that loss of state support would mean the decline of religion in America, but under the new "voluntary" system, church membership actually grew between 1800 and 1850. By mid-nineteenth century, one out of every seven Americans claimed church membership, compared with one out of fifteen in 1800.[59]

Disestablishment did, however, mean the decline of the *old* religion in America, for the denomination that had grown the largest and had become, by 1855, the most important religious group in America, was the Roman Catholic Church, with more than one-and-a-half million members. Next numerous were the Methodists, followed by the Baptists — each also claiming over a million congregants. In contrast, the once-powerful Congregationalists were reduced to a mere 207,508.[60]

This loss of political influence by the once-legally established churches, and the subsequent shift in power among Protestant denominations, define the status of religious life in the late 1800s, when Salmi Morse proposed producing America's first professional Passion play. Two manifestations of that status especially should be kept in mind:

First of all, the effect on society of the Catholic Church's phenomenal growth should not be underestimated. Some idea of the size of that increase can be gleaned from the fact that the first census in 1790 had recorded only 24,500 Catholics in the entire country.[61] But this new strength and increased visibility inevitably fueled anti–Catholic prejudices. Everything about the Catholic faith—from the foreign-sounding liturgy to the perceived subservience to the Pope in Rome—made the Roman Catholic Church seem sinister and subversive, something for Protestant Americans to fear and, at all costs, to suppress.

Indeed, during the late nineteenth century, the ecclesiastical struggles waged by the Protestant churches against the growing influence and power of the Catholic Church were expressed almost wholly in terms of war. Typical was the sermon delivered in the 1880s by a Presbyterian pastor, who, in a novel reading of Reformation history, boldly declared:

> I hold that if one Church was built upon the other, it was the Catholic built upon the Protestant. The former Church was a parasite: it had attached itself to the Protestant Church, and was sucking the life from it, and to prevent that the Roman Catholic Church should be killed.[62]

Refuting the assertion that both Catholics and Protestants might get to Heaven, only by different roads, the good Reverend flatly stated, "There might be different roads to Sacramento, but to Heaven there [leads] but one."

The second noteworthy element in religion in the 1800s was that, with disestablished churches now competing on the open market for communicants—not unlike rival theatres competing for audiences—the early and mid-nineteenth century witnessed the rise of a new kind of minister: part preacher, part politician, part rabble-rouser, and part performer. Ann Douglas, speaking of how competition among nineteenth-century clergymen inevitably led to a premium being placed on "novelty," notes:

> Disestablishment promoted a kind of star system which gave much, perhaps too much, to a few, and very little to the many. An enormously

> popular preacher like the Congregationalist Henry Ward Beecher (1813–87) could make a comfortable fortune; [while] the average minister at mid-century earned about four hundred dollars a year, less than many manual laborers....[63]

There was a very real motivation, then, for many ministers of the time to encourage notoriety, if not controversy, simply as a means of increasing earnings. Fiery, impassioned orators such as Beecher, or "the Methodist bulldog," Peter Cartwright (1785–1872), or the Presbyterian T. De Witt Talmage (1832–1902), quickly became expert at drawing public attention to their causes and, not coincidentally, to themselves. Obviously, a not-inconsiderable part of their pulpit technique was a decided flair for the theatrical.

These two factors—the Catholic/Protestant rivalry, and the competition among Protestant ministers for public recognition—were both to influence to a great degree the controversy that would surround Salmi Morse's *Passion*.

As for the theatre's relationship with the law at the time of *The Passion*, playhouses and theatrical managers were still tightly regulated in virtually every city in America. As we have seen, the precedent for law-enforcement officers to "clean up the stage" by legal means had been established both by tradition and by the actions of the Continental Congress. Likewise, the use of the law to "protect public morals." Victorian Americans expected the law to protect society from any kind of indecency, and because of these expectations, few nineteenth-century Americans would have thought to extend First Amendment protection to the stage. Freedom, after all, did not mean license; even Constitutionally protected free speech must have its limits. Despite a few romantics' claims that an "artist" should be above the restrictions of the bourgeoisie, the nineteenth century was on the whole an age of socially mandated moral censorship, and the majority of the artists of the time—playwrights as well as novelists—willingly subscribed to this philosophy by censoring themselves.[64] In any clash between the theatre and the church, the outcome, in most Victorians' minds, was all but inevitable.

The sociopolitical stage was thus set for the entrance of the eccentric, flamboyant Jew who devised the daring notion to produce a Passion play in San Francisco in 1879.

2
Don Quixote, Munchausen, and Salmi Morse

I

Most accounts of Salmi Morse's life record that he first arrived in San Francisco in 1875, some four years before bursting into the public eye with his production of *The Passion*. But his affiliation with the city actually dates back to 1848, when Morse, then twenty-two years old, moved west, presumably seeking his fortune in the newly discovered gold fields. Over the course of the next thirty years Morse would return to San Francisco time and again, still seeking that always-elusive "fortune." His story and the story of San Francisco's turbulent development, therefore, are closely intertwined.

Salmi Morse's emigrating to California in 1848 put him among the first to answer the call of easy riches; the discovery of gold at Sutter's Mill had been made only late that January, and the news had not hit the San Francisco papers until the middle of March. The first announcement in New York City, where young Salmi had been engaged in the garment business with an older brother, did not come until August 19, in a letter to the *Herald* from a New York soldier serving in California.[1] Even then, these alarums caused little real stir; what came to be known as the Gold Rush did not begin to hit its stride until 1849 and '50. So young Salmi Morse, rushing west in '48, would seem to have been something of a gambler and a restless dreamer even as a youth.

The San Francisco that greeted him that year was a town still unprepared for what was about to unfold. Only two years before, it had been a sleepy little Mexican port village named Yerba Buena — population, less than eight hundred. Wrested from Mexico, along with the rest of California, in the Mexican War of 1847, Yerba Buena had been resurveyed and renamed San Francisco; and now, with the discovery of gold, the population of the new American town would, within another two years, leap to over thirty thousand.[2]

The scene that engulfed Salmi has since become familiar through countless Western films: the frenzied activity; the hillsides dotted with tents and makeshift dwellings; the so-called argonauts crowding "Frisco" on their way to or from the mines; the astronomical prices for basic staples and services; the nonstop nightlife along the Barbary Coast. But there was another, less glamorous side to life in San Francisco in 1849. The streets were often unnavigable rivers of mud, and fires were common, some of which razed whole sections of the city. The growth was unmanaged, and unmanageable. Tintypes from the period show schooners packed so tightly in the bay that the distant horizon is actually obscured by their masts and riggings, looking like a child's web of scribbles across white paper. In fact, as dirt was dumped into the bay in an effort to increase salable real estate, beached ships simply became part of the newly extended city streets, and were used as hotels and retail shops. This "informal land filling" sometimes had its hazardous side — it is told that a theatre hastily erected on one such section of fill in the early '50s sank several inches beneath the weight of its first full house! In short, San Francisco of the Gold Rush was an improbably sudden metropolis, a noisy polyglot of both men and languages — what one diarist termed "a modern Babel."[3]

It seemed as if here men were removed not only from their homes and families but from society's restraints and prejudices as well. That perhaps explains why theatrical activity, like virtually everything else in town, also enjoyed immediate, unmanaged growth. It was literally everywhere. Even the American troops sent by President James K. Polk in 1847 to occupy Yerba Buena, in a curious echo of the occupying British armies during the Revolution, had set about giving plays "almost at once," according to Constance Rourke.[4] Professional theatricals in San Francisco are thought to have begun with a part-time lawyer and journalist named Stephen Massett, performing comic impersonations and songs under the name "Jeems Pipes of Pipesville," on June 22, 1849.[5] Other professional performers quickly followed, to provide the Forty-niners with the variety of entertainments they demanded. And while San Francisco could not claim the first actual theatre built in California — that honor would go to Sacramento, where the Eagle Theatre, a canvas-sided structure with a tin roof and a stage constructed of packing crates, was slapped together in October 1849[6] — the City by the Bay did enjoy minstrels and even a circus in this first year of the Gold Rush. What Rourke characterizes as "quickly contrived little halls" were the norm in early San Francisco, and no one can say with any authority just how many self-termed "theatres" there were.

However, San Francisco was quick to catch, and then surpass, Sacramento. By July 4, 1850, Dr. David "Yankee" Robinson, an eccentric actor and previous manager of several minor halls, had erected the first notable theatre building in the city, the 200-seat Dramatic Museum, on

2. *Don Quixote, Munchausen, and Salmi Morse* 31

Tom Maguire. Called the "Napoleon of the San Francisco Stage," the legendary manager had virtually led the theatrical world in San Francisco since the Gold Rush era. His production of "The Passion" marked the beginning of his decline. But it may have been his personal feud with an ambitious editor that prompted opposition to the play in the local press. (Courtesy San Francisco Archives, San Francisco Public Library)

California Street.⁷ San Francisco's bid for theatrical preeminence in California had begun.

It was at about this same time that the man who was to be by far the most influential of San Francisco's impresarios first entered the theatrical arena. Like Salmi Morse, Thomas Maguire had been among the first to follow the lure of money to California. Formerly a bartender and hack driver in New York City, Maguire quickly found he preferred the saloons of San Francisco to the muck and mire of the gold fields beyond. Already the proprietor of a successful gambling saloon, Tom Maguire quickly decided that El Dorado was ready for a truly first-class theatre. On the second floor of his Parker House, on October 30, 1850, he opened the 800-seat Jenny Lind Theater. Under the management of a recently emigrated eastern actor, James Stark, and a pioneering actress named Mrs. Sarah Kirby (later, Mrs. Stark), the Jenny Lind would set the theatrical standard for all of San Francisco, with comedies, farces, melodramas, tragedies—all kinds of "legit" drama. Miners would take breaks from the faro tables and whorehouses to line up for *King Lear* and *Hamlet* and the Jenny Lind was continually crowded.⁸ For Tom Maguire—whose illiteracy and whose ignorance of the stage were equally legendary—it was the auspicious beginning of what was to become one of the most remarkable producing careers in nineteenth-century American theatre, a career that would reach its climax, and begin its decline, with the production of Salmi Morse's *Passion*, almost thirty years later.

In an era when the stage still faced moral censure or strict legal regulation in most of the nation, it was welcomed with enthusiasm by the rowdy new society being created in San Francisco. According to *The Theatre of the Gold Rush Decade in San Francisco* (1935), which attempts to catalogue all the known plays and operas produced there during these years, the sheer numbers of theatrical offerings were astounding:

> In the ten years from 1850 to 1859, the rival companies lavished on their patrons over 1100 different theatrical pieces! That averages 110 new productions each year. Since touring companies were still unknown and each play was cast and rehearsed here, San Francisco emerges as an important independent producing center.⁹

Touring theatrical companies may have been scarce, but traveling stars were common attractions in San Francisco, even in the early years. The actor Walter M. Leman lists, among others, Junius Brutus Booth, James E. Murdoch, James Stark, Matilda Heron and Anna Thillon as all having appeared in San Francisco before 1854.¹⁰

"In one sense," write David Dempsey and Raymond P. Baldwin, "the theater typified the city's wild and freebooting kind of life, and, in another sense, it provided convenient, if momentary, refuge from it."¹¹ It is

2. Don Quixote, Munchausen, and Salmi Morse

certainly true that audiences comprised every intellectual level, and at the same time demanded every kind of entertainment possible, the more of it, the better. It is often noted that enthusiastic Forty-niner audiences jumped freely from Shakespeare to minstrels to burlesque to opera and music hall—sometimes all in one night—and demanded that their actors be able to keep up with them. Canny managers like Tom Maguire built their reputations, and their fortunes, by offering audiences just that kind of variety.

As was the case with certain other long-held moral teachings from back East, the two centuries of religious and political animus toward the stage in America meant little to the ethnoreligious mélange that was San Francisco in 1850. The church there was not yet powerful enough to abrogate the miners' hunger for entertainment, and the relationship between the stage and the law was the most desirable kind of laissez-faire. But like the wild and woolly side of San Francisco itself, that state of affairs would not last forever.

II

If San Francisco had created its identity out of whole cloth, the same might be said of Salmi Morse. Contemporary descriptions paint a portrait of a man whose flamboyance and self-promotion would have done a Barnum proud. In trying to characterize him, most writers could only resort to literary images: one San Francisco figure dubbed him "a perfect Don Quixote," while another spoke of "the harmless egotism of the man that led him through realms of Munchausenism, where even the most credulous and impressible listener declined to follow."[12] Upon his death in 1884, newspapermen in both San Francisco and New York recounted with relish all the whoppers Morse had told about himself. He had built a fantastic hotel in Australia. He had fought in the Crimean War. He had single-handedly put down native uprisings in Santo Domingo. He had wandered the Holy Land for twenty years. On and on the stories went, their outrageousness matched only by the bemused tolerance now voiced by those repeating them. "All who knew him felt some kind of regard for the old man," swore the drama editor of the *San Francisco Chronicle*, whose paper had evidenced no regard at all for Morse in 1879. "He had a marvelous fund of erroneous information. He had a wealth of ignorance that impressed one as genius.... It would not have taken more than an afternoon to have developed in his brain the belief that he was the original St. George of England."[13]

Yet, while he was alive, it had also been noted—albeit contemptuously—that he was considered by many to be "a ripe scholar and a linguist of pretension."[14] It can, perhaps, be said most charitably that there were always those who were willing to be persuaded by Morse that he was everything he said he was. It is also clear that, as he grew older, he was not above embellishing the truth about himself and his exploits. "He was, in my opinion," wrote George Barnes, drama editor of the San Francisco *Daily Morning Call*, in 1884,

> a victim of overweening vanity—a vanity so strong, so self-absorbing, that all judgment, not to say common sense, was destroyed by it as with a consuming fire.... His romancing, however, did no harm except to himself; ordinary intelligence soon ceased to be deceived by it. His life was a misdirected one, either by a mental twist of his own, or by circumstances of early years over which he had no control. He meant to do right as far as he knew how; but with imperfect rearing and shallow education, his knowledge did not extend very far. A weakly-supported ambition carried him into theatres of action for which, especially of late years, he was not qualified, and where there could be only one result—failure.[15]

Barnes's attempt at armchair psychoanalysis, aside from being remarkable for its time—Freud, after all, was not yet a household name—is one of the most sympathetic evaluations of Morse's eccentricities to come from any of his contemporaries.

Unfortunately, trying to separate fact from fiction in the biography of Salmi Morse is not made any easier by the subject's affinity for stretching the truth. Clearly, the braggart Morse of the 1870s and '80s, recalled with such glee by reporters after his death, had given every listener what he or she had wanted to hear, willingly making inflated claims for both himself and his past. But it is also clear that the truth, in those cases where it can be established, was quite remarkable in its own right.

Of his beginnings, for example, he once told a reporter for the *New York World*:

> I am an Englishman and was born in the city of Norwich. My father was of excellent family, our people having been leading Englishmen for a thousand years. My father was a Professor in Oxford University and I was educated partly there and partly in Heidelberg, Ger. When I was very young, like most English gentlemen of good family, I was sent abroad to travel. In that way I came to this country [i.e., the United States] a great many years ago.[16]

In reality, his heritage was a good deal less charmed.

Salmi Morse was actually born of Jewish parents in Germany in 1826. Christened Samuel Moss, he seems to have adopted the name "Salmi Morse" only toward the end of his life. As late as 1879, the year of *The*

2. Don Quixote, Munchausen, and Salmi Morse

Passion's premiere, he would still say that his name was "sometimes Morse — and sometimes Moss, and sometimes Salmi, and sometimes Samuel — I answer to both of them — they are both correct."[17]

His claim to having been educated both in England and in Germany, where he "graduated in" the University of Heidelberg, was also inflated. According to his sister Charlotte, "He was educated chiefly in England, [and] at an early age came to this country."[18] He was most certainly in America before he was twenty, for he and an older brother, Lewis, had operated a clothing and dry goods business in New York City for a long enough time for young Morse to make what Charlotte termed "a fortune" — with Salmi, it was *always* a "fortune" — which in this case meant at least enough to allow him to quit and head for the California gold fields at the age of twenty-two. While in New York, young Samuel Moss lived at 95 Greene Street, in what is now known as Soho; the firm, at 69 William Street, near the southern tip of the island, was known as "Moss, Friedenberg & Co."[19]

In addition to his brother Lewis and his sister Charlotte (who was married to Edward Behrend, a "segarmaker" and later a music-box salesman), there was one other sister known to be living in the United States when Salmi died in 1884 — Mrs. Mary Meyer, living in Chicago. Finally, there was also a report of a third brother, rather unkindly described as "a Chatham-street pawnbroker" who "died of softening of the brain"; but Charlotte, in her interviews after Salmi's death, mentions only Lewis and Salmi.[20]

There was nothing in Morse's early background that could explain his eventual drift into theatre, unless it was his restless nature. "Salmi was always rather erratic," Charlotte told one reporter, "and after he left the [clothing] business ... [he] disappeared for many years. He was always turning up unexpectedly and then dropping out of sight for years at a time."

Where he disappeared to that first time, of course, was San Francisco. What he did there is not known. Years later he told the *World* that he had been a banker. "There was a tremendous fire in San Francisco and I was ruined in consequence. But I was so popular, they thought so much of me as a financier, that I was offered all the berths I wanted in a ship going to Australia."[21]

To give him the benefit of the doubt, it should be noted that there was indeed a major fire in San Francisco, on May 4, 1851, in which he may very well have lost his business, banking or otherwise. Tom Maguire's first Parker House/Jenny Lind Theater was destroyed in this conflagration, as were most of the other early entertainment palaces of the city.[22] Since it was around this time that Morse left San Francisco, perhaps it was indeed this catastrophe that helped drive him away.

III

Whatever Salmi did in California in the first years of the Gold Rush, he did not stay long. But he next shows up in Australia, just as he claimed, not long after gold was discovered there in 1851.

"His Australian experience," wrote George Barnes in the *Call*, "was mostly confined to Melbourne during the first years of its growth." Melbourne's Gold Rush history closely paralleled that of San Francisco. According to one observer, within a year of the Australian gold strike four thousand new buildings went up in Melbourne alone, and its population multiplied almost tenfold.[23] As one goldseeker described it, "The goldfields came upon us with almost the suddenness of the changes of dreamland."[24] It all must have had a certain familiarity for Salmi. Perhaps here, too, young Morse had first come to dig gold, but if so, he never admitted to anything so plebeian. Instead, he would grandly brag that he had built and managed the Criterion Hotel—"the first hotel of any note in the city during the early gold days."

Morse's claim to have managed a Melbourne hotel is, in fact, documented. The Australian pioneer William Kelly, in his autobiographical *Life in Victoria* (1859), speaks of Melbourne's Criterion Hotel, which was started "by a Mr. M— —ss, a travelled Yankee, who was taken by the hand and put forward by a small company of Melbourne capitalists." Kelly further observes that the hotel "was conducted with a degree of enterprise and supervision beyond all praise ... and, as Mr. M— —ss sailed from the United States, it became the great Yankee rendesvous [sic]."[25]

There may have been one exaggeration to Morse's story, however. According to the present-day historian W. H. Newnham, the Criterion was not "built" by Salmi and his backers, but was simply the renamed old Royal Hotel, the site for which had been originally purchased in 1837. It was in 1853, writes Newnham, that an American, "Samuel Moss, renamed the Royal the Criterion and introduced American bartenders who looked like the traditional picture of Uncle Sam with white, pointed beards."[26]

Kelly describes other "American" features that Morse added to the Criterion—such as a billiard parlor, a barber shop and a "bowling saloon." But one of the features he mentions is of particular interest:

> a pretty ornate little vaudeville theatre, capable of containing an audience of five hundred, which was tolerably well supported for a time, and would have been continuously sustained if a suitable company could have been secured; but it soon lapsed into a concert-room, and then became the head-quarters, for a considerable time, of Rainer's celebrated troupe of Ethiopian serenaders.[27]

This enticing bit of information makes one wonder to what extent Morse

2. Don Quixote, Munchausen, and Salmi Morse 37

himself was involved in the management of that little theatre. For such involvement would indicate a much earlier introduction to the stage than previously supposed.

At any rate, Morse, at the age of twenty-seven, was now the successful proprietor of one of the most notable hotels in Melbourne, and a prime candidate for what parents with daughters then called "a good match." And it was during this period that he met his future bride, an Englishwoman by the name of Harriet Jay Elliott. It was *Mrs.* Elliott, however, for Harriet Jay was already married. Harriet told a *Chronicle* reporter in 1884 that she had first met Morse "in London, at my father's house." According to Morse, however, they met "in Australia in the year 1852–53," which would have been during his lesseeship of the Criterion. Their "acquaintanceship" there, he said, lasted "about a year."[28]

Then suddenly, inexplicably, Morse left his successful management of the Criterion. He would later say that his Melbourne years had netted him another "respectable fortune." But the *San Francisco Daily Examiner* would recall a "queer story [that] followed him in reference to a gigantic hotel scheme, which collapsed and stranded Morse upon the rocky shores of bankruptcy."[29]

William Kelly in his memoirs sheds some light on the circumstances of Morse's departure from the Criterion. Kelly describes a so-called "Peruvian swindle," for which, unfortunately, he gives no date. The Peruvian swindle "was an industriously circulated Yankee report" that gold had been discovered at the headwaters of the Amazon. Nearly three-quarters of the American contingent suddenly left Melbourne for Peru, according to Kelly, and "it was a general remark that the [Criterion] hotel was suddenly struck with a blight, which eventuated in the absconding of the proprietor and the entrée of a new lessee."[30]

Thus did Salmi Morse retire from the hotel business.

He did not, however, go to Peru. Instead, he suddenly found himself in Turkey during the Crimean War (1853–56). In Salmi's later accounts, he claimed to have "inherited a commission" in the British Army and to have fought on the side of Turkey in its struggle against Russia. His adventures were brazenly colored to fit the moment, according to George Barnes. "He was at one time a Colonel, and had been wounded in both ankles, at the head of his regiment, in a charge that decimated the redcoats; or he was connected with the commissariat and overcame untold difficulties in bringing up supplies; or, as an attaché of the medical staff, ran a perilous ordeal in getting quinine for the sick and suffering soldiers." He was always willing to display the "valuable decorations" he had received "from Abd-el-Aziz and Abdul-Mejid, for services during this brisk campaign."

Morse's wife, Harriet, however, had her own, far less romantic version of what happened to Salmi after he left Melbourne, and it did not include the British Army: "The nearest he ever was to the Crimea," she scoffed in her *Chronicle* interview, "was when he was a clerk to my father in Constantinople." That Harriet's father, a London merchant, would hire his daughter's fiancé to attend his interests in distant Turkey does not seem impossible. After all, Salmi had already proven himself to be a more-than-capable businessman. And for Morse, clearly an imaginative young man, being at Constantinople *was* being in the Crimean War; at the very least, his experiences would bring to his fanciful stories a disconcerting note of verisimilitude that would ever after keep his listeners wondering.

Three years later, Morse was again back in England. In 1858, at the Jay household in London, Salmi Morse and Harriet Jay Elliott became engaged. But their marriage was postponed until another family matter was settled. Harriet had a younger brother, Robert Jay, who was, to use Morse's word, "wild." As Salmi later told the story, "The order was given to me by his father to put the boy in business [in America].... I was to do all I could for him."[31] It would not be surprising to learn that the idea of returning to America had actually been initiated by Morse himself, but however it came about, Salmi brought young Robert Jay back to San Francisco in the early fall of '58. The plan was for Salmi to get them settled there, after which time Harriet would join him and they would be married.

By October, he had found a ranch in northern California, in upper Mendocino County, north of San Francisco. On November 2, 1858, Morse, countersigning for Robert Jay, bought the property for $4,000 cash, plus $1,000 mortgage; he claimed that the cash was his own: "I signed for [Robert] whenever he asked me, knowing his father was good for it," he said. The two men immediately moved from San Francisco to the Mendocino ranch, which soon became known locally as the Morse Ranch, where they settled down to a life of raising chickens and cattle. There Salmi awaited Harriet's arrival.

Evidence indicates, however, that the young Englishman Robert Jay was never happy with ranch life. Twice he deeded the land away, the first time to Morse, on November 17, 1858 — a mere fifteen days after they had bought it — and the second time to his sister Harriet, on May 30, 1859.[32] Some months after this second deed, Robert finally left the ranch for good; Morse said he never heard from him again.

Harriet finally arrived in San Francisco on July 9, 1859. Salmi had come down to the city to meet her, and they were wed that same day. It is noteworthy that they were married not by a rabbi or a justice of the peace, but by the Reverend Bishop Jesse Peck, the pastor of the Powell Street Methodist Church; the ceremony was held at the Tremont House, where Salmi had presumably taken rooms.[33] Twenty years later, much would be made of Morse's claim that he had converted to Christianity. The fact that he was married in a Christian, rather than a Jewish or civil

2. Don Quixote, Munchausen, and Salmi Morse 39

ceremony (there were at least two Jewish congregations in the city in 1859,[34] not to mention a justice of the peace), might indicate that his self-professed conversion was genuine, and may have occurred as early as 1859. Even if the Christian ceremony was at his bride's insistence, it showed, at the very least, that Morse's commitment to his own Jewish faith was not inviolable.

For the next five years, Salmi and Harriet Morse remained on the Morse Ranch in Mendocino. After Salmi's death in 1884, the Petaluma *Argus* reminded its readers of Morse the Rancher, as "many in Sonoma and adjoining counties who personally knew Mr. Morse, have never once thought of associating him with the Salmi Morse of 'Passion Play' fame." According to the *Argus* editor, Salmi had been a familiar figure in the lower valleys of Sonoma County throughout the early '60s. During the Civil War,

> Mr. Morse was a Unionist of the most radical type. He contributed many communications to the *Argus* on national politics. He was a vigorous and forcible writer, but so ultra that even the *Argus*, accounted among the most radical of journals, often found it necessary to tone down and extract some of the vinegar and gall from his articles.... He was a frequent visitor of the *Argus* sanctum during war time, and he never departed without leaving it vapory with his invective against those who were trying to found a government with human slavery as its "chief corner-stone." He was a great reader, and evidently a close student of the Bible.[35]

Editors in both San Francisco and New York would also mention Morse's penchant for visiting their "sanctums," where he would hold court for hours on any number of subjects. It was a practice that he had evidently fallen into early. Even more noteworthy is the fact that, as this report indicates, Morse was arguing constitutional issues as early as the Civil War.

Naturally, on those rare occasions when he spoke of his years as a rancher in Mendocino, Morse invariably cast them in the best possible light. He boasted to George Barnes that his own "improved methods of agriculture and cattle-treatment" had made it possible for him to supply his neighbors with dairy and garden produce when they "were going a-begging." But the *Argus* hinted that Morse may not have been so successful; Salmi, the editor recalled, came down into the valley each spring to hire himself out for "grafting and budding fruit trees."

Perhaps for this reason, Salmi in his reminiscences usually glossed over completely his years as a California rancher. Instead, after he had written *The Passion*, and especially as opposition to that play mounted, Salmi began to swear that it was during these years that he had lived in the Holy Land, either traveling in the company of Charles Dickens, or living as a monk in Jerusalem "for the purpose of studying the Syriac and Hebrew traditions."

"He never saw Charles Dickens in his life," Harriet would declare. "The closest relation he ever had with him was holding Dickens' autograph in his hand." Moreover: "He never was nearer to the Holy Land, of which he often used to prate, than Smyrna." The worse things got for Morse, the more elaborate became his stories of his long sojourn in the Holy Land. These all-important claims, by which he justified his authority to write *The Passion*, were sad fabrications, which only made him an easy object for ridicule even by those who were his friends.

By the end of 1864, after six years, Salmi was finally ready to give up ranching, either because the venture had been a financial failure or because his restless spirit would not allow him to stay in one place for long. Leasing out the land for a period of five years, Morse left the ranch for good that December and returned once again to San Francisco, this time in search of a house in which he and Harriet could live.

Thus did Salmi Morse retire from ranching.

IV

The San Francisco to which Salmi returned in 1865 was a city marked by a sort of civic schizophrenia. On the one hand, the lawless, brawling "Frisco" of the Days of '49 could still be found, as the old-time Frontier Code of Justice still held sway in many quarters. Periodic resurgences of citizens' Vigilance Committees throughout the fifties and early sixties, while ostensibly undertaken to demonstrate a desire for law and order, had only served to hinder efforts to build a workable system of law enforcement. Petty personal quarrels were still being decided by means of Colt .45s.

On the other hand, as many of the Forty-niners began giving up and trudging wearily back home to Indiana or Pennsylvania, the city's merchants who stayed behind—and especially their wives—were undertaking a drive to remake San Francisco in their own image. Throughout the sixties, and with increasing urgency in the seventies, this newly entrenched bourgeoisie strove to determine not only its own social agenda—which could be characterized in one word, "respectability"—but state and local political courses as well. As yet, however, the two San Franciscos existed side by side.

Even so, the shape of the future city could already be discerned beneath the physical changes that had marked San Francisco's growth in the past fifteen years. William Issel and Robert W. Cherny observe that, with half of the city's merchants hailing from either Massachusetts or New York,

> San Francisco's social structure assumed a shape similar to that of New York, Boston, Philadelphia, or Brooklyn. Fewer than 5 percent of the male labor force of the city owned between 75 and 80 percent of personal

and real property.... Six of every ten very wealthy men came from the merchant class.³⁶

They formed a "permanent core of settled wealthy [New England] merchants," who were gradually coming to dominate almost every aspect of public life in San Francisco.

The importance of these merchants' shared geographical background is obvious, for it meant the importation not only of New England industriousness but also of New England Protestantism. And, surprisingly, the old Puritan values were finding fertile ground in El Dorado, especially as the Gold Rush era began to slacken. Nor had this simply been coincidental.

Had Morse been looking, he might have noticed the proliferation of churches throughout the city. Protestant ministers back in New England had from the first seen the possibilities inherent in California, and had urged gold-seeking parishioners to take their Protestant faith west with them. The Reverend Timothy Dwight Hunt had gone so far as to demand that California be made "the Massachusetts of the Pacific." By some accounts, San Francisco's Yankee Protestants had almost succeeded in doing just that: by 1854, the visiting former mayor of Salem, Massachusetts, was congratulating members of the Sons of New England that they had "built up a city [in] which ... everywhere over its surface, in New England fashion, arise the spires of churches and schoolhouses."³⁷

Unfortunately for them, however, not all of those spires were Congregationalist or Presbyterian; the Yankee merchants still had to share their city with large groups of non–Protestants, and even non–Christians, who had also come to San Francisco seeking riches. Adding to their ranks, upon completion of the transcontinental railroad in 1869, would come thousands of foreign-born railroad workers, many of them immigrant Irish Catholics. By the end of the sixties, one-third of the city's population would comprise native Irish, Germans, Chinese or Italians.³⁸ With a working class consisting largely of Irish Catholics, and a merchant class of mostly New England Protestants, it was inevitable that any class conflict should also take on the colorings of religious warfare. This is exactly what would happen in the next decade, coming to a climax in 1879 — at the very time Salmi Morse was announcing the completion of his biblical pageant.

The theatre in San Francisco had also been maturing since the wilder days of the Gold Rush era. Many of the first rough halls were gone, having been supplanted by newer, more substantial structures. Tom Maguire, who had (in a much-debated transaction) sold his third Jenny Lind to the city in 1852 for use as a City Hall, had built in 1856 what was now considered the city's finest theatre, the Maguire Opera House.³⁹ Here, in state-of-the-art, gaslit splendor, he had been showcasing some of the best-known dramatic talent in America. Seeming to thrive on controversy, as when he shocked (and thrilled) San Franciscans with the importation of the infamous Adah Isaacs Menken in *Mazeppa*, in 1863,[40] Maguire had grown considerably as a manager. Like most astute producers before and since, Tom Maguire was not unaware of the correlation between public controversy and cash receipts. More and more, however, his old-time brand of managing was coming under pressure from "decent" citizens.

Like every western American town, San Francisco had always paid lip-service to "decency" and "morality." Just as civic pride demanded that every new building, no matter how humble, be hailed as proof of the community's progress and stability, so Victorian moral propriety demanded that every theatre advertise its offerings as fit for the sensitivities of the most delicate lady — even if such a creature was as yet a rare commodity in town. But now, in the mid-sixties, respectability did indeed seem to be catching up to the San Francisco stage. Community interest was as strong as ever. Virtually every newspaper had its regular theatrical column, and rivalry was strong; several even offered their subscribers the latest theatre gossip from New York, via telegraph. This same year, 1865, had seen the inauguration of a new newspaper in San Francisco ostensibly devoted solely to local theatrical news, called *The Daily Dramatic Chronicle*. Started on twenty-five dollars, which had to be borrowed by its founders, Gustavus and Charles de Young, the new publication's very first edition, of January 16, 1865, had promised its readers complete coverage of "the actions, intentions, sayings, doings, movements, successes, failures, oddities, perceptions and speculations of us poor mortals here below."[41] While such a promise went far beyond normal theatrical news, the de Youngs and their newspaper — as both Maguire and Salmi Morse would later learn — were determined to be more than average chroniclers.

Along with the high level of interest in things theatrical, however, had come more and more cries for reform, or at least, rehabilitation. To be sure, the battle was not yet decided, but the theatre's foes had every reason to be heartened. There had always been those reformist-minded few determined to drag San Francisco into Civilization, despite itself. Attempts to force Sunday closings of gambling houses and theatres had begun as early as 1850. In 1855, an act forbidding "noisy and barbarous amusements" on the Sabbath had been passed by the legislature, only to be contemptuously ignored in San Francisco. One editor of the time ridiculed the Puritanical "Sabbath-keepers-by-compulsion" for attempting to "carry out the Blue Laws of Connecticut on the Pacific." A second such law had also been largely ignored. But in 1864, following another wave of moral fervor during which Maguire and several other managers had been arrested, they determined to fight the ban in court. Using Maguire's as a test case, the managers took their fight all the way to the State Supreme Court — where, on December 20, 1864, they were finally forced to agree to Sunday closings.[42] It was an important battle, and the Court had decided on the side of the moralists. Maguire should have seen it for the omen that it was.

V

As was his pattern by now, the restless Salmi Morse did not remain long in San Francisco. He and Harriet were there for only a short time before moving on again. By October 1868, they had emigrated to the Caribbean country of Santo Domingo (the Dominican Republic), in the West Indies.[43]

While Morse was always more than happy to recount his many improbable adventures in Santo Domingo, he seems never to have satisfactorily explained how and why he went there in the first place. Not surprisingly, the move may have involved another scheme for easy wealth. But this one carried with it a fair amount of national controversy.

According to Harriet, she and Morse went to the Caribbean "with a surveying party commanded by Professor Gabbe [sic] at the time President Grant wanted to annex Santo Domingo." "Professor Gabbe" was William More Gabb (1839–1878), an eminent paleontologist and geologist, who did indeed head a party surveying Santo Domingo at this time. Gabb's survey was not funded by the Grant administration, as Harriet supposed, but rather was sponsored by a private consortium with political ties to Grant's White House. Composed chiefly of "New York capitalists," this consortium was to receive from the Santo Domingan government, in "compensation" for their work, one-fifth of all lands they surveyed.

Santo Domingo officials sought annexation primarily because it meant protection from the many insurrections and attempted coups being directed almost daily from neighboring "Hayti" (Haiti). The consortium of capitalists lobbied for annexation because, obviously, with territorial status would come a phenomenal rise in the value of their own Dominican lands. With the plan so vehemently opposed by Congress, still struggling with Reconstruction at home, poor Professor Gabb found his surveying party in the middle of a political tug-of-war.[44]

Salmi Morse's connection to this controversial scheme can only be surmised. Perhaps he knew one or more of the wealthy California investors involved[45]; perhaps he knew Professor Gabb himself — Gabb had spent the years 1861–65 in California, preparing a monumental geological survey of the state, published in 1865,[46] and Morse may have met him there; or perhaps Salmi had simply invested in some of the land himself, in hopes that he, too, would make a killing when annexation came. However they came to be there, Morse and Harriet remained for the next seven years, until long after Professor Gabb had completed his work, and long after any hope of annexation to the U.S. had passed.[47]

Their only documented address in Santo Domingo was the seaport town of Monte Cristo (now Monte Cristi), on the northern coast of the island.[48] The village of Monte Cristo was dangerously close to the Haitian border, and, based on an old map, was even being claimed by Haitian authorities. The town was, therefore, subject to frequent raids from guerrilla forces. Such skirmishes became prime material for the Revised Standard Version of Salmi Morse's Life. "One time," Barnes recalled him saying,

> I had a narrow squeak of it: the natives were more than usually desperate and bloodthirsty, and I was seized, carried off to the interior and thrust into a prison, where I remained for some time, taking it easy and beguiling the hours with a huge rat that became so tame as to eat a portion of the scanty jail rations out of my hand. At length, some of my friends, learning where I was, organized a party and released me one night by tearing off the roof.

He told the *New York World* that he had such "stupendous influence" with the local natives, that he once "stopped an army of 8000 men on the march and turned homeward an insurrectionary force."

As she had with all the rest of his imaginings, Harriet mocked Morse's grandiose Santo Domingo adventures, too. And yet, in her sarcastic put-down, she inadvertently made it plain that their situation had been, in fact, a dangerous one. "Why," she said, "he'd have been shot if I hadn't been an Englishwoman and kept that flag hanging over my door-sill."

It could not have been easy for Harriet. Living with a man like Morse was no doubt trial enough, but having to cope with life in primitive Santo Domingo on top of that was only adding to her discontent. "He was totally unreliable," she complained to the *Chronicle*, "and I think always a crank.... Oh, I think he was crazy." It is not surprising to learn that their relationship was deteriorating during these last years.

Morse himself may have felt equally stuck in a hopeless situation, but a means of escape presented itself in 1875, when Salmi's brother Lewis forwarded to him an advertisement that had been published in newspapers back in the States:

> Salmi Morse and his wife, a lady said to be from Leeds, Eng., who occupied lands in Mendocino county from 1859 to 1864-65, will hear of something to their advantage by addressing John J. Haley, railroad offices, Fourth and Townsend streets [in San Francisco].[49]

John J. Haley, a former broker, hotel keeper and land speculator, was now working as a land agent and supervisorial lobbyist for the Central Pacific Railroad Company.[50] It is not known exactly what his offer was,

2. Don Quixote, Munchausen, and Salmi Morse 45

but according to Harriet, it ultimately involved selling the Morse Ranch in Mendocino. Naturally, Salmi leapt at the chance to return to San Francisco, and soon was on a ship sailing back to the States to meet with Haley. Harriet remained in Monte Cristo, evidently thinking that Morse would send for her when matters were settled.

Back in California, Morse, armed with Robert Jay's first deed (assigning the property to him), sold the Morse Ranch for $12,000 on November 29, 1875.[51] According to a bitter Harriet, who still held her brother's second deed, "that was my land," and Morse "squandered" the money in mining property "with a man named Blumenberg." As for Harriet, Salmi never bothered to send for her. As far as he was concerned, evidently, the marriage was over. "He left me destitute," Harriet charged in the *Chronicle*, "...suffering terrible hardships in that tropical country." She would later follow him back to San Francisco and unsuccessfully sue to regain the ranch. But she and Salmi would never again live together as husband and wife.

Thus did Salmi Morse return to San Francisco for the last time.

VI

Salmi Morse was now forty-nine years old, on his own again, and still casting about for a means of making a comfortable living without having to work too hard at it so far. By any standards, his had been an incredible life: New York merchant; the California Gold Rush; the Australian Gold Rush; Turkey during the Crimean War; ranching in California during the Civil War; and then on to the primitive outposts of Santo Domingo. Only the most insecure sort of egotist would feel compelled to embellish on experiences such as these. But Salmi Morse felt so compelled. Whatever he had been, he always had to be more.

Salmi, supported by the money from the sale of the ranch, set out to present himself to all of San Francisco as a man of means, returned in glory, never defeat. It was an accepted practice during this period for gentlemen of wealth—especially single gentlemen—to live in hotels rather than in houses. By 1875, the tradition had become so codified in San Francisco that Samuel Williams could offer readers of *Scribner's Monthly* the following pointers:

> Living at a first-class hotel is a strong presumption of social availability, but living in a boarding-house, excepting two or three which society had indorsed as fashionable, is to incur grave suspicions that you are a mere nobody. But even in a boarding-house the lines may be drawn between those who have a single room and those who have a suite.[52]

Eschewing boardinghouses, Salmi took rooms at the Park Hotel and had himself listed in the *City Directory* as a "rancher." By 1877, when he had moved to better quarters on Van Ness Avenue, he had changed his entry to read, "Moss, Samuel, capitalist."[53]

According to Barnes and others, Morse was now telling anyone who would listen that he had been born in England and that he "drew an allowance" from his mother in Australia. He also claimed to have recently read law with a prominent San Francisco lawyer, simply because "he knew a great deal of every other subject except law, and would like to get a smattering of that." But the law didn't satisfy him either. As Barnes recalled it, Salmi "never got beyond Kent."[54]

Instead, it was another chance acquaintance at around this time that was to prove far more decisive. Sometime around 1877, Morse, then living at the Florence House, struck up a friendship with a fellow boarder, an actor named James A. Herne. Herne had first come to San Francisco in 1868 as the leading man in Lucille Western's company; since that time he had become a prominent actor in the city and had managed several theatres, including Tom Maguire's New Theatre. Currently Herne was the stage manager for the Baldwin Theatre, on Market Street, a position he had held since its opening in 1876. His assistant — but, according to most historians, the stage manager in fact — was an ambitious young 25-year-old named David Belasco.[55] The manager was none other than Tom Maguire.

The Baldwin Theatre, along with the California and the Bush Street theatres, dominated theatrical life in San Francisco in the late 1870s. Elias J. "Lucky" Baldwin, a lecherous, profane, cigar-smoking gambler who had made a fortune in the Comstock Lode, evidenced little or no actual interest in his theatre beyond its usefulness as a speculative venture and public relations ploy; therefore, he had simply turned the management over to Maguire. As stormy as was the relationship between the two men, this partnership was propitious for both, and was even more so for the city of San Francisco. Always willing to spend someone else's money, Maguire, now popularly known as the "Napoleon" of the San Francisco stage, had set out to gather one of the finest stock companies outside of New York. By 1877, that company included, in addition to Herne and Belasco, Samuel Piercy, Kate Denin, Olive West and Katherine Corcoran (who was soon to marry Herne). To further bolster the Baldwin Stock Company, Maguire was in 1877 about to bring from the east several other young actors just beginning to establish themselves: Rose Wood and her husband Lewis Morrison, and a dashing 31-year-old Irish leading man named James O'Neill.[56]

Through Herne, Salmi Morse was introduced into this rarefied world of San Francisco theatre. Typically, he was in no way intimidated by any aspect of it. In fact, Salmi would seem to have been more than ready for this chance. According to Barnes, he immediately "read some of his plays" to Herne. The actor's reaction to Morse's efforts has never been recorded,

2. Don Quixote, Munchausen, and Salmi Morse

but Barnes says that Herne "recommended [Morse] to Manager [F. W.] Bert of the Grand Opera House as a moneyed Australian with histrionic tendencies." Going into partnership with Bert and Howard P. Taylor, Salmi thus became co-manager of his first documented theatrical venture: the production at the Grand Opera House of one of his own plays, a futuristic drama entitled *Anno Domini 1900*.[57] Salmi, naturally, was to put up the cash.

Nothing is known about *Anno Domini 1900*, especially where it came from. Indeed, no one knows when—or why—Salmi Morse began writing plays at all. Harriet in her interview swore that he "never wrote anything that I know of" before he returned to San Francisco in 1875; the Petaluma *Argus*, it will be recalled, claimed several Morse contributions during the Civil War. But playwriting seems to have come to him inexplicably. All of a sudden, Salmi Morse was a dramatist, reading "some of his plays"—or, more probably, *describing* plays that were only in his mind—to one of San Francisco's leading young actors (who was himself a neophyte dramatist). And despite alleged disparagement from his friends, or so they all claimed afterwards, Morse was now firmly convinced that the theatre was, at last, his life's true calling.

Morse could not have chosen a riskier time to go into theatrical management—especially in the guise of a "moneyed Australian." For, beginning in 1877, the hard times that had been plaguing the rest of the nation for over twenty years were finally beginning to be felt in El Dorado. Even the millionaire mining men, who in the past could afford to throw large chunks of their fortunes at the chimerical whims of the theatre, were beginning to question the wisdom of supporting such a losing operation. "Lucky" Baldwin reengaged Tom Maguire as manager of the Baldwin Theatre's 1877–78 season despite Maguire's reported loss his previous season of over fifty thousand dollars.[58] Similar losses were being chalked up at every other theatre in town. The golden era of the San Francisco stage was, unfortunately, coming to an end.

Increasingly, San Francisco managers, like their counterparts in the commercial theatres of New York City, were forced to compete for two commodities: backers with money; and novel properties with large box office potential. And here, now, was Salmi Morse, brashly presenting himself at the Grand Opera House in 1877 as a man who possessed both, but who, in reality, had neither. The end result was practically a blueprint for every one of Morse's later theatrical sallies. As George Barnes continues the story in the *Call*:

> He took hold at once and commenced a series of broad-gauge improvements, preparatory to producing ... Anno Domini 1900. He also endeavored to forward the fortunes of a young married lady who had dramatic ambition. The expense account would have been startling had

> it not been ordered by an Australian "capitalist," but Morse quelled the uneasiness of the manager, engaged people, encouraged his protégé with the promise that her brightest dreams would be realized, and cut a wide swathe generally.... And so he carried on for about three weeks, until, to use the expression of an attaché, it was necessary to "dish up some sugar," and then it was found that the Australian capital was mythical.... [Morse told everyone that] he had "shorted Sierra Nevada," and his immense fortune had gone at one fell swoop. That finished the business.[59]

But far from finishing Salmi Morse's desire for theatrical glory, the experience only served to whet it. For here at last was a world that suited his eccentricities perfectly. Here the outrageous was the ordinary; here fame could come in spite of failure—perhaps, even, because of it. Here he had found an arena large enough to accommodate a restless imagination fueled by thirty years of disappointments and near misses.

With no embarrassment at all over this first fiasco, Morse made himself a familiar fixture in the city's theatrical circles. He continued his regular visits to the various newspapers, but now spent much of his time at the desks of the drama editors. "For two years I used to get an hour every afternoon of Salmi's vainglory," recalled the editor of the *Chronicle*; "he compared himself quite frequently with Shakespeare; sometimes with Dickens; always with any writer of eminence whom you happened to mention."[60] George Barnes recalled a frequent evening gathering at this time, which some wag had dubbed "The Round Table":

> Hither came Fred Harriott, nice, gentlemanly, debonair, with the latest news and gossip from the foyers of the New York theatres; Percy Wilson, with his memories of the old-world actors and actresses, and dead-and-gone celebrities generally; James O'Neill, with a modest hesitation that assumed nothing, but took advice from everybody; Fred Lyster, with his Johnsonian intolerance of conventional proprieties, never so happy as when he was dashing to pieces somebody's favorite idol; Manager Maguire—the silent Thomas—with his restless, roving glances, that seemed to take toll of all of the grist of gossip and information poured into the hopper of that social mill; and many others, including [Salmi Morse], who seemed happy in the society of the people around him, because they were fresh listeners, and who rolled a cigarette [of reputed "Haytian tobacco"] for every one who requested it. Sometimes Morse would be exceedingly loquacious; sometimes sit silent for hours, in a state of mental introversion; hunting, mayhap, in the fields of his own fancy for some quiddet or quillet to startle his companions.[61]

Excelling as a raconteur, Morse fine-tuned on this captive audience some of his wilder tales, such as a "shocking" story he called "The Doctor of Lima," a variation on the Frankenstein tale, which he claimed to have written for Charles Dickens.

2. Don Quixote, Munchausen, and Salmi Morse

It was also at the "Round Table" that Barnes first heard Salmi talk about his latest, most ambitious project, "his dramatized story of the evangelists." He had first "commenced agitating" about it during his unfortunate managerial stint at the Grand Opera House, Barnes says, and "more stoutly after his 'shorting Nevada' had briefed his usefulness" to that company. Now, in the presence of Maguire, O'Neill, Lyster and the others, Morse began speaking more and more of "my Pawssion." It would, he announced, rival Milton in its depiction of "the omnipotent power."[62]

By late 1878 Morse had actually finished his "masterwork," now entitled, simply, *The Passion: A Miracle Play in Ten Acts.* Barnes noted its completion in his column in the *Call*, October 6, 1878, noting, "It is a bold experiment on the part of Mr. Morse to make the manner of man's salvation the subject of a stage drama."

Indeed it was. For no known American theatre company had ever before attempted such a presentation. Old Testament stories had often been dramatized—America's first produced playwright, Royall Tyler, for example, had penned several such poetic dramas, including *Joseph and His Brethren* and *The Judgement of Solomon*[63]—and "living statue" troupes, popular throughout the nineteenth century, had immobilely reproduced famous paintings of biblical scenes (including the Crucifixion) in *tableaux vivants*. Ministers and other religious figures had also been seen on stage— Bulwer-Lytton's *Richelieu* (1830) being the most famous example. But as far as is known, no professional American acting company had ever attempted to mount a New Testament drama in which Jesus Christ was presented onstage. George Barnes couldn't help but wonder if anyone would, even now. "Where is the manager who will be bold enough to place it on the stage?" he asked his readers. "Will the manager of the Standard do it?"*

Ironically, the manager who would, indeed, very soon be "bold enough" to present the country's first professional Passion play had been sitting all that time with Barnes at the "Round Table." The actor who would play Jesus Christ was at the "Round Table." One of the musicians who would supervise the music was a regular participant as well. And much sooner than he ever expected, George Barnes himself would face the possibility of passing judgment on Salmi Morse's folly in the pages of the *Call*.

Thus did Salmi Morse finally embark on a career in American show business, and enter into history in the bargain.

---

*The Standard Theatre specialized in burlesque and low comedy.

3
"A Miracle Play in Ten Acts"

I

From the very first, Salmi Morse was convinced that *The Passion* would be a major contribution to American arts and letters. He envisioned it "gracing" the shelves of future libraries, and being revived at regular intervals, much like the famous *Passionsspiel* at Oberammergau. To ensure that his masterwork had the sanction of the church, moreover, Morse took his initial draft to California's prominent Catholic Archbishop, Joseph Sadoc Alemany. His reason for seeking Catholic approval, he later claimed grandly, was because

> ... the only sound learning among churchmen [in the Holy Land] is among the Catholics. I had extensive intercourse, during my sojourn in Palestine[,] with many of the holy fathers, whose remembrance I shall always call to mind with utmost veneration and delight. Twenty years ago, at the express desire of the Bishop of Jerusalem, I witnessed the *Passion Play*, rendered upon the sacred grounds of Mount Calvary proper, in the church of the Holy Sepulchre.... My poem [i.e., *The Passion*] being finished, I went (without introduction) to the Most Reverend Arch Bishop [Alemany], counting securely on finding learning and truth.[1]

It will be recalled that "twenty years ago" — 1860 — Morse had actually been living on his Mendocino ranch with Harriet.

According to Salmi, Archbishop Alemany "not only approved of [*The Passion*], but revised it at the same time." Morse, not surprisingly, then inflated the Archbishop's polite critique into a full-blown public testimonial. When George Barnes first announced completion of the manuscript in the *Call*, on October 6, 1878, he gave the full title of the work as:

> THE PASSIONS [sic]: A Miracle Play in Ten Acts. By Salmi Morse. Revised and approved by the Most Reverend Joseph Allemany [sic], Archbishop of California.

Furthermore, when Morse had the play printed in early 1879, the title

… "A Miracle Play in Ten Acts"

THE PASSION

A MIRACLE PLAY

IN TEN ACTS.

By

SALMI MORSE.

REVISED AND APPROVED BY THE

Most Reverend JOSEPH S. ALEMANY, Archbishop of California.

———

SAN FRANCISCO:
Edward Bosqui & Co., Printers, Cor. Clay and Leidesdorff Sts.
1879.

"The Passion," when published in 1879, was first hailed as a reverent work of literary merit. But its endorsement by the Catholic prelate of San Francisco was one important reason why Protestant ministers suddenly found it "blasphemous" when it was announced for production on the professional stage. The title page reads, "Revised and Approved by the Most Reverend JOSEPH S. ALEMANY, Archbishop of California." (Library of Congress) page repeated this credit, and the Archbishop's suggested changes were included as an Appendix. There is no record that Alemany ever objected to any of this publicity.

The Archbishop's revisions consisted of several pages of specific notes, broken down scene by scene. Some suggestions corrected historical inaccuracies: "Caiaphas was not High Priest at the time of the birth of Christ, nor for many years after"; some corrected doctrinal errors: "For 'beyond our control' say 'beyond our designs,' because man by his free will can control"; and some were actual rewrites of Morse's text: "'All men's lives are suborned by Providence' (better than 'destiny')." And in one case, he even changed the dramatic action of an important scene, altering the Jewish rite of circumcision to a less-ethnic "presentation at the Temple," because, in the Archbishop's words, "an assembly of Christian spectators is not now prepared for such [a] scene."[2] Surprisingly, considering it meant tampering with the text of a self-proclaimed genius, Morse accepted most of Alemany's revisions. But this only underscores how desperately he wanted the endorsement of the church for his Passion.

To further demonstrate his belief in *The Passion*'s importance, Morse took the precaution of immediately applying for a copyright of the work.[3] (It was the only one of his several known plays for which he took this step.) Although copyright laws had existed in the United States since 1790, they were at this time a confusing, piecemeal jumble of legislation, the legal effectiveness of which was questionable — especially when it came to plays. The old eighteenth-century intellectual separation of drama from the rest of the arts still prevailed, leaving playwrights to fend for themselves in many cases. Furthermore, there was as yet no such thing as an international copyright agreement — a condition which allowed many an American melodramatist to build a career by plagiarizing European originals[4] — and many prominent playwrights still refused to publish their works for fear of having them stolen by eager rivals. Salmi's copyrighting of *The Passion* was proof, at the very least, of his belief in the piece as a literary, if not necessarily a dramatic, work.

As to why Morse should choose such a subject to dramatize, there were any number of explanations. Morse himself claimed to have seen various Passion dramas presented at Jerusalem, Oberammergau, Madrid and Rondo (Spain).[5] Of these, the only one that logic tells us he *might* have seen would have been the decennial pageant presented in his native Germany, at Oberammergau; and even then, there were only two years in which he could have seen it: in 1830, when he was four years old, or 1840, when he was fourteen. In all of the other years in which the pageant was presented, his whereabouts have been accounted for: in 1850, Salmi was in San Francisco; in 1860, at the Mendocino ranch; in 1871, in Santo Domingo. But even if Morse had not actually seen any of these Passion plays,

3. "A Miracle Play in Ten Acts"   53

his cognizance of them makes it clear that he was well-read on the subject.

According to William Winter, Morse (whom Winter calls "an apostate Hebrew") had written his *Passion* in direct refutation of the Oberammergau presentation, which he felt "had been devised and performed for the purpose of arousing and stimulating hostility against the Jews, and he profoundly disapproved of it. His purpose, he avowed, was simply to present an epitome of the life of Jesus, as described in the gospels."[6] If Morse did indeed object to anti-Semitism in the Oberammergau text, he would not have been the first.[7] And, in truth, as will be seen, Morse's *Passion* was less rabidly anti-Jewish than the Oberammergau script, if only by degrees. But since his commitment to his own Jewish roots does not appear to have been strong, such a purely altruistic motive seems highly suspect. Then, too, as we shall see, New York journalists, including Winter, refused to accept Morse's claim of Christian conversion, and instead consistently depicted him as a crackpot Jew with delusions of grandeur.

At the same time, however, Winter also ascribes a purely literary motive to Morse's penning a Passion play:

> Salmi Morse, in conversation with me and my old comrade Dr. Charles Phelps..., [in 1880] said that he began "The Passion Play" with the intention of writing a poem like Milton's "Paradise Lost," but soon discovered that the Byronic style, as evinced in "Cain," was more consonant than the Miltonic style with his subject and his genius, and accordingly determined to write not like Milton but like Byron; and he added that his drama was really not, at first, intended for the Stage, but for publication in a book.[8]

This motivation seems more to fit Salmi Morse, whose literary pretensions were notorious.

Morse's wife, Harriet, also had her explanation. In fact, she claimed credit for giving Salmi the initial idea to write *The Passion*. As she told the *Chronicle* reporter, after Salmi's death:

> The *Passion Play* he got from an article in an Edinburgh *Review* that I put into his trunk for him to read when he took ship at Santo Domingo to answer John J. Haley's advertisement [in 1875]. The paper that he got it from had a graphic description and dialogue of the Italian *Passion Play*. There was nothing original in his treatment of it.[9]

He may well have gotten his inspiration from a magazine she gave him to read, but it probably wasn't the Edinburgh *Review*. Inspection of that magazine's issues from 1870 to 1875 reveals no such article concerning an Italian (or Latin) Passion play. The issue of April 1875 did feature an essay entitled "Supernatural Religion," which examined the historicity of Gospel accounts of Christ's life, and included lengthy quotes from both Scriptures and contemporary critical commentaries.[10] But again, there was no mention of an Italian Passion play, nor was there any "dialogue" quoted.

The notion that Morse got his inspiration from a magazine or newspaper article, however, cannot be discounted. For beginning at this same time, the villagers of Oberammergau were gearing up for their next presentation, in 1880, and interest was already running high worldwide. The history of the Oberammergau *Passionsspiel* was by then well known: how it began with a town promise in 1633, to present the Passion play every ten years from then on until "the end of time," if God would spare the remote Bavarian village from a plague that had been ravaging all of Europe. How, according to the legend, God complied, and the first presentation of the Oberammergau Passion play took place the following year. Modern scholarship tends to dispute the contention that 1634 marked the clear beginning of Passion presentations in Oberammergau,[11] but nonetheless, the decennial event has continued, with minor interruptions and scheduling adjustments, down to the present day.

Until 1800, the performances were largely private; but that year, the Austrian Army was called upon to protect the village from Napoleon's troops, and they carried the word to the outside world. By 1840, nobility from all over Europe had turned the arduous journey to remote Oberammergau into an upper-class pilgrimage.

It was not until 1850, however, that Oberammergau was truly "discovered" by the world-at-large, via the writings of the actor-historian Eduard Devrient, who witnessed the staging that year. His enthusiastic endorsement heightened the interest of the general public, and from then on, magazine articles and travelogue descriptions of the tiny Bavarian village had brought increased notoriety. *MacMillan's Magazine* had done a piece on the Passion play in 1860, and ten years later Hans Christian Andersen described the production in his book *Pictures of Travel* (1871). That same year also saw the publication, and, more importantly, the English translation, of Franz Schoebel's *The Passion-Play at Ober-Ammergau*. By 1881, Captain Richard F. Burton, in his own book, *A Glance at the Passion-Play*, could count "some 30 books and brochures" in English on the subject.[12] So Morse certainly had a wealth of information to which he could refer.

Naturally, along with increased fame for the pageant came an increase in attendance. And profits. Where the town had lost money on every presentation prior to 1800, from 1850 on, after it had become *de rigueur* for European royalty to be seen at the Passion play, income began to soar. According to Burton:

> [I]n 1850 the income was 24,000 [florins] to 7000 outlay; in 1860 the figures were 54,000 to 15,000; in 1871 they rose to 117,000 and 15,000;

and in 1880 they will be 300,000, while expenses may be from 70,000 to 80,000 marks. This means that the pious villagers have monopolised the most practical and profitable of theatrical "specs," now known to the civilized world.[13]

Burton's views were not shared by most Americans, however, who preferred to romanticize the Oberammergauers as simple peasantfolk faithfully fulfilling their Christian vow.

This leads us to the most obvious motive for Morse's writing *The Passion*, and the one most often ascribed to him by the preachers and the press: money. Certainly, after a lifetime of pursuing aborted get-rich-quick schemes, he must have viewed *The Passion*, if only initially, as another offensive in his ongoing battle for fame and the ubiquitous fortune. The novelty of it, the scope of it, the sheer audacity of it, all meant box office potential, no matter how self-righteously he tried to deny it. How else could he have persuaded so many otherwise-intelligent businessmen to invest in its production — and to keep on investing — if it were not the promise of some ultimate reward?

Yet if money were the only motivation involved, why would Morse have continued once it became clear that its production could not succeed as he hoped? Despite the coming ministerial condemnation, ridicule in the press, public outrage and, finally, legal suppression, Morse would refuse to simply accept his losses, as any mere speculator should have done, and go on to something new. Instead, it was as if he became determined to make his claims of purely Christian motives be true. Thus, this money-making venture was to prove far different from all of his others — the Criterion Hotel, the Mendocino ranch, the Santo Domingo land scheme — in that, this time, Morse would refuse to accept defeat.

Perhaps he was, as Harriet and many others believed, a bit crazy. But somewhere along the line, *The Passion* became a true obsession for Salmi Morse. And at that moment, the charge that his only motive was to make money ceased being at all valid.

II

This, however, was yet to come. In October 1878, when George Barnes first announced in his column the completion of Morse's manuscript, reaction was far from censorious. In fact, Barnes may have been skeptical about its future, but Salmi was receiving other, more positive responses, especially from the Catholic Church.

In January, he was invited to read *The Passion* for Catholic officials and the public at St. Ignatius College. The event was announced in all of the local papers, and Salmi reportedly invited civic figures and clergymen of every faith to attend.[14] Of course, because this was a Catholic-sponsored event, the Protestant clergy did not deem it important enough to accept the invitation. Archbishop Alemany was there, however, as were "a large number of the Catholic clergy and many prominent citizens" of San Francisco.[15]

The reading was held on a rainy Wednesday afternoon, January 22, 1879, commencing at a quarter past three. The auditorium was crowded as Morse stepped to the podium and read the complete manuscript of *The Passion*, taking time only for two five-minute intermissions. The reading itself was not reviewed by every newspaper—George Barnes, for some reason, made no note of it—but the *Daily Alta California* gave a detailed account of that afternoon, and its report makes it clear that, despite the reviewer's own criticism of Morse's overblown prose, the general response to the work that day was unreservedly enthusiastic. Pronouncing *The Passion* "a very powerful religious drama," the *Alta*'s critic went on to say of Morse that

> In dealing with his subject he has evinced great talent, poetic and dramatic power, and yet, interesting and well treated as are many of the situations, there is ground for revision. The language at times, more especially in the dialogues, paraphrases and descriptive portions, is not sufficiently simple, and contrasts almost painfully with the pure, pathetic, terse and beautiful English of the Bible versions, wherever used, more especially when emanating from the lips of the Savior. In one instance there is put into the mouth of Jesus a phrase which approaches so closely to the California "slang"—"come to grief"—that a perceptible effect was noticed in the audience. "Cock-crow" is translated "the cock's morning orisons," and so on. In spite, however, of a few imperfections, the work is undoubtedly one of great merit, and the situations are extremely dramatic, and although it is impossible for mortal man to do full justice to such a theme, as the "Life and Death of Christ," Mr. Salmi Morse has succeeded in composing a Passion Play which heartily gained for him the warmest congratulations and applause of all present, and which will rank as a literary labor of importance.[16]

The Argonaut, too, noted that "one and all, pronounced the work to be good, pure, and free from all taint of irreverence." Furthermore: "Many Jewish and Protestant leaders of the people were also consulted, and a like verdict was obtained."[17]

It is usually written that *The Passion* was branded "sacrilegious" from the moment it was announced, but this was clearly not so. In the beginning it was praised as a highly reverent work, and if the Protestant ministers did not join in its notice, neither did they condemn it. Morse was praised so long as *The Passion* was a "literary labor"—that is, a "drama." It would become "sacrilege" only when it became "theatre."

Unfortunately, Morse was not aware that such fine distinctions might exist. With the echo of applause—clergymen's applause, at that—ringing in his ears, Salmi was now determined to find a backer who could bring "my Pawssion" to glorious life on the stage.

III

Reading Salmi Morse's *The Passion* today, one is immediately struck with how slight and innocuous a work it is. Inarguably, the storm of controversy that raged around its production says more about the sheer power of the theatre, and the church's continuing fear of that power, than it does about this specific script. Again, this only serves to illustrate the fact that its suppression was the result of many factors, social and political, other than the purely religious charges of blasphemy.

To begin with, *The Passion* is not, strictly speaking, a true "Passion play," as that term has traditionally been understood, for Morse's pageant does not confine itself to the events of Easter Week. Whereas the Oberammergau *Passionsspiel* opens with Christ's triumphal entry into Jerusalem (Palm Sunday), Morse begins with the presentation of the infant Jesus at the Temple, by the Virgin Mary, a part of the traditional Christmas story. In fact, the adult Christ does not appear until Act IV, almost halfway through the play, and the first true "Passion" scene is the Last Supper, Act V. Nor can *The Passion* be called a "miracle play," for only one miraculous event is actually enacted onstage — the restoring of the Roman soldier's severed ear (Act V) — and this miracle, obviously, is not the central action of the play.

Morse's script, as read before the Catholic clergy at St. Ignatius College and as printed in 1879, employs an episodic, open structure, with the dramatic action built around a series of elaborate tableaux. This original version consists of ten scenes, called "Acts," ordered as follows:

Act I. Presentation in the Temple. Mary brings the infant Jesus to the Temple for presentation; aged Simeon, upon seeing the child, hails him as the promised Messiah. The High Priest, overhearing this and terming it "apostasy," hurries to take the news to Herod. Herod's messenger quickly arrives, with orders to kill the infant, but cannot bring himself to do so once he has seen the child. The chastened messenger advises Mary and Joseph to flee with the child for their lives.

Act II. Massacre of the Innocents. Basically only a tableau, in which the Holy Family is hidden by a sycamore tree as Roman soldiers across the land carry out Herod's orders and murder all newborn sons of Jewish mothers.

Act III. The Death of John the Baptist. "Salomi" [sic], at the request of her mother, dances before Herod and demands the head of John the Baptist. During this scene, various messengers and priests discuss the growing reputation of Jesus of Nazareth. Herod is portrayed as a compassionate man, unwilling to kill the hermit John but goaded into it by his conniving wife and stepdaughter.

Act IV. The Brook of Cedron. Jesus delivers parables while His Disciples plan the return to Jerusalem; Christ chides Judas for his "aptitude for barter" — "One cannot serve both God and Mammon, Judas" — and such dressing down seems to be Judas's sole motivation for betrayal:

JUDAS [*aside* —]By this *last* stab shall Jesus die!

Act V. The Lord's Last Supper. A divided stage, with a cottage Stage Right, in which the Last Supper takes place, and the Garden Stage Left, in which Christ periodically retires to pray. Judas, soldiers and priests arrive; Christ is betrayed and arrested.

Act VI. The Gabatha, or the Pavement. Christ tried before Pilate. This act opens with a remarkable exchange between Pilate and Eliezer, "a Jewish notable," a creation of Morse's, in which the two discuss the Roman occupation of Judea and what an offense it is to the Jewish God; Pilate, impressed with the Jews' "patriotism," agrees to protect their faith and their Temple from any defilement. This promise is immediately turned against him, however, for the Jews then demand the crucifixion of Christ on charges of just such defilement. Pilate, like Herod, is presented as a compassionate ruler who is loath to kill an innocent man, but, trapped by his own rash promise, must do so.

Act VII. On the Road to Golgotha. Basically another tableau, depicting Christ on the way to His execution.

Act VIII. Crucifixion. Christ on the cross, "realistically portrayed."

Act IX. Taking Down from the Cross. Two Centurions discuss the aftermath of Christ's crucifixion; Joseph of Aramathea removes the body, an action presented as a "grand tableaux [sic] of Ruben's [sic] celebrated painting."

Act X. The Resurrection and Ascension. "According to the painting of Rubens' [sic] at the Vatican."

This outline provided the basic core of the work, with scenes added and discarded over the years, seemingly at will. In New York, Morse would ultimately claim his full text had twenty-four "acts," but only these original ten figured in San Francisco.

If it was Morse's intention, as Winter contends, to compose a Passion drama less prejudicial toward the Jews, he succeeded only minimally. Aside from Judas, who acts out of a childish resentment, the only villains in the piece are still the Jewish priests and rabbis (whom Morse, perhaps so as not to offend, identifies by the French term "rabbins"). If these Jewish stereotypes are not as reprehensible as those portrayed in Oberammergau's Passion play, it is only because they are not given comparable stage time (the

Oberammergau presentation lasts for over eight hours), and so the Jewish cries for crucifixion in Morse's *Passion* do not seem as relentlessly incessant. Still, from a purely dramatic standpoint, Morse's play does not exonerate, or even forgive, the Jews. Like the Oberammergau script (and the Bible), it portrays the Romans as essentially blameless in the death of Jesus Christ, with the entire burden falling only on the Jewish people.

However, there is so little dramatic tension or growth to any of Morse's scenes, as written, that it is questionable whether the cumulative effect could ever direct any audience's hatred specifically toward Jews. Any dramatic impact would depend almost solely on the visual power of the tableaux, an emotional stimulus which — like viewing a painting — needs a far less-complex motivational subtext. But there were few reviewers at the time who recognized this. Perhaps the most level-headed critique of the script came not from a San Francisco critic but from the California correspondent to the *New York Sun*, who wrote, "It is destitute of merit as a literary work but, *like the libretto of an opera*, it serves its purpose, which is to connect and explain a series of tableaus"[18] [emphasis added].

Far more damning than the script's lack of dramatic depth, however, is the superficiality of its biblical scholarship, about which Morse continually bragged. There is no evidence that Salmi did any reading beyond the King James Version of the Bible. Nor is an effort made to shape that material in any meaningful way, to guide the viewer to interpret familiar events in a new or different light. Aside from the aforementioned exchange between Pilate and Eliezer (Act VI), which must certainly be seen as a sympathetic portrayal of Jewish feelings toward the Roman occupation, virtually every action in the play is simply copied from one of the four Gospel accounts, with little or no further dramatic or intellectual illumination added — a feat any writer could have accomplished. Even then, Morse sometimes got his facts wrong. Alemany's notes indicate that Morse mistakenly placed St. Paul among Christ's twelve disciples; at the end of Act I, the Jewish Priests and Levites sing the praises of the Holy Trinity — a purely Christian, not Jewish, doctrine; in the Crucifixion (Act VIII), the two thieves are nailed to their respective crosses, a barbaric act that Christian tradition reserves solely for Jesus Christ (according to that tradition, the two thieves were tied to their crosses).

Those additions that Morse does make to the story are inevitably the result, not of scholarship, but of the need to interject a little drama into the otherwise reverential proceedings. Not surprisingly for this period, these dramatic interpolations more often reflect the school of melodrama than any school of theology. The villains speak in asides. Messengers appear at opportune moments to report on distant battles or offstage intrigues, and to comment on events we have just seen. The assassin sent by Herod to murder the infant Jesus, upon seeing the child, "recoils, staggers, lets drop the dagger, kneels," and is instantly converted. The only reason Salome demands the head of John the Baptist is that, like any good Victorian ingénue, she loves her mother.

The language, too, often reflects the melodrama stage. Winter scornfully skewered Morse's poetic abilities.

> [Morse's play] purports to be written in blank verse, but it is, in fact, written in nondescript lines of unequal length, halting, irregular, formless, weak, and diffuse. Choruses of rhymed doggerel occur in it, at intervals, sometimes uttered by women, sometimes, — on the contrary, — by angels.[19]

In short, *The Passion* was, in Winter's stern opinion, "Merely a goody-goody, tiresome composition, full of moral twaddle, and consisting in about equal degree of platitude and bombast."

It is true that Morse's poetic gifts were anything but "Byronic." His imagery in *The Passion* is confined almost completely to agrarian metaphors: "seedlets" vegetate, deeds "bear fruit," Christ is a "plant" that "blooms but once." All of the characters speak with basically the same voice, and aphorisms flow with equal facility from king, rabbi and messenger alike. The quality of his verse runs from the merely pedestrian—

> **JESUS**
> Oh, Jerusalem, Jerusalem, thou that *killeth* thy prophets,
> And *stonest* them which are sent unto thee!
>   How often would I
> Have gathered thy children together even as a hen
> Gathereth her chickens under her wings, and ye would not.
> Behold the result of your iniquity! Your house
> Is left unto you desolate and neglected,
> Like a thing worthless. It is for this I say unto you,
> You shall not see me henceforth, *till* ye shall say:
> "*Blessed* is he who comes in the name of the Lord!"
>   (Act IV; Scene 1)

to the wholly incomprehensible—

> **HEROD ANTIPAS**
> Importune me no more with this, my queen,
> All seeds placed in the ground vegetate
> To their kind. What other result could be
> Hoped for us? [C]ruelty may exasperate example,
> But convert no scandal into slander.
> Leave this persistency: the blame lies
> More with us than him. Had we not
> Furnished material, he were no expert mechanic.

HERODIAS

To not be considered more than thus
Were not to be fathered and husbanded
Of kings, as I am. There is a Herod living
Who acquiesced to dissolve his marital ties
With the one he loved, and all only
For the love he bore her. But here
Herodias can broach no desire
But which is peremptorily gainsaid.

(Act III; Scene I)

One might sympathize with Lewis Morrison, whom George Barnes recalled as lamenting, "I speak the lines of Pilate, which I have acquired with difficulty; but for their significance or meaning I am utterly at a loss."[20]

Yet, on the whole, these archpoetical excesses are remarkably few. Speaking solely from an actor's standpoint, *The Passion* contains many other speeches written with a clarity and emotional "throughline" that make them eminently playable, even by today's standards. For example, take the following exchange between Pontius Pilate and Jesus:

PONTIUS PILATE
Art thou called Jesus of Nazareth?

JESUS
Thou sayest it[.]

PONTIUS PILATE
Is this true
That thou art King of the Jews?
Thy dress becomes thee most royally.

All laugh derisively.

JESUS
Mine enemies have put this mockery
Upon me. It is a derision which brings
Neither pleasure nor pain with it.

PONTIUS PILATE
Say, art thou really the King of the Jews?

JESUS
Is it perhaps
Of thyself thou sayest this, or have others
Told it to thee of me?

PONTIUS PILATE
Am I a Jew
That I shall know your origin or your kindred?

Your own people and priesthood
Have delivered you to me, and demand
Your execution. Tell me wherefore
Have you thus offended?

JESUS

              I am a King!
But not one of ostentatious vanity,
Vain pomp and glory, or other
Earthly triumphs; mine is the kingdom
Without end, in the after world.
Were I king of this world retinues of armed men
Had followed and guarded me; these would
Have killed or died in defence of me.
But I am a king of that meek order
Whose rule has no need of men of battle.

PONTIUS PILATE

And only thuswise you are king?

JESUS

As you say, I am king! to this end
Was I born, and for this cause
Came I into the world, that I should
Bear witness to the truth.

PONTIUS PILATE

What is truth? a shield of cobweb
And a lance of straw, to combat fanaticism,
Barbarous as this is. [*To the crowd:*] Caiaphas and Jews!
Here is simply a schism with which
I have no cause to wrangle, but
Which perhaps may be at variance
With the established tenets of
Orthodox mosaism. To me it appears only
A freedom of thought freely expressed.
In Athens one elbows with such,
Without limit each day. But of really malpractice,
I can detect not a jot. Let us, like men
Convened for justice only, adopt
A mutual compromise. The clemency
Of the Caesars have [sic] graciously
Retained to you the time-honored custom
Of pardoning one criminal at each
Passover feast. Let this man, therefore,
At once stand condemned and freed.
Say, will you be content, that I
Release unto you this king of
The Jews?

3. "A Miracle Play in Ten Acts"

>   JEWS
> No! no! release Barabbas, the robber!
> This man dies! free Barabbas! &c., [&c.]
> . . . .
>
>   PONTIUS PILATE
> Men of Judah! that quality of soul
> Which a benign instrumentality inclines
> To justice, mercy and charity, appears
> So completely extinct in you, that not a Cicero,
> With all his rhetoric[,] may convince you.
> It is your zealotry which kills this man
> Rather than his own malpractice. You are
> Determined upon his destruction, and he dies.
> But before all the gods I pronounce him
> Guilty of no malfeasance whatsoever.
> He may have a delusion, but is innocent.
> Still you clamour for his death, and he dies.
> Were he a Roman, not all Rome, with
> The Emperor at its head, would have power
> To gratify your bloodthirsty desires. But
> He is a Jew and is yours. — Have this man
> Prepared for sentence, and Barabbas released.
>
>   JEWS
> Long live Caesar! long live Pontius Pilate.
>   (Act VI)

Overwritten, certainly. But, nonetheless, *playable*.

Besides which, George Barnes, looking back in 1884, may have remembered Lewis Morrison and others only complaining about their speeches, but he seems to have forgotten that he also wrote, in 1879, when *The Passion* was still playing in San Francisco:

> It is mooted that the work may be transferred to New York, and be given at one of the principal theatres there.... *Most of the actors are so enthused with their parts, on account of the admirable opportunity given for declamations,* that they are anxious to present themselves to a wider field....[21] [emphasis added]

Given some of the convoluted dialogue being declaimed nightly from many a Victorian stage—"Rags are royal raiment when worn for virtue's sake!" and so on—one can perhaps understand why the actor Jefferson De Angelis could view *The Passion* as a literary "work of genius," and, further, why a young actor of the ability and growing reputation of James O'Neill might be drawn to the histrionic challenge represented by the extraordinary role of Jesus Christ.

IV

Just how and when James O'Neill actually accepted the leading role in *The Passion* is not entirely clear. O'Neill himself gave several conflicting accounts in later years. The one thing he always insisted on, however, was that it took a great deal of persuading. He gave one version of the story to Ada Patterson, who reported, in 1908:

> At first the actor had been reluctant to undertake the role. He prophesied defeat and ignominy.... He invoked the sentiment of his connection with the Roman Catholic Church. He gave his two weeks' notice. But the author was tearfully persistent. He asserted that if Mr. O'Neill did not play it, another actor would, that it was not in his power to prevent [the production]. The subtle author carelessly opened the first leaf of his play and showed thereon the written endorsement of an archbishop then at the head of the Jesuit Order.... Seeing which the churchman [i.e., O'Neill] yielded.[22]

According to what "the churchman" told a different reporter, however, it was "Manager Maguire [who] asked me to take the part of Christ. At first I refused, although, according to the terms of my contract, I had no choice but to play any part for which I was cast by the management."[23] It was William Winter's sarcastic opinion, however, that "O'Neill was desirous of impersonating Jesus Christ, a part to which he considered himself peculiarly fitted." Accordingly, wrote Winter, it was O'Neill who then convinced "Lucky" Baldwin to put up the money and to round out the cast with other members of the Baldwin Stock Company.[24] This seems to agree with David Belasco's memory. He painted a vivid picture of James O'Neill, obsessed with the play, excitedly "acting passages on the sidewalk night after night" in order to persuade Maguire and Baldwin to stage it.[25]

The newspapers of the time record only that "Mr. Morse is in negotiation with the management of Baldwin's Theatre, with the purpose of producing his 'Passion Play' at that theatre." It was alleged that Baldwin, Maguire and Fred Lyster had all "shed tears over it when it was read to them."[26]

Fate certainly played its part in bringing Morse together with Baldwin and Maguire. As it happened, the Baldwin Theatre had just been turned over to the Barlow, Wilson, Primrose and West Minstrel Troupe for an exclusive engagement, leaving Maguire casting about for another suitable theatre in which his own stock company could take up residence. In February he booked the huge Grand Opera House, on Mission Street, which was once again standing empty after the failure of its most recent management the month before. The Grand had had a rocky history. Begun in 1873 as Wade's Opera House, it was designed to be the most elegant in America.

Clockwise, from top left: E. J. "Lucky" Baldwin. The profane, cigar-smoking Baldwin had made his fortune in the Comstock Lode, which helped support the theatre and hotel that bore Baldwin's name. It was his money that financed "The Passion" in San Francisco; he was said to have lost his entire investment — $25,000 — when the City Supervisors suppressed the play. (Courtesy San Francisco Archives, San Francisco Public Library) / James O'Neill, c. 1879. The dashing Irish actor was 32 and still struggling in stock companies when he assumed the role of Christ in 1879. He had been so excited by the prospect that he reportedly acted out scenes on the street for his employers in an effort to convince them to stage the play. (Courtesy Billy Rose Theatre Collection, The New York Public Library) / The young David Belasco. As an assistant to Tom Maguire, the 25-year-old Belasco filled many shoes in the Baldwin company. For "The Passion" he recalled that he not only helped design the massive sets and innovative lighting effects, but assumed the staging of the play as well. In later years, at the height of his own success, he still defended the production as "holy" and "reverent." (Courtesy Billy Rose Theatre Collection, The New York Public Library at Lincoln Center)

Part One: *The Passion* in San Francisco, 1879

The Grand Opera House on Mission Street in San Francisco. The Grand's massive stage was ideally suited to the scenic grand-scale realism of "The Passion." On the night of the premiere, the street outside the opera house was crowded with spectators hoping to see the police close down the performance. (Courtesy Bancroft Library)

It could seat nearly four thousand, and its colossal stage, built in removable sections, measured 87 feet deep by 106 feet wide. But the Wade was a conspicuous victim of the economic disasters of the mid-1870s; its builder and namesake, a local dentist, had gone broke before he could finish his monument to himself, and the theatre had had to be completed by other, more fortunate speculators. Renamed the Grand Opera House, it finally opened on January 17, 1876, and promptly became a huge white elephant.[27]

Undaunted by the Grand's history of failure, the Baldwin Stock Company opened its run with *Within an Inch of His Life,* young David Belasco's adaptation of a French melodrama. But Maguire still needed other, more adventurous fare if he intended to avoid the fate of so many managers before him. *The Passion,* with its complex, spectacular scenic effects, its large cast, its music, color and opportunities for visual panorama, must have appealed to Tom Maguire's managerial instincts every bit as much as did the epic story itself. Here was a pageant whose scope virtually demanded the peculiar attributes of the Grand's huge stage. Further, the canny manager who had brought the city *Mazeppa, The Black Crook* and *Camille*—all three of which had been opposed by the local clergy and, consequently, had proved highly profitable—would not have shied away from

3. "A Miracle Play in Ten Acts"

this opportunity to try their side of the street and present the nation's first professional Passion play, not when it seemed to call for his own special brand of gambler's luck.

However it came about, Morse now had his Manager and his cast. In addition to James O'Neill as Christ, other actors included Lewis Morrison as Pontius Pilate; Samuel W. Piercy as Herod; King Hedly as Judas Iscariot; J. N. Long as Joseph; Olive West as the Virgin Mary; Kate Denin, Herodias; and May Wilkes, Salome.[28] The music was overseen by Henry E. Widmer, a violinist and composer, and husband of the popular actress Katie Mayhew.[29] Widmer not only adapted sacred works from the Baroque repertoire by Bach, Handel and others, but also wrote original music to Morse's verses and supervised the large chorus and orchestra hired for the production.

The play's actual "direction," in the modern sense of that term, is open to dispute, although most historians, such as Arthur Hornblow, simply accept David Belasco's later assertion that he staged it. However, Belasco's name is never mentioned in any of the contemporary coverage, not even in connection with the elaborate settings and scenic effects, which are credited to "Mr. Dayton and associates." Winter writes that Henry Brown supervised early rehearsals (with Belasco taking over the final preparations), while Jerome Hart, an eyewitness of the San Francisco production, credits William Seymour (who played "A Magi") with its direction. At least one San Francisco reviewer in 1879 gave the honor to Salmi Morse himself, although that is highly improbable, given the fact that Belasco, Seymour, Brown and other more-experienced talents were on hand.[30]

From Belasco comes the most vivid description of the rehearsal period. While this has been often quoted before, it is worth repeating here for the light it sheds on the scope of the production:

> How we scoured San Francisco, — school, church, and theatre, — for people to put in our cast! Every actor who was out of employment was sure of finding something to do in our mob scenes. I cannot conceive, in the history of the Theatre, a more complete or a more perfect cast.
>
> We engaged 200 singers;[31] we marshalled 400 men, women, children, and infants in our *ensembles*. And in the preparation every one seemed to be inspired.... O'Neill, as the preparations progressed, grew more and more obsessed. He gave up smoking; all the little pleasures of life he denied himself. Any man who used a coarse word during rehearsals was dismissed. He walked the streets of the city with the expression of a holy man on his face. Whenever he drew near a hush prevailed such as one does not often find outside a church. The boards of the stage became Holy Land. I also became a veritable monomaniac on the subject; I was never without a Bible under my arm. I went to the Mercantile Library and there studied the color effects in the two memorable canvases there hung, depicting the dance of Salome and the Lord's Supper. My life

seemed changed as never before, and once more my thoughts began to play with monastery life....[32]

I remember how many effects we had to evolve for ourselves. In the Massacre of the Innocents we had a hundred mothers on the stage, with their babes in their arms. In the scene where *Joseph* and *Mary* came down the mountain side we had a flock of real sheep following in their wake. The entire performance was given with a simplicity that amounted to grandeur. All was accomplished by fabrics and stage lighting....[33]

Lise-Lone Marker has elaborated on some of Belasco's staging techniques for *The Passion:* "The whole production is a typical illustration of the nineteenth-century emphasis on picturesque groupings and folk scenes," she writes,

> highlighted by colorful costumes and atmospheric surroundings. Its vivid panoramas were made further remarkable through the lighting effects introduced by Belasco for the first time. He eliminated the floats, or footlights, and lit his stage from the front with old locomotive bull's-eye lanterns, strung along the balcony railing, to obtain the effect of level rays. In carrying out this unusual experiment, he actually anticipated the methods of Reinhardt and Granville Barker by more than a quarter of a century.[34]

It is obvious that Maguire and Baldwin, once committed to this production, were going to spare no expense in bringing Salmi Morse's sacred vision to the stage.

Belasco's account also makes it quite clear that the mounting of *The Passion* was undertaken on a grand—and public—scale. There was certainly nothing secretive or clandestine about the preparations; how could there have been, with Belasco scooting about with a Bible under his arm and O'Neill sedately roaming the streets wreathed in a benignant smile? The events transpiring at the Grand Opera House were, in fact, the talk of the town.

By mid-February, the object of everyone's curiosity was finally being discussed in print, in the theatre columns of the city's papers. On February 16, the *Alta* mentioned the "long deferred 'Passion Play,'" unnecessarily adding that "the event will be looked forward to with considerable interest by the religious element in our community." Despite such misgivings, however, the majority of San Francisco's dailies—or at least their drama editors—seemed to try at first to be wholly objective and even supportive of the controversial project. On February 22, "Philo Judaeus," in *The Argonaut*, announced that he could see "no impiety" in such a play, "and, provided that the *Passion Play* be rendered truthfully, reverently, and, above all, artistically, we heartily wish it success whenever and wherever it may be given to the public." The following day, the theatre columns of

3. "A Miracle Play in Ten Acts"

both the *Morning Call* and the *Chronicle* took note of the upcoming pageant, both without rancor. The former mentioned the tears the work had allegedly elicited thus far, from Maguire, Baldwin, *et al.*, and observed, "If it be thus effective for good in its incipiency, what may we not expect when it is presented in its completeness." The latter opined that, as Morse had made such "a serious study" of Passion plays, "it may be inferred that his work will be presented in a very artistic manner."[35]

But if the dramatic editors were going out of their way to promote a wait-and-see attitude on the part of their readers, another influential segment of San Francisco society was not willing to be so patient. Or so forgiving.

On Monday, February 24, 1879, the long-anticipated formal announcement finally appeared in the city's dailies:

> **GRAND OPERA HOUSE. ANNOUNCEMENT.** During the Lenten Season will be rendered, with every circumstance of solemnity and preparation, Full Chorus and largely-increased Band, **THE PASSION PLAY.**

By then, however, *The Passion* had already become the topic of outraged Sunday sermons preached from certain pulpits throughout the city.

Salmi Morse's "literary labor" was about to become "theatre," and the opposition was taking up arms.

4
Preachers, the Press, and Politics as Usual

I

Everyone in San Francisco had an opinion about *The Passion*. Not only from pulpits, but in barbershops, saloons, retail shops, restaurants, office buildings and drawing-rooms, Salmi Morse and his Passion play were the primary topic of conversation. Even before any official announcement had been printed in the papers, *The Passion* had been debated. By February 26 — a mere two days after the first paid advertisement, and only five days before its scheduled opening — public debate had already become so heated that the *Call* could report that "there is some doubt of its production" ever taking place.[1]

"During the week [*The Passion*] was given, nothing else was thought of or discussed in the city," wrote M. B. Leavitt, one of Maguire's fellow theatrical managers, "and business almost came to a standstill."[2] That a theatrical event, no matter how controversial, could galvanize the attention of virtually every San Franciscan in 1879 is indeed remarkable, for the city had more than its share of other pressing problems, social, political and religious. But, as Craig Timberlake has suggested,[3] perhaps the Sturm and Drang that raged around *The Passion* represented a desire on the parts of many San Franciscans to set aside, at least for the moment, those other, more-serious issues vying for attention.

For 1879 was a crucial year in the city's history. The economic depression that had begun in the mid-'70s had by now brought the city to near anarchy. The collapse in 1877 of the Consolidated Virginia Mine of Nevada, a part of the Comstock Lode, had "busted" the entire silver bonanza; that same year, the worst drought in a decade had brought ruin first to farmers then to businesses; real estate prices fell; a railway strike in the East brought pay cuts for California railroad workers. As bankrupt farmers joined unemployed laborers and down-on-their-luck miners wandering the streets of San Francisco, the city's population swelled to over

4. Preachers, the Press, and Politics as Usual

230,000 and the unemployment rate reached an estimated 15 percent, perhaps more.[4]

Frustrated and angry, these workers—mostly Irish Catholic—began meeting in the sandlots south of City Hall, staging a series of mass rallies, several of which ended in riots. The "Sandlotters," as they were called, blamed most of their problems on the glut of low-paid Chinese laborers living in Chinatown. Also coming in for their share of the workers' anger were the wealthy merchants of Nob Hill—mostly Protestant—who were getting richer by employing this underpaid labor force. The Workingmen's Party of California (WPC), which emerged in 1877 from these sandlot meetings, rose to political power over the next two years almost solely on the battle cry, "The Chinese Must Go!" Under the leadership of an excitable Irish drayman, Denis Kearney, the WPC had been instrumental in dictating "anticoolie" provisions into the new state constitution, which was, at the time of Salmi Morse's *Passion* in the spring of 1879, being debated prior to ratification. The WPC was also about to name its own candidate for the mayoral election that fall. The columns of the increasingly powerful *San Francisco Chronicle*, which supported the new constitution, added to the din of the hour with inflammatory exhortations against the "Pig-Tails" making "Asiatic Inroads" on American soil.[5] The fact that the workingmen were themselves immigrants was a glaring irony that seemed to be lost on the *Chronicle*. Obviously, the issues were complex, but, as previously noted, the ongoing battle between the primarily Irish Catholic workingmen and the primarily Protestant merchant class—a class war with the added overtones of religious intolerance—was just approaching its climax that spring of 1879.

In many ways, the political events of that year represented the last gasp of old-time Gold Rush San Francisco. All three of the social forces of interest to us here—religion, the press and politics—were still jockeying for position in the city's power structure during this period, and their respective individual interests were by no means exclusive. Yet each had different reasons for wanting *The Passion* suppressed.

II

The Preachers

On February 13, 1879, the Reverend Allen Curr, a Scots cleric visiting San Francisco, delivered a farewell lecture at the First Baptist Church. His topic was "What a Scotchman Thinks of San Francisco, socially, morally, commercially and religiously." His analysis of the city's moral and religious state was not encouraging, according to the *Daily Alta*:

> he had never been in a city where the Gospel word reached fewer hearers, [and] preachers were less respected. San Francisco has not much to be proud of in her Sabbath breaking and open violation of God's law.... It is painful to say this, but it is true, and to prevent this evil all good and true men and women must pray and work.[6]

Naturally, the theatres, which had resumed Sunday performances, were given the requisite condemnation: "In no other city," the *Alta* continued, "will you find on Sabbath evenings licentious plays produced in crowded theatres. He hoped a public sentiment would be started sufficiently strong to compel a decent observance of God's day."

It is certainly no surprise to find that men of the cloth might feel ignored in a frontier town like San Francisco. But the Protestant ministers' fear that they had become "less respected" was not confined to the outposts of the Wild West, by any means. Across the continent, similar dark prognoses on the course of American Protestantism in general were being heard, from small town and large, East and West. Protestant pastors throughout the late 1870s and early '80s were looking at America and seeing a frightening loss of moral ground.

To many ministers, the end was already a *fait accompli*. Half a million New York Protesants were not going to church, claimed the Reverend Dr. Henry W. Bellows, the acknowledged Unitarian leader of the nation, who cried, "How can we call New York a Christian city?" And in 1880, the Presbyterian Dr. T. De Witt Talmage of the Brooklyn Tabernacle would finally state what the ministers of America most feared: after a recent twenty-day trip covering some two thousand miles, Talmage would say, he had concluded that religion in America "was dead." What did Talmage feel was the answer? "We want a revival like that of 1857, when 20,000 souls were saved." Or, even better: "We want a revival like that of 1831, when the old Chatham Street theatre was turned into a church."[7]

Of course, declaring the death of religion (or, for that matter, the theatre) in America has always been a good way of grabbing headlines. But these remarks only serve to reveal the real sense of helplessness being felt by Protestant ministers in the late nineteenth century, especially as they watched Irish Catholic immigration figures soar.

Furthermore, as Talmage's remarks demonstrate, the age-old religious prejudice against the stage was still very much a central tenet in the doctrines of most Protestant sects in America at the time of *The Passion*. The Presbyterian Assembly that same year debated a resolution condemning the playhouse (but, curiously, not the opera). The Methodist Episcopal Church had instituted an "amusement ban" in 1877, by which church members could be excommunicated for attending the theatre. (This ban would not be revoked until 1924.) The *Baptist Weekly*, while diplomatically leaving it up to each individual's conscience to decide the matter, at the same

4. Preachers, the Press, and Politics as Usual

time warned, "there ought to be manifest in Christians a nobler disposition than that which is constantly craving excitement and amusement." And while the majority of such condemnations were still being directed at actors (the Congregationalist Reverend Thomas K. Beecher in 1882 compared actors with "monkeys and idiots"), a Helena, Montana, minister in 1879 expelled two members of his congregation simply because they held jobs at the local playhouse.[8]

This was all, in part, a reaction to the urbanization of industrial America. In the larger cities, theatre had been gaining perceptibly in influence and economic power, especially among Robert Toll's immigrant "common men"; the American stage was, in fact, enjoying what some historians call its "Golden Age." Obviously, despite the ministers' most vehement denunciations, among any given theatre audience on any given night must be found a good many Methodists, Baptists and Episcopalians. Benjamin McArthur has noted: "As Protestant and, to a lesser degree, Catholic clergy witnessed the increasing rush to the theatre's door, they realized that its growing influence would have to come at their expense."[9] Thus, making a pronounced, public stand against *The Passion* was a way by which the Protestant ministers of San Francisco could prove that they, at least, were very much a force to be "respected" in their community, a force whose power must be reckoned with, whose social position and religious sanctity must be protected by law, if necessary.

What were the ministers objecting to, in a production that could only be described as fulfilling to the nth degree all of their demands for moral and uplifting plays? Wasn't this exactly what the church had always wanted from the stage? While the examples of sermons that have survived are limited, in general there were four main thrusts to the Protestant ministers' complaints:

First, and perhaps the most-often heard charge, was that *The Passion* must be blasphemous, no matter how respectfully presented, simply *because* it was a product of the hated stage. "To think," cried a horrified Reverend W. J. Smith, of the Central Presbyterian Church,

> that to-morrow night that cross will be raised, and that James O'Neill will hang there, and that actors, in mimicry, will drive the nails through his hands, and that he ... shall stand in the centre of that Grand Opera House and cry, 'My God, my God, why have you forsaken me?"... My friends, it is an awful thing, and you tell me, standing here, that I am too severe in this measure, and I tell you nay; and I hope to God that if those with high hand dare to put that on the stage that there may be a true accompaniment of that scene of Calvary, and that the lightning that played around the crest of Sinai may rend that stage from end to end, and the earthquake throes that rent the rocks to twain on Mount Calvary shake the foundations of that building; and that the pall of darkness that fell with all its midday gloom, may descend upon them, until actors and

spectators shall fall like that Centurion, and with aching knees cry out, 'Truly this is the Son of God.'"[10]

"Think of the Redeemer of the world personified by a play actor!" shuddered the Episcopal Bishop, William Ingraham Kip. "Than such a representation on the public stage of a theatre, a more fearful impiety could not be devised."[11]

Not only were theatre professionals presenting this "impiety," but all those involved could clearly have only one motive, in the minds of these preachers—profit. "It is the production of Judas selling his master for thirty pieces of silver," Reverend Smith believed, while the Reverend T. K. Noble, of Plymouth Congregational Church, considered it "an outrage" that this "irreverent" representation should be undertaken solely "for the purpose of gain." "When it is performed in the Alps by the simple peasants at Ober-Ammergau," declared Bishop Kip, "it is a strictly religious service, under the direction of the priests."[12] Once again, the myth of the ignorant Tyrolean peasants fulfilling their Christian vow blinded men like Kip to the fact that the Oberammergauers, too, were charging admission and were, as Richard Burton had pointed out, making a tidy profit of their own.

As, indeed, were many of the Protestant churches in San Francisco. For they did not object to using the "sinful stage" when it could benefit their own coffers. On February 19, 1879—at the very time ministers were denouncing Morse, Maguire and O'Neill for presenting *The Passion* for profit—St. Peter's Episcopal Church sponsored a fundraiser at Platt's Hall, one of the city's smaller auditoriums used for touring theatrical companies, boxing matches, dances and so on. At any rate, the St. Peter's fundraiser that night comprised an operetta, *The Crimson Scarf,* followed by a concert and a farce; ticket prices ranged from fifty cents to a dollar. Platt's Hall was also hired that week by the Presbyterians, the Episcopalians, the Methodists, Congregationalists and Baptists for a weeklong series of ladies' lunches—with entertainments—to benefit the YWCA. Even more to the point, the Young Men's Hebrew Association on March 25, 1879, presented, "with appropriate Music and Scenery," the dramatic oratorio *Cantata of Esther*—based on a biblical story—at the Grand Opera House—the same stage on which *The Passion* had been enacted—also for the purpose of making money. Ticket prices ranged from fifty cents to a dollar fifty (the same as for *The Passion*). Not one Protestant leader objected.[13] Of course, these monies were being raised (usually) by amateurs, not "professionals," and were earmarked for the church, not the stage; even so, the fact that religious organizations could use these same "sinful" theatres to present dramatic and musical works for their own profits only betrayed their tenuous position in condemning the professional stage for doing the same.

What seemed to be at issue here was addressed in the preachers' second objection: that *The Passion* was a "secular spectacle," that is, outside the control of the church. This somehow implied that the most sacred—most *hidden*—aspects of the Christian religion were being publicly ridiculed. Sounding for all the world like the eighteenth-century Freemasons who, legend has it, accused Mozart of putting their secret rituals on the stage in *The Magic Flute*,[14] so San Francisco preachers accused Salmi Morse of betraying Christianity's most profound secrets. This viewpoint would best be phrased by the *Argonaut*'s critic, "Betsy B.," who would write that "the veil [has] been lifted from our Holy of Holies with a ruthless hand"; but ministers were earlier making the same accusation. Calvary's Reverend John Hemphill included the production in a sermon on "The Jonahs That Endanger the Ship of State," charging that, in *The Passion*, "everything that we hold sacred in religion is burlesqued or profaned." And the vituperative Reverend Smith had decried:

> It is enough to make the blood of this so-called Christian nation curdle in its veins to see that scene—the holiest and most awful in a Christian religion,...—put on the stage with caricature and burlesque, to be laughed at by the public and the throng that may go to look at it.[15]

Thus, not only was *The Passion* a secular offering, but because it was, its presentation would be—the preachers' third objection—"a pernicious influence on the thoughtless and profane."[16]

The notion that the Great Ignorant Unwashed would be harmed by religious subject matter if it were represented on a theatre stage rather than narrated by a minister from his pulpit might indicate that many in the clergy were simply afraid of losing control of their own personal domain. But this argument also reveals a deeper fear, one that strikes at the heart of the theatrical experience and helps explain why some preachers so opposed *The Passion*: that the realistic depiction of these sacred events onstage would have an emotional power far beyond that which any mere minister, no matter how gifted, could give them, a power, moreover, that no one could control. Such a stand, intentional or not, further made it clear that these men feared that religious faith might only be maintained in the comfortable distance afforded by literature, or mythology, if you will. Physicalization might force the faithful—and certainly must force the "ignorant" lower classes—to confront a reality for which they were unprepared, and which made most Victorian Americans uncomfortable. This was, after all, the self-confessed experience of no less an educated man than William Winter, who, apropos of *The Passion*, wrote:

> In the end of a church in Heidelberg there is, or was, visible, through a long window, a full-length effigy of Christ on the Cross, which swings to and fro as a pendulum to the clock, and in a church at Mayence there

> is a life-size figure of the Virgin Mary, seated, with the body of the dead Christ, also life-size, lying across her knees. I remember looking on those objects with aversion. To *see*, in a theatre, a man, impersonating the *Christ*, washing the feet of another man will, generally, give offence.[17]

Merely hearing the act described from a pulpit, however — imagining it in your mind's eye — reading the account in the poetry of the Scriptures — none of these evoked the kinds of troubling reactions that might be raised by *seeing* the biblical story realistically enacted onstage by living beings.

Another justification for this argument was that the people behind *The Passion*, not being ministers of the Gospel, could not possibly understand — or sympathize with — religious subject matter, and thus did not really care what effect they might have on the uneducated viewer. While this may have been a backhanded way of pointing out that Morse was a Jew, far worse than that, for these Protestant leaders, was the fact that both O'Neill and Maguire were Irish Catholics. "Even though the managers of the affair lack Christian education or feeling," said Reverend Noble, "they ought not to mock the feelings of others and blaspheme their God." (Obviously, for Noble, Catholics were not Christians.) The *Pacific Methodist* at least gave Salmi the benefit of the doubt, stating that, since he was not a Christian, it was "possible that Mr. Morse does not know his own turpitude."[18] That, however, did not excuse Maguire or O'Neill.

In fact, judging from the newspaper accounts of Sunday sermons — which are all we have to go on — it is remarkable that the Protestant leaders made very little of Morse's Jewish background. They accused him of blasphemy, of profiteering, of sacrilege, immorality and a lack of taste, but seemingly few of the Protestant preachers in San Francisco got much mileage out of a Jew writing a Christian Passion play. Indeed, in a comic twist on the expected, it was a Jewish reader of *The Argonaut* who took offense that the Hebrew Christ was to be played by the Irishman O'Neill. It is possible, of course, that anti-Semitism was so open and accepted that they did not feel the need to mention it; however, most social analysts for this period make the point, as do Issel and Cherny, that Jews suffered less discrimination on the West Coast than on the East.[19]

But perhaps the Protestant clergy's lack of concern over Morse's Jewishness is better understood in light of their fourth — and, given the religious tensions in the city in 1879, certainly their most self-revealing — accusation: that *The Passion* was in actuality a product of the Catholic Church.

The Congregationalist newspaper, *The Pacific*, set forth this charge most bluntly, writing:

> We have it on good authority that this play was first performed at St. Ignatius College; that the funds by which it has been placed upon the

4. Preachers, the Press, and Politics as Usual

stage were furnished by a prominent capitalist of this city [i.e., Baldwin], whose antecedents and relations are all Romish, and that the net proceeds, if any, will go to aid in the erection of the Jesuit College on Van Ness avenue. All this may be nothing strange, but for some of our readers it may add emphasis to that scriptural and prophetic title of the Romish hierarchy, "Mother of abominations."[20]

The errors of this report notwithstanding, Protestant mistrust of the Catholics, fueled by such alarmist reports that *The Passion* was a conspiracy hatched by "the Romish altar and the priest's chamber," undeniably played a major part in the Protestant ministers' wholesale condemnation of Salmi Morse's drama. Morse himself was convinced that this was the only reason his play was so opposed. He wrote:

> The chief sin ... which I committed with the *Passion Play*, and for which the Protestant Clergy will never forgive me, is the fact of my having submitted it for approval to the Catholic clergy and not to themselves. This step alone goes on to refute as low bred slander, any and every thought upon its "offensiveness" or upon its being an "outrage...."[21]

There can be no doubt that the Catholic connection, more so than the fact that Morse was a Jew, proved the major liability for *The Passion*.

As for the Catholics, they did their best to distance themselves from further connection with the controversy. It didn't help Morse's position when an enterprising *Chronicle* reporter called upon Archbishop Alemany himself, seeking his opinion of the play; unfortunately, Alemany's response was not exactly destined to assuage Protestant criticism. The Archbishop, once so impressed with *The Passion* that he himself suggested improvements in the text, was now diplomatically "non-committal." Neatly explaining away his own earlier enthusiasm, the Archbishop "thought that the Passion play, as a literary production, reflected credit on its author, but not being himself in the habit of attending theatres, he did not care to say whether or not it could with propriety be placed upon the stage."[22] And so the circumspect Archbishop removed himself completely from the field of battle.

During this entire controversy, in fact, not one Catholic clergyman in San Francisco is on record as having defended—or, for that matter, condemned—*The Passion*. Alemany's silence no doubt spoke volumes to the Protestant clergy, however. Alemany had already been, for more than two years, lambasted in the Protestant press and from Protestant pulpits for his perceived lack of control over Denis Kearney and the violence-prone Irish Catholic "sandlotters" of the Workingmen's Party, and it was therefore understandable that he might be reluctant to tangle with his enemies and face more of the same, certainly not for the sake of a mere stage production. Instead, it was easier for him to simply walk away.[23]

What of the Jewish community? There had been Jews in San Francisco since 1848, as Morse's presence would attest. As previously noted, the first Jewish service, numbering fifty, had been held on the Day of Atonement, 1849, and by 1854 two synagogues, Emanuel and Sherith Israel, had been built.[24] Just as the theatre had benefited from the nonjudgmental attitudes of the Forty-niners, so too had racial and religious minorities; Jews, although in small numbers, could be found among the city's commercial community, Levi Strauss being perhaps the most obvious example, and they fairly dominated banking. The same opportunities were extended to blacks. (This would change as the city became more "civilized.") But the small Jewish community was itself divided theologically between Orthodox and Reform, a situation that caused Gustav Adolf Danziger to lament that his fellow Jews in San Francisco had always lacked the kind of religious zeal and political cohesiveness demonstrated by the Protestants and Catholics.

"The Jew," Danziger wrote in 1895, "is a Jew only in the synagogue, *i.e.* in his religion but not in politics or business."[25] Relatively small in number and politically powerless, the Jewish community hardly seemed to figure at all in the *Passion* controversy. Later, it would be said that they opposed the play, but at the time, no reporters sought the rabbis' opinions on the matter. Nor did the cautious rabbis seem eager to volunteer them.[26]

Thus, clerical opposition to *The Passion* in San Francisco was a peculiarly Protestant affair; and theirs was an uphill battle. *The Passion*, after all, was not a typical "evil play." It contained no profanity. There was not the slightest hint of sexual licentiousness, innuendo or nudity. Despite what its opponents claimed, it ridiculed no revered teaching or figure. *It was an evil only because the Protestant ministers proclaimed it so.* And in their need to flex their ministerial muscle, it was, perhaps, inevitable that their campaign for the play's suppression would not be confined to the pulpit, but would drive them to do what their colonial forebears had done: seek a political solution to what was basically a religious problem.

Ironically, however, many of these same Protestant ministers were already on record as highly disapproving just such pulpit activism, a stand prompted by their disavowal of the political shenanigans of one of their own—the notorious Reverend Isaac Smith Kalloch, shepherd of the downtown Metropolitan Temple, the largest Baptist church in the United States.[27] The vain, ambitious Kalloch, a burly, handsome redhead with a magnetic personality and a shady past (he had been dubbed "The Sorrel Stallion" by a Kansas editor), had set Protestant parish houses reeling by zealously aligning himself with the anti-Chinese causes of the Workingmen's Party. To Kalloch, power in the pulpit and power in the polling booth were interchangeable, and his blatant politicking from his own

4. Preachers, the Press, and Politics as Usual

pulpit would soon lead to the supreme political act. He would run for the office of Mayor on the 1879 WPC ticket.

Kalloch's fellow ministers were appalled — not least because the Protestant Kalloch had committed the ultimate betrayal by joining ranks with the Catholic-infested WPC. Sermons were preached and articles written denouncing Kalloch as the "chaplain of the sand lots" and tagging the WPC as "hoodlums." (Yet, given the turbulence of the times, many ministers, Protestant as well as Catholic, publicly supported restricting Chinese immigration.)

When *The Passion* controversy suddenly erupted, the quandary it presented was obvious. Protestant ministers, having for the most part already disavowed preachers mixing in politics, now had to backpedal in order to justify their own activist stands in calling for local politicians to legally suppress a secular play. The Reverend Hemphill, for example, now defended his "right, as a minister of the Gospel, to speak of matters, political or otherwise, which his intelligence told him were dangerous to the prosperity and well-being of the people." He pointed to "the political services" of Jesus Christ, the Apostle John, Martin Luther and John Calvin, among others, to justify his political actions, saying that "Religion should pervade every relation of life, and has a great deal to do with politics."[28] Kalloch's example had clearly set a precedent that his former critics were now all too willing to follow. Although criticized by some for standing on such questionable ground,[29] the Protestant clergy forged ahead with its campaign against *The Passion*, increasing the pressure on city officials as the March 3 opening drew nearer. It is safe to assume that on Sunday, March 2, 1879, there was not a Protestant pulpit in the city of San Francisco that did not hear a prayer to the Almighty on the subject of Salmi Morse's blasphemy.

Prompted to action, then — partly out of fear of having lost power within the community, partly out of spite for this "Catholic-influenced secular sacrilege," and, mostly, out of a genuine moral outrage at seeing sacred matters presented in a public theatre — the Protestant preachers sought, first, to mobilize the entire community against Maguire, Morse and company, and, second, by doing so, to effect civil legislation that would close the presentation once and for all by force of law.

This second step was dependent upon the duly elected public authorities, mainly, the San Francisco Board of Supervisors. But molding the public opinion necessary to convince the Supervisors that such a decisive step was politically expedient in an election year depended upon the sympathies and alliance of that other powerful community force — the press. Luckily for the preachers, the most influential of the city's dailies had its own reason for agreeing that *The Passion* should fail.

III

The Press

Like most American cities of any size in 1879, San Francisco had a wealth of competing periodicals from which to take its news — at least half a dozen city dailies, plus assorted weeklies, monthlies, literary and special-interest publications (including the religious press), and various national journals and reviews. Each of the San Francisco papers had its distinctive editorial style, its particular political sympathies, and its own peculiar social prejudices.

"Journalism," wrote George Henry Payne in 1920, "is the only profession where prejudice, like versatility, may be an asset."[30] This was certainly true of the late nineteenth century, which Payne dubbed the era of the "personal journalist," when a newspaper was almost expected to reflect the individual tastes and political biases of its owner/editor. *The New York Herald* of the 1840s through '60s *was* the opinionated James Gordon Bennett; the *Tribune*, the more socialistic Horace Greeley. Competitive, combative and aggressive, these flamboyant Victorian editors constantly pushed the boundaries of freedom of the press. They took on all opponents — including their journalistic rivals — in the columns of their papers, and street fights with unhappy victims of their attacks were a legendary hazard of the trade.

San Francisco editors were no exception. Their papers made little attempt to hide the editors' political loyalties or social ideologies. The *San Francisco Chronicle* had always been, in John P. Young's phrase, "pronouncedly Republican," while the *Illustrated Wasp* in its inaugural edition declared itself Democrat — indeed, was founded in 1876 in part to support Tilden's Presidential bid. The *Daily Alta California* was conservative and pro-business, the *Bulletin* socially aggressive, the *Call* determinedly neutral. And while none of the major dailies would have admitted allegiance to any specific religious denomination, all freely gave lip service to "Christian" values.[31]

The editors themselves were a colorful lot, epitomizing perfectly the stereotyped frontier newspaperman. James King of William — his unusual name was meant to set him apart from several other James Kings in town — used the pages of his *Daily Evening Bulletin* to attack local political corruption; his opponents had him assassinated in the street as he left his office one night.[32] Charles de Young, co-owner and editor of the *Chronicle*, was so controversial and malignant in print toward his enemies that both he and his brother went armed, "prepared," says John Bruce, "to defend their editorial viewpoint with vigor." Charles had already been involved in several shooting matches, one of them described by Richard Rapaport as "a running gun battle that raged up and down Battery." Luckily, in this case, no one was killed: the "only casualty was a young messenger boy, who was slightly wounded."[33] But the use of the printed page to vent the personal spleen of an editor was well established in San Francisco by 1879. So the Protestant ministers, in seeking the editors' support in their campaign against *The Passion*, were not misdirecting their energies.

At first, however, as we have seen, their urgings fell on relatively deaf ears. Most of the drama editors, at least, were reluctant to denounce the production without a hearing, merely to appease religious prejudice. Generally, their approach was to urge restraint on the part of the outraged moralists.

One notable exception was the critic for *The Argonaut*, the pseudonymous "Betsy B.," who from the very beginning found the production "simply an outrage." As she wrote to her fictitious correspondent, "Madge,"

> No one is deeply religious in these latter times, but . . . *per contra*, we are not irreligious enough to accept [the "Passion Play"] as a theatric [sic] spectacle. . . . Public feeling runs high, and, in point of fact, Madge, the whole affair is simply awful. I can not imagine even an atheist, who has ever sat at a mother's knee, lolling carelessly in an orchestra seat and regarding the spectacle of the Crucifixion, for they intend to go even so far as presenting that. . . .
> I hope, Madge, that they will not try to force it upon the public.

At the same time, "Betsy B." admitted facetiously,

> Of course, we should all go out of sheer curiosity. We could not stay away. But we shall be outraged and shocked to the last fibre.[34]

Other drama critics were not so quick to condemn. Their managing editors, on the other hand, tended to agree with "Betsy B.," although many of them supported the ministers' movement in a rather singular manner. The *Morning Call*, for instance, after printing a cautious notice in George Barnes's column on February 23 and publishing the first paid announcement three days later, thereafter simply stopped accepting any advertising from *The Passion* and allowed no further mention of the play in its theatre columns. Nor was Barnes sent to review it. On the other hand, neither did the *Call*'s editor rage on incessantly about it, as many no doubt wished he would. While covering the denunciations emanating from Sunday pulpits, the *Call*, much like Archbishop Alemany, remained for the most part above the fray. Likewise, the *Bulletin*, after a brief initial flurry of editorial condemnation, allowed no further advertising and never ran a review of the production; the evening edition of the *Bulletin*, in fact, carried this editorial policy to its extreme. Anyone reading only that journal for this period would hardly even know that anything like *The Passion* had ever been presented in San Francisco.[35]

A similar approach to the controversy was adopted by the *Daily Alta California*, which also gave no free column space to *The Passion*; it did, however, continue to accept paid advertising. But this sort of pragmatism was perhaps to be expected from the mouthpiece of the city's business community, a paper whose own course was "conservative," in John P. Young's biased opinion, "even in the matter of gathering and presenting the news." The *Alta*, says Young, "was regarded by the community as the representative of the substantial elements."[36]

Then, too, the *Alta* had a special problem. That paper, it will be recalled, had praised *The Passion* in January as a "literary labor of importance"; now the editor was compelled to explain why, one month later, it had suddenly become a sacrilege:

> While recognizing to the fullest extent the talent displayed by Mr. Salmi Morse in his literary creation, "The Passion Play," not only his friends, but the public at large must regret the indiscretion of himself and his advisors in arranging for its production upon the stage in this city. Such performances ... are entirely in antagonism with the more advanced civilization of today.[37]

It is ironic that the dubious assertion that San Francisco was far too civilized for *The Passion* was being offered by editors who carried guns in order to protect themselves from outraged enemies whom they might have slighted in their own injudicious editorials.

While condemnation in the press was virtually universal, then, it was by no means ubiquitous. In fact, compared to the amount of column space editors would give *The Passion* in New York, San Francisco papers were practically mute on the subject. The stubborn silence seemed so ridiculous to their rival editor at *The Argonaut* that he later lashed out at the hypocrisy of their ploy:

> Two newspapers in this city, which habitually criticise plays, appear to have known nothing of this one—did not discover that it had been put upon the stage, were unaware that anybody had been to see it. It was not advertised in their columns—they did not permit it to be. Now, *what* are the *Bulletin* and the *Call?*—they are certainly not newspapers.
>
> The *Bulletin* and *Call*, that is to say, do not advertise anything which has not their sanction, do not relate anything of the occurrence of which they disprove [sic]. *Ergo*, they *do* approve of "magnetic healing," fortune telling, abortion, quack doctoring, and "procuring"—for all these things they advertise. They *do* approve of murder, arson, theft, swindling, adultery, and rape, for all these things they recount with minute particularity. On the whole, are Messrs. [George K.] Fitch [of the *Bulletin*]

4. Preachers, the Press, and Politics as Usual 83

and [Loring] Pickering [the *Call*] any better as moral protectors of the public than they would be as purveyors of news?³⁸

"Betsy B." to the contrary, *The Argonaut* was the only major San Francisco journal to give even token support to Morse editorially. As for its froward critic, Miss "B" in this instance agreed with her editor:

The newspapers alone, strangely enough, have kept out of the discussion. Why? I can not say. Perhaps to discourage [the play's] continuance by refraining from a notice, which would be an advertisement. Perhaps because they see nothing wrong in the production, but hesitate to say so while the present state of feeling exists.³⁹

Still, the pointed avoidance of any mention of *The Passion* whatsoever, much like Archbishop Alemany's profound silence on the subject, did effectively keep these several papers from appearing to condone its presentation, and gave tacit approval to the growing movement for its legal suppression.

However, if *The Argonaut* and, in their own ways, the *Call*, *Bulletin* and *Alta*, were not enthusiastically beating the drums in the ministers' cause, there was one journal willing enough to join — if not to lead — the parade. But its reasons for doing so may have been more than simple concern for the community's threatened moral fabric.

As luck would have it, the paper in question was arguably the most influential daily in San Francisco. The *San Francisco Chronicle* had come a long way from its humble beginnings in 1865 as a theatrical throwaway. The de Young brothers, Charles and Michael (M. H.) — brother Gustavus had since been sent to an insane asylum in Stockton — had dropped the word *Dramatic* from their masthead in 1868, and cut back on theatrical coverage, in an ambitious bid to become the paper of record for San Francisco — indeed, for all of northern California. The *Chronicle's* new course would finally be set by M. H., whose "master plan," Richard Rapaport writes, "was to use the influence of the *San Francisco Chronicle* to revise a less than illustrious family history and then, through his paper's society pages, remake the social order of San Francisco in the image of that family."⁴⁰ Employing, under Charles's editorship, "scandal, controversy, and lively writing," the *Chronicle* had, throughout the 1870s, grown in wealth, in notoriety and, as a result, in power.

Naturally, this increased status had given rise to any number of rumors about how it had been achieved — rumors that usually involved blackmail, stock swindles or other unsavory practices. Stories about the de Youngs' origins also abounded, the most inflammatory of which held that their mother had been a St. Louis prostitute.⁴¹ It is known that they, like Morse and Belasco, were born Jewish and embraced Christianity (M. H.

converted to Catholicism). They were also ardent Republicans. Therefore, it is not surprising to find their *Daily Chronicle* stumping for the new state constitution of 1879, in alliance with the Workingmen's Party.

It was to be the powerful *Chronicle* that would now take up the banner and most effectively fulfill the Protestant ministers' need for an ally among the press — a fact that may sound surprising in light of M. H.'s own ties with the Catholic Church. Nonetheless, on Wednesday, February 26, two days after printing the official announcement of *The Passion*, the *Chronicle* became one of the first major dailies to editorially demand that "the management" of the production "respect the religious sentiments of the citizens of San Francisco and withdraw the objectionable spectacular play." The editorial, entitled "A Threatened Sacrilege," echoed the standard ministerial line:

> Any attempt to imitate the sacred drama by a theatrical company must necessarily degenerate into a travesty or caricature of the most holy event in sacred writ. An audience that is familiar with Mr. O'NEIL [sic] in his ordinary round of characters can only regard as sacrilege his assumption of the principal role in a representation of the crucifixion of Christ.[42]

Again the charge was made that professional actors could never display the kind of simple "religious enthusiasm" ascribed by de Young to the "illiterate" peasants of Oberammergau.

Such remarks would be repeated in the *Chronicle* over the four days remaining prior to the March 3 opening. Admittedly, its coverage comes off seeming more extensive than it might simply because of the almost total lack of mention in the rest of the San Francisco secular press. The day before the premiere, for example, the Sunday *Chronicle* included not one but two lengthy articles about *The Passion*, one on the front page, the second in the regular theatre column. The first more or less accurately recounted the history of religious drama in Medieval Europe; the second focused more on Morse's new text. Both pieces, however, came to the same negative conclusion: *The Passion* was "a hazardous experiment that ought never to have been undertaken."[43] Again, the message was clear. The management ought to respect the inviolability of the church in San Francisco and withdraw the proposed blasphemous presentation immediately.

The *Chronicle* editorially developed the motifs of the Protestant ministers — arguments based on emotional rather than intellectual or legal grounds. But if the de Youngs' denunciation of the production added little to the debate that was new, or well-reasoned, their attack had one other significant aspect to it, evidenced from their first editorial of February 26. In that opening broadside, apart from O'Neill, the only other individual singled out for reproach by the *Chronicle* was neither Salmi Morse nor "Lucky" Baldwin, but the nominal manager of the Grand Opera House —

4. Preachers, the Press, and Politics as Usual

Tom Maguire. In the opinion of the de Youngs, it was Maguire alone who had "entirely mistaken the sentiments of the reputable citizens of San Francisco, who have supported him through a long managerial career," by "fancying" that they would "sustain" him in "an attempt to caricature" the crucifixion of Jesus Christ. With his announcement that *The Passion* was in preparation, the paper charged, Maguire had "shocked the sensibilities of every citizen who reverences the religion which, under various forms, we all profess to respect."

The de Youngs' singling out of Maguire for vilification betrays a far more human motivation for their using their *Chronicle* to call for the closing of this particular play. For Charles de Young and Tom Maguire had been carrying on a personal feud that dated back more than a dozen years.[44]

The bad blood had begun in 1866, when Maguire presented the actress Matilda Heron in *Camille*. Tremenhere Johns, the drama critic for the de Youngs' *Daily Dramatic Chronicle* at the time, was of the opinion that Miss Heron's two hundred pounds made it a little hard to believe she was wasting away from consumption, and said so in print. The actress, naturally, took offense, and demanded that Maguire revenge her honor.

Maguire banished critic Johns from his Opera House (including once physically throwing him out when Johns tried to defy the ban). Then Maguire further decreed that the de Youngs' fledgling *Dramatic Chronicle* would no longer be sold in any opera house he managed. Charles de Young, already well versed in the effect a good fight might have on circulation, took on Maguire in the pages of his paper, and the feud was on.

John Young, the *Chronicle* historian and apologist, says that Maguire "provoked" the *Chronicle* with a series of articles in an unnamed paper, in which he denounced the de Youngs. The brothers struck back with scathing editorials in which they accused Maguire of, among other things, freely admitting to his Opera House "improper and notorious characters, and that his negligence in this regard was resented by the public."[45] This kind of slander prompted Maguire to sue the *Chronicle* for ciminal libel, a suit that Young claims "was never prosecuted because the paper was fully prepared to substantiate its allegation." According to other sources, however, the suit was indeed prosecuted, and Maguire won. He was awarded $2,500 — which the prosecuting attorney later reduced to a mere $5.[46] Even with a judgment of only five dollars against them, the de Youngs must have rankled at the decision. At any rate, this early skirmish set the stage for continual sniping between Maguire and the de Youngs over the years. As far as the *Chronicle* was concerned, therefore, any controversy touching Tom Maguire was fair game. And *The Passion* definitely touched Tom Maguire.

Morse tried to defuse any rancor by immediately issuing a card in which he announced that "neither Mr. Baldwin nor Mr. Maguire are in any way interested in the production of the *Passion*, beyond having contracted for the talented company to me at so much per week."⁴⁷ But it was widely believed that both Maguire and Baldwin were very much "interested" — as, it turned out, they were — and rumors of their involvement continued, despite official denials from all three.

So it was that the de Youngs' *Chronicle* was the only major newspaper offering almost daily coverage of the controversy as it unfolded. But its vociferous campaigning was more than adequate. Besides, their later silences notwithstanding, the other San Francisco papers were also at least on record as disapproving the production.

The Argonaut alone of all the major dailies failed to editorially condemn the play without reservation. (Of course, *The Argonaut* was the means through which "Betsy B." flailed away at it.) Finally, however, even that sympathetic organ could defy public pressure no longer — although it did wait until the initial run of *The Passion* was almost over, and the eye of the storm had seemingly passed, before coming out against it. It was not until March 8, 1879, that the editor of *The Argonaut* resignedly conceded that "the world has changed, the church has changed, the stage has changed," and what once was a means of worship "comes in these enlightened times to be but an absurd and irreverent money-making spectacle."⁴⁸

Even so, the editor was still not about to accept that the church had the right to legislate *The Passion* out of existence:

> The stage has its privileges; the church has its higher duties and responsibilities. The law can not define the boundary line between them, and only good sense and right feeling may determine where the feather-edge of amusement, pleasure, and innocent folly shades into the deeper lines of spiritual concern.

And even while bowing to public opinion, the editor argued in defense of the play:

> As to the propriety of presenting this play upon the stage, we have no especial feeling. We are not prepared to admit that it would do any harm at all to those who did not go to witness it, nor work any serious injury to those who did. We do not believe it would undermine any of the eternal truths upon which the Christian church is founded. We know its author, Mr. Salmi Morse, heard his play read at the church of the Jesuit fathers, and were impressed with the beauty of the sacred story told in the elegant diction of literature.

Then why was the editor finally joining the throng?

> Upon this question we have no fixed opinions, and because we have none of our own we accept those of the clergy of the Christian church. If, in

the opinion of religious and intelligent persons, this spectacle shall be regarded as hurtful and sacrilegious; if it wound the feelings of our Christian community, and by our Christian teachers shall be deemed of evil influence, then we say it should be withdrawn from the stage. We would respect the sensibilities of our Christian people, and in this respect allow their judgment to control ours.

As Morse would have been the first to point out, Pontius Pilate once said essentially the same thing.

By the time that *The Argonaut* came out against *The Passion*, however, its support was not really needed, for the ministers by then had not only the other San Francisco papers in their corner, but much of the national press as well. In Chicago, Philadelphia, Boston, Atlanta and New York — even in London[49] — subscribers had been informed of the events in the far western city, and in most cases, freely given their own editors' observations on the matter. Some agreed with their San Francisco colleagues and condemned the production as blasphemous. The outraged editor of the *New York Daily Mirror* called for a nationwide "popular condemnation" of both the play and of Tom Maguire, while the *Boston Times* chastised the entire cast on behalf of "all thinking, right-minded people."[50]

There were others, however, for whom the advantage of distance provided a comfortable objectivity. Charles Dana, the editor/owner of the *New York Sun*, reminded his readers that Passion plays, *per se*, had never been considered blasphemous in the past. "Perhaps the religious zeal of San Francisco," Dana noted wryly, "is just now stimulated by the necessity of demonstrating itself to the heathen Chinese and showing them how earnest California is in defence of religion."[51] But then, Dana could afford to be impertinent. *The Passion* wasn't in his backyard. Yet.

IV

The Politicians

Of course, there is no way of knowing just what proportion of the San Francisco public actually supported the demand for suppression of *The Passion*. Both the Protestant clergy and the newspapers claimed that they spoke for the "overwhelming majority," but the play's supporters — and there were many[52] — could point with equal justification to that segment of the public whose opinions were being voiced by purchasing tickets to the play. This willing audience, however, figured little in either pulpit or press.

At any rate, those moral citizens who denounced the production as sacrilege and demanded that it be closed were many — and loud. However, by Monday, March 3, the day of the scheduled opening, it was obvious even to them that their demonstrations, petitions and angry editorials were not going to stop the play. So that evening, the religious activists took their protest directly to their final ally, City Hall.

At this point, it is worth remembering that the time span for all of these events was very short.[53] Only two weeks had elapsed since the earliest rumors of the upcoming production had appeared in the theatrical columns; only *one* week since the first formal advertisement had been published; and a mere five days since the *Chronicle's* first editorial calling for the play's withdrawal. So the eleventh-hour march on the City Supervisors' offices on the very evening of the premiere was a reflection of the protesters' desperation as time ran out, and with it, their options. This is not to say that they had been idle; steps had been taken to find a legal means of forcing Maguire, Baldwin and Morse to close the play.

Among those who crowded into the Supervisors' offices that evening was an Episcopal rector, the Reverend Dr. Platt. Dr. Platt had on his own applied for an injunction to prevent the management from presenting *The Passion*. Unfortunately, the San Francisco Police Department authorities had been unsure whether or not they had the legal authority to interfere with what was advertised as a religious service.[54] Now Dr. Platt was here with the others, noisily demanding that the Supervisors pass their own law, if necessary, giving the police that authority.

The San Francisco Board of Supervisors was a twelve-member body, each Supervisor elected from one of the city's dozen wards. Its membership had long reflected the political entrenchment of the Yankee business community, and was, as a rule, dominated by the merchant class; therefore, it was also often heavily Protestant, as it was now. However, the Consolidation Act of 1856 had removed most of the real powers from the San Francisco Board—as it had from the city's mayor—in an effort to control corruption among elected local officials. Instead, the most routine city business had to be approved by the State Legislature.[55] Because of this, it was now a question whether even the Board of Supervisors had the legal authority to outlaw *The Passion*.

The present Board was, to say the least, a beleaguered one. In an election year, all were already feeling threatened by the phenomenal growth of the Workingmen's Party, and the loss of public confidence that denoted. Their unease was not unwarranted: not one of these men would be reelected that coming fall. Now, asked to judge between their Protestant constituents and a disruptive, sacrilegious theatrical production, the Board had a chance to demonstrate that it had not lost its ability to be effective. It could not opt for the Archbishop's diplomatic silence, as had some editors. This was a decision that would unavoidably be made in the glare of public scrutiny; also among the crowd this night was a reporter for the powerful *Chronicle*.

4. Preachers, the Press, and Politics as Usual

Not that the Supervisors had merely been waiting for just such a committee to descend on their City Hall offices. Earlier that very day, two of them had "constituted themselves as a committee" to try and settle the matter on their own. Supervisors James O. Rountree and E. Danforth, both stern-visaged Yankees sporting long, full whiskers, were the two most vociferous anti-*Passion* spokesmen on the Board of Supervisors. Mr. Rountree represented the city's Sixth Ward, which included Nob Hill, the wealthiest area in the city. Mr. Danforth had been elected from the neighboring Fourth Ward, not quite so upper class, but, still, home primarily to merchants, professionals and others in white-collar occupations.[56] Both were Protestants. Rountree, in fact, was reportedly the brother-in-law of the Reverend Mr. Hemphill.[57]

The two determined Supervisors had that morning first called upon Tom Maguire, at the Baldwin Theatre, to demand that the play not be opened. "I explained to them," Maguire said later, "in the strongest terms, that I had nothing whatever to do with the matter, and referred them to the author, manager and responsible person, Mr. Salmi Morse, whom they subsequently interviewed at the Grand Opera House." Morse's reaction to their visit was predictable: "a decisive refusal to withdraw it."[58]

Now, at this emotional, last-minute meeting in the new City Hall offices of the Board of Supervisors, it was the rebuffed Mr. Rountree who introduced a resolution requesting the City District Attorney to

> take such legal steps as will suppress the production and exhibition at the Grand Opera House, or at any other place within the city and county, of the play entitled The Passion, or of any other play illustrative of scriptural subjects or characters, the same being subversive to good morals and an outrage upon religion, making it subject to ridicule and contempt.

It was hoped that this resolution might be enough to stop the play's opening, now mere hours away; but in no way had it the force of law. Therefore, Rountree further introduced a draft of an official order

> making it a misdemeanor to exhibit, or take any part in exhibiting, in any theater or any other place where money is charged for admission, any play, performance or representation displaying, or intended to display, the life and death of Jesus Christ, or any play, performance or representation calculated or tending to profane or degrade religion, and making any person violating any of the provisions of the order guilty of such misdemeanor, to be punished by a fine of not more than $1,000, or imprisonment for not more than six months, or both.[59]

Rountree's first resolution was adopted unanimously; his proposed General Order was immediately passed to print without debate, and referred to the Judiciary Committee.

Something was happening, at last.

Rountree's hasty proposals were drafted in the heat of the moment, admittedly, but even so, the possible legal problems inherent in both measures should have been obvious to any rational analyst. To begin with, empowering the District Attorney to suppress not only *The Passion* specifically, but "any other play illustrative of scriptural subjects or characters," made the upcoming Young Men's Hebrew Association presentation, *Cantata of Esther*, equally subject to city censorship. Moreover, Rountree's sweeping General Order, if adopted, making it a misdemeanor to represent "in any play, performance or representation," the life and or death of Jesus Christ, in any venue "where money is charged for admission," would have to apply equally to every annual presentation of Handel's *Messiah* or Bach's *St. Matthew Passion* presented by any glee club — or church group — in any auditorium or parish hall in San Francisco. Even ignoring these potential sticking points, his proposal to make it illegal simply to hold in "contempt" religion — again, "religion" here clearly meaning Protestant Christianity — was a violation of the First Amendment of the United States Constitution. "It does me no injury for my neighbor to say there are twenty gods, or no God," Thomas Jefferson had written some hundred years before; had he so publicly spoken those sentiments in San Francisco in 1879, for remuneration, the Board of Supervisors might well have sent him to jail.

Making these measures so sadly ironic was the fact that it had never been Morse's intention to "degrade" or "ridicule" religion, but only to glorify it. Again, it was the Protestant clergy who decreed that *The Passion* was an "outrage upon religion." And for that very reason, the greatest problem with Rountree's knee-jerk resolutions was that they put San Francisco law enforcement officials in the same position that seventeenth-century religious colonists had found so untenable. They made city government responsible for enforcing and punishing what was or what was not morally acceptable to one specific branch of religion.

The twentieth-century reader comprehends that this last condition was, again, in clear violation of the First Amendment's "establishment clause." No religion, not even the vaguely nonspecific "Christian religion," could have its teachings or, in this case, its public image protected by law. The legal scholar and First Amendment historian Harry Kalven, Jr., has recently written that the Constitution made religious censorship in this country impossible. "There is in the United States," Kalven says, "no heresy, no blasphemy."[60] As Salmi Morse's plight demonstrates, however, legal opinion in the late nineteenth century was not yet so sure. The emotionally heightened times demanded that some legislation — even bad legislation — be quickly forthcoming, and so it was.

There were, however, the formalities to complete, and so Rountree's draft was referred to the Judiciary Committee, which in turn would submit it to City and County Attorney Burnett for a final ruling on its legality. Then it would go to Mayor Andrew J. Bryant for his signature. As Burnett's ruling might take days, in the meantime there was the stopgap request that the District Attorney find some way to intervene within the next few hours. Danforth, naturally, applauded Rountree's measures, saying that the Board of Supervisors, as a body, "should put itself upon record as against such exhibitions—a measure demanded by the community generally."[61]

Those shouting, angry citizens crowded into the Supervisors' offices that evening certainly seemed to support Danforth's claim that the community as a whole was outraged. And they must have sighed a collective sigh of relief to see that action was finally being taken, even if it was literally at the last possible moment.

At least *something* was going to happen.

Meanwhile, a far larger crowd of equally noisy citizens—many of them, in the *Chronicle*'s malicious view, "of a class too ready to improve any opportunity that might occur for the creation of tumult and disorder"[62]—was at that same moment gathering in the streets outside the Grand Opera House, several blocks away.

Inside the Grand, there were still more citizens. The auditorium was "nearly filled," the parquet and dress circle peopled with "a very select" audience, the galleries crowded with the usual noisome "gods." "About one-fifth were fashionably dressed women," according to one report, while the bigoted "Betsy B." would exaggeratedly scoff that "seven-eighths of the first audience" were Jews.[63] There were some Protestant ministers seen in attendance, come to dislike what they had already denounced. There were members of the press there, too, including several critics who knew their opinions would never see the light of day. Finally, there were a few who could qualify as politicians—including the Mayor.

Backstage, the actors nervously prepared for the moment of truth. James O'Neill later told a friend, "I was uncertain up to ten minutes before I went to the theatre whether I should not give up the whole thing. My wife threw herself upon her knees at my feet and pleaded with me to send word that I would not go on. She said the people would kill me."[64] At 32, having labored as a stock star in both New York and San Francisco companies, he had yet to find that one perfect play that would catapult him into national prominence, that one role that would forever be stamped his. Would this be it? If O'Neill had once thought so, he may now have had his doubts. But here he was, in his dressing room below the stage, staring into the mirror at the reflection of Jesus Christ.

Everywhere, inside the theatre and out, everyone anxiously waited. Whispering, watching. Waiting with a mixture of excitement and apprehension for the night's entertainment—onstage or off—to begin.

Something was going to happen.

5
The Passion Premieres

I

What happened that night was surely not what most San Franciscans expected.

Those who stood in the misty night outside the Grand Opera House on Mission Street, hoping for a battle royal, were left with disappointment. Either because there was no such law clearly empowering him to do so, or simply because he had no desire to suppress the production, the city district attorney chose not to carry out Supervisor Rountree's directive. No brigades of mounted police came barreling down Mission Street at the last minute to halt the production and carry everyone off in paddy wagons. Neither were there bands of irate churchgoers marching around the corner, armed with bricks and clubs, intending to do the job themselves. Instead, the appointed hour of performance arrived with no move being made by the city authorities. The "show" remained entirely indoors, and those outside simply stood in the drizzle and waited until, one by one, their numbers dwindled.

For the Protestant ministers and their followers, hoping to see Divine retribution, this night was equally disappointing. The fervent prayers of the Reverend Smith notwithstanding, no heavenly earthquake cleft the Grand in twain. No ethereal darkness covered the moon and made all time stand still. True enough, the entire city, figuratively speaking, may have come to a halt at that very hour, but not *The Passion.* That spectacle went on regardless. And the following morning the dawn would come, and San Francisco would stand, unchanged.

For those *inside* the Grand Opera House, however, the night's events would bring the greatest surprise. Even many who came to scoff were to leave impressed by what one reporter would call "a representation of uninterrupted solemnity—one that is in some respects sublime."[1] Maguire and Belasco had made every effort to minimize the production's kinship with everyday Victorian theatre. The regular Act Curtain was gone, replaced by a specially painted drop depicting "a distant view of Calvary"; there was

5. The Passion *Premieres*

MISSION STREET, BET. THIRD AND FOURTH.

SALMI MORSE, - - - - - Lessee and Manager.

Orchestra, Dress Circle and Parquette, One Dollar, (Reserved seats, Fifty Cents Extra.) Family Circle, Fifty Cents. Gallery Twenty-five cents.

LENTEN SEASON.

EVERY EVENING, SUNDAY INCLUDED,

Will be rendered with every circumstance of Solemnity and attention to historical facts,

"THE PASSION"

A Choir of Eighty Voices. A Full Band of Instruments.

Views in the Holy Land and Jerusalem.

1. THE PRESENTATION IN THE TEMPLE.
2. THE MASSACRE OF THE INNOCENTS.
3. THE DEATH OF ST. JOHN THE BAPTIST.
4. BY THE BROOK OF KEDRON.
5. THE GARDEN OF GETHSEMANE.
6. THE GABATHA.

"IT IS FINISHED."

☞ Owing to the sacred character of the representation, the audience is respectfully requested to suppress all outbursts of applause until the drop of the Curtain.

"THE PASSION"

Will be rendered on Saturday Afternoon at 2 o'clock.

Programme for "The Passion," 1879. The simple, black-bordered programme omitted the usual theatrical trappings, such as the cast list. Also note that the final, climactic scenes — of the Crucifixion, Resurrection and Ascension — were not presented, in deference to religious opposition. (Courtesy San Francisco Archives, San Francisco Public Library) no preshow concert, no curtain-raiser, no after-piece; even the four-page program pointedly omitted the standard Cast of Characters, and listed only the order of scenes. A printed admonition further warned the attendees: *"Owing to the sacred character of the representation, the audience is respectfully requested to suppress all outbursts of applause until the drop of the Curtain."*[2] "There was some manifestation of a disorderly element in the gallery," the *Chronicle* was to report, "but after a few slight attempts at ridicule at the outset, it subsided into respectful attention, and any interruptions were suppressed with marked expressions of disapproval by the audience generally."[3] From the moment Henry Widmer stepped to the podium and began conducting the Overture—based on Bach's *St. Matthew Passion*—the spell was cast and the evening, it seems, unequivocally belonged to Salmi Morse and the members of the Baldwin Stock Company.

Few latter-day historians have stopped to ponder the production itself; following William Winter's lead, they tend to condescendingly dismiss it as "goody-goody moral twaddle," and concentrate instead on the religious controversy that surrounded it.[4] But what must it have been like, with young David Belasco experimenting in "grand-scale realism" on a stage that could accommodate such excesses; with the legendary Tom Maguire as Manager, funded by the willing "Lucky" Baldwin; with James O'Neill, a still-exciting young actor, searching and unafraid to reach, heading a large and talented cast of San Francisco's best? What, indeed, must it have been like?

A rather curiously gushing article in the otherwise unfriendly *San Francisco Chronicle* describes firsthand the San Francisco production of *The Passion*, and gives us the closest approximation to the performance itself. It is worth reprinting here:

> The music [of the Overture] ceases; there is a silent pause, during which it is evident that the audience is more curious than reverent. The lights are turned low; the curtain rises upon an impressive tableau—"The Presentation in the Temple." There is an altar and a high priest; a large chorus of male voices; troupes of acolytes swinging censers; a chorus of mothers bearing their babes in their arms. The costuming is brilliant. In the dramatis personae the Jewish type prevails and is strongly marked; the effect is realistic to the last degree. From the opening of the act ... the sublime choruses sustain the [scene] and it is brought to a close amid irrepressible bursts of applause. The act-drop is a distant view of Calvary, with the three crosses in relief against a lurid sky; a flight of angels brightens the somberness of the scene. The effect produced upon the audience by the act is undoubtedly favorable.... During the interlude the music is again resumed, with an introduction to Act II, "The Massacre of the Innocents." The scene is a wild gorge in the desolate mountains of Judea. The lights are subdued; amid the wailing of the orchestra the holy family descends; there are but few words exchanged; it is rather a living picture, vivid and by no means displeasing.... [The

5. The Passion *Premieres*

brilliant grouping as the curtain descends, arouse[s] the audience to something like enthusiasm, and the curtain is again raised for a moment upon the final tableau.... [In Act III, Salome] and her attendants dance before the throne of Herod; baby harpers sit upon each hand; a multitude of retainers gather to feast their eyes upon the sensuous beauty of Salome.... The costuming of the chief actors is magnificent. Thus far there has been nothing repellent in the Passion play. It is merely an historical drama possessing few good lines and a great number of ungraceful ones, that seem to half-paralyze the tongues of the actors.... We are the solemn witnesses of a solemn tragedy presented with the utmost solemnity. Act IV, "By the Brook of Kedron" [sic]. The test has come; the curtain rises on a scene of surpassing beauty. It is a touch of Eden — the umbrageous groves, the green pastures, the still waters, and in the foreground a group of silent figures. There is not a sound in all the house save the low moan of the music, every note of which seems to throb upon sympathetic strings.... [The figures] are still silent, still motionless. A dazzling light surrounds the central figure, a light that follows him like a glory at every step. It is the unmistakable face.... It is the Christ and his apostles!... Act V, "The Garden of Gethsemane" ... —it is all vividly represented. Even in the sacred mysteries — the breaking of the bread, the pouring of the wine, the prayer in the garden — there was no visible evidence that the audience was scandalized. Act VI ["The Gabatha"] ... is the least agreeable of the acts, for in it the spectator's indignation is aroused; not at anything which may be called sacrilegious, but at the turbulent Jews who are clamoring for their innocent victim. We have heard him deliver the word of life more impressively than it has ever been our lot to hear it delivered from the pulpit. We have followed him with

A PECULIAR SYMPATHY

That no actor has ever before aroused. The Christ of this Passion play is a chaste, reverential and in some respects a very extraordinary impersonation. It may be said of the dramatis personae that without exception they were assumed with impressive reverence.[5]

In short, whatever the script's deficiencies, the San Francisco production of *The Passion* cannot be fairly dismissed merely as "moral twaddle." It was not an embarrassingly shoddy affair, nor, for that matter, a piously untheatrical one. It was like no other play ever produced in San Francisco. It virtually demanded the audience's attention and respect, and won both.

By common consensus, the acting honors went to James O'Neill. Virtually every eyewitness account had nothing but praise for his understated, deeply felt interpretation of the Messiah. The correspondent for the *New York Sun* applauded him for making "no effort to elicit applause by theatrical display," and O'Neill's fellow actors related how, during the performance, he would often be in tears and would retire alone to his dressing room after every scene.[6] David Belasco later recalled that such emotional immersion paid off, for O'Neill's effect on his audience was electrifying:

> [W]hen O'Neill came up from his dressing room and appeared on the stage with a halo about him women sank on their knees and prayed, and when he was stripped and dragged before *Pontius Pilate*, crowned with a crown of thorns, many fainted.
>
> I have produced many plays in many parts of the world, but never have I seen an audience awed as by "The Passion Play."[7]

Belasco (as did O'Neill) ever after defended *The Passion*, and one must accept as sincere his opinion — still heartily expressed thirty-five years later — that "the greatest performance of a generation was the *Christus* of James O'Neill."

As the performance progressed that opening night, it soon became obvious to everyone in the theatre, even those who had come to criticize, that there was nothing profane or sacrilegious about *The Passion*. Rather, as one journalist reported, "The more impressive scenes were received with a reverential silence, which their deep solemnity seemed to command, without exception." ("Solemn" appeared to be the catchword of the hour.) Certainly, few in the audience that night could have expected the play to be so genuinely powerful. According to that same reporter, from first to last, "the interest of the numerous spectators was riveted, as if spell bound, and it was only at the fall of the curtain that long and well-merited applause was bestowed on those who so ably had impersonated the author's ideas and characters in this divine history."[8]

The final curtain descended after Act VI, "The Gabatha," which depicted Christ's trial before Pontius Pilate, and there the play abruptly ended. There was no Crucifixion. No Resurrection or Ascension.

> The audience still tarried, uncertain whether the exhibition had concluded, until the manager [i.e., Salmi Morse] finally appeared in front of the curtain in response to a clamorous appeal for explanation. He stated that the play embraced four additional scenes, which had been prepared, but in consequence of the violent opposition that had been raised against the exhibition by the press and pulpit, it had been deemed advisable to omit them, and he asked the indulgence of the audience for the obedience to the antagonistic sentiment. The audience then quietly withdrew.[9]

This artistic capitulation to the religious community reveals how keenly Morse and Maguire must have felt the threat of public censure. These final acts — the Crucifixion, Resurrection and Ascension — were the narrative and visual highpoints of the play. They were, in fact, the very scenes that gave the story any significance, religious or dramatic, and to sacrifice them represented a major compromise.

Furthermore, while this tactic may have been undertaken in order to lessen moralists' objections to the production, omitting the miraculous

5. The Passion Premieres 97

climax opened the door for religious protestations of another sort. The *New York Sun*'s reviewer seemed to sense this:

> It seemed to me, last evening, that while the humanity of Christ was depicted with all becoming reverence, the divinity was obscured and almost forgotten, as the action of the play progressed. Judged by the orthodox interpretation of Christ's divine origin and holy mission upon earth, the drama is irreverent.[10]

Self-censored so as not to seem too religious, in its truncated form *The Passion* could now be criticized for not being religious enough.

Still, unease over the actual staging of the Crucifixion and Ascension is certainly understandable. Having heard nothing but the direct predictions from ministers, newspapers and city officials for the past two weeks, which of these men could really say what effect it would have on the audience? Indeed, the story is widely held that the play was, in fact, "incentive to some public disturbances and breaches of the peace." This is repeated as fact by Timberlake, the Gelbs, by Bennett and Kibbee—in almost every later account.[11] But the only source for this story seems to be William Winter, who wrote that "ignorant Irish who witnessed it were so distempered that, on going forth, some of them, from time to time, assaulted peaceable Jews in the public streets."[12] However, there is no historical evidence to corroborate this report; neither the *Chronicle* nor the *Call*, the *Bulletin*, *The Argonaut* or the *Alta* contains any such reports of racial attacks instigated by a performance of *The Passion*. Had any such public disturbances taken place, one would expect that the play's opponents would have loudly exploited the fact in renewed attacks on the production; but none did. Editorials—especially from the *Chronicle*—would have cited anti-Semitic reprisals as a further reason for shutting down the play; there were no such editorials. Instead, as the *Chronicle* story clearly states: "The audience then quietly withdrew."

Thus *The Passion* had its premiere despite all moves against it, and showed itself to be much less—and much more—than anyone expected. But if Morse was convinced that this would vindicate his play and end the attacks, he was mistaken. On the contrary, the artistic success of *The Passion* only made it that much more troubling to its opponents, who could never accept that a stage play might be more powerful at delivering the Gospel message than a Protestant minister. (One plank in the opposition's platform did have to be dropped, however: the charge that *The Passion* would have an immoral influence on its ignorant audience. Not only was it obvious that the production had been mounted with impeccable care, but its audience was turning out to include most of San Francisco's finest citizens, who all week long clamored for tickets.[13])

Nor was *The Passion* soundly panned by the critics, as received wisdom would have it. At worst, it might be said that reviewers tried to have it both ways. For no one, least of all those few critics whose reviews were actually printed, quite knew how to respond to the production. After all, most opinions had been delivered long before the play had ever opened. Now, faced with the reality of its physical production, they could only echo Albert Sutliffe, the *Chronicle* reviewer, who, after praising virtually every aspect of the production—excepting Morse's dialogue, of course—went on to condemn the play anyway, merely on principle. "It is impossible to write on such a subject as this in the vein of usual theatrical criticism," Sutliffe admitted; therefore, his conclusion did not, perhaps could not, challenge the position already laid out so strongly by his bosses, the de Youngs: "Admitting even that the presentation was viewed with reverential attention," Sutliffe concluded lamely, "it cannot be accepted that a theater is the proper place for a Passion play."[14] The other major reviewer, *The Argonaut's* "Betsy B.," likewise remained unconverted by what she saw, although she, too, was forced to praise its many merits. She erroneously credited Salmi Morse with being "an admirable stage manager. The costumes, the chorus, the tableaux, the music, were arranged with a taste which is beyond cavil." In the early scenes, she found "nothing absolutely sacrilegious excepting that a very unpleasant-looking infant in [the Virgin Mary's] arms is hailed as the Son of God." As for the *last* third of the play, however—even without the Crucifixion—

> [W]hat follows should not be allowed—the Last Supper, the Agony in the Garden, the Crowning of Thorns.... Whatever delight the cold artistic eye may have taken in the picture of the Last Supper, the most callous could not fail to be shocked at the literal rendering. It was blasphemous, desecrating, unholy.[15]

There were the "deeper feelings and holier prejudices of nine-tenths of the community" to consider, she felt, and so the play ought to be closed, not because it was a bad play, but merely "upon the simple doctrine of good will."

The same kind of moral obstinacy was echoed by Protestant ministers that week, as they kept up their efforts to force city authorities to suppress the production. First Universalist's pastor, the Reverend Dr. B. F. Bowles, for example, who attended the opening performance on March 3, freely admitted the following Sunday that the play was "solemn and reverent" and "of a high degree of excellence"; even so, it should not be encouraged, he preached, because the character of Jesus—"that life of lives which should ever stand in our minds apart from and above common humanity"—was necessarily tainted through its association with "the imperfect and comparatively unworthy character of the actor" playing Him.[16]

As is so often the case in religious controversies, few minds were

5. The Passion *Premieres*   99

changed by the actual production of *The Passion*. Stunning it may have been. Groundbreaking it may have been. Respectful and reverent, as well. But it had been pronounced a great sacrilege before it ever opened, and a great sacrilege it would remain.

II

Performances of *The Passion* continued throughout the week of March 3, while the Board of Supervisors awaited City and County Attorney Burnett's ruling on the legality of Rountree's opening-night anti-*Passion* resolution. Crowds continued to be respectable, although not large enough to fill the elephantine Grand. Then, too, attendance was reportedly kept low by bad weather. By the end of the week, the *Call* was predicting that the production would "probably" lose at least two thousand dollars.[17] But Morse was exuberant. Rumors began to circulate of his taking the play to New York, and within another week he was promising the "early production of a spectacular play under the title of 'A Midwinter's Night [sic] Dream.'"[18] Salmi Morse the Playwright had arrived.

The Passion also remained the object of nationwide curiosity and innumerable rumors.[19] Not to be outdone, New York papers began directing their readers' attention to an alleged "Passion play" then being presented right in their own midst by the Religious Plastic Art Company. Actually a series of *tableaux vivants* recreating famous paintings of biblical stories, this amateur program had been presented—"unopposed," in the dire words of the *New York Sun*—in Catholic parishes and public halls throughout New York City since Christmas 1878.[20] While designating this program a "Passion play" was exaggerating the case—there were no dialogues, no plot, no dramatic movement, no *play*—the presentation enjoyed a brief notoriety in the pages of New York journals, thanks to its approximation to *The Passion* in San Francisco. At the very least, the *Sun* wanted to believe, the Religious Plastic Art Company's untroubled presence in the city seemed to imply that New Yorkers were far more tolerant and sophisticated than their comically outraged brethren in San Francisco. Apropos of which, the *San Francisco Chronicle* reminded its readers of similar dramatic *tableaux vivants* presented in San Francisco "twenty years ago" by the famous Keller Troupe. "These Living Pictures were, we believe, licensed in every city of the land," the *Chronicle* noted, sagely concluding that perhaps the only difference between the Kellers' static, arty poses and Salmi Morse's dramatic extravaganza finally came down to a question of "the propriety or the impropriety of *Realism!*"[21]

On Friday night, March 7, the Judiciary Committee of the Board of Supervisors finally held its meeting to consider, among other business,

Rountree's proposed ordinance outlawing religious plays in San Francisco. Some committee members felt that the best course at this late date was to simply let the present play "die a natural death at the hands of an unsympathizing public. Non-paying houses would have a greater effect than a prohibition."[22] The committee had still not heard a word from Attorney Burnett regarding the legality of the Rountree ordinance. Nevertheless, it was decided to recommend, at next Monday's meeting of the entire Board, that it be passed. This would ensure that no future Passion plays would ever see the stage in San Francisco.

Three days later, on March 10, Burnett legitimized the Judiciary Committee's decision by finally submitting his opinion: the proposed order was, he wrote, "well drawn," and "if passed it will be legal."[23] That same night, at the Board of Supervisors' regular Monday meeting, the Judiciary Committee introduced its slightly reworded version of the order from Rountree, which read, in whole:

> It shall be unlawful for any person to exhibit, or take any part in exhibiting in any theatre, or other place, where money is charged for admission, any play, or performance, or representation, displaying, or intended to display, the life or death of Jesus Christ, or any play, performance, or representation, calculated or tending to profane or degrade religion.[24]

The Board passed the ordinance unanimously. It would now be forwarded to Mayor Bryant for his signature — or veto. Should the Mayor neither sign nor veto the legislation within ten days, it would automatically become law.

Curiously, it was at first rumored that Bryant would, indeed, veto the ordinance, despite City Attorney Burnett's favorable opinion, as Bryant himself thought it "unconstitutional." He had thoroughly examined the law, Bryant would tell the *Call*, and he had conferred with members of the judiciary; and it was his fear, he said, that "such a law would conflict with the rendition of oratorios."[25] The real reason for his reluctance to sign such a bill would come out later: he had seen *The Passion* himself and personally found nothing objectionable in it.[26] For the time being, however, the Mayor did nothing about the act and the city had to wait impatiently for the question to be resolved.

Even at that, the Mayor's legal dallying was already beside the point, as the city's dramatic columns had unexpectedly announced that *The Passion* would close after the March 9 (Sunday) performance — only one week after its premiere. This surprising development is usually credited to the continuing efforts of the angry moralists; David Belasco wrote in his memoirs that such was the case. According to him, threatening letters had been sent that week to Maguire and, presumably, to Morse. Moreover, Belasco

5. The Passion *Premieres*

wrote, yet another "committee of citizens" called upon Tom Maguire (although he may have been referring to Supervisors Danforth and Rountree's meeting of March 3). At any rate, Belasco recounted that these good citizens "worked upon [Maguire's] credulous nature until he believed that he was marked by the devil for sacrifice and would meet with instant death if he did not withdraw the play." As a result, said Belasco, "in a fever of fear he closed the theatre."[27] The Gelbs, among others, further elaborate that the cowed Maguire then "hastily substituted" a run of *The Miner's Daughter*, starring Rose Eytinge, for the abruptly canceled *Passion*.[28]

According to the historical record, however, it was not that way. To begin with, Rose Eytinge's return to the Baldwin in *The Miner's Daughter* was anything but "hastily substituted." It had been promised as early as February 23, when the *Call* reported that Miss Eytinge, then appearing at Baldwin's with Cyril Searle, had been "engaged to play at Baldwin's for a [three-week] season" minus her costar. She was to be supported by the members of the Baldwin Stock Company—including James O'Neill and Olive West. While no specific dates for this "season" were given at that time, by March 2—a day *before The Passion* opened—the *Alta* could be a bit more specific, saying her engagement would probably commence on "Monday a week," i.e., March 9.[29] *The Miner's Daughter* was no last-minute substitution; on the contrary, it is clear that from the beginning *The Passion* was expected to run for no more than a week.

Secondly, Miss Eytinge's engagement was to be staged at the Baldwin, not at the Grand Opera House. It will be recalled that the Baldwin had been housing the Barlow, Wilson, Primrose and West Minstrels (which was one reason *The Passion* was staged at the Grand in the first place); therefore, the specific dates for Miss Eytinge's return were dependent upon the closing of the Minstrels, as well as *The Passion*.

Further casting doubt on Belasco's "fevered" closing story is the fact that *The Passion*, in the end, did not in fact close on the ninth of March, but continued for another two performances—"In deference," said the ads, "to a widely expressed desire on the part of the many, whom the inclemency of the weather prevented from witnessing this sublime work."[30] Forced to wait for the Stock Company, *The Miner's Daughter* was delayed until Wednesday, March 12. Even then, the seeming continued success of *The Passion* almost prevented that opening from taking place.

"It was proposed to continue [*The Passion*] during the [second] week," the *Call* reported later, "as attendance was large enough to warrant this course; but a difficulty arose in finding an actor to fill the principal personation."[31] This was, to say the least, an understatement. For Salmi did attempt to keep *The Passion* running at the Grand Opera House despite the loss of his leading actors to Rose Eytinge's melodrama at the Baldwin. Miss Eytinge, already miffed at the two-day postponement, adamantly refused to wait another week for her leading man, James O'Neill, to finish at the Grand. Morse then proposed to replace O'Neill in the role of Christ with John N. Long, who had been playing Joseph, but to this O'Neill himself "offered the most strenuous objections, even to the cancelling of his contract." As the *Chronicle* explained O'Neill's position,

> With grave misgivings he had assumed the sacred character and bearing the brunt of the general condemnation of the press as to its production, he had earned, in his opinion, a well-merited approval to his efforts and he would not resign the part, and so the further presentation of *The Passion* had to be postponed.[32]

According to the *New York Mirror*, this little offstage melodrama was played out right down to the wire:

> The managers had slyly ordered everybody concerned in *The Passion* to be on hand at the Grand Opera House, and even got so far as to have everybody dressed for the performance, when Mr. O'Neil [sic] came to front with the surprising knowledge of the duplicity and emphatically refused to be enticed to Baldwin's until the Grand Opera was closed and the performers dismissed. At this late hour, after much persuasion, he was induced to go to his post at the Baldwin, and finally the curtain went up [almost an hour late] on an impatient audience....
> In consequence of these troublesome circumstances, Mr. O'Neil seemed distracted and ill at ease [in *The Miner's Daughter*] and gave a very unsatisfactory performance of Fergus Derrick.[33]

It is no wonder Miss Eytinge never mentions this Baldwin season (much less anything about *The Passion*) in her memoirs.

On that startling dramatic note, *The Passion* closed its doors, March 11, 1879. It had run for ten performances. But far from responding to a "fever of fear," this closing was seen as a temporary measure only. Within days, the city's newspapers were running a hyperbolic advertisement promising *The Passion*'s return:

> **NOTICE.** Notwithstanding the immense crowds that regularly attended the representations of this sublime work, they will be suspended for a few days, in order to reproduce the sacred drama with increased splendor and solemnity.
> Due notice will be given of the first representation.

If Maguire was not exactly in a fever, others were. A rumor immediately made the rounds of theatrical circles that the Mayor, despite his reluctance, had that very day, upon learning of the production's proposed revival, signed the Supervisors' ordinance into law, "but further inquiry" by the *Chronicle* "showed that this news was at least premature."[34]

III

Now it was Salmi Morse who had to wait, while Rose Eytinge played out her three-week season at Baldwin's. In the meantime, the ten-day period in which the Mayor had to decide the fate of the Supervisors' ordinance was passing, with Mayor Bryant still opting to take no action at all. He freely admitted to the *Call* that, while he himself saw nothing irreverent in the production, he had decided to yield to "the outraged sense of the religious community" by doing nothing to prevent the ordinance from taking effect. Thus, by default, Ordinance Number 1493 became Section 62 of General Order Number 1,587, of the laws of San Francisco, on March 21, 1879.[35] It was no longer Pulpit and Press vs. Playhouse; the church's position was now law.

Four days later came the first test of the widest possible interpretation of that ordinance. The Young Men's Hebrew Association staged the religious oratorio *Cantata of Esther* at the Grand Opera House, March 25.[36] The authorities ignored it. Six days after that, the Handel and Haydn Society offered Mendelssohn's Old Testament oratorio *Athalie*, at Platt's Hall. Again the new law was not invoked. Clearly, the Supervisors had decided, these works did not "profane religion." Then, everyone knew that the law was intended to stop only one specific production — Salmi Morse's *Passion*.

Nevertheless, confidence was running high among the play's backers. Pointing to the fact that public interest had been "on the increase" when the play was forced to close, they seem to have still been convinced that, as O'Neill would later put it, there was "a fortune in the piece,"[37] and it was very much worth the gamble. "Lucky" Baldwin reportedly felt so strongly about the production's possibilities that on April 10 he and Morse signed a contract under which the entire company would afterward be taken east, to play *The Passion* in leading cities across the country, culminating with a run in New York. The *Chronicle* reported that this contract had Baldwin "assuming all expenses and allowing Mr. Morse fifty per cent of the net receipts,"[38] but such liberal terms for a Victorian playwright seem highly doubtful and may have been the product of more of Salmi's shameless self-aggrandizement. Whatever the terms of the agreement, however, it is important to note that everyone — including Baldwin — was confident that the endeavor would, in the end, succeed and that the city authorities would not interfere after all.

Unfortunately, some of the actors were not so sanguine, and a few withdrew from the revival rather than face a possible jail sentence. Samuel Piercy, for one, gave up his tongue-twisting role of Herod, and was replaced by "Mr. Walton," an Australian actor. O'Neill, Lewis Morrison and most of the other leads, however, were perfectly willing to resume their parts, regardless of any threat.

No one, of course, was as confident as Salmi Morse that *The Passion* could vindicate itself. In fact, no sooner had Rountree's ordinance taken effect than Morse was telling the *Chronicle* that *The Passion* would reopen "despite the prohibition of the authorities." Furthermore, far from backing away from a confrontation, it was now Morse's novel intention to deliberately "test whether the municipal ordinance is constitutional or not." For the first time, he began speaking of "defend[ing] his rights before the Courts of law."[39] To question the constitutionality of a city's antitheatre ordinance was virtually unheard of in nineteenth-century America. But to argue a constitutional "right" to write a play was radically new. To make such a claim was to take that crucial leap from viewing Drama as Theatre, to seeing Drama as Speech, and no court had ever been asked to make that leap before. It might be said that few Victorian American playwrights would themselves have made such a claim. "With so much prejudice to overcome," warned the *Chronicle*, "this would appear to be a hazardous experiment."[40]

There were others, however, who just as quickly saw Morse's point about the thorny question of constitutionality, albeit approaching the question from a different side. *The Argonaut*, which had earlier supported Morse, angrily took the San Francisco Board of Supervisors to task for its new law that would, in effect, protect "religion." "Whose religion?" the editor demanded.

> If they do not mean religion in the abstract, they must mean the Christian religion; which, obviously, is just what they do mean. We are clearly of the opinion ... [that] the organic law of the nation [is] based partly on the theory that all religions are entitled to equal protection, and each can better be left to the protection of public opinion than given that of the law. Would the Supervisors stop a play that ridiculed the worship of a Chinese joss?[41]

Whether one viewed the issue as did Morse, who claimed constitutional protection as a playwright; or as did *The Argonaut*, which argued the unconstitutionality of protecting the Christian religion—it was obvious that the First Amendment was going to play an important part in the uncertain future of *The Passion*.

Thus, as Rose Eytinge neared the end of her run the first week of April 1879, the city's attention was once again focused on the Grand Opera House, and the showdown that was now inevitable. *The Passion* was scheduled to reopen on April 15, Easter Tuesday, and tickets went back on sale the Thursday before; demand for the first night was heavy. The revival was to be "new and improved," and this time the final climactic scenes and tableaux which had been previously omitted were to be reinstated *in toto*. This time there would be no capitulating to religious sensibilities. This time *The Passion* would be seen as Salmi Morse had always intended.

5. The Passion *Premieres*

This time, too, the city's newspapers were all represented at the second opening on April 15 — if still not to review the production, then at least to cover the newsworthy events promised by the ominous presence in the house of Police Officer A. E. C. Bradford, Jr. As it had been on the first opening night, the auditorium was once again crowded with "a large and attentive audience," come to be both witness and participant in the drama.

Like all good actors, though, Bradford made them wait for his entrance. Scene by scene, *The Passion* progressed, with the policeman remaining implacably in his place, and tension rising palpably. Act Six, the point at which the previous production had ended, came and passed without his stirring; Act Seven, the realistic Crucifixion, evoking audible gasps from some in the audience, segued into the sorrowful Descent from the Cross; then came the triumph of the Resurrection and finally, after almost three hours, the emotionally cathartic Ascension. The audience, having finally seen *The Passion* in its entirety, was left, in Belasco's words, "hushed and breathless."

George Barnes, finally given his chance to comment on the play in the pages of the *Call*, wrote: "With the exception of the Herod scene, the drama is amplified and improved in many particulars." Barnes was most favorably impressed with the new scenes and music, especially the staging of the Ascension — "a strikingly beautiful mechanical effect" — in which O'Neill as Christ was physically raised off the stage and lifted toward the heavens.[42] Albert Sutliffe, of the *Chronicle*, was likewise impressed by the additions, calling the Descent from the Cross and the Ascension scenes "beautiful in design, admirable in color and grand in effect."[43]

Having witnessed for himself the entire spectacle, Officer Bradford finally exercised his own opinion of the play, and thus began his portion of the evening's entertainment. He walked backstage and presented James O'Neill with a warrant for his arrest, for impersonating Jesus Christ in violation of a city ordinance. O'Neill, perhaps (the newspaper reports aren't clear on this) still in the costume of the Messiah, was hustled offstage, through the thronging crowd and into the night, where a waiting police wagon noisily carried him away to a cell at the city jail.[44]

6
"It Is the Cross Strangled by the Cross"

I

Even though his arrest had been expected, the reality of incarceration under such public circumstances could not have been easy for James O'Neill, whose very livelihood, not to mention his ego, depended on public acceptance. Looking back on the experience later, he would admit, "I firmly believed myself at the end of all success as an actor." He sat in his jail cell for two hours that night, before "Lucky" Baldwin could arrange for his release by posting one hundred dollars bail.[1] The next morning—Wednesday, April 16—the actor found himself in Police Court, rising before Judge Davis Louderback for preliminary arraignment on the misdemeanor charge. O'Neill's counsel, no doubt also secured by "Lucky" Baldwin, was Edward C. Marshall.[2]

Salmi Morse, from the relative safety of the sidelines, had confidently declared that O'Neill's arrest and trial would constitute a "test case" by which the "validity" of the Supervisors' order could be challenged. He wanted his day in court, to claim his "Constitutional rights." But O'Neill's attorney shied away from raising constitutional issues at first. Instead, he announced, he wished to get right to the heart of the matter. As the new law—constitutional or not—made it a misdemeanor to produce a play which "tended to degrade religion," Marshall wanted to determine whether Morse's play did, in fact, fall under its jurisdiction. In other words, was *The Passion* really sacrilegious, as the Supervisors charged, or did their law simply legalize the church's antitheatrical bias? In order to determine this fundamental question, Marshall shrewdly requested a jury trial,

> that the jury might witness a representation of the play, which he felt certain would convince them that no religious scruples could sensibly be entertained against it. The same scenes had been reproduced in spirit, in marble and on canvas, yet they were no more faithful representations, and not a tithe more conscientiously presented . . . than was the Passion

play. Rather than degrade religion, such a piece was calculated to eminently better it.[3]

This maneuver had the further advantage of shifting the emphasis from the clear legal issue of law-breaking, to the murkier moral context of the law's intent and purpose.

Marshall seemed reluctant to directly attack the Supervisors' ordinance as unconstitutional — Morse's defense of choice — and with good reason. No precedent had been set prior to 1879 establishing a play as a form of speech, protected by the First Amendment. Nor was there much chance in Victorian America that the theatre could win against the church in a secular court. So rather than attack the law, Marshall intended to turn it to his own advantage. If a jury were to declare *The Passion* free of sacrilege, then, technically, James O'Neill had not broken any law. No crime had been committed, the ministers had no case, and both the production *and the ordinance* could go on, unchanged.

Judge Louderback ordered the case continued until the next morning, while he considered Marshall's request for a jury trial.

It has been generally assumed by historians that O'Neill's arrest ended *The Passion* in San Francisco. It did not. That Wednesday evening, April 16, 1879, James O'Neill and the entire cast at the Grand Opera House again presented Morse's play, despite the star's arrest the night before. It is a powerful witness to O'Neill's belief in the project that he would continue defying the authorities.

Officer Bradford, this time accompanied by Sergeant Bethel, was also again in attendance, and this time at the conclusion of the performance he arrested Lewis Morrison, John Long, William Seymour, J. H. Wooland, E. A. Ambrose, W. J. Duignan, J. McConnell, Forrest Brooks and A. D. Bradley. The warrants also named David Belasco, but according to William Winter, Belasco had been warned of the impending arrest by "the local Sheriff, a friend of his." Winter writes that this Sheriff forcibly kept Belasco away from the theatre while the others were being carted off; the Gelbs say Belasco "foiled arrest by hiding in the cellar." The *Chronicle*, the *Call* and the *Alta*, however, all list Belasco as among the men arrested that night. Each of the ten immediately furnished bail, and none was actually taken to jail.[4]

The following morning, Thursday, April 17, James O'Neill was joined at the Police Court by the ten of his fellow lawbreakers (including Belasco) arrested after that second performance. While the new cases were now continued until a later date, O'Neill's hearing resumed as scheduled.

Court records have not survived, but evidence suggests that the prosecution had now withdrawn the complaint of immorality — in part, perhaps, to keep a jury from passing judgment on the production — and argued instead that the case should be confined to the narrower charge of defying a city ordinance. This meant that Marshall would not be allowed to address the larger question of sacrilege. Whether he had wanted to or not, the defense now had to challenge the law on the grounds of its legality.

Still attempting to avoid that challenge, O'Neill's attorneys first "demurred to the complaint, on the grounds that it does not contain facts sufficient to constitute a public offense."[5] Louderback overruled the demurrer; the charges would stand. O'Neill then pleaded not guilty, and the trial, such as it was, began.

Only one prosecution witness was called—Officer Bradford, the arresting officer who had filed the complaint. He carefully outlined the case against O'Neill: that he, Bradford, had personally observed O'Neill acting in a play that represented the life and death of Jesus Christ, in a production at which money was charged for admission, in direct violation of an ordinance of the Board of Supervisors.

There was no challenge from the defense, nor were any witnesses called on its behalf. O'Neill sat by in silence as Louderback declared him guilty as charged, and ordered him to appear in court again the next morning for sentencing. The entire proceeding had lasted less than an hour.

Morse immediately fired off a letter to the public, which he sent to every newspaper editor in the city:

> SIR: Do me the justice to explain to the public the result of Mr. O'Neill's arrest. Mr. O'Neill's prosecutors, finding their position untenable, withdrew entirely from the charge of pronouncing the *Passion* play indecorous and damaging to religious sentiment, thereby pronouncing it pure, instructive and elevating. But the fact stands bare that the odious ordinance, whilst its illegality is still unproven, has been infringed upon, and to this Mr. O'Neill pleaded guilty, as to prove its unconstitutionality this step was necessary. Yours, very respectfully, Salmi Morse.[6]

For Salmi, the very fact that the court would not allow them to argue the morality of his play—what had, in other words, been the reason for the law's adoption in the first place—represented on his enemies' parts an admission of defeat.

As far as the lawyers were concerned, however, it was simply good legal strategy. Marshall explained for the *Call* why he had allowed O'Neill to be found guilty:

> In order to test the validity of the ordinance under which the proceedings were instituted, the counsel for the defendant will allow him to go into the custody of the Sheriff after sentence, and then apply to one of the Supreme or District Judges for a writ of habeas corpus. Upon the hearing

of the writ, counsel will argue that the Board of Supervisors exceeded its authority in passing the ordinance...."[7]

It was O'Neill, of course, who stood to lose the most in this legal/political wrangle, and the possibility of spending more time in a jail cell once again loomed before him.

In the meantime, he was still free, as were his ten fellow defendants. And they all returned to the Grand Opera House that night for yet another performance of *The Passion*. The advertisements were now promising that the play would continue, "Notwithstanding the legal proceedings pending," and George Barnes reported in the *Call* that the production was still "attracting attention."[8] These performances were evidently uninterrupted by further arrests. But by now, public interest in the *cause célèbre* seems to have peaked, and attendance figures were beginning to fall.

On Friday morning, April 18, at ten o'clock, O'Neill made his third appearance in Judge Louderback's Police Court. Louderback pronounced a sentence of fifty dollars or twenty-five days' imprisonment. O'Neill, upon the advisement of his counsel, refused to pay the fine and was remanded to the custody of the city sheriff. At the same time, according to plan, Salmi Morse was petitioning Judge Robert Francis Morrison, of the Fourth District Court, for a writ of habeas corpus on O'Neill's behalf, to keep him out of jail. Morse argued that "the ordinance referred to is illegal and void, because the Board of Supervisors have not the power and authority to pass the same."[9] The judge granted a temporary writ, setting aside ten o'clock Saturday morning to hear arguments. O'Neill was released after posting another fifty dollars in bail.

Due to various delays, the hearing would not actually take place until the following Monday, April 21. Meanwhile, O'Neill remained free on bail, and over the weekend *The Passion* brazenly continued its performances. But, perhaps because they could sense the inevitable, or perhaps simply because audiences were smaller, by the morning of the hearing before Judge Morrison the producers were announcing *The Passion*'s "Last Week." A spectacular English melodrama, with the ironically biblical title of *The New Babylon*, was scheduled to open on Monday, April 28.[10]

II

I heard a voice from out of heaven crying —
I heard a voice from the earth replying.
FIRST VOICE:
  The Savior once was made to feel
  Men's wrath at his behavior;

> And now they lock up James O'Neill
> For looking like the Savior.
> SECOND VOICE;
> What earth attests let heaven record,
> Men's wrath at James they level
> Because, while looking like the Lord,
> He's acting like the Devil![11]

This was how *The Argonaut* expressed itself on the arrest and trial of James O'Neill. The local *News Letter*, on the other hand, saw nothing funny at all in the situation:

> It is not decorous England, or puritan Boston, that convicts Mr. O'Neill, nor is it some obscure, little village vestry board, which might well be pardoned for narrow-mindedness. But in San Francisco — wicked, reckless, dashing San Francisco, and her Board of Supervisors.... We expect next to hear of an ordinance for the burning of all old women who keep cats or have a mole on their noses.[12]

Such editorial favor, however, was not to be found in the major dailies. The editors of the *Call* and the *Bulletin*, as they had throughout the run of the production, maintained an obstinate silence on the subject of *The Passion*, while at the same time publishing reports on James O'Neill's appearances in Police Court. The de Youngs' *Chronicle*, too, dished up the most detailed stories of the event, but tactfully refrained from saying "We told you so" — at least, during the trials.

Still, it was the *Chronicle* we have to thank for the most complete record of the arguments presented before Judge Morrison at the hearing on Salmi's writ of habeas corpus for James O'Neill, held in Fourth District Court that Monday morning.[13] This was Morse's prized opportunity for a hearing before a higher court, and O'Neill's attorneys, Marshall and Harpham, covered all the requisite bases.

Marshall argued that under the Consolidation Act of 1856, which, as previously noted, had all but stripped the San Francisco Board of Supervisors of their powers, the present Board had in passing the ordinance exceeded its legislative mandate. Furthermore, the ordinance was clearly an arbitrary one, forbidding *The Passion* but no other religious presentation; it was also "so cunningly worded as to debar the defendant of his right of the trial by jury as to whether the act forbidden was, in itself, in contravention of any law of the land or against public morality, or decency, or safety."

Most important, Marshall argued, was the fact that the Supervisors' act "was an encroachment on the constitutional rights of citizens, and could not justly be sustained." Not only the play*makers'* but also the play*goers'*

6. "It Is the Cross Strangled by the Cross"

rights had been abridged: audiences had been "of the best social element of the community," and municipal interference with the production was "a wrong and an outrage."[14] Finally, protesting the lower court's refusal to allow him to challenge the moral basis for the law, Marshall warned that

> [I]f the Supervisors had power to make this ordinance they could ordain what shape of hat a citizen should wear, or that churches should not be permitted to perform their religious services, and that if the Court had not power to go back of the ordinance and inquire into the real nature of the act prohibited we were living under a worse and more unquestionable despotism than that of Constantinople.

Marshall supported his position, noted the *Chronicle*, by reading "many authorities."

The People, represented by District Attorney Murphy and Alfred Clarke, had their authorities, too—all of them strictly pertaining to the question of legality, rather than morality. In essence, Murphy argued that the state legislature had indeed delegated authority to the Board of Supervisors—in implication if not in fact—simply by its upholding of similar prohibitions of "acts not evil in themselves." Among the examples he cited were:

> Andrews, a Hebrew, convicted of prosecuting his secular business on the Christian Sabbath, in violation of the Sunday law; of Scorader, convicted of maintaining a slaughter-house within limits forbidden by a San Francisco ordinance; of Smith and Keating, female beer dispensers, convicted of distributing tipple in a Sacramento groggery after 12 o'clock midnight contrary to a Sacramento ordinance.

Once again, justification for a "religious" law was found to be the "public good." Theatres were, like slaughterhouses and beer halls, *entirely within the sphere of civil authority*. Whereas a newspaper or, more rarely, a book might address any issue, social, political or religious, the stage could not. The Supervisors, Murphy claimed, "as guardians of the city, have full authority to prevent the performance of anything on a public stage that might be regarded as improper or inadmissable,"[15] and it must be accepted by the Court that the Supervisors had, before enacting the ordinance, "duly ascertained" the "quality of the act forbidden." Hence, the actual morality or immorality of *The Passion* was immaterial, since it had already been officially deemed "an offense to the religious feelings of a civilized community" by the Board of Supervisors, acting in its capacity as a sort of Chief Censor for the city.

Judge Morrison's reaction, as noted by the *Chronicle*, must have given

Morse and O'Neill cause for both despair and hope. "From the questions asked by his honor Judge Morrison," the paper said, "it is inferable that he had no doubt of the power of the Supervisors to prohibit things not bad in themselves, but it is also inferable that he is equally strong in the opinion that there must be some principle governing the power that prevents it from becoming arbitrary." Morrison adjourned the hearing, saying he would rule on making the writ permanent "at an early date."

Such slim hope, however, was not enough; that evening saw the last performance in San Francisco of Salmi Morse's *Passion*. Not waiting for Judge Morrison to deliver a verdict, Maguire, Baldwin and Morse elected to close the play. The morning newspapers, April 22, carried the announcement:

> The Management has the honor to announce that in deference to public opinion "The Passion" will no longer be presented.[16]

The *Chronicle*, naturally, could not refrain from gloating. Applauding their own sagacity and ignoring entirely the religious/legal controversy in which they had played no small part, the de Youngs finally allowed themselves their editorial comment: "As was predicted," they wrote, "the revival of *The Passion* did not prove a financial success, and the theatre is closed...."[17]

III

Certainly, *The Passion* was a financial failure for Baldwin; it was estimated that he had lost his entire investment of $25,000.[18] But to credit poor box office alone for its demise is to whitewash not only the facts of the case, but the deeper social and historical attitudes that those facts reveal. Moreover, the implication that the play had failed simply because it did not make money disregards the important fact that at this time no *other* theatre in San Francisco was making money either. For, in the end, the truth is that *The Passion* had been doomed to fail from the beginning, for reasons other than its controversy.

It seems obvious in hindsight that nothing could have attracted the large numbers of spectators Maguire needed to make the Grand Opera House turn a profit. His hope that *The Passion* could do so was a misguided one. M. B. Leavitt's description of the city during this period reveals the problem:

> At this time, I was playing many attractions in ... the Bush Street Theatre and the Baldwin. There were then five other houses, the Grand

6. "It Is the Cross Strangled by the Cross"

[Opera House], the California, Billy Emerson's Minstrels, Morosco's Theatre and the Tivoli Opera House. In addition to these, were Platt's Hall, devoted to miscellaneous entertainments; the Wigwam, a large Chinese theatre in Jackson Street; the Orpheum, the Adelphi, the Bella Union, other small variety establishments, and almost numberless concert places, dives and cellars, wherein some sort of show was given. *In short, San Francisco was asked to support more resorts of amusement than any other city of its size, or even double its size, in the world* [emphasis added.][19]

In the midst of this plethora of theatrical competitors, the Grand, with its seating of nearly four thousand, was considered by many to be "too extravagant for a city of less than 300,000 people."[20] Thus, even with fairly sizable houses, such as those *The Passion* seems to have drawn, the possibility of a profitable run was remote.

More importantly, the Grand Opera House was not the only San Francisco theatre in financial trouble. As previously noted, the hard times that had descended on California theatres by the late seventies, which had made a novelty like *The Passion* seem a viable property, also helped make the entire gamble that much riskier. The frantic theatregoing of the Gold Rush days had passed. Only three months after the closing of *The Passion*, the San Francisco correspondent to the *New York Daily Mirror* was writing, "There is [sic] not in San Francisco enough people [who go to the theatre] ... to support one theatre one week.... It is an unpleasant truth, and is consequently seldom told." In fact, *within another fifteen months, four of the city's five "first-class" houses would close for want of patronage*, prompting the editors of the *Call* to lament, "for the time being the drama [in San Francisco] has been taken down with paralysis."[21]

Even had *The Passion* never provoked a single preacher, then, it is doubtful that the production could ever have returned the kind of profit that Maguire and Baldwin had hoped for. But a lack of profit does not necessarily denote a lack of interest, nor does it reflect on the merit or importance of a theatrical venture. Therefore, it does not follow, as the *Chronicle* and, later, some New York papers would have it, that *The Passion*'s failure was due not to the public controversy but, rather, solely to a lack of patronage.

IV

On Wednesday, April 23, 1879, two days after the closing of the play, Judge Morrison handed down his decision on James O'Neill's petition to make the writ of habeas corpus permanent. "The only question to be considered," Morrison stated, "is the legality of the order under which the petitioner was convicted." Accepting the prosecution's reasoning, Morrison, too, looked to other local statutes enacted for the control of public nuisances, in order to rationalize the so-called anti–*Passion* ordinance. That these acts had been upheld by the state Supreme Court was for Morrison proof enough that the San Francisco Board of Supervisors did indeed have the legal power, as well as the right, to suppress *The Passion*. Following the judicial tradition and thinking of the time, Morrison never questioned the advisability of a civic body's granting, in effect, a protected legal status to the Christian religion. To him, the threat to the "public good" represented by *The Passion* was all too clear:

> The Board of Supervisors has seen fit to prohibit the exhibition in question because such exhibition is, in their opinion, against good morals, because it is calculated to bring religion, which is the foundation of all morality, into ridicule and contempt, and because the sacred mysteries of the passion and death of the Redeemer upon the cross are too solemn and sacred to be made the subject of a theatrical exhibition.
>
> [T]he character of this performance has been determined by the "verdict" of the Board of Supervisors, and I have neither the right nor the inclination to set aside that verdict. The writ is discharged and the petitioner remanded to the proper custody.[22]

Morse had lost the appeal.

The next morning, O'Neill paid his fifty-dollar fine. (Considering that the maximum allowable fine was $1,000, this represented considerable leniency on the judge's part.) Counsel for Belasco, Morrison and the other actors arrested on April 16, was also present, and argued that, since the accused had performed "under advice of counsel that the ordinance was unconstitutional," they should not be blamed for intentionally breaking the law. "He then suggested that the defendants be allowed to pay a fine of $5 each. The suggestion was concurred in by the Prosecuting Attorney, and the Court made an order accordingly." According to Morrison's granddaughter, Joan Bennett, it was James O'Neill who graciously paid the fines of all the others, in addition to his own.[23]

V

With the passing of *The Passion*, San Francisco returned to business more or less as usual. O'Neill, Morrison and the rest of the Baldwin Stock Company went back to performing less-controversial fare to less-than-overwhelming audiences, all talk of a Passion Play Combination going East seemingly forgotten. The city's attention turned once again to the upcoming local elections. The ministers returned to their pulpits none the worse

6. "It Is the Cross Strangled by the Cross"

for their foray into moral activism; in fact, according to one eastern newspaper, Protestant clergymen in San Francisco were boldly "united in a movement 'for the reformation of public affairs through religion,'" and were "delivering sermons on the subject."[24] Morse later claimed that he dropped in on the indomitable Reverend Platt one evening, not long after *The Passion* had closed, to personally give the minister a copy of the printed script and to assure him there were no hard feelings.[25]

As for Salmi himself, he, too, returned to more mundane pursuits. He had for some months past been serving as editor of the satirical weekly newspaper, *The Illustrated Wasp* (he was not, as he would later claim, that journal's first editor). The *Wasp* had been founded in 1876 by a pair of cigar makers, the Korbel Brothers, primarily as a means of justifying the expense of their lithographic press, then being used only to print the colorful labels for their cigar boxes. An illustrated newspaper, they reasoned, would not only showcase their printmaker's art, but advertise the Korbels' cigars as well—and promote their beloved Democratic Party in the bargain. The paper's philosophy was summarized in its name—to sting like a wasp. But under Morse's editorship, the satire was, as George Barnes would later put it, about as stinging "as a wasp in a tar barrel":

> If [Denis] Kearney was not in the habit of letting main chances slip, he'd slip down to Maine.

Or:

> Is tearing your pants whilst sliding down to a stream a riparian damage?[26]

How Morse had been able to talk himself into the editorship of the *Wasp* is an open question. Salmi, said Barnes, "had no more idea of wit than a horse has of the alphabet." But it was the *Call* critic's opinion that perhaps Morse had "impressed" the Korbel Brothers with his "manner and talk," or perhaps with his penning of *The Passion*. However it came about, by spring of 1879 he was no longer listing himself in the City Directory as "rancher" or "capitalist," but, for the first time, as "ed., S. F. Illus. Wasp."

And now, following the suppression of his play, Salmi began to learn for himself the difference between the theatre and the press in Victorian America—at least as far as freedom of speech was concerned. For he had his own personal weapon of attack now, and none of his perceived enemies could touch him. In a column uncharitably titled "Human Trash and Their Desserts," Morse in the *Wasp* began to hold every decision of Judges Louderback and Morrison, and most of the actions of the Board of Supervisors, up to the closest, most scathing kind of scrutiny. The Supervisors became "Rountree, Danforth & Co.," while the ministers were "the white-chokered fraternity," and "the great suppressionists of *The Passion Play.*"

Not insignificantly, Morse also began to fine-tune his view of the First Amendment, at least as it applied to cultural domination by religion. "Be it understood, once for all, that the WASP is in favor of any measure conducive to the well being of morality and religion," he wrote at one point,

> but it most emphatically protests to anything savoring of infringement upon the Constitution of the United States. It goes further yet, it would even favor the amendment of that particular clause [i.e., the First Amendment] . . . but until that is done, legally and squarely by popular ballot, we protest against the right of any bigoted sect to intermeddle with the character of its inviolable sacredness.[27]

Paradoxically, Morse was, at the same time, bringing about a significant change in the *Wasp's* editorial direction. His publication, he now claimed, was "a *strictly moral family weekly magazine for gentlemen, wives, daughters and little children*" [his emphasis].[28] It was "worth preserving as an heirloom," and, more importantly, it avowedly represented "a mere continuance of the teachings commenced by the memorable Passion Play."[29] Of course, with his continuing personal attacks on every preacher and politician who had opposed him, such moral posturing could be called equally hypocritical.

Nonetheless, the *Wasp* under Morse could be seen as epitomizing the unique dichotomy that was Salmi Morse. On the one hand, he railed against the moral tyranny imposed upon society by organized churches; but like a small child maligning the members of a club to which he desperately wants to belong, Morse devoted his life—and the pages of the *Wasp*—to proselytizing for that same mainstream Christian morality.

His supreme accomplishment at the *Wasp* came that Christmas 1879, with the publication of a nine-page religious epic poem entitled "The Bell of the Cross." Lovingly illustrated on every page with beautiful, full-color lithographs by the *Wasp's* illustrator, G. F. Keller, Morse's unmetered and often ungracefully written opus covered exactly the same territory as his suppressed play, climaxing with a description of the Death, Resurrection and Ascension of Jesus Christ.[30]

As poetry, "The Bell of the Cross" was neither better nor worse than *The Passion.* What was dramatically different, however, was the reception it received. "A beautiful Christmas Carol in eight cantos," gushed the *Christian Advocate,* while the *Evening Post* felt it reflected creditably on "the good taste and artistic skill of the publishers." The *Chronicle* dubbed it a "commendable enterprise," and the neighboring *Watsonville Pajaronian* pronounced it "written in good style." The *Alta* praised the artwork while tactfully ignoring the poem and the *Bulletin* and the *Call* simply noted its publication—in exactly identical wording.³¹ Not one Protestant minister called it sacrilegious. Not one Supervisor moved to have it banned. Not one theatre critic dubbed it "moral twaddle." Had publication of this poem been a deliberate ploy on Salmi's part, it could not have made the point with greater irony.

While *The Passion* was being kept alive in the pages of *The Illustrated Wasp*, Morse was making sporadic attempts to keep it before the public in other city journals, too. In June, two moths after the closing at the Grand, Morse planted an item with George Barnes of the *Call* about a production of *The Passion* being planned in Boston by Henry Edwards, an actor formerly with San Francisco's California Theater. Supposedly, Edwards had met with the president of a "Society recently formed in the Hub to discountenance plays objectionable in tone and influence," and Morse's work had been accepted by all as suitably pure. "Mr. Edwards and the Boston coterie express surprise," said Barnes, "that the play could have been opposed in this city."³² Nothing more was heard of this production.

Meanwhile, on another front, the citywide elections were held that September 1879, and the Workingman's Party swept to victory with its candidate for mayor, the Reverend Isaac Kalloch. Kalloch himself almost didn't live to see it, though. Shortly before the election, *Chronicle* owner Charles de Young, bitterly opposed to Kalloch, attempted to cast the deciding ballot himself by shooting the candidate in the street outside Kalloch's Metropolitan Temple. This was, of course, the same Charles de Young who, among other reasons, had opposed *The Passion* on the grounds that San Francisco was far too "civilized" to need it. Kalloch lived and went on to win the mayoralty. (De Young was not so lucky; eight months later Kalloch's twenty-eight-year-old minister son revenged his father's honor by bursting into the *Chronicle* offices and killing the editor before he could get his gun out of its holster.³³)

The new mayor presided over a whole new Board of Supervisors, also elected that September. So Morse, taking advantage of the WPC's animosity toward the previous administration, decided to petition this new Board to rescind Rountree's Supervisorial ordinance banning Passion plays. Perhaps as a symbolic gesture, he waited until April 1880—one year after *The Passion* had been closed by the previous Board. It is not recorded that either Baldwin or Maguire was involved in the petition in any way, but their later financial claims on the property are well enough documented to suppose that, at the very least, they followed the attempt with great interest.

On Saturday, April 9, 1880, a hearing was held on Salmi's petition, by the new Joint Committee on Health and Police and Licenses and Orders. Morse appeared on his own behalf to present his case. But he was outnumbered by the Protestant ministers also present to oppose him, the Episcopal Reverend Platt and the Presbyterian Reverends John Hemphill and W. J. Smith among them. Each minister in turn delivered a lengthy condemnation of the play and urged the committee not to rescind the order. Morse, left to the last, quietly told the committee that, given the opportunity, "he could refute the statements made by the gentlemen, to the effect that the play was impious."[34]

The committee adjourned until the following Tuesday.

That Sunday, Protestant ministers across the city once again took to their pulpits to denounce Salmi Morse and *The Passion*. It was as if the controversy had never ended; all of the church's objections to the theatre in general and *The Passion* in particular were once again paraded before captive congregations. At Calvary Church, the Reverend Hemphill dramatically held up a letter that he said had been sent him from Baltimore, and which told of a Passion play supposedly once presented in that city. As in several other such apocryphal tales trotted out by newspapers a year ago, this purported Passion play in Baltimore had suffered the requisite unexplained tragedies—the most common of which had the offending theatre inexplicably burn down—but Baltimore did them one better. Not only did their theatre mysteriously catch fire, but during the performance the actor playing Jesus Christ was accidentally "stabbed and killed by one of the Roman soldiers"![35] No wonder the good Reverend Hemphill, "in the name of our Saviour," protested the presenting of a Passion drama "in a play-house."

On Tuesday afternoon, the hearing of the Joint Committee was resumed. Once again, Morse faced off against a formidable lineup of ministerial ire. This time, though, he was allowed to go first, and he began with an appeal for both freedom of speech and for simple reason. First of all, he argued, Milton, Byron and Bunyon had also written on the subject—"Had anyone a copyright on the Bible?" he asked—and his own play had been approved by Archbishop Alemany, so where was the impiety? After all, he was only presenting what was presented in every house of worship every day—only better. He cited the favorable reviews from a year ago, and then made an astonishing promise: James O'Neill had originally been educated for the priesthood, Morse said, and had only become an actor "as the result of circumstances"; therefore, if the Board would rescind the ordinance, and allow Morse and the Baldwin Stock Company to mount another production, O'Neill "would never assume any other character than the one he had enacted in 'The Passion Play.'" As O'Neill would later make this promise himself, one is again impressed by the actor's total commitment to this play.

After the multitude of ministers had reiterated their objections, the committee went into executive session, and unanimously voted to deny Morse's petition for a rescinding of the law.[36]

Salmi returned to the pages of the *Wasp* to lick his wounds, in an almost tearfully self-indulgent "Letter to the Public of San Francisco." "When not a San Francisco preacher will be remembered," he predicted,

6. "It Is the Cross Strangled by the Cross"

the *Passion Play* will grace libraries and work benignant influence by its representation upon the stage; the passages pertaining to the scandalous interdiction at iniquitous San Francisco, will be approached with disgust as when reading the life of Shakespeare and coming upon the name of the vindictive De Lacy, or alighting upon the persecutors of the sublime "Cain" maligned Lord Byron.

He was most grieved, he said, by the "source from which the opposition comes": "It is the Cross strangled by the Cross, and the bloody intentions of the dark ages over again . . . when every new dogma was denounced by the established older ones." Salmi promised that this would be the last he would ever write in his defense; no, *he* would not stoop to the mudslinging level of the ministers. After all, he lied, he had always "peremptorily declined to say one single word in [the play's] defense or my own in this paper, upon the ground that the sacred subject was not a fit theme for bitter tirade or cavil."[37] In fact, defending this play had been practically all he *had* been doing for the past twelve months.

With this, Salmi Morse seemed to give up on San Francisco as a suitable site for his own kind of moral ministrations. Within another month, he would resign as editor of *The Illustrated Wasp*.

VI

Whatever bitter memories Morse's surprise petition to the Board of Supervisors may have resurrected, on either side, one thing it did accomplish was to bring both *The Passion* and its eccentric author back into the center of public consciousness. Stories of Salmi's other dramatic "masterworks" resurfaced—he claimed he now had seventy-two plays ready for the boards[38]—and by the end of the summer he was talking once again about taking *The Passion* east. Now that he was free of his journalistic duties, Salmi threw himself back into the theatre wholeheartedly. "My venerable friend has a fresh idea about every other day," the *New York Dramatic News*'s San Francisco correspondent wrote, "and his latest inspiration is to secure the production of his original comedy, A Bustle Among the Petticoats, at Baldwin's." Morse ("the talented author") was already "training a young lady" to play the leading role, that of a small boy.[39]

In August, James O'Neill went to George B. Rieman's photogrpahy studio on Montgomery Street, where he had his portrait taken in the costume and makeup of Jesus Christ, just as he had appeared in *The Passion*. This immediately raised new rumors—was *The Passion* to be revived despite the law?, was it going to be produced in the East at last?—and the

O'Neill as Christ in "The Passion," 1879. It was, said David Belasco, "the performance of a generation." The effect of O'Neill's first appearance was so startling that some spectators fell to their knees. The role had its effect on O'Neill as well; he gave up smoking, drinking and swearing. But in the end the actor was arrested and jailed for impersonating Jesus Christ in violation of a newly passed city ordinance protecting the Christian religion. (Courtesy Billy Rose Theatre Collection, The New York Public Library)

sitting also resulted in "severe censure" directed toward both O'Neill and the unsuspecting Riemer.[40]

This photograph, however, had nothing to do with San Francisco. Not long after it was taken, Tom Maguire suddenly departed for New York, followed about ten days later by Salmi Morse.[41] These trips were far from secret; Morse's stopover at Chicago's Palmer House, for example, was noted in the local papers: "He has his renowned play with him, as well as several others that he will submit to New York managers."[42] San Francisco

6. "It Is the Cross Strangled by the Cross"

fairly buzzed with rumors of what and where and *who* would possibly produce *The Passion* in New York.

There were also reports that indicate Tom Maguire's trip to New York on behalf of Morse's play may not have had "Lucky" Baldwin's blessing. While Maguire was wooing managers in the east, A. M. Palmer, of New York's Union Square Theatre, showed up unexpectedly in San Francisco. He protested loudly that he had come to the Bay City only for "a holiday," but one reporter observed that Palmer had "several lengthy interviews with Mr. Baldwin and Mr. O'Neill." New rumors began: had Baldwin called Palmer to California as a possible replacement for the absent Maguire? Or had he been asked west so that Baldwin could offer him *The Passion* for New York, thus beating out Morse and Maguire completely? As the *New York Dramatic News* analyzed the situation, it had all the makings of a plot by James Clavell:

> Palmer appears to recognize Baldwin's claim to the Passion Play, although Salmi Morse, the author, and Maguire are also both interested in securing its production in New York, in conjunction with ... any other metropolitan manager that will take hold of it with them. Maguire and Morse expect O'Neill to go East and appear in his original character of the Messiah. Palmer, of course, intends to get in ahead of them and secure O'Neill by making him a partner in the concern with Baldwin. It cost Baldwin something like $25,000 for the Grand Opera House production, and as this was a dead loss ... some arrangement was made which gave him a prior claim to it in case it should be produced elsewhere. Palmer has, no doubt, been apprised of all the facts by O'Neill, and if this speculation is the real motive which prompted the Union Square manager's quiet little holiday trip out this way, the indications certainly are that while O'Neill aspires to be recognized as the only J. C. (dramatically speaking, of course) of modern times, he is not unwilling to descend to the character of Judas, when it comes to a matter of silver....
>
> Mr. Palmer isn't supposed to know that the houses are papered night after night, slim as the average audiences are, to induce people to witness O'Neill's acting. This is an unpleasant acknowledgement, but it is nonetheless true.[43]

For his part, Palmer flatly denied everything.

It all made for exciting speculation, but if Baldwin had been trying to beat his cagey manager and wayward author to the punch, he did not succeed. Even as he and Palmer were engaged in their "lengthy interviews" in San Francisco in early September, Salmi Morse was cabling the happy news from New York to his friend George Barnes at the *Call:*

> NEW YORK, September 7, 1880. — Contract signed with Booth's Theatre to produce "Passion" in December. SALMI MORSE.[44]

If Salmi could not vindicate his *Passion* in San Francisco, he now had another chance for his lifework, not to mention a new stage on which Salmi Morse himself could shine. As will be seen, it meant new chapters as well for almost everyone else involved—James O'Neill, Lewis Morrison, Henry Widmer, Fred Lyster, David Belasco, and, most especially, Tom Maguire.

But it also meant the end of a major chapter for the city of San Francisco, although residents were unaware of it at the time. The last vestige of the Gold Rush theatre, epitomized so well in the career of Tom Maguire, "who [had] built up most of that golden legend . . . and sustained it,"[45] had begun its culmination with *The Passion* in 1879. The stage in San Francisco would never again be so daring, so important—so *welcome*, as it had been when the Forty-niners reigned.

So Salmi Morse turned his back on San Francisco and returned from whence he had started some thirty years before, New York City. And while San Franciscans would follow Morse's misfortunes with great interest over the next four years, the city would never see the author of *The Passion* again.

Part Two:
The Passion in New York, 1880–1884

7
"The Grandest Thing I Ever Listened To" ... "A National Disaster"

I

It had been thirty-two years since the young Salmi Morse had abandoned New York for adventuring in the California gold fields. Since then, the eastern metropolis had grown to become the largest city in the Western Hemisphere. In 1880, the population of New York City, not counting the boroughs, was 1,206,299[1] — double that, it was joked at the time, if one counted the tourists, visitors and commuters on any given day. And while small farms could still be found on the northern half of Manhattan, the commercial areas at the southern end were already feeling the pinch of finite space. As a result, Manhattanites were creating room for themselves by building skyward. "Land being very high in price, the buldings are generally lofty," wrote James D. McCabe, Jr., in his 1882 guidebook *New York by Sunlight and Gaslight*, "often reaching an altitude of seven and eight, and sometimes ten and twelve stories." Here, said McCabe, was gathered "the wealth of the world."[2]

If one word could capture the pure essence of New York City in the late nineteenth century, that word would be "money." The Civil War had spurred industrial growth throughout the northern states and with that growth had come enormous wealth, as well as enormous corruption. The Rockefellers, the Carnegies, the Vanderbilts, J. P. Morgan, E. H. Harriman, Henry C. Frick, Jay Gould — the "oil kings," the "railroad millionaires," the "robber barons" — America's *nouveaux riches* — all called New York City home. The plays in American theatre of the time may have been glorifying the simple virtues of *Davy Crockett* and the homespun pieties of *Joshua Whitcomb*, but in reality the true cultural hero was the businessman.[3]

The entire city seemed to be on the move. The new steam-powered elevated railroads could now speed passengers from 59th Street to City Hall in an impressive twenty-eight minutes flat. The restless, inexorable crawl northward was turning 14th and 23rd streets into the busiest crosstown arteries in the city. McCabe noted that the "superb mansions" that once could be found north of 14th Street only twenty years before had now disappeared, "and in their places stand huge iron, marble, and stone structures, devoted to the various branches of the retail trade."[4]

The mansions in question had simply moved further uptown. There were as yet few businesses to speak of north of 34th Street (in what is now Midtown); in that vast, sparsely populated area could be found several hotels, some new-fangled "Apartment Houses," the relocated estates of the well-to-do, and Central Park. Further north was the old Dutch town of Harlem. The Astors were living on the future site of the Empire State Building; the Brooklyn Bridge was still under construction; there was no Statue of Liberty. The new uptown St. Patrick's Cathedral was still missing two towers on its Fifth Avenue façade. Macy's was on 14th Street and Sixth Avenue, while Brentano's News Depot, Lord & Taylor's drygoods emporium and the famous jewelry establishment of Tiffany & Co., all ringed Union Square. Salmi's old drygoods concern on Williams Street, of course, had long been out of business, his late brother Lewis having moved into partnership with Charlotte's husband, Edward Behrend, who had gone from selling cigars to selling musical instruments; his store was on Broadway near Chambers. Edward and Charlotte lived far out of town, at 130 East 105th Street.[5]

Socially, New York was a city without a middle class. Due in large part to Manhattan's high cost of living, McCabe noted that "persons of moderate means doing business in New York, who desire the comforts of a home for their families, are, as a rule, obliged to reside out of the city." As a result, New York was a study in economic extremes. "The pauper population is large," McCabe wrote, "the number of those who live by manual labor is larger, and against these are set the rich men of the city. The class which should be strongest [i.e., the middle class] is conspicuous by its absence."[6]

Nevertheless, the commuting bourgeoisie made its presence felt. The Victorian moral structure, so reflective of the middle class, was firmly in place in New York City. Unlike in San Francisco, where the church had been relatively late in influencing public behavior, in New York the tradition of social and political power wielded by organized religion had been observed since colonial times, and religion, in one way or another, affected the life of almost every inhabitant. Sunday Blue Laws had long been enforced and religiously motivated private pressure groups, such as the New York Society for the Suppression of Vice, or the Society for the Reformation of Juvenile Delinquents, carried great weight in the corridors of City Hall — as

7. "The Grandest Thing I Ever Listened To"

Salmi himself would learn. Such "vice societies" were born of the same impulse that had brought together the pulpit, the press and politics to fight *The Passion* in San Francisco; and if they were not yet so organized a force in that western city, they were common in the East in the latter half of the nineteenth century. Funded by the wealthy, ostensibly for the purpose of "protecting" the morals of the underclasses, many of these societies were all too often a means of keeping those classes under control. Although unallied with any specific sect, they sought to promote Christian morality—in the arts, as in society at large—through individual self-censorship and public conformity. Censorious and self-righteous sometimes to extremes, their spiritual father was most certainly Anthony Comstock, the namesake of the Comstock Act of 1873 and later the bane of George Bernard Shaw.

David J. Pivar writes that organized Victorian purity movements reduced the religious sentiment to three components: "obedience to authority, reverence, and worship." As religious values were transformed into social values, churches were increasingly expected to assume social functions. In essence, it was a philosophy not far removed from the old colonial doctrine of moral law. In the words of one reformer, it was a matter of "Christianizing Democracy."[7]

Coincidentally, the National Reform Association was convening that fall of 1880 to "secure the recognition of the Christian religion by the Government of the United States." The convention called for a constitutional amendment to legalize already "existing features of the American Government, such as the Bible in the schools, the Christian law of marriage, the Sabbath laws, the national and State thanksgivings, fasts, &c." They did not see this as a union of church and state, but merely a way of bringing the U. S. Constitution "into harmony" with some thirty state constitutions in which "acknowledgements, more or less explicit of God and the Christian religion, are to be found."[8]

As for organized religion in New York in 1880, James McCabe counted more than five hundred churches, chapels and other "places used for religious worship" in the city, "with seating accommodations for about 600,000 people"—or, put another way, for almost sixty percent of the population. Of these religious houses, nearly 450 were Protestant, fifty Catholic, five Quaker, one Greek Orthodox, and twenty-seven Jewish. True to the spirit of the age, these churches were also profiting from wise investments. McCabe attempted to compute the value—in 1880 dollars, bear in mind—of church-owned property in New York City: "Protestant, $30,000,000, exclusive of endowments; Catholic, $8,000,000; Jews, $2,000,000; the Greek Church, $10,000."[9] Finally, McCabe noted that the various hospitals, schools and charitable institutions built on such property had swelled the value of the churches' tax-free real estate to "an enormous figure."

The Revs. Crosby, Talmage, Potter and Newman. These four Protestant clerics, among the most powerful in the nation, led the ministerial opposition to "The Passion" in New York City. Beginning in 1880 and continuing through Morse's final attempts to stage the play in 1883, they tirelessly opposed any presentation, whether in a professional theatre or in its own special "Temple." (As sketched by the artist for the "New York World," March 2, 1884.)

Leading these churches were some of the most famous ecclesiastics of the era — Ann Douglas's "star preachers" — many of whom were extremely popular on the speaking circuits and commanded large fees for their services. The Reverend John P. Newman, of the Central Methodist Episcopal Church, reportedly doubled his $10,000 annual income with lecture fees; the Reverend Morgan Dix, the rector of Trinity Church, likewise earned around $20,000 a year in salary and fees. By far the titan of the New York clergy at this time, however, was the 68-year-old Reverend Henry Ward Beecher, "the great divine of Plymouth Church, Brooklyn," whose various lecture fees raised his annual salary of $25,000 to an impressive $50,000 per year.[10] Beecher's influence was so strong that many newspapers referred to Brooklyn as "Beecher Town."

Brooklyn, in fact, was the locus for the socially directed nonsectarianism spoken of by Pivar. Following the lead of Beecher, whose preachments against slavery during the Civil War had been instrumental in establishing the right of the pulpit to direct social agendas, the new generation of independent preachers had evolved what were known as "Ethical Churches," where hellfire and damnation made way for politics and civic reform. Men like the Reverend T. De Witt Talmage, of the Brooklyn Tabernacle, became national figures — and further supplemented their incomes — by following another practice established by Beecher: syndicating their Sunday sermons for publication in newspapers all across America.[11]

With great power, inevitably, had come arrogance and abuses, and many of these preachers were, like Isaac Kalloch in San Francisco, figures of great controversy. Beecher himself had been involved in a notorious adultery trial in 1875; the Reverend Stephen H. Tyng, Jr., would, within a year, resign his post as rector of the Church of the Holy Trinity, accused of stock swindling and "improper relations" with his parishioners; and the aforementioned Reverend Talmage, an unyieldingly orthodox Scotch Presbyterian, had only the year before been brought to trial before his own Brooklyn Presbytery on charges of "false-hood and deceit." In a split decision, he had been exonerated, and now he continued to hold forth every Sunday from his pulpit at the Brooklyn Tabernacle, his base of support inexplicably stronger than ever. Talmage was, said one newspaper editor in 1880, "an anachronism." He might have been "a respectable and useful member of society in the time of the Crusades."[12] The object of contempt for many, Talmage was, after Beecher, arguably the best-known of the New York ministers.

Judging from the numbers of their respective churches, one would suppose that the Protestants far outnumbered the Catholics in New York, but, in fact, a situation existed there similar to that in San Francisco. The most numerous single sect in the city was the Roman Catholic, thanks especially to the vast numbers of Irish immigrants jammed into the area north of Canal Street. If the majority of these Catholics were working class, as they were in San Francisco, their numbers represented no less a threat to the wealthier uptown Protestants. McCabe tellingly observed that "almost the only churches in the poorer and more crowded sections of the city are Catholic, and this immense field is being cultivated by them with an energy and zeal well worthy of imitation."[13]

There was a practical side to such cultivation, however, for those same working-class Irish kept the mighty Tammany Hall in power, and Tammany's Irish politicos in turn awarded liberal political support and even economic gratuities to the Roman Catholic Church via the city government. In the city elections now under way in 1880, Tammany Hall had succeeded in nominating, and would secure the election of, New York's first Irish Catholic mayor, William R. Grace.[14] Considering the religious tensions of the times, it was an arrogant action that could only exacerbate the worst of Protestant fears: Catholics would take control of the public schools; the Papacy in Rome would be governing New York; the Catholics would censor newspapers and books; it would mean the end of religious freedom, and the blurring forever of church/state separation in New York City. "The Church of Rome," one agitated Methodist minister warned, "is the most masterly piece of human organism on the globe, whether taken for collecting money, for propagandism or for gaining political power." "Citizens," cried the Reverend John P. Newman three days before the November 2 election, "in God's name, in the name of Washington, in the name of Abraham Lincoln, in the name of Grant, in the name of childhood, in the name of womanhood, in the name of manhood, in the name of liberty, vote for Dowd!"[15] To the utter horror of the city's Protestants, the power of Tammany Hall would carry Grace to his bitter victory.

Thus, Protestant-Catholic antagonisms, already at the forefront of American religious life nationwide in 1880, were being dangerously compounded via politics in New York City at the very time that Salmi Morse arrived from the West with his Catholic-tainted *Passion* in tow.

II

If the story of *The Passion* is a tale of two cities, it is also the tale of two different kinds of theatre. The phenomenal rise and public support of the unbounded stage in early San Francisco simply had no parallel anywhere else in the country. We have already seen the long struggle fought by acting companies for footholds in colonial cities, including in New York. But while theatre now proliferated there, remnants of religious censoriousness still hampered the New York stage to a frustrating degree.

Under an 1872 state law, every theatre in the city of New York had to be licensed. Each license cost $500 per year and was granted at the mayor's discretion. Few theatre owners begrudged the city an annual license fee; however, what made the $500 Theatre Tax so galling to the theatre community was the fact that under it all license monies and penalty fees went not to the city but, rather, "shall be paid over to the treasurer of the Society for the Reformation of Juvenile Delinquents in the city of New York, for use of said society."[16] This arrangement only perpetuated the old moral prejudice against the stage, complained the *New York Mirror*, because it implied that theatres were somehow "responsible for the delinquencies of youth." "Why," the editor demanded, "this invidious selection of the theatre for the payment of a penalty which aligns it with the criminal classes and the violators of social order?"[17] Worse, since it was now in the Society's financial interest to oversee theatrical licensing, the law, in effect, made the Society for the Reformation of Juvenile Delinquents the real arbiter of who had a theatre license in New York City and who didn't. Charles Byrne, editor of the *Dramatic News*, thought this nothing less than state-sanctioned "annual blackmail." He estimated in 1880 that this "association of voracious phantoms," as he termed it, was earning some $35,000 a year from theatre licenses and penalty fees, for which sums the privately run organization was publicly unaccountable. Obviously, the more prosecutions initiated by the Society, the more fees and penalties it accrued. The situation had reached the point where, according to Byrne, if an agent of the Society, walking down the street, heard a piano playing in any public building, the Society would immediately serve a summons on the proprietor for operating a place of amusement without a license.[18] Judging from the number of extant letters of complaint to the various mayors from Edward R. Robinson, the Counsel for the Society, demanding its due fees, Byrne's outlandish charge may have had some truth to it.[19]

Even if a theatre owner paid his fee to the S.R.J.D. and was allowed to keep his doors open, he was still at the mercy of other societal watchdogs, such as Comstock's Society for the Supression of Vice, or, more notably, Elbridge T. Gerry's feared Society for the Prevention of Cruelty to Children, known far and wide as the Gerry Society. Organized in 1875, before child labor laws were enacted, this group took many a nineteenth-century manager to court to stop the exploitation of child performers; its seeming overzealousness in this regard has often been the comical butt of theatrical memoirs, but the Gerry Society's awesome power in these early years was virtually unassailable.[20]

Despite all the obstacles, however—perhaps because of them—the theatre in New York was well-organized, methodically professional, and thriving. While the general hard times had reduced San Francisco to one first-class theatre by the time Morse left there in the fall of 1880, New York had fifteen, plus more than fifty second-class and variety establishments, not to mention the "third-rate theatres of the Bowery." "It is estimated," wrote James McCabe, "that from $30,000 to $40,000 are nightly expended in the city in the purchase of theatre tickets, or from seven to eight million dollars in a single season." The *Mirror* would pronounce the 1880 season one of "unprecedented prosperity."[21]

Morse would have quickly found that most of the city's theatrical life centered on Union Square, where dramatic agencies, play publishers, costumers and other auxiliary businesses were located; the south side of 14th opposite the Square was known as "The Slave Market," because of the large numbers of actors "hanging around there in the summer, looking for engagements."[22] But, like the rest of the city, theatres were gradually moving uptown, too. Daly's Theatre, built in 1866; the magnificent Booth's (1869); the Park (1874); the Standard (1875) and Madison Square (1879) theatres all were found above 14th Street. Even now, Lester Wallack was in the process of joining the migration, moving soon from his theatre on 13th Street to a new facility on 39th and Broadway, opposite Daly's.[23]

The theatre community in New York even had its own press. The self-proclaimed Oldest American Theatrical Journal was the *New York Clipper*, founded in 1853 as a sporting and theatrical paper. It had since minimized its general theatrical coverage, and was now more a trade sheet, in which both actors and managers advertised.[24] Its position as a newspaper had been taken over by the *Dramatic News*, edited since 1875 by Charles Alfred Byrne. With correspondents in every major city of the country, the *Dramatic News*'s coverage of American theatre was as impressive as it was important; but Byrne himself was notorious for his personal attacks on prominent members of the profession and was considered by many to be a "blackguard." He once bragged in his paper that he had been physically attacked sixteen times in his first few years as a publisher.[25] Lately, the prominence of the *Dramatic News* was being challenged by the newest theatrical entry, the *New York Mirror*, founded in 1879 by Ernest Harvier and only recently come under the editorship of a 19-year-old college dropout by the name of Harrison Grey Fiske. The teen-aged editor was still an unknown quantity in the theatre world; aside from his precociousness he had yet to make his mark.[26]

Despite the hatred that many ministers still harbored for the stage, the theatre by 1880 was beginning to rise a bit in public estimation. The most visible sign of this change was society's growing interest in and acceptance of prominent actors. Benjamin McArthur, in *Actors and American Culture, 1880–1920* (1984), in which he chronicles this change in social status of American performers, dates the beginnings of our national "cult of celebrity" to the early 1880s. It had long been the practice that almost every local theatre had its own resident stock company (Baldwin's was

7. "The Grandest Thing I Ever Listened To"

typical), which offered a regular season of plays as well as supporting the occasional visiting star. But with the expansion of the railroads in the 1870s, major actors could tour the country with their own complete companies, called "combinations." And feeding the nation's growing hunger for popular stars and pre-packaged plays was New York City, the home base for many of the finest combination companies. Over one hundred touring theatrical troupes would set out from New York in 1880,[27] carrying the latest Broadway fare to even the smallest towns. While this new system would in time mean the end of the old stock companies, including Baldwin's in San Francisco, the popularity of combinations helped ensure that New York's influence on the American theatre would be widespread and long-lasting.[28]

The rise in combinations also resulted, as McArthur has noted, in a new kind of theatrical manager, as yet relatively unnoticed, but nonetheless representing the future of stage producing in America. This powerful, independent producer, schooled in the ways of business, would replace the old local actor-manager, and would make obsolete the kind of relaxed management style practiced by Tom Maguire. The new breed would soon be seen in producers like Charles and Daniel Frohman, and later, ironically enough, Maguire's protégé, David Belasco.[29] And, in 1880, another early harbinger of the future could be discerned in the person of the ambitious young manager who had agreed to produce Salmi Morse's *Passion* in New York, a 34-year-old impresario on the rise named Henry E. Abbey.

III

Henry Abbey (1846–1896) had begun his theatrical career in Ohio in the early 1870s, selling tickets for the Akron Opera House. After box-office stints in Cleveland and Pittsburgh, between which times he oversaw several stars' tours, Abbey lucked into partnership with Charlotte (Lotta) Crabtree in 1876. There were rumors of an affair, although Lotta's later biographers generally doubt it.[30] Lotta, the darling of the California mining camps, had long wanted to take New York by storm, and now put up the money for Abbey to lease the Park Theatre, on Broadway and 23rd Street, wherein he could showcase her talents. Thus, with Miss Crabtree's backing, young Abbey was launched on a managerial career in New York City. Unfortunately, Lotta's season at the Park proved to be a failure. But Abbey continued as manager, and one of his subsequent productions—Leonard Grover's bucolic comedy *Our Boardinghouse*—was an instant and phenomenal hit.

The series of successes that followed made Abbey's seeming ability to second-guess the public the topic of envious comment by his many rivals.

His wedding of sharp business practices with traditional theatrical management made him very *un*traditional, which was all to the better, in the view of some. "Probably nobody else knows so little as Manager Abbey of the details of the performances that are going on in his different theatres," wrote an admiring journalist; but his "placid exterior and indifferent demeanor" hid "an acute and shrewd knowledge of his business."³¹ A handsome man, tall, thin and dark, Henry Abbey had in little more than two years become one of the New York theatre's prizes, singled out by the *Mirror* in 1879 as bringing "new ideas" to the scene. What New York needed, sighed the *Mirror*, was "half a dozen of such men located here."³²

He had just capped his rising career with what was surely the coup of the decade, if not the century. Returning from Europe this summer of 1880, Abbey had announced that he had arranged for the notorious French actress Sarah Bernhardt to make her first American tour, commencing in November. It was an announcement that had propelled Abbey himself into the national spotlight. Clearly, Henry Abbey in 1880 was a young man on the threshold of a spectacular career in the American theatre.

IV

When Tom Maguire and Salmi Morse approached Henry Abbey with the idea of presenting *The Passion* in New York, it was, in a sense, history being repeated. Just as Maguire himself in San Francisco had been leasing the expensive Grand Opera House and in need of a property to fill it when Morse fortuitously came along in 1879, so Abbey now stood in New York with the massive Booth's Theatre under lease and in need of something spectacular to draw a paying crowd. There were unluckier parallels, as well. Booth's, like the Grand, had a history of financial problems. Built in 1869 by the great tragedian Edwin Booth, the building had from the first been plagued by poor management; the national Panic of 1873 had brought all of the actor's creditors down on him at once, and in January 1874 he filed a petition of bankruptcy. A year later—six years after he had built it— Edwin Booth surrendered his theatre on foreclosure.³³ Its several lessees since had enjoyed little more success. Even the popular playwright/actor Dion Boucicault couldn't make a go of it, and had sold the remainder of his lease to a confident Henry Abbey earlier this year.³⁴ And now Abbey was stuck with it. Of course, Bernhardt would be the Booth's drawing card in November, but what, Abbey must have wondered, could he possibly do for an encore? How could he top the Bernhardt?

Enter Salmi Morse with *The Passion*.

It is not entirely clear just how Henry Abbey first learned of Morse's work. Dempsey and Baldwin, in their biography of Lotta Crabtree, assert that she was somehow involved,[35] but there is no public record to corroborate this claim. Abbey himself said that "it was first called to my notice by the author," who then "induced" him to hear it read. But according to Morse: "I did not come to Mr. Abbey with my poem. He sent for me, and when he heard me read, he paid me the highest compliment I ever received from a manager"—mainly, the immediate promise of a production. Salmi claimed that it was the comedian Nat Goodwin who, having seen *The Passion* in San Francisco, had first recommended it to Abbey.[36]

Whatever the case, Salmi Morse, after following Tom Maguire east in September 1880, upon his arrival in New York did read the play for Henry Abbey, and, evidently, that was all it took. As Abbey told the *Tribune* a few days later, "I consider it the grandest thing I ever listened to, and shall try to present it on a grand scale.... I would not undertake this if I were not sure that I am right."[37] San Francisco's George Barnes, with whom Salmi maintained a running correspondence about the affair, told his readers that "there was quite a race to get in first on the 'Passion' venture. Abbey won by clenching [sic] the bargain after but few words." It was Barnes, in turn, who informed Morse of A.M. Palmer's secretive visit to California. Palmer, Barnes related, "rather regrets that he was not approached in regard to it."[38]

While the possibility of a New York production had long been the subject of speculation in California, the first newspaper in New York to pick up on the story was the *New York Tribune*, on September 10, a mere three days after the deal had been concluded. Abbey was apparently caught off guard by the *Tribune* reporter who showed up at his office on the 9th, asking for the details, but the manager nevertheless granted a lengthy interview, in which he confidently asserted, "There is no doubt that I shall meet with some opposition in the production of this play; but I believe it will be witnessed everywhere with the greatest respect. I intend, therefore, to present it all through the United States and Canada."[39] Everything had been settled. Barring an act of God, the play was scheduled to open at Booth's on December 6.

And so Salmi Morse returned to New York a playwright of some notoriety. He rented rooms at 65 West 21st Street, in a boardinghouse run by Mrs. Isabella Gault, and settled down to the daunting task of restaging his controversial masterwork. Of course, now that the story had broken, he also made himself available for interviews, freely extemporizing on his colorful career and the genius behind *The Passion*.[40] "You can have no idea how full of this subject I am," he told one journalist, assuming the role of tormented genius.

> Everything I write is flavored with it. I refused to write a play for Clara Morris on this account, and after writing two acts of a play for Sol Smith

Russell the same cause compelled me to throw it away. I think any author becomes encrusted, as it were, in a certain style, and that is one reason why I could never believe that Boucicault wrote London Assurance, his other works are so trashy.[41]

When asked about the Supervisors' ordinance, which had stopped the play in San Francisco, Morse admitted that it was still on the books, "but," he lied, "that is because I thought too much of the theme upon which my work is based to drag it through the mire of the courts, although I was told by the best lawyers in California that I would win." Evidently, what New Yorkers didn't know about Judge Morrison's Fourth District Court in San Francisco would never hurt them.

For another reporter, Morse elaborately improvised new variations on his old theme of "Passion Plays I Have Known and Loved." After describing in detail for the umpteenth time the presentations he had supposedly seen at Mount Calvary, Rondo, Madrid, and so on, he said he had then somehow found himself at Malta, where, the reporter recounted,

> he found a manuscript on parchment, to unravel which he was compelled to construct a key. It was partly Arabic, partly Romanic, and, strange to say, was written in Chaldean characters. It was the work of a Maronite monk, one of a curious sect, a cross between Christians, Mohammedans and all other known sects.[42]

This story was later gleefully retold in the *San Francisco Chronicle*, which called it "the crowning romance of all."

Watching the press devour Morse — or, perhaps, it was the other way around — Abbey was understandably made uneasy by all the attention and speculation being concentrated on his newest acquisition. "If it could have been done," he grumbled to a reporter for the *Dramatic News*, "I would have preferred to have never said a word about the play until it was ready to be brought out."[43] Given the notoriety of *The Passion*, and of its author, he should hardly have expected such a luxury.

Still, Abbey, too — sharp managerial talent that he was — seems to have believed wholeheartedly in Salmi Morse, for he freely turned over to him "the direction of the whole affair," allegedly in the interest of historical accuracy.[44] The contract agreed to between Abbey, Morse and Maguire, in fact, was in the form of a copartnership, in which Abbey was to provide the theatre and most of the money. Maguire, presumably backed by some of Morse's wealthy friends in San Francisco, was to put up the rest, and Salmi, the self-proclaimed expert on ancient Hebraic customs, was to actually stage the production. As Abbey explained to the *Dramatic News*:

> To show you what pains are really being taken, some of the cloths to be used in the costumes are being dyed four and five times in order to get

> the exact tint of the garments worn by Christ and the people who surrounded him in his lifetime. All this is under the supervision of Mr. Morse, who has made this matter the study of his life, and the consequence will be that we shall produce a play which, in point of the historical knowledge alone which it will impart, will be worth far more than the price of admission.[45]

Even his severest critics, including William Winter, conceded to Salmi some superiority in historical knowledge.[46]

A great part of Salmi's ability to flim-flam everyone was certainly his image. Now 54 years of age, but looking older, his thick white hair and mustache neatly trimmed, he had taken to assuming the daunting black suit and dark colors of a man of the cloth. A little over six feet tall and slender, "with a slight tendency to angularity," Morse struck most people at first meeting as extremely sincere and knowledgeable. George Barnes's description in his Eulogy is the most oft-quoted: "a tall, rabbinical-looking Hebrew, scrupulously dressed in black, with reverent gray hairs, mild benignant eyes, and somewhat heavily moulded features." In addition, Salmi was an accomplished orator, despite his penchant for obscure terms and convoluted phrases. In short, "his whole contour," as one reporter put it, "is more that of a Protestant clergyman than anything else."[47] It is clear enough why so many people felt they could trust him.

Certainly, Morse was not all bluff; and it is reasonable to assume that his fanaticism about *The Passion* had driven him to some further study since 1879 — if only to be able to defend what he had already written. Moreover, his love of arcane Eastern cultures, so evident in his writings for the *Wasp*, was not fostered in total ignorance, no matter how absurdly he embellished his adventures. At the very least, it could be said that Salmi had more knowledge — accurate or not — about the subject at hand than anyone else on the scene; therefore, putting him in charge of the production must have certainly seemed logical.

Through late September and into early October, Morse and Abbey plunged ahead with preliminary preparations for *The Passion* in New York, while Tom Maguire returned to San Francisco carrying contracts for O'Neill, Lewis Morrison, Henry Widmer and several others in the original San Francisco production.[48] Hoping to avoid Maguire's unhappy experience, Abbey early on promised New York audiences that his production would be unlike anything they had ever witnessed. Everything about it would eschew the theatrical, and would be "carried on in a solemn and profound manner." To begin with, Booth's Theatre was to be renovated *à la* the Grand Opera House in San Francisco. Abbey ordered workers to remove some of the "improvements" made during Boucicault's recent tenure, and Morse announced that one of the more distinctively theatrical features of the proscenium arch — a massive niched statue of Shakespeare "meditating and in act to write" — would be removed and replaced with a large cross. During the run, Booth's Theatre would be rechristened Booth's Temple.[49] Sets were ordered, a new drop-curtain modeled on the one used in San Francisco (depicting "the flight of angels at the dawn of Easter morning") was designed, and some three hundred costumes begun. In all, it was estimated that Abbey, like E. J. Baldwin before him, would wind up spending anywhere from twenty to twenty-five thousand dollars on Salmi Morse's sacred drama.[50]

To further ward off any moral objections to *The Passion* as a theatrical event, Abbey promised that neither the usual posters nor any advertising handbills would be printed, nor would he publish a cast list. "We shall make it a condition of the contracts," he vowed, "that the people engaged shall in no wise make known their connection with the piece." And finally, to ensure that all spectators stayed suitably sober, Abbey promised that no intermission "return checks" would be issued, despite a running time estimated at three hours or more.[51] In return, all he asked was that his production not be hastily prejudged — by preachers, by the press, not by anyone. "The public will accept no judgment save their own," he said, "and they can form none until they can see for themselves. I await their verdict without apprehension."[52]

Even as he spoke those words the verdict was already rolling in.

V

As in San Francisco, attention in New York quickly focused on the city's ministers. And even more so than in the western press, New York dailies willingly gave full coverage to clerical objections. Virtually every pastor in the city, Protestant, Catholic or Jewish, was besieged by reporters, fairly tripping over one another to secure an interview. The better-known clerics, such as Howard Crosby, Chancellor of the University of the City of New York and pastor of the Fourth Avenue Presbyterian Church; John P. Newman, of the Central M. E. Church; Henry C. Potter, Rector of Grace Church; Henry W. Bellows, of All Souls Church (Unitarian); and the theatre-hating T. De Witt Talmage, of the Brooklyn Tabernacle, were approached by nearly every paper in town, while even some of the lesser lights were finding themselves quoted in the pages of the most powerful dailies in America.

This was a heady forum indeed. Yet on the whole, their initial responses were cautious; surprisingly few said they would preach against the play from their pulpits, for fear of advertising it. "I never preach against particular instances of this kind," said one unperturbed Presbyterian shepherd. "I believe it to be the duty of a minister to teach his people the principles of religion, and to let their consciences make the application."[53] Such responses were not exactly destined to sell papers. But then, this was a very busy time for the Protestant ministers. They not only had *The Passion* to worry about, but a Catholic was running for mayor, and Bernhardt was coming to town.

At the same time, if they were not going to preach against *The Passion* from their pulpits, they willingly offered their personal opinions of the work for the eager reporters. Most such comments echoed the familiar litany of objections heard out west: *The Passion* was sacrilegious. It was blasphemous. It was a profanation of a sacred subject and an irreverent money-making scheme. It was an insult to the religious sentiments of right-thinking Christians everywhere. "The nearest approach to blasphemy that I know of," said one Congregationalist pastor; a Baptist minister felt that it would "shock the public mind," and "such shocks [are] generally followed by a reaction in the direction of evil"; a Methodist opposed it "because it is an attempt to make theatre going respectable.... Christians should find enjoyment in church entertainments, the home circle, in society, and a pure and elevated literature"; and a Unitarian pronounced it nothing less than "a national disaster." As for the Jewish community, some rabbis adopted a philosophical view: the Jew, said the prominent Rabbi F. de Sola Mendes diplomatically, "knows that religion is necessary to the safety of society." Therefore, he seemed to be saying, no Jew would interfere in this Christian tempest.[54]

While most of the clerical comments were predictable, there were some that were, at least, novel. Several of the city's ministers—fittingly, given New York's growing reputation as a national theatrical center—tried to phrase their objections to *The Passion* in the jargon of dramatic criticism. The Presbyterian Reverend William Lloyd denounced "any effort to drag Christ down to the level of an earthly hero": "The whole life of Christ," he opined, "was totally free from anything like striving after dramatic effect. Sometimes a dramatic effect was produced, but He immediately retired [i.e., left the stage]. All His miracles were performed with the injunction that silence should be maintained concerning them. His life was intended to influence by its moral character and not by its dramatic effect." The Reverend Dr. Llewellyn Bevan was an even more literate critic, pronouncing the play "an outrage on the dramatic proprieties. Aristotle describes tragedy as a means of elevating the moral nature by exciting the sentiments of pity and terror; but I should think that the representation of the Passion of Christ upon the stage would only excite disgust." As the plot was so well known to one and all, postulated Bevan, it could not produce catharsis but only revulsion. It would be "like putting the life of my own father or mother on the stage to make money."[55]

Abbey attempted to defuse the old charge of profiting from religion by announcing in late October that he would donate all of his profits to the poor. "Humph," one cleric stubbornly responded, "you can tell Mr. Abbey we are not in need of charity." Another pointedly asked, "How much of the proceeds will be devoted to charity after the salaries of managers and actors have been paid?" Still another adroitly deflated the claim by saying, "We should not do evil that good may come of it."[56]

Many of the ministers may wisely have been reluctant to promote the production with their opposition to it. But whether they preached against it or not, frankly, mattered very little. For the controversy quickly began to assume a life of its own quite beyond their special circles, and by the beginning of November nothing Abbey could have promised or done would have made the slightest difference to his detractors. Worsening the situation for him was the fact that the story had broken so early. Whereas in San Francisco all of the events had transpired in only a matter of weeks, in New York the play's opponents had almost *three months* in which to stir up public antagonism. The point at which reason can no longer be swayed was quickly being passed.

John F. Flanagan's editorial in the October issue of the Catholic *Celtic Monthly* provides a perfect illustration. Told by several Catholics who had seen the San Francisco production that the play was, in fact, "elevating and instructive," Flanagan obstinately wrote, "We care not ... for the individual opinion of anybody upon this subject; such a representation ... is an insult." Further informed of Archbishop Alemany's participation in the preparation of the original manuscript, Flanagan retorted, "We doubt this statement; and even if it turns out to be true, it will not change our opinion." Any such defenses of the play were the "prattle" of "booby freethinkers," in Flanagan's view, and would have "little to do with popular sentiment.... Let the public authorities immediately find out whether they are legally vested with power to prevent a spectacle degrading to man and insulting to God."[57]

As Flanagan's comments demonstrate, Gotham's Catholics were free to oppose *The Passion* as vehemently as the Protestants. After all, *their* Archbishop had never sanctioned the script. Surprisingly, however, considering the heat Alemany took for being silent in California, Catholic denunciations in New York were generally understated. Cardinal McCloskey, when asked for his views, regally issued the following terse statement: "His Eminence has nothing to say on the subject at present. When the proper time comes he will speak."[58] Of course, it is not beside the point to remember once again that the city was in the midst of the hotly contested 1880 city election and so the Cardinal, like many prominent Catholics, may have simply desired to maintain as low a public profile as possible.

However, neither the Catholic Church nor Tammany Hall could

afford the appearance of condoning the hated play, not even after Grace's election in November. It is certainly no coincidence that, on November 6 — four days after Grace's victory — it was being reported that

> the Roman Catholic clergy of New York have been instructed to use every means in their power to stop Abbey from producing it. A regular organization has been made, and they will push the thing to the end. Already Catholic legislators are interesting themselves, and considerable lobbying is being done in anticipation of the necessity, as a last resort, of creating a law that will make its presentation impossible.[59]

Morse, who had counted on Catholic support in New York City, was once again thwarted by political expediency. Quoting Jesus (*John* 7:24), he pleaded with all of the ministers and the public, "Judge not by appearances, but judge righteous judgment." "They should at least," he said, "be charitable enough to see the work before they condemn it."[60]

VI

Unlike in San Francisco, then, opposition to *The Passion* in New York was not confined to the Protestant sects but encompassed every religious creed. But if, in the beginning, many New York clergymen expressed a reluctance to preach against *The Passion* from their pulpits, public outrage was soon being stimulated from another quarter, the city's secular press.

Like San Francisco, New York in 1880 supported a large number of newspapers. James McCabe counted twelve daily morning and seven evening papers; ten semi-weekly; almost two hundred weeklies (including the religious press); and about twenty-five magazines, reviews and other journals. The principal ones in terms of power and influence were all morning papers: the *Tribune*, the *Herald*, *Times*, *World* and *Sun*.[61]

Just as the Civil War had helped establish that Victorian ministers like Henry Ward Beecher could be social/political activists, so that great conflict had cemented the power of the eastern press to dictate public opinion, even on a national scale. In the words of George Henry Payne, "The question [after the Civil War] is no longer one of the newspaper in its proper field, representing the people, but of its controlling the machinery of politics."[62] With a national distribution system to disseminate their viewpoints throughout the country, the New York editors enjoyed an audience the size of which the California papers were denied. And whereas in San Francisco the city newspapers, with a few important exceptions, chose to all but ignore the production, in New York the aggressive spirit of competition among the daily papers drove them all, without exception, to join the battle lines early. Indeed, in New York it was the press rather than the pulpit that spearheaded the assault on *The Passion* and first raised the cry for its suppression. Therefore, their individual arguments against its staging are worth noting.

The venerable *Tribune*, the first daily to learn of Abbey's production, had been established by the late Horace Greeley in 1841, and was now managed by Whitelaw Reid.[63] The socially minded *Tribune* editorially opposed *The Passion* on populist grounds, dubbing it an offense "to the popular sense of decorum. The American, whatever his life, is at heart reverent of the name of Jesus." It was a "gratuitous insult," said the editor, to "bill the Saviour" between "the burlesque blondes and Sarah Bernhardt."[64]

The more sensationally inclined *New York Herald* had been around since 1835, even longer than the *Tribune*, and now edited by the founder's son, James Gordon Bennett, Jr., was the most powerful newspaper in America.[65] Ordinarily, Bennett had little sympathy for religious propaganda, and his paper usually reflected that view. Defending its refusal to take a sectarian stand in the recent election, for example, the *Herald* had flatly declared, "It is not for secular newspapers to take sides in [religious] questions." Nevertheless, when it came to *The Passion*, Bennett's paper suddenly grew very sanctimonious indeed, unashamedly using such churchly terms as "blasphemy" and "sacrilege" to characterize the production. Like the de Youngs' *Chronicle* in San Francisco, Bennett's *Herald* belittled the stage's assumption of a higher purpose. "Heaven spare us," the offended editor now prayed, "the apings of comic actors and buffoons in such scenes as the life of Christ."[66] As the storm of denunciations increased, fed to a large degree by its own sensationalized coverage, the *Herald* would be among the first to advocate use of the law to stop the play. Inarguably, the *Herald*'s national reputation and eminence made it one of Morse's most powerful foes.

The third major New York morning daily was the younger *New York Times*, founded in 1851 by Henry Jarvis Raymond.[67] Whereas both the *Tribune*, with its radical social views, and the *Herald*, with its emphasis on crime and scandal, had alienated the conservative upper and middle classes, the *Times* had avowedly set out to claim the middle road, "to allay, rather than excite, agitation," and to "substitute reason for prejudice."[68] Now under the editorship of George Jones, the *Times* chose for its point of attack the same bigoted territory staked out in San Francisco by "Betsy B.":

> To the Jew or the infidel there seems to be no reason why the sufferings of Jesus, whom they regard as a mere man, should not be illustrated on the stage.... We need not be surprised if a Jewish manager is unable to comprehend the feeling of the Christian community in regard to this matter, and if he feels that any attempt to prevent the representation of the Passion Play is an outrage on his rights. Though Christian people will

stay away from the play, the manager calculates that he can draw large audiences from the other classes of the community and can thus make the play a source of profit.[69]

So much for substituting "reason for prejudice."

Charles A. Dana, the owner/editor of the *Sun*, had once served as city editor under Horace Greeley, and, like him, was fond of underdog social causes. But he had no sympathy for *The Passion*, either; in fact, Dana's was the first editorial voice to raise the alarm.[70] Virtually all of the other smaller papers would come to follow his lead.

Every major newspaper in the city also had its own theatre editor-cum-critic, each of whom addressed the problem in his own respective column. The *Herald*'s chief dramatic critic in 1880 was Felix Gregory de Fontaine (1834–1896); the *Times* employed at least two critics, George E. Montgomery (1858–1898) and Frederick Schwab (1844–1927); at the *Evening Post*, the desk had been filled since 1874 by the English-born John Ranken Towse (1845–1933).[71] Not unexpectedly, the consensus among these men was overwhelmingly against the purported sacrilege, and in favor of Abbey's withdrawing it.

The most powerful theatre editor in New York in 1880, arguably the finest critical voice of the day, worked for the *New York Tribune*. He was William Winter.

Winter (1836–1909) had been hired by the *Tribune* in 1865, following stints as literary editor and drama critic at several other papers. His erudition, his extensive knowledge of theatrical history and theory, and his open-mindedness had distinguished his early writings. Of all the critics of the era, the prolific William Winter was the most widely read.[72] It was, therefore, worth the risk, or so Salmi apparently thought, of reading to Winter several acts of *The Passion*, in the confident hope that Winter himself might become a convert to the cause. This Salmi did, one pleasant mid-October afternoon, in the vestibule of Abbey's Park Theatre.[73]

Unfortunately, Morse should have known that Winter was, as Benjamin McArthur puts it, of "the genteel tradition," given to "Victorian sentimentalizing."[74] Something of a poet himself, Winter believed that the theatre "should be the home of beauty, poetry, and art"; the drama, "a repository of noble thought, romantic imagery, and pure influence." It should not be the province of the stage, Winter would write, to offend social conventions, "which, gradually, have been evolved and established for the advancement and welfare of civilization and the elevation of man from the state of a mere animal."[75]

Winter's reaction to Morse's work, therefore, could have been predicted. On October 18, following Salmi's special reading for his benefit, Winter's column in the *Tribune* was completely given over to a consideration of Morse's text. And William Winter said: "It is one of the most tedious compositions that ever were written," full of "moral twaddle," a "goody-goody affair." At the same time, it is significant that he, at least, did not call for city ordinances, or even picket lines. He thought the production might get "one full house" and then die a quick death at the box office. But blasphemy? No. "That the Passion Play can exercise an immoral influence we do not believe," he offered. "There is no irreverence in either its spirit or its incidents." Rather than injure morals, a play like *The Passion* could only injure the community's self-respect. "It is best, with a people like ours — intellectual, sceptical, prone to satire, and quick to see the ridiculous side of everything — that sacred words and images and ideas should not be made commonplace."[76] Once again, the nineteenth century was seen as far too civilized a time for a Passion drama.

The ruminations of William Winter and the other drama critics only added to the pounds of lead type being expended daily on the story by every newspaper in the city. As the weeks passed and the announced opening date of December 6 drew nearer, the volume and hysterical tenor of the press coverage escalated sharply. But all of this attention only served to advertise the play. By mid-November, with Abbey and Morse still obstinately holding on and rehearsals scheduled to commence at Booth's, many drama critics, like their editors, began to argue that *The Passion* could only be stopped by immediate passage of specific legislation. Editorial objectivity in the matter was, to say the least, open to question. "To have this august and sacred personality [of Jesus Christ] brought down to the level of a negro minstrel show is a crime," preached the *Herald*. "And we trust that our authorities will do what was done in San Francisco — make the performance a crime."[77] Gradually, the newspapers convinced not only the public, but the pulpit as well, to agitate for the direct intervention of the law.

Even more noteworthy, the cumulative effect of all the interviews, articles and editorials was, first, to elevate the protest into a local *cause célèbre*, and then, because of the New York papers' wide distributions, to turn the local protest into a national scandal to a degree of which the San Francisco press a year earlier had never dreamed. Indeed, the western papers, watching the circus unfold from two thousand miles away, could only marvel at the scene.

VII

If the aggressiveness of the secular dailies in helping mold public outrage was one of the distinguishing features of the *Passion* controversy in New York, a second, even more interesting element could be seen in the

7. "The Grandest Thing I Ever Listened To"

reactions of the theatre community to the furor. In that quarter, especially, where the stakes were so much more personal, emotions ran high on both sides of the issue, dividing actors, critics and managers alike. In fact, the one city journal most personally committed to stopping Abbey and Morse—the one newspaper that tirelessly ferreted out and quoted opponents from every walk of life—that sponsored its own anti-*Passion* petition drive—that urged its readers to boycott the production—that cried the loudest for the law to suppress a theatrical work—was the theatre's own newest trade journal, the *New York Mirror*, led by its neophyte editor/owner, Harrison Grey Fiske.

The untried Mr. Fiske was about to make his mark.

8
The Mirror's War on Mr. Abbey

I

In San Francisco, it was reported that New York was "about evenly divided" over *The Passion*. Ignoring the fact that the New York scenario of the controversy was basically replaying that of the West Coast, the *San Francisco Chronicle* now reported the affair with an air of detached sarcasm:

> Between those [in New York] who favor and those who oppose, there is ... this great difference: that the pro-*Passion*ists are moderate in tone, whilst the anti-*Passion*ists are as bitter as we Christians so well know how to be. Some of the offended have actually howled at the sacrilege.[1]

If this tone of self-deprecatory bemusement seems surprising coming from the journal that had so eagerly led the anti-*Passion*ists in San Francisco, it can be credited in part to the simple fact that now Morse and his play were someone else's problem and San Francisco could well afford to laugh.

However, the *Chronicle*'s remark that the "anti-"s in New York were out-shouting the "pro-"s was very much on the mark. And in no segment of the community was this division more evident than in the New York professional theatre.

On the one side, there were those actors who were every bit as morally offended by *The Passion* as any minister. "Is there a living mother who could consent to have her darling babe held up to the view of a gaping crowd?" a "RETIRED ACTRESS" asked rhetorically. "How then can we bear to think of our blessed Lord in all His sufferings, our only sure hope and comfort in this life, being so insulted?" The young Frederick Paulding had no sympathy for any actor who would attempt the role of the Divine Master. "As an actor," Paulding wrote, "I think there are enough human passions to portray without meddling with divine ones." An anonymous "ACTOR" of "thirty years' experience" asserted that this was all the fault of the new breed of managers; such a thing could never have happened in the

8. The Mirror's War on Mr. Abbey   147

Harrison Grey Fiske. Only 19 years old when he assumed the editorship of the "New York Mirror," Fiske set out to make "The Passion" his first great public cause. Expressing concern only for the good of the theatre, Fiske vehemently attacked everyone connected with the play and actively lobbied the city government to suppress it by law. (Courtesy Billy Rose Theatre Collection, The New York Public Library)

good old days. "Nearly all the theatres in the United States at the present day are managed by persons who are not, and never were, actors," he complained; "neither have they any affinity with the actor or his calling. The play house, under their control is a thing of speculation only." An ex-drama critic, who signed himself "B.E.N.," advised that people only go to the theatre "to be amused, and not to have their prejudices stirred up," while another Victorian lady, speaking on behalf of her entire sex, wished to protest—"in the most earnest and forcible manner of which I am capable"—that condoning a sacrilege such as *The Passion* threatened to turn New York into a modern Sodom and Gomorrah. "It seems as if we might be prepared to reap the consequences in some such calamity as befell those cities," she ominously warned.[2]

On the other side of the theatrical coin, however, the production did have its supporters, most of whom saw the question in terms of, if not constitutional rights, at least the right of the theatre to treat of religious subject matter. A letter written to the *Herald* and signed by "AN ACTOR" angrily lambasted the editor for continually caricaturing actors only as "buffoons" and "variety players," and for assuming that the play would necessarily be no better than a minstrel show. The erudite ACTOR scolded the *Herald* by calmly pointing out the obvious: "Mr. Abbey will not, I am sure, put buffoons and ballet dancers into the cast, and so far from the performance being a burlesque it will undoubtedly be one of the grandest and most impressive representations ever seen." The only worthwhile argument against the play seemed to be that a theatre might not be the proper place for a sacred drama. Well, the ACTOR demanded, "will some one tell us on what ground they thus limit the province of the stage?" A "UTILITY MAN" some days before had raised the same point: "The poet may sing the praises of the Master, the painter canvas the sufferings of His sinless life, but the player has no such rights; his art is circumscribed. And yet the year is 1880!"[3]

Another, not-so-anonymous defense from a theatre practitioner came from the most successful American dramatist then living, Bartley Campbell (1843-1888). The author of such popular Western dramas as *The Vigilantes* (1877), *My Partner* (1879) and the hugely successful melodrama *The Galley Slave* (1879), Bartley Campbell had been hailed by many critics as the best playwright America had ever produced. At the height of his popularity when he sat down to write the *Herald*, his voice was not an unimportant one. He wrote:

> TO THE EDITOR OF THE HERALD: —
> In behalf of that consistency which is said to be a jewel of great price let us give the producers of the "Passion Play" a fair hearing. For myself, I know nothing of its argument, its performance or its effect upon an average audience. If it should prove to lessen the dignity or mar the Christian conception of the Redeemer, or in anywise impair the pathos and power of the lesson of Calvary, . . . [then] its managers should be held up to public reprobation.
> But the proposition to condemn [it] in advance of its production is, to say the least, illogical. It smacks too much of that intolerance which has fought every advance of civilization. . . .
> I could more readily comprehend the opposition to the "Passion Play" if Colonel Ingersoll had not occupied the same stage within the year to attack and ridicule not only Christ, but every form of revealed religion, . . . while a packed auditorium applauded him to the echo.
> If Ingersoll is permitted to ridicule Christ, what consistency is there in preventing a representation consisting of sacred music and speaking tableaux, which the managers claim is reverently done? Where Ingersoll has a hearing the "Passion Play" should not be silenced.[4]

Campbell's remarks represented an argument adopted by many in defense of *The Passion*. The lawyer Robert Ingersoll (1833–1899) was an infamously accomplished orator of the day, known as "The Great Agnostic," whose attacks on organized religion had prompted many preachers to brand him the anti-Christ. But his power to sway an audience also made him one of the most successful—and highly paid—speakers of the age, rivaling the great Beecher himself in the number of hearers that mere mention of an appearance could command.[5] If Ingersoll were allowed to debunk the divinity of Christ, why indeed should not *The Passion* be allowed to celebrate it?

Finally, there were also within the theatrical community those few who did defend *The Passion* on constitutional grounds, who framed the debate, as Morse did, in the radical terms of freedom of speech. The most vociferous, publicly visible exponent of this position was Charles A. Byrne, the editor of the *Dramatic News*. From the very beginning of the controversy Byrne used his columns—not only in the *Dramatic News* but in his newly founded secular paper, the *New York Truth*—to put the tempest in some sort of legal perspective. Responding to yet another cry from the *Herald* for the authorities to decree *The Passion* a crime, Byrne sarcastically chided,

> the *Herald* must know, if it knows anything, that "the authorities" have no rights in the matter. In the eye of the law the legend of the Christian faith is not more sacred than that of the Jew or the Mahometan ... and the lawmakers are forbidden to make enactments affecting any of them.... While legislatures cannot abridge religious freedom in any way, they are equally powerless to abridge the right to deride religion.... The dramatist may use the sacred legend of Christianity with as much impunity as the preacher or the priest. These are the legal points of the question, and the *Herald* only makes a fool of itself when it counsels "the authorities" to disregard them.
>
> [*The Passion*'s] representation abridges no man's right and interferes with no man's religion. Opposition to it is mere cant, and cant in a country which protects neither sect nor creed is despicable.[6]

Byrne's was practically the only editorial voice consistently, and from the first, raised in defense of Morse and Abbey. And, even though his theatrical paper was of relatively minor import, as compared with the *Herald* or *Tribune*, his editorials were nonetheless quoted in other parts of the country as representative of the pro-*Passion*ist faction.[7]

Of course, it is arguable that Byrne defended the production simply *because* it was the unpopular position; this was, after all, the same "blackguard" editor who took delight in attacking the sacred cows of the profession, who impertinently referred to William Winter as "Wee Willy" and regularly accused the distinguished critic of being a drunkard.[8] However, his ardent defense of the play put Byrne at odds with a far greater constituency than his usual audience, the small, socially unimportant theatre community. His position placed him on the side opposed by virtually every major newspaper editor of his time, by every prominent clergyman, and by many of New York's most powerful citizens. In short, it was not a position for an editor, no matter how iconoclastic, to take without some measure of sincerity. At the very least, Byrne must be acknowledged—as must Morse himself—for attempting to define and defend, in a culture that so admired conformity, the difficult legal concept that linked artistic expression with freedom of speech, i.e., the right of the individual artist to be heard *despite* the majority sentiment.

Not insignificantly, Byrne's editorial position also placed him in polar opposition to his rival theatre editor, Harrison Grey Fiske. And therein, perhaps, lies the real tale of *The Passion* in New York. For it was young Fiske who picked up the story of *The Passion* and ran with it. Looking back at Fiske's behavior, there can be little doubt that he exploited the controversy in an effort to establish the still-struggling *New York Mirror* as the preeminent journal of the theatrical profession, over Byrne's *Dramatic News*.

III

Even as a teenager, Harrison Grey Fiske (1861–1942) had exhibited both a love for the theatre and a tendency toward the romantic gesture. The son of a wealthy New York hotel owner, the teen-aged Fiske had once served briefly as drama critic for the New Jersey *Argus*—but quit when he learned he had been hired only because the editor was in debt to his father. Still, these scruples did not impel him to object when, in 1880, that latter gentleman bought the 19-year-old Harry a one-third interest in a year-old dramatic weekly called the *New York Mirror*. Fiske immediately assumed the editorship of the *Mirror*, and within months had begun moves to supplant his two partners.[9] Thus, at the time of *The Passion* controversy, young Harrison Fiske's financial as well as professional fortunes were tied up in the future of the struggling *Mirror*.

Fiske was a crusader. Already he had begun to take on Charles Byrne and the *Dramatic News*, and in years to come he would fight the $500 theatre tax, lobby for the Actor's Fund and for an international copyright law, and continually urge theatre people to comport themselves with utmost decorum, that the profession might become socially acceptable. His enthusiastic embracement of Victorian morality for the theatre community betrayed the fact that he had been, in Archie Binns's phrase, "born into a gentleman's world."[10] This would sometimes lead him into a kind of snobbery, as when he applauded the formation in 1882 of a social club along the

8. The Mirror's *War on Mr. Abbey*

lines of the later Players' Club, in which actors and dramatists could hobnob with artists, musicians and "society men." This club was being organized "on the right sort of principles," Fiske remarked, as "none but desirable persons will be admitted."[11] In another revealing editorial from these early years, Fiske, noting that attitudes toward actors showed some signs of softening, fancifully envisioned that very soon

> the actor can at pleasure breathe the heavy-scented atmosphere of Society's drawing-room, jostle the claw-hammered swell, hear the sweet rustle of silks and satins and listen to the well-bred buzz of fashionable scandalmongering. It is questionable whether the privilege is worth enjoying; but there can be no doubt that its enjoyment is valuable as an indication of the modern estimation in which the player and his art are held.[12]

It also seems certain that Harry Fiske, for one, thought the "privilege" very much worth enjoying.

In 1880, however, nineteen years old and editor of the fledgling *Mirror* for only a few months,[13] Fiske had yet to find his first major crusade. Salmi Morse was about to provide him with one.

The *Mirror* first noted Abbey's intentions to produce *The Passion* on September 25, fifteen days after the news had appeared in the *Tribune*. In the meantime, first the *Sun* and then the *Herald* had both already gone on record as being opposed to the production. In fact, Fiske reprinted both of these editorials along with his own, on September 25.

As for Fiske himself, his initial editorial reaction was negative but circumspect, couched in the phrases of a warning:

> The question that interests the dramatic profession with reference to this matter is this: will its production in New York and other cities cast discredit upon the stage, and still further strengthen or revive the prejudices that exist or existed against the theatre? Should this be the case, *The Mirror* would most decidedly take a stand against the proposal, and beg of Mr. Abbey to reconsider his intention before it be too late. He is a manager who has the best interests of the drama at heart, and should it be proven to him conclusively that his action would have a deleterious effect, no doubt he would be the first to come forward and acknowledge the error of judgment he has made, by giving up all idea of bringing it out.[14]

In young Fiske's ideal world of gentlemen and ladies, such a gracious warning should have done the trick.

This first editorial established the argument on which the *Mirror*'s entire crusade would be based: that Mr. Abbey, in producing a play that would make society angry, was the enemy of the theatre; Mr. Fiske, in protecting the theatre from such antagonism, was its friend. The issue, to Fiske, was just that simple — and that simplistic. "In setting out to prevent the production of the Passion Play in New York," Fiske wrote, "we have no other motive than that which characterizes our fight against anything and everything which we consider in the light of an evil endangering the welfare of the profession and the drama."[15] That such moral/religious censorship might represent an evil and a danger of a different kind seems never to have occurred to him.

Fiske's concern for the state of the theatre in 1880 is commendable, but in such statements there was also a certain smugness, a growing tone of self-righteousness that assumed for the young editor and for his paper an importance they had yet to merit. It was an attitude that went quite beyond the controversy itself, and it grew more presumptuous with every editorial. At the height of the controversy, Fiske was announcing:

> Here in America we have no Lord Chamberlain, as in London, to judge of the fitness of a play for prodution, but the need of some voice to advise and counsel for such purposes is universally recognized. This right *The Mirror*, as the dramatic organ of the country, lays claim to, and if its censorship has never been called into action heretofore, it is because no occasion has offered. The press is the safeguard of the community. *The Mirror* is the safeguard of the Stage.... It is our particular province ... to protect the stage, and in this, as in all other instances, we propose to fulfill it to the letter.[16]

In the pages of the *Mirror*, at least, *The Passion* was the personal crusade of the *Mirror* alone. It wasn't long before Fiske was earnestly claiming that the *Mirror* had been first to publish an article condemning the idea. According to the *Mirror*'s self-serving scenario, "The *Herald, Sun, Spirit, Tribune, Star,* and *Times, following the initiative of The Mirror,* have printed strongly worded editorials *supporting our course* and reiterating the caution we had given Mr. Abbey" [emphasis added]. Even clergymen "of widely different creeds" were harmoniously "drawn up in battle array behind *The Mirror*."[17]

Sending his reporters out to interview every minister of note in the city, Fiske further pronounced his theatrical journal the medium through which the clergy now spoke. His editorials, too, began to address theological concerns. Commenting on Abbey's proposed gift to the poor, Fiske sermonized, "The poor, of course, should be fed, but only on nutritious food. Blasphemous bread and unsanctified meat would prove neither palatable nor healthful."[18]

Fiske was not without critics of his own for this pseudo-religious stance. Chastised by an acquaintance for being in the wrong "from a politic standpoint" — "*The Mirror* is not a Church journal. It is the organ of the dramatic profession" — Fiske acknowledged that the church had its own press, as did the theatre, but "for the moment ... the batteries of each [are centered] upon a common enemy"—mainly, Henry Abbey. Again, Fiske protested, society's approval of the stage was at stake: "We must not place a sword in the hands of an enemy to destroy our dearly-bought claims to public consideration and support." That, he said, was why he was publishing the opinions of the clergy—"to show what sort of endorsement Mr. Abbey's project would receive from the people to whose patronage it is intended to appeal."[19]

What the excited young editor failed to grasp, of course, was that much of the blame for the degree of heat being fanned was directly attributable to him. Worse, his policy of publishing clerical protests only served to exacerbate what he claimed to fear the most, religious opposition to the stage. To see it unfold in the columns of the *Mirror* is almost comic. Commenting on the number of ministers his staff had been able to interview, Fiske rhapsodized: "Twenty-five years ago, you could not have found a single minister who would have talked temperately and kindly about the theatre, much less venture opinions for publication in the organ of the dramatic profession. How different is all this now!"[20] Three weeks later—after publishing their objections, plus liberally quoting attacks from other journals—Fiske was rather ludicrously pointing to all the vitriol and melodramatically crying,

> Henry E. Abbey is doubtless responsible for this.... This is a precise illustration of the baleful influence the presentation of a sacrilege would work upon the stage.... The danger that *The Mirror* predicted is imminent. The dark clouds of superstition, bigotry and prejudice are lowering. Will they break?[21]

Of course they broke, but when they did it was not the churches who had summoned up the storm. If anything, it was the *Mirror* itself.

Henry Abbey, as the manager behind both *The Passion* and Sarah Bernhardt, was already being daily bombarded with invective from the religious and secular press; he was, therefore, disinclined to seeing himself branded as "evil" and an "enemy" of the stage in the pages of one of his own profession's journals as well. Early in November he sent a letter to Fiske, informing the combative editor that, due to its inflammatory editorials, the *Mirror* would no longer receive any of Abbey's advertising support—from either Booth's or the Park Theatre. The outrageously wounded Fiske immediately took up his pen and loudly asked the public what he had done:

> Our articles have been written in the spirit of true and legitimate journalism, never stooping to the level of personality, abuse or blackguardism.... We did [Abbey] a service in showing the public opposition he must expect.[22]

The "pig-headed" Abbey, said Fiske, had "flung down the gauntlet," and he promised his readers that the fight would be "a bitter one. *The Mirror* is on the right side, and the one that will come off victorious."

Within a week, Fiske had composed a piously worded petition addressed to the Mayor and the New York City Board of Aldermen, calling for the legal suppression of *The Passion:*

> **WHEREAS,** Public advertisement has been made of an attempt to degrade religion and to divert the playhouse from its proper sphere by representing at Booth's Theatre ... a so-called Passion Play depicting the life and sufferings of Jesus Christ and his Disciples by hired performers, upon the public stage, to the detriment of morality and the endangering of the peace;
>
> **THEREFORE,** The undersigned, citizens and residents of New York City, respectfully petition the Board of Aldermen to enact, and the Mayor to approve, the following ordinance, in order that the aforesaid desecration of religion and malversion of the theatre may be prevented by law....[23]

The resolution that followed was copied verbatim from the San Francisco ordinance, which Fiske had published in the *Mirror* on November 13.

Fiske placed copies of this petition in the leading hotels and in the offices of the *Herald, Times, World, Tribune, Sun* and *Star*, as well as in his own offices at 12 Union Square, and "at numerous public places." In addition, he dispatched a number of women — "distinguished leaders of society" — to collect signatures door-to-door. "These ladies," Fiske bragged, "represent a class of our people whose attendance is vital to our best theatres."[24]

As if Abbey's withdrawal of advertising from the *Mirror* had voided all the rules of gentlemanly combat, Fiske also now increased his personal attacks on the manager. In his editorial of November 20, Fiske compared Abbey's obstinacy to the rantings of a madman. But the *Mirror*, good physician that it was, was there to cure Abbey "in spite of himself." And of what did Fiske's cure consist? Just as an insane man, for his own protection and for the protection of society, would be placed in a "strait-waistcoat," "now we intend to put Manager Abbey in the strait-waistcoat of the Law."[25]

So eager was he to rid the country of *The Passion*, that Fiske willingly aligned himself with what were for him some strange bedfellows. One of the *Mirror*'s favorite enemies was the pietistic Reverend T. De Witt Talmage. Fiske, of course, despised Talmage for his antitheatrical tirades, and characterized him at other times as a "charlatan," a "loud-mouthed pastor," "an agregious [sic] ass" and a "dangerous fool."[26]

But Talmage opposed *The Passion*.

8. The Mirror's War on Mr. Abbey

So, among those pastors whose denunciations Fiske approvingly printed was the "charlatan" De Witt Talmage.[27]

Likewise, Fiske regularly opposed the various vice societies—especially the Gerry Society and the Society for the Reformation of Juvenile Delinquents—for their meddling in the free operation of the city's theatres. But these groups also opposed *The Passion*. So it is that one finds Fiske willingly brandishing the threat represented by these same societies in order to bring a stubborn Henry Abbey into line.

Finally, despite the fact that he vehemently opposed the censorious tendencies of the "invidious" theatre-licensing laws, Fiske was suddenly eager to call the Board of Aldermen's attention to the fact that "the section of an act passed in 1839, relating to theatres, which was amended in 1860 ... distinctly provides that 'License shall be issued *under such terms and under such regulations* as the municipal authorities may respectively present'" [his emphasis].[28]

"We have no desire," Fiske disingenuously claimed, "to see [Abbey's] theatre closed by the officers of the law, as it certainly will be closed; himself and his company arrested, as they certainly will be arrested." And yet, he also wrote in the same issue,

> we urge every reader to sign the petition which is republished in another column, and to aid us in locking the doors of our theatres against the contemplated outrage at Booth's, and against any recurrence of such an attempt hereafter. Manager Abbey has one more week to repent; but we intend to make his repentance final and to take bonds against any relapse.[29]

Certainly, under any other circumstances, had anyone outside the theatre made such open threats against a manager or a production, one hopes that Fiske would have been among the first to cry "Interference," or even "Censorship." But *The Passion* had now become Fiske's obsession, and his desire to see it suppressed blinded him to the thoughtlessness of his own inflammatory editorials.

But then, it would have been folly for Fiske to back down now. For his breathless campaign to suppress *The Passion* was gaining him notice throughout the country—indeed, throughout the world. Not only had the tiny *New York Mirror* been credited approvingly by important city dailies, such as the *Herald* and the *Tribune*, and by the city's religious weeklies, but editors in cities as far away as Houston, Texas, and Ottawa, Canada, were remarking favorably on the fact that no one in New York opposed the theatrical production more violently than the self-professed "organ of the stage." A correspondent from Geneva, Switzerland, wrote Fiske that *The Passion* and the *Mirror*'s campaign against it were being discussed in that city by the English, the Americans and even the Swiss. More significantly,

Fiske began to see the *Mirror*'s circulation climb.³⁰ The little *New York Mirror* and its "plucky editor" were being noticed indeed.

At the same time, Henry Abbey's commercial boycott of the *Mirror* did cause Fiske to alter, if not the number, then at least the *aim* of his personal attacks. After November 13 *The Passion* was no longer the folly of Abbey alone. Now it was Abbey and "a small clique of California speculators" who were perpetrating the outrage; Abbey had "foolishly [become] the tool of the broken-down California schemers who have entrapped him."³¹ Whereas Tom Maguire and Salmi Morse had been, for the most part, noticeably missing heretofore from the paper's editorial denunciations of *The Passion*, Fiske now widened his sights to include them in his harangues.

As proof that this was all a plot imported from the far-off Pacific, and as a further reason for New York to drive the sacrilege from its midst, Fiske pointed to the fact that no local actor had been found to play the leading role, but rather, Abbey "has been obliged to send to California for the people to cast and rehearse the Passion Play."³² As those same actors and actresses began arriving from the west early in November, they were greeted with a hostility that already equaled, if it did not exceed, the storm they had braved more than a year before in San Francisco.

IV

One by one, the prominent members of Baldwin's Stock Company had been hired away, many of them by Henry E. Abbey. Henry Widmer, who was to lead the *Passion* orchestra in New York, took his farewell benefit in San Francisco on Monday evening, October 18.³³ Five nights later, before a full house, James O'Neill performed for the last time on the Baldwin stage in his own benefit. George Barnes, while bemoaning the loss of San Francisco's favorite star, nonetheless wished the actor well.

> It is a more important turning point in *his* career, for he goes East to play a character hitherto looked upon as too sacred for the stage, an impersonation which will make him a very prominent figure in the civilized world.... Widely different as opinions here were as to the wisdom of presenting [*The Passion*] ... there was but one opinion as to the representation given by Mr. O'Neill. It was simply *grand.* If he creates the effect we anticipate, he will never again descend even to the legitimate, so those who will see him play "Fairfax" tonight may see the last *theatrical* performance he will give.³⁴

It was widely rumored in San Francisco that O'Neill, who had been earning $175 a week as a stock star, would be making $500 per week during the two-month run of *The Passion* in New York City.³⁵

8. The Mirror's *War on Mr. Abbey*

San Franciscans did not seem to begrudge him his success. Instead, they became protective of him; New York newspaper attacks on James O'Neill became attacks on San Francisco. A sort of perverse local chauvinism began to take effect, a sense of pride that defended not only James O'Neill but even Salmi Morse. Loring Pickering, the editor of the *Call*, who had been so silent during the run of *The Passion* in San Francisco, now complained that the play's opponents in New York "are not fully informed of the exact nature of the production." *The Passion*, he explained, was simply a series of tableaux, "put in a perfectly reverential spirit, and, so far as they can offend anybody, . . . [they are] not open to cavil." Even more surprising, Pickering now argued that if the authorities in New York would only allow the play to open, they would readily see that it

> might really turn out to have a strong moral effect on the side of religion.... That it can have any direct evil effect, we doubt. That Mr. Salmi Morse is a Jew, is sufficient reason why its motives cannot be impugned. And it must, in justice to him, be said, that in spite of literary peculiarities, he has treated the subject with a high respect and reverence not necessarily required in the work of one whose creed is opposed to that which holds the divinity of our Saviour.[36]

Now it was almost as if the play had never been suppressed in San Francisco. As previously noted, even the *Chronicle* looked upon *The Passion* now with an almost nostalgic tolerance.

By the end of October, Tom Maguire had said goodbye to San Francisco and joined O'Neill, the Morrisons, Forrest Robinson and the other actors heading east. According to one San Francisco observer, it was commonly held that Maguire, whose fortunes had changed so dramatically since meeting Salmi Morse, desperately needed for *The Passion* to succeed in New York; poor Tom was already being ungraciously referred to as "the ex–Napoleon of the California stage." "The Baldwin Theatre is now almost stripped of its stock company," Barnes noted with genuine sadness.[37]

V

Back in New York, auditions for *The Passion* began on the afternoon of November 11. Abbey had advertised for two hundred supernumeraries, but perhaps because of the controversy — or perhaps because the audition notices had stressed "respectable young men" — only about half that number had showed up this first day, from whom some sixty were hired. More auditions were to be held the following week. It was one of Morse's stringent requirements, the *World* reported (with a straight face), "that the Romans and the rabble shall be persons of exemplary character." They would be "required to conduct themselves behind the scenes with the strictest propriety, and avoid all laughter or light behavior."³⁸ For this, they were to be paid from twenty-five to fifty cents a performance.

James O'Neill arrived in New York City on Sunday, November 14, and the following Wednesday, the seventeenth, the entire cast gathered for the first reading of the play. O'Neill, justifiably skittish at the amount of press animosity he had already garnered before he had even arrived, attempted to deflect any more attacks by divorcing himself as much as possible from his own "disreputable" calling. He desperately told reporters that, "If the public will support me, I shall devote the remainder of my life to this great work. I have no desire to go back to the routine work of the stage at all. I believe I can do more good by this presentation than any of the ministers from their pulpits."³⁹

Although Abbey and Morse, true to their promise, never allowed an official cast list to be published, the *San Francisco Daily Examiner* later printed what it claimed was a record of the cast. If the *Examiner's* list is accurate, in addition to James O'Neill as Christ, and Lewis Morrison and Forrest Robinson repeating their respective roles of Pontius Pilate and the High Priest, Abbey's cast included Charles Burton as Judas; Lewis Barrett as Herod; and Thomas Jackson as Joseph. W. C. Whitecar, George Jordan and Russell Bassett were also named. Among the actresses, only Nellie Wetherell was mentioned; she played Anna. According to the *Dramatic News*, the part of the Virgin Mary was being assumed by "a young Hebrew girl of [New York], who is not connected with the profession." The *San Francisco Examiner* further noted that this anonymous young lady was "a friend of the author." In addition, it was reported that there were 130 male and 100 female supers, plus a twenty-five-piece orchestra ("the largest ever seen in a theatre") and a sixty-voice mixed chorus.⁴⁰

Ignoring the weekly sermons assigning them all to perdition, the large cast and crew began the grueling task of rehearsing and restaging the monumental spectacle. "Mr. Morse is keeping eleven painters busy," Barnes reported. In fact, Salmi told Barnes that the famous scenic designer and painter William T. Voegtlin, who had designed the ornate sets for the 1870 revival of *The Black Crook*, was "getting up a scene for the death of John the Baptist at his own price."⁴¹ The number of costumes ordered had now escalated to seven hundred, and included thirty-two "real India shawls" cut up for dresses. "A hundred Levites and six *real* harpists and six real lyrists, will play to the dancing of Salomi [sic], all fully according to the best authorities." Morse was said to be at the theatre day and night, which (if even remotely true) meant rehearsals were being held on the upper floors of Booth's at the same time that the divine Miss Sarah, who had opened on November 8, was packing them in downstairs.

The pressure on Henry Abbey must have been tremendous. Protestant ministers' tirades against the "sinful French Jewess," "the Bernhardt," had been bad enough. But now, on top of juggling that temperamental star's publicity and supervising her daily schedule, Abbey had to contend with reporters demanding that he answer each and every new attack upon *The Passion*. And although he had acknowledged from the very first that he expected some opposition to Morse's work, it is clear that he never anticipated the amount — or degree — of viciousness now being directed his way. Moreover, he had always maintained that he would fight for his right to produce the play all the way to the higher courts, if necessary.[42] Unfortunately, now he found his case being tried in that most hackneyed and capricious of journalistic forums, the "Court of Public Opinion."

Two weeks before *The Passion* was scheduled to open the final blows were struck. The first of these fell on Tuesday afternoon, November 24, 1880, when the New York City Board of Aldermen met to address the problem of *The Passion*. Like San Francisco and her Board of Supervisors, the city of New York was governed by a mayor and a board of twenty-two aldermen, who together oversaw the various boards of commissioners. The mayor was elected every two years, the aldermen annually. The boards' chief legal resource, the Corporation Counsel, was appointed for a four-year term.[43] It was to the Mayor and the Board of Aldermen that Fiske had addressed his anti–*Passion* petition. In fact, his was only one of many such petitions pressed upon the harried aldermen, demanding that they find some way to legally stop *The Passion* before it could ever open.

At this momentous Tuesday meeting, the Board's President, Alderman Morris, offered his own resolution, requesting the Corporation Counsel to

> give the Board of Aldermen an opinion as to whether any of the laws now in force would be sufficient to prevent [*The Passion's*] introduction; and, if none now exists, whether the Common Council have the power to pass an ordinance prohibiting the introduction and exhibition of this play before the public.
> And if they have the power to pass such an act, then he, the Corporation Counsel, shall prepare such an ordinance as will cover this case and all other cases that may arise in the future, and send the same to this Board of Aldermen for its immediate passage.[44]

In the discussion that followed, the obligatory arguments supporting suppression for religious reasons were offered. But the Board also included at least one member who was troubled by the larger constitutional issues. Alderman Marshall objected to the resolution on the grounds that it would "introduce a religious element into the Board, which all of us should deprecate." While he hastened to add that he was not advocating the play in any way, still, "We have no right to anticipate that it is going to degenerate into a burlesque." For Marshall, who had seen the Oberammergau

Passionsspiel earlier that summer, the issue finally came down to a question of "public freedom. I can see no possible objection to the play so long as it is properly and reverentially presented and does not become a mere vulgar show."

A second alderman also objected to the resolution "so far as it pretends to criticize the play." After all, he remarked, there were plenty of other shows in town that ought to be closed down. He proposed that the preamble to Morris's request, which established that *The Passion*, specifically, was "an insult to the Christian community," be stricken out. Otherwise, he was not opposed to hearing, at least, what the Corporation Counsel might have to say as to "whether this Board has power to pass an ordinance of the character proposed," and so he approved of the resolution itself.

In the end, theirs were the only two voices heard in favor of civic caution. And when the resolution was put before the Board, Alderman Marshall's was the only dissenting vote. By a margin of twenty to one (President Morris abstaining), the resolution requesting legal options was forwarded to both the Corporation Counsel and the Mayor.

The Corporation Counsel, W. C. Whitney, told a reporter that offhand he knew of no such law to stop Abbey. There wasn't even a law making blasphemy a crime anymore (a claim many other states could not have made at the time). Regardless of that pessimistic outlook, however, on Friday, November 26, the Mayor signed Morris's resolution requesting that the Corporation Counsel look into the matter.[45]

New York City, following San Francisco, moved one step closer to legalized religious censorship.

Surprisingly, the aldermen's sudden step caused several newspapers to rethink their positions on legal suppression. Whitelaw Reid, in the *Tribune*, cautiously suggested that it might be "a much more effective and useful veto upon the project . . . if the play should be presented and fail utterly because a self-respecting public refused to go see it." The *Evening Express* was far more blunt, saying that any legislation undertaken would mean

> restraining the liberty of speech — for to suppress the production of a play is to suppress free speech. No journal in this city has protested more earnestly against the production of this blasphemous play than the *Express*, but if its suppression can only be obtained by violation of the law, the performance should be allowed to go on, and the public can take the matter in its own hands by staying away.[46]

The majority of the other city papers, not surprisingly, applauded the aldermen's decisive action.

The second blow to hit *The Passion* at this time, while not as potentially devastating as the first, was perhaps the more painful to Abbey. On November 24, 1880, the day after the Board of Aldermen's meeting, the

8. The Mirror's War on Mr. Abbey

Herald published interviews with eight of Abbey's fellow theatrical managers, including Lester Wallack, A.M. Palmer, Augustin Daly and Steele MacKaye. If earlier they each may have held back from publicly criticizing a professional colleague, there was no sign of reticence now. Abbey's peers were ready to take a stand.

Wallack willingly endorsed legal censorship ("The best time to stop an evil is at the start"); Palmer once again denied that he had ever wanted to produce it himself; E.G. Gilmore, the co-manager of Niblo's Garden, claimed that "the same parties were here last year and tried to get me to take the play on," but Gilmore had sent them packing; similarly, the manager of New York's Grand Opera House on Eighth Avenue said he had turned down Abbey's more recent request to use the Grand for rehearsal space ("for $1,000 a minute he would not have his name connected with it in any shape or form").

Augustin Daly, too, said he would never have attempted such a project, but when asked if the play should be stopped by the law, Daly bristled. "The law has nothing to do with it," he said. "This is a matter for the people and only the people. It would be un-American for the law to interfere. It would be introducing a system that should never be introduced in this country and I hope never will." Of the eight men interviewed, however, only Steele MacKaye refused to condemn for publication one of his brother managers. But that didn't matter to the *Herald*, which noted: "As he [MacKaye] announced this [refusal] to the reporter his tone and manner gave a sufficient proof that he was greatly opposed to it."[47]

Capping these managers' condemnations was that of America's most famous tragedian, Edwin Booth, then appearing in London. Even though he no longer owned the theatre in which Abbey proposed to produce *The Passion*, as the actor after whom that theatre had been named Edwin Booth represented a sentimental as well as symbolic force; his pronouncement on the play, therefore, carried more weight with the public than perhaps all of the other managers combined. Consequently, his opinion was sought by the *Herald*, the *Tribune*, by Harrison Grey Fiske for the *Mirror*, even by Henry E. Abbey. Booth's answer to one and all was a forcefully declared "No." "It is not a proper subject for the play house," he cabled the *Mirror*. Privately, he expressed himself to his close friend William Winter in even stronger terms: "Abbey is mad & will regret his obstinacy in this matter. I hope you'll let the people know that though the theatre bears my name I have no connection or authority — if I had I'd put a stop to the profanation."[48]

The disavowal of these men, among the most important figures in the American theatre in 1880, was the final straw for Henry Abbey. What he had defended as a matter of legality and freedom of speech, was for them, as it was for Harrison Grey Fiske and the other editors, a matter of the greater good. This troublesome controversy was harming the theatre; never mind that any one of them might be faced with similar community outrage, for whatever reason, some day in the future. *The Passion* was here and now, and, for their own sakes, they had to dissociate themselves from it. Henry E. Abbey was on his own.

Four days later, on November 28, just eight days before the scheduled opening, the New York Sunday morning papers simultaneously published Abbey's notice to the public that he was withdrawing his production of *The Passion*.

VI

To the Public:
In all my managerial experience in the City of New York and elsewhere, I have never before found it necessary or advisable to address the public in regard to any intended production upon the stage of my theatre. So much, however, has been said and urged against the representation of this particular drama, (if, in the general acceptation of that term, it may be so called,) that it appears incumbent upon me to acquaint the public with the circumstances surrounding my intended presentation of it....

Upon the primary suggestion of its production ... at my theatre, I felt as I believe the majority of Christian people feel now, a natural repugnance to its representation on the stage. I was induced, however, to hear it read by its author.... I was so impressed with the subject and its treatment by him that I signed a contract for its production at Booth's under his personal supervision. My part of such contract was to furnish the edifice and the money needed. Strange as it may appear, the idea of making money from its representation did not influence me in the slightest degree....

It seemed, however, to be the settled determination to condemn its production in advance, and not to consider that I was as much moved by the sacredness of the subject as any one in the community, and that it was my purpose to have it treated only in the most reverential spirit.

It is my conviction that no man whose business success depends upon the approval and patronage of the public has any right to represent that which is regarded with a disapproval so positive and expressed in terms so denunciatory, as those which greet[ed] the mere announcement of an intention to produce the Passion Play.

While ... I have always entertained the belief that the representation would inevitably inspire feelings of reverence and awaken devotional emotions, ... yet I feel that I have no right to set my single opinion against that of an almost entire community, and thus to outrage any sentiment they may possess, no matter how unjust I may consider the existence of such sentiment to be.

I have therefore concluded not to produce or give any representation whatever of the Passion Play.

HENRY E. ABBEY[49]

VII

Salmi Morse complained that the first he knew of Abbey's decision was when he, like the rest of New York, read about it in the Sunday papers.[50] But the *Herald* intimated that Abbey, having already spent $15,000, had been trying for at least two weeks to negotiate with Maguire and Morse an "honourable way to be released from his engagement." It was explained that Abbey could not just abandon the project on his own because the agreement he had made with Maguire and Morse was in the form of a copartnership rather than a standard contract, and Abbey's two partners "were most anxious to go ahead." But Abbey, said the *Herald*, "pressed by his other cares and thoroughly alive to the power and influence of the press, and fully posted as to the unanimity of public disapproval, . . . brought the matter to a head yesterday afternoon [Saturday, November 26], and, having paid Mr. Maguire a satisfactory amount, announced to the *Herald* his conclusion."[51] It was reported that part of Abbey's pay-off to Maguire included bringing Sarah Bernhardt out to Baldwin's Theatre in San Francisco.[52]

The first to react to the news were the city's ministers. Abbey's eleventh-hour announcement caught most of them ready to loose a barrage of Sunday-morning pulpit rhetoric. Suddenly deprived of their target, but profoundly relieved, they quickly rewrote their sermons in an effort to show they could put the matter behind them. All, that is, except De Witt Talmage. His face reportedly "illumined with gladness," he mounted his pulpit and, saying he had not seen the papers in time, delivered his anti-*Passion* sermon anyway.[53]

The defeat of *The Passion* had proved that this is a Christian nation, Talmage exulted. "The Christian people hold the balance of power in the United States to-day. No man can be elected to a Legislature or Congress or to the Presidential chair if he be pronounced infidel." Furthermore,

> out of this great excitement grand and good results have followed. The first is that we stand to-day in the presence of an almost omnipotent power—that of the newspaper press. This is a force that has not created public sentiment, but has aroused it. . . . Let us give credit to whom it is due, to the press; the great metropolitan press of the city, which having seen proposed the shamefulness, the iniquity, the sacrilege, has not ceased seven days in the week to discourage it by powerful argument and earnest appeal. The power of the press has been acknowledged as rarely ever before. The voice of the pulpit has been esteemed the voice of God.[54]

The resounding failure of this Passion play, said Talmage, meant that no other American manager would wish to make the same mistake in the future. And to underscore that point, he flatly warned all American playwrights to "keep their hands off the Cross. There is only one stage for that—the hill back of Jerusalem."

For their own part, the city newspapers were far more gracious in their victory. They warmly congratulated Abbey on his decision, most of them pronouncing it the "manly" thing to do. Theatres, said the *Herald*, should always be in "the hands of men so happily enlightened on the subject of the relations of the stage to the current of opinion." The *World* went so far as to sympathize with Mr. Abbey that *The Passion* should be suppressed by that same public opinion "which partly tolerates Talmage."[55] And the *Evening Post* helpfully suggested a means by which the poor manager could recoup his losses and still take advantage of the heightened public interest in the subject of the Passion play: have someone dramatize George Croly's 1827 religious novel, *Salathiel, the Wandering Jew*. Abbey could use the same costumes, props, sets, etc., and all that would be missing would be "the chief figure" of *The Passion*. Thus, the new play could not offend anyone. (Except, perhaps, the Jews.)[56] At any rate, the editors were, on the whole, magnanimous. Victorian propriety had been satisfied and excessive jubilation was unseemly.

One exception to this gentlemanly rule was the editor of the *New York Mirror*. Fiske fairly crowed. "This is a great victory for *The Mirror*," he gloated,

> because it vindicates the stand we have taken in regard to Church and Stage. But we hasten to divide the honors of the victory among those who rallied to our support, in the pulpit and the press, and especially among those professional allies—from Edwin Booth in London to the leading managers of this city—who gave us their hearty endorsement and indispensable cooperation.
>
> Without the interference of *The Mirror* the Passion Play would not have been withdrawn, or else its withdrawal would have been claimed as a triumph of religious bigotry. We were determined to prevent its production, but we were also determined that the profession should have the credit of withdrawing it.... [W]hen Manager Abbey awakes from his long dream and reflects upon what we have done for the profession, he will be one of the first to tender *The Mirror* his hearty congratulations.[57]

Fiske was wrong, however. One year later, he would complain that the grudging Abbey was still boycotting the *Mirror*, refusing to advertise in the pages of the accredited organ of the American stage.[58]

Fiske's rival at the *Dramatic News* was, in an opposite way, equally ungracious in his acceptance of the news. Charles Byrne felt utterly betrayed by Abbey's withdrawal of *The Passion*. "We should never have cared to defend him and his production of the Passion Play unless we had felt that we had a man to deal with who meant precisely what he said," Byrne griped bitterly. Abbey, charged Byrne, had been unfaithful to his oft-made pledge to fight for his constitutional rights, even so far as the higher courts. In another editorial gesture worthy of Pontius Pilate,

Charles A. Byrne now angrily washed his hands of Henry Abbey: "It is a great thing to have a strong man to fight with—one who never quails. But to be allied to a poltroon is humiliating.... Now let them fall on him and devour him. We have nothing to say."[59]

In his own defense, when challenged directly by one of Byrne's reporters, Abbey tried to bluff it through. Rather awkwardly, he explained his move by saying that he was not so much backing out of *The Passion* because of public pressure but because of the unexpected demands placed upon his time by Sarah Bernhardt's upcoming tour. "I did not dare let others handle the Passion Play," he told the *News* reporter. "Had I been able to remain in New York, I should have done it spite of all the clamor of Press and Pulpit. But my reputation was at stake. One mistake on the part of subordinates and a torrent of vituperation would have opened on me."[60] In short, as the old saying goes, he had suddenly found that his presence was required elsewhere.

Both Tom Maguire and James O'Neill felt similarly betrayed. Maguire told the *Herald* that, had he "control of a theatre here, nothing would please him better than to try the experiment." O'Neill criticized the managers who had come out against the play, saying that by their opposition to a sacred pageant like *The Passion* they were no better than the moralists; they had, in effect, declared the stage fit only for "adulterous and licentious" melodramas. Furthermore, O'Neill hinted at "a concealed power," more potent than either the press or the pulpit, that had worked behind the scenes to bring about Abbey's decision. "I saw work being done which astonished me," he said darkly; "silent, inside work, which was not noised abroad, but which was none the less effective." He was convinced that Abbey's rival, the powerful producer J. H. Haverly, for one, was "at the bottom of it."[61]

Abbey had done what he could to appease both of these men. Maguire had evidently received a large cash payment; O'Neill, along with Lewis Morrison and Forrest Robinson, was immediately cast in Abbey's next production at the Park Theatre, *A Celebrated Case*. Henry Widmer was awarded the post of musical director for the Park. And even J.H. Vincent, the stage manager brought from San Francisco for *The Passion*, had been made permanent stage manager of the Park.[62] Only Salmi Morse, as Charles Byrne noted, seemed to be "left out in the cold."

"I suffer a greater loss than any monetary deprivation," a bereft Morse said. "The work upon which I have spent the better part of my life, upon whose perfection I have exerted my every energy, in which I have become utterly wrapped up, is stamped as some villainous thing too morally hideous for a Christian public to look upon. They have cried it down as rankest blasphemy, and I am looked upon as a blackguard, an enemy to society, condemned before allowed the semblance of a trial. It is no enviable position to occupy, I assure you."[63] At first, he claimed that he had another backer—"a gentleman, a man of wealth ... I am not at liberty to give his name"—who would bring out the play "in the face of all opposition," but that seems to have been mere bravado. Such desperation drove him to make other surprising claims as well. To another reporter, after describing in more detail his supposed sojourn in Palestine—where, he said, for five and a half years he had stayed in a monastery, "in filth and vermin, living on bread and water half the time"—he implied for the first time that he had actually been converted to Christianity:

> "When I travelled over the same hills that He travelled over," Mr. Morse continued; "when I visited the same spots that He visited, and when my shadow fell in the same places in the holy land that His fell in, I was struck with awe, and I determined to learn the whole of the life of the Saviour...."[64]

He could not understand, he said, the churches' opposition to his *Passion*. "They don't know anything about it; they haven't seen it." And would they only give it a chance, "they dare not say one word against it."

He determined to give them the chance to at least hear what they would not see. He announced that he would read *The Passion* to the public, as he had done in San Francisco when the work was newly finished, and to that end he began to negotiate for the large basement lecture hall at Cooper Institute on 7th Street and the Bowery. Free lectures were regularly scheduled in the hall during the winter months, and such notorious speakers as Bob Ingersoll and Denis Kearny had recently lectured there. Because of the kind of controversy surrounding *The Passion*, however, Morse had some trouble securing the site for his reading. "I actually had to get the [endorsement] of a Christian minister before they would rent me the hall," he complained.[65]

Confident as always that *The Passion* would redeem itself to even its worst opponent, Salmi sent out personal invitations to all of the city newspaper editors, as well as the major critics, such as William Winter. In return, he asked that each "do me the courtesy to properly notice it in your columns."[66]

On a cold Friday evening, December 3, at precisely 8 p.m., Salmi stepped onto the Cooper Union's lecture-hall platform, enlarged to accommodate Henry Widmer's orchestra and chorus, to offer his masterwork to the city of New York. The city of New York, in turn, was represented by approximately one hundred persons—only a handful in the large auditorium—who had paid one dollar apiece for the privilege, and among whom, sniffed the *Times*, "there was not a person of prominence." But as that journal described the reading, there was obviously nothing really offensive about the work—except for the very *idea* of it:

> Mr. Morse is a tall, finely built man, with gray hair, and a face which gives him the appearance of a High Priest of the Temple. He is a fine elocutionist and, despite a severe cold, which frequently interrupted his reading, he gave a fine rendition of the lines of his "Passion." In justice to him, it should be said that he treats his theme in a perfectly reverential spirit. The objection to the Passion Play is not to the sentiments, but to the outrage to Christianity which any stage treatment of the agony of Christ is calculated to produce.[67]

The *Times* reporter found the musical portions of the presentation to be "really impressive," and noted further that "during the reading, which occupied two hours and three quarters, the audience was very attentive, and at times rewarded Mr. Morse with applause." The *Sun*, too, found nothing objectionable in Morse's play and reported that "the small audience applauded him frequently, and remained interested throughout the recitation."

Other papers, however, were not so kind. The major portion of the *Tribune*'s report maliciously described every *dis*interested member of the audience, while the *World* found the work itself laughable, especially Morse's grasp of history: "The man who in his attempts to be realistic copies Leonardo da Vinci for his conception of the Lord's supper had better study a few years until he learns that Judea was completely Hellenized, and that the disciples ate that supper on triclinia." But the *World* did agree with Salmi that *The Passion* should be published, and should grace library shelves for future generations: "It would be," said the paper, "a joy and a source of laughter forever."[68]

As might have been expected, the greatest horselaughs came from Harrison Grey Fiske, who contemptuously labeled the work "the most revolting, sacrilegious, ridiculous composition ever designed for the stage." Pointing to the opening scene, the one involving one hundred mothers and their babies, Fiske scoffed, "Imagine the row these youngsters would probably have created at their first appearance behind the glare of the footlights before a crowded auditorium." And, showing his own bigoted view of Christian history, Fiske berated Morse for depicting a Jesus who "shows a knowledge of the Hebrew tongue." In short, Fiske wrote, Morse's reading was a gross error in judgment. Even the fact that no one had showed up, he said, proved that no one was really very interested (which made his own campaign against its production, at the least, a fantastic waste of energy). Finally, the "pure, unadulterated inanity" of the writing made it highly doubtful that any manager would ever be so foolish as to try to revive it in the future. In a single stroke, the question of any such sacrilegious biblical Passion drama in New York had been summarily settled.[69] It would simply not be worth it.

VIII

One week after Salmi Morse read his play at the Cooper Institute, John L. Stoddard appeared at Chickering Hall with a stereopticon presentation of the 1880 Oberammergau *Passionsspiel.* "As it is pictorial and not dramatic," William Winter advised, "it escapes the reproach of being a mummery."

Two weeks after that, the Oratorio Society offered its annual staging of *The Messiah* at Steinway Hall.

Both played to crowded houses.

Life returned to normal in New York City.[70]

IX

Henry Abbey's sudden and ignominious withdrawal of his planned production of *The Passion* in late November 1880 effectively ended his association with Salmi Morse and his problematical pageant. But the aftermath of Abbey's aborted presentation would be felt — by Abbey personally, and, indirectly, by the American theatre — for many years thereafter.

Arguably, the most profound ramification of the *Passion* fiasco was its possible effect on Henry Abbey and his subsequent contribution to the American stage. He continued his boycott of Harrison Fiske and the *Mirror* for at least a year, perhaps longer, which would indicate that his anger and sense of betrayal were deep and not easily forgotten. Fiske, in turn, repaid Abbey with continued sniping. He lectured him in December for allowing both the Park and Booth's to fall into artistic disarray. The *Mirror,* Fiske chided, had warned him to be ready with another production when *The Passion* failed, but Abbey had not heeded the advice, and now he himself was failing. At year's end, the *Mirror* ran a large cover lithograph depicting the most successful theatrical events of 1880. In one lowly corner stood a monk-robed Henry Abbey, clutching the manuscript of *The Passion* to his breast and skulking away by himself, miserably alone and completely outside the circle of the year's financial successes.[71] This one-sided depiction completely ignored Abbey's tremendous artistic (and financial) triumph as manager of Sarah Bernhardt. But what Fiske had intended as a satirical jibe — Abbey's supposed separation from the theatrical mainstream because of *The Passion* — would soon become more than symbolic, for, where once he had demonstrated "an intense desire to become the manager of a theatre," Abbey after *The Passion* began to turn away from producing new plays, leaving that task more and more in the hands of those same "subordinates" with whom he would not trust *The Passion.* Instead, Abbey began to spend his creative energies on managing well-known European celebrities

8. The Mirror's *War on Mr. Abbey*

Cover of the "New York Mirror," December 25, 1880 (detail). In an illustration celebrating the theatrical successes of the 1880 season, Fiske had producer Henry E. Abbey depicted in the lower-right corner as a monk, skulking away in disgrace while clutching a copy of "The Passion" to his breast. Such editorial attacks prompted Abbey to refuse to advertise further any of his productions in Fiske's paper. (Courtesy Billy Rose Theatre Collection, The New York Public Library)

and already established acting companies. A biographical portrait written in 1884 illustrates this change of direction: "The burning of the Park Theatre [in 1883], on the very night that Mrs. [Lillie] Langtry was to make her New York debut there . . . was at once a misfortune and a benefit to Manager Abbey. . . . It was a benefit, because it left him free to devote himself to his real vocation, which is *not theatrical management, but speculation in stars*"[72] [emphasis added]. By 1884, he would move even further from the legitimate theatre by accepting the directorship of the new Metropolitan Opera House.

Ever the alert businessman, Abbey would never completely dissociate himself from the commercial stage; in 1893 he would even build his own theatre on Broadway. But his personal commitment seems never again to have been as great, and, as Gerald Bordman remarks in noting Abbey's untimely death in 1896: "his growing interest in musical affairs makes moot just what his future importance to the American theatre might have been."[73] Of course, it is equally debatable to speculate on how much his later career was motivated by his thwarted attempt to stage *The Passion*; it will probably not be answered until a major biography on Abbey has been written. But the question nonetheless remains.

For Tom Maguire, too, the withdrawal of *The Passion* in New York meant another dramatic change in personal fortune. While he continued to act as de facto manager of Baldwin's Theatre in San Francisco, the times he actually spent in the city would become less and less lengthy, and his contributions to the theatre less and less successful. Finally, in 1882, "Lucky" Baldwin would dissolve the partnership completely and close down his theatre for good. Returning permanently to New York in 1884, Tom Maguire would try unsuccessfully to find his niche in the professional theatre there, ending his days in poverty, supported by the Actor's Fund — which, ironically, owed its existence to Harrison Grey Fiske and the *New York Mirror*. Tom Maguire, once the mighty Napoleon of the California Stage, would die penniless in New York in 1896, the same year as Henry Abbey.[74]

The Passion would mean better fortunes for several of the other California participants. Lewis Morrison and his wife Rose Wood, as noted, were cast in *A Celebrated Case*, along with James O'Neill, and both would remain in Abbey's employ for a time. Their successes at the Park and at Booth's would enable them later to organize their own touring companies. And Henry Widmer, the composer for *The Passion*, would also relocate permanently to New York, serving as musical director at the Park Theatre for the next several years and quickly becoming one of the most respected theatre conductors in New York.[75]

Of them all, though, James O'Neill perhaps benefited most from *The Passion*'s attempted production in New York. For, in the very broadest sense, it was *The Passion* that had brought him east again; and, just as George Barnes had predicted, it was in the east that he would finally become a star—but not in the role of Jesus Christ. As he would later recall, after *The Passion* "I was facing the beginning of the most progressive experience of my whole professional life."[76] This is not to say that it would be easy. The *Dramatic News*, noting O'Neill's "run of ill fortune" in his choice of plays immediately after *The Passion*, urged him not to lose heart, and, "above all, let him not go away again. In New York lies his chance to make fame and fortune, and both are bound to come sooner or later—with his ability."[77] This prediction was prescient, if premature. It would take two more years of struggling before the actor would finally stumble upon the role for which he had been searching.

X

With Abbey, Maguire and O'Neill now out of the picture, it fell upon Salmi Morse to keep the dream alive on his own. But his entire life's saga had been one of bouncing back from adversity, and this minor setback would be no different. As long as he had his wits and his tongue, he could convince men of vision to believe in him. He would find such men now to help him produce his *Passion*.

"Yes sir," he had promised the *Dramatic News* right after Abbey had left him stranded. "Yes sir; the Passion Play will be produced, and right here in New York."

It would be another three years before he would accomplish it, but Salmi Morse would prove to be a man of his word.

9
The Shrine of the Holy Passion

I

For the next year and a half, Salmi searched in vain for a manager who would accomplish what Abbey had not. It was a quest that would lead him into several minor skirmishes with the courts, and finally a full-blown trial, with an intermediate stop at the city jail. It was also a search that would turn the spotlight onto Salmi Morse himself. This time there would be no James O'Neill, no Henry E. Abbey to bear the brunt of public censure. This time the object of scorn would be the playwright alone. But he had vowed that he would see *The Passion* produced in New York City "if it takes twenty years," and so he diligently approached every manager in town.[1]

For a while, he still had the willing support of O'Neill, whose own career was floundering. In January 1881 the *Dramatic News* reported that O'Neill "is still anxious as ever to find some manager who will do the Passion Play. He wants to prove that popular opinion was wrong on the subject. There is a fortune in the piece."[2] A month later, there was a brief flurry of alarm over a report that the New York manager Frank Gardner had agreed to produce it. "Those petitions," Harrison Fiske warned in the *Mirror*, "are all ready, with the signatures of a thousand prominent citizens, and I advise Gardner, who is a personal friend and a good fellow, to let the thing drop before he experiences disastrous loss, as was Abbey's case."[3]

Gardner bowed out, and Salmi resumed his search.

He managed to eke out an existence by giving elocution lessons and by selling articles to city journals and newspapers.[4] Surprisingly, he also sold the rights to some of his other dramatic works. The first of these was his "sensational play," *The Doctor of Lima*, a dramatized version of the story he had once told at the old San Francisco "Round Table," the one he claimed to have written for Charles Dickens. A variation on the Frankenstein tale, Salmi's play involved a dead woman restored to life. It was reportedly because of the "unsurpassed opportunities for a versatile emotional depictment" offered by the role of the revitalized woman that the famous Czech actress Fanny Janauschek decided to produce the play in late 1881.[5]

9. The Shrine of the Holy Passion

Madame Janauschek (1830–1904) was in her early fifties at this time, a tempestuous European star of formidable mien who had learned English only eight years before (in her earliest American appearances, she had performed her roles in German while her American costars declaimed in English). Years later John Ranken Towse would remember her as "an artistic jewel of great brilliancy and worth":

> It was in great dramas that she shone, and when they disappeared from the stage her occupation, like Othello's, was gone. After holding a high seat among the queens of tragedy, she was, in her declining years, reduced to the necessity — as a mere means of livelihood — of appearing in the cheaper kinds of melodrama, which she often made extraordinarily effective by her still undimmed dramatic genius. No matter what the nature of her surroundings, she was a grand artist to the last, but the spectacle of her great abilities [wasted] on unworthy purpose was a melancholy one.[6]

Unfortunately, *The Doctor of Lima* was, in Towse's opinion, just such an "unworthy purpose."

The plot of the play concerns "The Subject" (Madame Janauschek), a corpse revitalized "by galvanic shock" by James Austin, the Doctor of Lima (Alexander H. Stuart), who has discovered the body on the dissecting table of a medical student. Austin falls in love with her and they marry, "only to find her bad former husband (James H. Taylor) returning to make trouble," as George Odell dryly summarized it. "Of course," said Odell, "some god from the machine brings a suitable solution to the difficulty."[7]

The critics were unanimous in panning the play. Said the *Times*, "Mr. Morse's English, like his dramatic instinct, is pretentious tom-foolery.... As a physiological study, 'The Doctor of Lima' aims very deep indeed — but it can hardly be viewed with sustained solemnity. If Mr. Morse will bury his corpse again and then bury his play he will certainly win the applause of an astonished community." Towse, the *Evening Post* critic, would remember the play as "a perfect miracle of ineptitude, but the pathos with which [Janauschek] filled her own part was supreme. While she was on the stage the audience was sympathetic and tearful; when she was 'off' it was shaken with irreverent laughter." Harrison Grey Fiske had already announced two months before, "The subject could not be better — for a failure — and I look forward to the Doctor and his anatomical demonstrations with the liveliest anticipations of rare fun." He was not disappointed. It was "torture," Fiske finally wrote in his review, and he helpfully offered the playwright Morse ("the Passion Play fiend") some advice: "until Mr. Morse ... thoroughly familiarizes himself with stage business, and can understand that scientific disquisitions and large words are not the condiments with which to season plays, he need never expect to reach fame through this channel."[8]

However, in spite of the failure of *The Doctor of Lima*, six months later Salmi announced the sale of yet another of his plays, *King Rene's Daughter*, this one to the prominent manager J. M. Hill.[9]

It was primarily through the graces of his mysterious backers, though, that Salmi Morse managed to survive in New York City during this bleak period. Chief among these capitalists, it would later be revealed, was the well-known costumer Albert J. (some reports say Henry J.) Eaves. Eaves Costumes, located at 63 East 12th Street, had been founded by Charles Eaves in 1864, and had grown into one of the most important costume houses in the city; it was Eaves Costumes that had built the wardrobe for Henry Abbey's production of *The Passion* in 1880. Both Albert and his wife had become ardent converts to Salmi's cause, generously encouraging his efforts to find another manager to mount the play.[10] When virtually every avenue that Salmi tried proved hopeless, Eaves finally stepped forward with a daring plan of his own.

Since two of the church's primary objections to *The Passion*, he pointed out, were that it would be housed in a theatre and staged by professional actors, why not secure a nontheatrical site, the sole purpose of which would be to showcase *The Passion*, and have the work performed by amateurs who would not then go on to play *Camille* immediately thereafter? The new site would be consecrated as a place of worship, not as a theatre, thus eliminating all possible objections to the play.

The audacious idea must have seemed as brilliant as it was obvious. In a way, both Maguire and Abbey had attempted the same ploy on a smaller scale, disclaiming their theatres as theatres. Salmi immediately agreed. If they could not find anyone else to produce *The Passion*, he and his backers would produce it themselves. Eaves reportedly "purchased part of Morse's copyright for $5,000, and put up a good deal more." Salmi later told George Barnes that he had been down to his last fifty cents on the day that the new agreement was made. "In the evening of the same day," Barnes wrote, "he drew his check against $12,000 advanced on account for 'current expenses.' He was justified in saying to a friend, 'God is good to the Jews. He never forsakes His chosen people.'"[11] (From a self-proclaimed Christian convert, this was a rather curious remark to make.)

Salmi was flush again. Immediately, he reassumed his old public persona of a wealthy capitalist expansively putting his own money into *The Passion*. Perhaps Eaves, and the others whom he would soon find to join him in the new venture, preferred to remain anonymous. But whether they wanted it that way or not, it was Salmi Morse alone who claimed center stage.

II

By the latter part of October 1882, Morse and Eaves had located an old building on 23rd Street between Fifth and Sixth avenues that seemed to suit their purposes. Situated next to the boisterous Koster and Bial's Music Hall and, ironically, down the street from Booth's, the building they now leased for a ten thousand-dollar down payment had originally been used as a church, then an armory, and most recently a livery stable. It was a large building, taking up three city lots—its official address was listed as 139, 141 and 143 West 23rd—and sported an impressive Moresque façade "rendered ancient-looking by the action of the weather." While the necessary remodeling work began on the main floor interior, Salmi converted several rooms at the rear and on the second story into offices and his own private living quarters, and immediately moved in.[12]

Morse could not restrain himself from announcing his plans to the press, proudly pointing out that the building's former life as a Protestant church made it especially suited to become what he now called "The Shrine of the Holy Passion." He intended to erect a large stage, 130 feet deep; to dig an orchestra pit ("which will be covered by a hood like that of Wagner's Theatre in Bayreuth"); and to install theatre seats on both the main floor and in the balcony, with seating for approximately fifteen hundred people. The Shrine was to be completed in time for a Christmas dedication, to which the clergy, newspaper editors and legal representatives would be invited; following the dedicatory rites, these guests would be treated to a tour of the facilities and a performance of *The Passion*. Then the Shrine would be opened to the general public. Morse planned to present daily performances of his epic work, he said, and no other play would ever be staged in the Shrine. Preparations were already under way: he had hired an experienced business manager/press agent, Everard Stuart; he had sent to San Francisco for a new composer and conductor—respectively, Oscar Weil and Fred Lyster (once a member of the "Round Table" and former musical director at Baldwin's Theatre); and, of course, he already had a costumer in Albert J. Eaves.[13]

Finally, it was also reported that Salmi was trying to coax James O'Neill, then on tour with his own company, to return to New York and resume his prized role as Jesus Christ. While a key part of the new plan was to employ only amateurs instead of professional actors, presumably Salmi believed that O'Neill was still willing to make good his previous claim that he would devote the rest of his life to playing *The Passion* and nothing else. Thus his status as a "professional" actor could thereafter be technically denied. But after two years of decidedly modest success, O'Neill's career finally seemed to be on the rise. He was currently finding some favor in Charles T. Dazey's *An American King*, and was finally beginning to win praise from both the public and the profession alike. Not wishing to jeopardize his newly budding career — or, not ready to face another fight, which he felt was inevitable — O'Neill declined Salmi's offer and judiciously stayed on tour, and away from New York, for as long as he could.[14] Salmi was forced to look elsewhere for his Christ.

On another front, however, things were looking up. Following an unsuccessful attempt to entice the Methodist Book Concern into the project,[15] Eaves and Morse managed to enlist the financial support of John Ferris and M. Severance, both former San Francisco businessmen; Ferris, in fact, had reportedly known Morse in California.[16] A third new investor was another former San Francisco speculator and current Wall Street broker named George D. Roberts, who had made his money in California mining stock and now had his offices at 155 Broadway in New York. If Morse had not known Roberts in California, it is almost certain that Roberts had heard of Morse. At any rate, Roberts alone reportedly advanced as much as $30,000 for the venture; according to George Barnes, Roberts was also paying Salmi's personal expenses, to the tune of $100 per week.[17] All told, the entire production would finally be reported to have cost from $60,000 to $100,000 for both the renovation of the stable and the mounting of the play.[18]

Typically for Morse, all of this was begun before he had ever approached the city authorities for permission to do any of it. He was firmly convinced that he had found a way around every religious objection, so why should the city oppose him now? True, the newspapers and the clergy had begun to make noises, but not nearly to the extent that they had two years before. Even Harrison Fiske had only half-heartedly protested, taking the position that since, this time around, Morse proposed "to desecrate the church — not the stage," therefore, this time it was up to the clergy "to repeat the job that the *Mirror* did effectually two years ago."[19] But Fiske had no time to worry about Morse; his newest crusade was to lobby for the passage of a bill that would amend the 1872 Licensing Act to channel all monies away from the Society for the Reformation of Juvenile Delinquents and into the coffers of the Actor's Fund, which had been organized in 1881. It was Fiske's goal to remove the meddling S.R.J.D. from any role in the licensing or policing of New York theatres.

By early November, with the Shrine still not finished, *The Passion* had been cast and Fred Lyster had begun to rehearse the large chorus. As planned, Salmi's players comprised unknown amateurs. The role of Christ had gone to a young man named Wannemaker (or Wannamaker), "a Baptist minister — an American of German descent," while another of Salmi's protégées, a "comely young Jewess, a very excellent young lady," would enact the Virgin Mary. It is also known that a man named A.H. Warren ultimately assayed two roles: that of Pontius Pilate and of the tongue-twisting King Herod.[20]

As opposition began to increase, Morse took a defiant stance. Abbey may have failed in his resolve, but this time, Salmi promised ("threatened" was the word the *Mirror* used), if the authorities interfered he himself would pursue his cause all the way "to the Supreme Court of the United States, claiming a Constitutional right." This got a slight rise out of Harrison Fiske, who made a rather veiled "promise" of his own. "There is a class of men," Fiske warned, "who will be apt, by force if necessary, to compel the doors of the 'Sanctuary' to remain closed."[21]

For a while, it looked as if the City Building Department and its strict theatre-safety codes would save Fiske's men the trouble. "If Morse wants to use the building as a theatre," an inspector told a reporter after touring the Shrine in mid-December, "he must build a wall between the stage and the auditorium, extending four feet above the roof, and the roof must have four skylights. There are other changes which will have to be made." All of this was going to be very expensive, but, the inspector shrugged, "that is not my fault."[22] Salmi's reply was just as Eaves had planned: he was not building a theatre, but a holy shrine, a place of worship — in time, he would even claim that it was his place of residence and that *The Passion* was nothing more than a home entertainment. In short, it was anything but a theatre.

Fiske saw through this, of course, calling it a patent "religious dodge," totally indefensible "in the face of the negotiations for a star actor, the press agent, the musical conductor and the costume-maker."[23]

He certainly had a point. But Morse seemed convinced that "The Shrine of the Holy Passion" would prove the acceptable venue in which his sacred lifework would find a home.

III

In late December, mere days before the date of his promised consecration ceremony, Salmi finally applied to Mayor Grace for a permit to open his Shrine. The meeting was held at 10:30 on Saturday morning, December 23.

When Salmi entered the Mayor's office, he was dismayed to find the ubiquitous large reception committee awaiting him, including the Reverend Drs. Howard Crosby, Henry E. Bellew, Howard Potter and Stephen P. Nash, plus Elbridge T. Gerry and Lewis L. Delafield (counsel since 1876 to Gerry's Society for the Prevention of Cruelty to Children), and the lawyer E. R. Robinson, representing the Society for the Reformation of Juvenile Delinquents. Poor Salmi "seemed to be disconcerted at the large gathering," remarked the *Evening Post* (whose reporter was also there), but [he] took a chair in the circle surrounding the Mayor's desk, and in a somewhat apologetic tone opened the proceedings by saying that he was there to ask and pay for a license to open a new house in 23rd Street. He had supposed, he said, that his application would be received by the Mayor, in private, and hoped that the large gathering of citizens was not an indication of a determination to prejudge his case.[24]

The lawyer for the S.R.J.D., Mr. Robinson, ignored that remark and sternly asked Salmi to tell them all "as clearly as possible" exactly what it was he proposed to do.

Obviously, it was going to be another one of those meetings. Salmi rose from his chair and, looking around the room, replied: "I propose to do a good work." He carefully set forth his new line of argument: this establishment was not a theatre, "but a hall, to be devoted solely to this performance." He assured them that the hall "could not be used as an ordinary theatre; there is no stage entrance in the rear, and no proscenium boxes. It is not a theatre," he repeated, "but a shrine, dedicated to the work of instructing the people as to the scenes and incidents of Christ's life." In a blatant appeal to Grace's Catholicism, Salmi slyly described Archbishop Alemany's endorsement of the play in San Francisco. Then he attempted to explain, as eloquently as he could, the finer points of his production.

All of the fabrics, the costumes and all of the properties, he told them, were modeled after artifacts he himself had seen. The Crown of Herod, for example, was copied from "a stone found in the ruins of Samara [sic], and also the sceptre of Herod, which was over seven feet long." The costumes of the Medes, Persians, Babylonians and other nationalities would be "just such as were worn in Christ's time." Even many of the colors were tints "then in use, but not now known." As for the dialogue, he continued, it was taken "mostly from a book written by myself" about the life and death of Christ. However, he assured them, the actual sufferings and Crucifixion would be omitted from his presentation.

Morse's application was based on the slimmest of legal technicalities. He requested a theatre license only for his "house," which was not a theatre, and it should make no difference to the law, in advance, what he might produce there; and yet, at the same time, he was compelled to defend the play that everyone knew was going to be produced there anyway. (His lawyer would also try later to keep *The Passion* out of the argument, putting his case in the twisted logic of legalese: "All the talk about producing the Passion Play was mere conjecture, and no person in the room could say what play Mr. Morse intended to produce.") Obviously, Salmi was trying to protect himself by applying for a license, even though he was arguing at the same time that he didn't need one. Unfortunately, his requesting a theatre license for what he claimed was not a theatre would later be

9. The Shrine of the Holy Passion

used against him as proof that even *he* considered the Shrine to be a playhouse.

Even in this first meeting that issue was tentatively being raised. Didn't his so-called "Shrine," someone wanted to know, have scenery, a curtain, footlights and a box office for taking in money? Yes, replied Morse, "but it is not a theatre."

Wasn't it true that there would be dancing on stage? Yes, "there will be dancing before Herod, but it will be done in precisely the same way that the nuns dance in Eastern convents on St. John's Day."

So it went through the rest of the meeting. The Reverend Dr. Crosby resurrected the charge that the results of Morse's Passion play, performed in an "unconsecrated hall" before "a promiscuous audience," could not help but be "horrible." Crosby reminded the Mayor that the press, which represented "the public sentiment," without exception agreed with him. Stephen Nash added that even the Jews of the city were opposed to *The Passion*'s receiving a license.

Morse, who for the first time was coming face to face with some of his harshest critics, tried to deflect such moral criticisms by reiterating that he was not here to request a license for a theatre, nor even a license for *The Passion*. The Mayor did not license particular plays anyway, he pointed out, only buildings, and he had come to obtain a permit merely for "a certain house" on 23rd Street which he wished to open. If any play which he might bring out there was "injurious in character," *then* the Mayor could stop it. But he had no legal right to censor it before the fact.

Mr. Robinson answered that of course the Mayor—and Robinson's Society—had every right to consider how the hall in question would be used. "The law [has] established over and over again that the Christian religion [is] to be protected from ridicule and injury," he said.

Elbridge T. Gerry threatened to bring the law down on Morse if he used small children, as Gerry had heard he would, in the opening scenes. Salmi "quietly replied" that any infants in the play were to be made out of *papier-mâché*. In that case, said Gerry, his Society would still be opposed "because the children who would be taken to see it would suffer moral injury in consequence." *Anything* tending to bring the Christian religion "into disrepute" was against the law, Gerry declared, "and hence the Passion Play should not be produced."

Clearly, religious opposition to the play was not being satisfied by the ruse of the Shrine. Growing increasingly frustrated, Salmi finally turned again to Mayor Grace. He had not anticipated this sort of meeting, he said, and these gentlemen insisted upon prejudging his work. Therefore, he asked for a postponement until he could consult with his own counsel. Grace adjourned the hearing until the following Thursday.

IV

Christmas Day came and passed with no dedication ceremonies at the still-unfinished Shrine of the Holy Passion. There were, however, the expected sermons, newspaper editorials and angry letters-to-the-editor protesting the resurgent sacrilege. The *Times* was in an especially anti–Semitic mood on Christmas Day, comparing Morse and his claims of "doing good" to the phony obsequiousness of the hard-selling "Hebraic clothes dealers" on Chatham Street:

> In the earnest effort to sell a second-hand coat the enthusiastic dealer will sacrifice his own feelings and interests to an almost unlimited extent.... [The] typical Chatham-street Hebrew ... [claims he] sells secondhand coats solely to do good and without a thought of profit.[25]

Salmi's "extraordinary pretensions as a Christian evangelist," the editor implied, were, at heart, no different. Morse ought to be "sent back to his legitimate business in Chatham-street" where all good Jews belonged.

On Thursday morning, December 28, the hearing in the Mayor's office resumed. Morse entered the room precisely at half past ten and, without preamble, laid out five hundred dollars on the Mayor's desk. "Mr. Mayor," Salmi brusquely began, "I am not here to argue as to the merits of my representation or as to its effect upon the public, but to demand a license for my house, in accordance with my rights as a man, my privileges as a citizen of the United States, my liberty, and my freedom of conscience. I am told that in order to protect myself I must come forward and pay the license fee; so here it is." Again, he reiterated his belief that the Mayor could not reject a legitimate request for a theatre license; if his play was improper, then it could be stopped, but not before. "I shall spend $150,000 in this enterprise," he said grandly, "and have risked all that I am worth. I owe no man a dollar, and shall open my house free of debt." (Not one word was mentioned about Eaves, Roberts, Severance or Ferris.) However, he continued, "as you will see by these letters, which are taken at random from my daily mail, there are many persons in all parts of the country who encourage me to go on."[26]

Lewis L. Delafield was again in attendance, and he quickly called attention to a letter published that morning in the *Herald*, from the actress Rose Eytinge, "who was in San Francisco," Delafield noted, "at the time the Passion Play was produced there, and who says that the play was injurious in its effect and was looked upon with abhorrence by the best people of the community." Miss Eytinge in her letter further reported that the city authorities there had had to step in and put a stop to it.[27]

The lawyer Delafield now turned to the Mayor. "You sit here," he said,

9. The Shrine of the Holy Passion

with power as a magistrate; you are to decide whether or not an act which annoys, injures, and insults the Christian people of this city—a majority of the population—is to be allowed. It has been decided over and over again, notably for this State by Chief Justice Kent, that the Christian religion is part of our law, and is to be respected and protected from injury or contempt.... [And] as this Passion Play certainly comes under the head of a public nuisance, no license can be granted for its performance.

Salmi, who, according to the *Evening Post*, had been "impatiently listening" to Delafield's oration, "jumped up, and, flourishing a copy of the *Herald* at the Mayor, said: 'Here is the letter from this woman, and I will explain how it came to be written.'" He then proceeded to provide a rather slanted version of the events in San Francisco in 1879. In Salmi's recounting, Miss Eytinge had been playing at the California Theatre in direct competition with *The Passion* and because of its success she had been unable to draw enough people "to pay for the gas consumed." As a result her contract was canceled by the manager. "Miss Eytinge," Morse explained, then "went to Mr. Maguire and induced him to withdraw Mr. O'Neill from ... the Passion Play, and to form a combination with her to open his [Maguire's] theatre. When I came to the opera house one night I found a young man named Long dressed for the part that Mr. O'Neill had assumed.... I refused to accept the exchange. Mr. Maguire refused to send Mr. O'Neill back to me," said Morse; and so he himself had nobly closed his own play. "The receipts [of *The Passion*] used to be from $1,800 to $1,900 a night," he claimed. As for Miss Eytinge: "This woman then made as much of a wreck of the theatre she went to as the one she had been turned away from."

Grace listened patiently to more such arguments and then, rather than accept Morse's license fee before he had made his ruling, he returned it and called the hearing to a close. He would announce his decision, Grace said, by the end of the week. That was cutting it close for Grace, as his two-year term as Mayor was coming to an end. The 1882 mayoral election had been won the previous November by Franklin Edson, and Edson was to assume the office the first week in January 1883, less than a week away.

The very next day, December 29, Grace carried out one of the last official acts of his term as Mayor. He denied Salmi Morse's application for a theatre license.[28]

Morse was outraged and all but undone by the decision. Now he had no choice, he told the *Times*, in a rambling, almost incoherent interview, but to do what he swore he never wanted to do: take his case to the courts. His enemies had compelled him "to go to [the] law to prove the justice of my exalted cause. I will have spent $150,000 in producing the play," he said again, "and [I] will sacrifice that sum or even my life to its subject."[29]

V

Cooler heads evidently convinced Salmi not to turn to the courts immediately. First, he resubmitted his request for a license to the city's new mayor, Franklin Edson, just three days after Edson had been sworn in, and five days after Grace had turned down the same. This time he was accompanied by a lawyer of his own, William F. Howe, of Howe and Hummel. Together they appeared in the mayor's office on Wednesday, January 3, with Salmi's application in hand.

Was this license for *The Passion*?, the new mayor asked. Salmi's lawyer carefully replied, "We don't say that." According to Edson's official report of the meeting (which makes it clear that the new mayor also considered *The Passion* a play and the Shrine a theatre),

> Howe continued then to state the general nature of the plays to be produced in this theatre, having the Passion Play in mind without doubt; the plays were to inculcate "sublime moral lessons" . . . &c &c. Howe added that Morse courts the fullest investigation as to the nature of the play. . . .
> Mr. Morse then said that his intention was to start a "New Era in Drama"; if his plays [should] not be permitted while low dives are, all he [could] say was that he lived before his time.[30]

Edson set aside the following Friday for his decision.

On Friday, Franklin Edson initiated one of the first official acts of *his* term as mayor. He refused to grant a theatre license to Salmi Morse.

Salmi—by now it almost seemed as if he were reading his lines by rote—swore that he would now seek redress from the courts. Editors threw their hands in the air and asked "Why?" Why wouldn't the man just give up and go home? "So loud and wide-spread has been the opposition to the play that it seems as if Mr. Morse could hardly have the heart to take any further steps in the matter," marveled Whitelaw Reid in the *Tribune*. Yet some of the editors who had for so long opposed him had to credit Salmi's fortitude in the face of that overwhelming public enmity. Even Fiske conceded, "He is a man of enterpise, and he willingly invests his fortune and that of some enthusiastic partners with a liberality that commands our admiration. But his persistence seems foolhardy."[31]

Foolhardy it may have been, but his persistence was taken seriously by Mayor Edson and the legal advisors to the Society for the Reformation of Juvenile Delinquents. Edson, after he had refused the license, quietly requested E. R. Robinson to furnish him with "any authorities in support" of the position he had already taken, mainly, "that the Mayor has a discretion to grant or refuse a license and that the provisions of the play in question shocks [sic] public decency and therefore violates [sic] the statute." A four-

9. The Shrine of the Holy Passion

page legal brief was then prepared by Robinson, dated January 10, 1883, and privately submitted to the mayor's office.

It is an enlightening document. "I cannot furnish you with any case in which the question, whether the Mayor has or has not a discretion, has come up directly before the Courts," Robinson admitted, "but the Courts have always incidentally recognized that such discretion exists." Reviewing how the licensing system had worked in the past, Robinson advised that mayors had refused a license when it had been feared that the theatre in question was "an objectionable place, as being a disorderly house, a place where female attendants were employed etc." But "it has never before, to my knowledge," wrote Robinson, "been questioned, that the Mayor had the power to refuse, or that the language of the Act [of 1872] authorizing him to grant licenses, is mandatory and not permissive." It would be absurd, he said, to contend, as Morse was, that the mayor must grant a license when he already knew that the performance to be given would be offensive—"that is to say, it is his duty to issue a license which it is also his duty to immediately revoke."

Obviously, Morse's *Passion* represented a different kind of legal problem. Refusing a license for a rowdy beer hall was one thing, but in this case, the mayor was attempting to use the Licensing Act in order to censor a play offensive mainly to Protestant constituents. Therefore, the question Edson was really asking was whether that outraged religious sentiment against the *The Passion* provided a legally defensible justification for his refusing the license. Advised Robinson:

> [I]t seems to me that the court will not enter in to the consideration of the question if satisfied that the Mayor has a discretion in the matter.... The sentiment which the Mayor respected, is, it seems to me, as much entitled to consideration from him as the sentiment which is shocked by nude and lascivious exhibitions, although such exhibitions may seem unobjectionable to some persons in the community and have as a matter of fact been tolerated in many countries.[32]

In conclusion, Robinson had "very little doubt" that Edson's ruling could withstand any challenge in a higher court. But should Morse win, Robinson said it was the mayor's duty to follow Salmi's lead and take the matter all the way to the Supreme Court. "The society which I have the honor to represent," he encouraged, "has always been solicitous [sic] that licenses should be refused for improper performances, although its revenues are diminished by its failure to receive the license fees which would otherwise come to it."

The outcome, Robinson implied, was in doubt to an uncomfortable degree. If Salmi Morse had no clear legal precedents with which to back his case, neither, evidently, had the mayor. What the mayor did have, however, was the long tradition of "majority rule."

VI

In late January, Harrison Fiske's drive to remove the Society for the Reformation of Juvenile Delinquents from all theatrical affairs took an important step forward. State Senator Grady presented an amendment to the New York State Legislature calling for an end to the consigning of theatre license monies to the S.R.J.D. Fiske was hopeful that the fees could now go to the Actor's Fund, as he had long been urging. "Every Manager in this city should bring what influence he possesses to bear on the Albany Legislature to help get this measure adopted," Fiske pleaded. The Grady amendment was also applauded by the powerful *Herald*, which said it was high time the theatre stopped being penalized "for the support of juvenile delinquents."[33]

Henry Abbey at this time was supervising the American tour of England's Lillie Langtry, another of his imported stars. The Park Theatre had been destroyed the previous October, catching fire on the very evening Miss Langtry was to have made her debut. Booth's had also proved a continuing economic drain for Abbey, and was hardly paying its way. Baldwin's Theatre in San Francisco had finally been closed the year before, and young David Belasco was also now in New York, managing the Madison Square Theatre. In his reminiscences in *Hearst's Magazine*, Belasco wrote that he did see Salmi Morse in New York during this period, when Morse was "attempting to resurrect his play."[34]

As for James O'Neill, in late January 1883 he was completing his tour of *An American King*, and was scheduled to begin rehearsals at Booth's in New York City the first weeks in February. He was about to open in an old melodrama, several versions of which had been around since 1848. O'Neill had even played another version of the story, but this was his first appearance in Charles Fechter's script, in which Fechter (1824–1879) himself had starred from 1870–'77. The role was Edmund Dantes in *The Count of Monte Cristo*.[35]

VII

Meanwhile, Salmi Morse had, as promised, applied to the Supreme Court of the State of New York for a mandamus with which to compel Mayor Edson to grant him a theatre license. On Saturday, February 3, 1883, arguments were heard in the Supreme Court Chambers of Judge Ingraham.[36]

9. The Shrine of the Holy Passion

Salmi's case was presented by William Howe, his lawyer. As his client had submitted his fee, Howe said, and had complied with every requirement of the 1872 law, the Mayor had no legal right to deny him a license. The "merits or demerits of any play," Howe argued, were not to be considered in advance; the act was not, after all, designed to set up the Mayor as an arbitrary censor. Morse had complied with the letter of the law. Now the Mayor must do the same.

The Corporate Counsel George P. Andrews defended the Mayor's refusal by stating that the license requested was actually to produce *The Passion* and everyone knew it. The question at issue, Andrews argued, was precisely "the morality or immorality of the Passion Play." This was, it will be remembered, the same legal stance originally taken—and then retracted—by the lawyers for the city of San Francisco in 1879.

Ingraham reserved his decision until a later date.

Salmi had been rashly promising that he would open his Shrine and "bring things to a crisis" by presenting *The Passion* with or without a license. When asked now by a reporter whether he still intended to open his theatre, Salmi replied, "No, sir; but *The Passion* will be presented at my *church* during the latter part of next week" (on Friday, February 9, near the beginning of Lent). "Why should [the authorities] interfere with me?" he asked confidently. "I tendered my money for the license and they refused it. What more can they ask?" As ever, he was firmly convinced that the entire problem would be magically solved with the very first public presentation of his play. "When *The Passion* has once been seen, those who have opposed it will feel sorry that they have done so," he said. "My people are devoted to me and there is no demoralization. The people engaged are not members of a theatrical company, but are my choir. In fact, I have no theatre."[37]

Theatre or no, the renovations at the "house" on 23rd Street continued, as did rehearsals with the large cast, orchestra and stage crew (personnel were now said to number seven hundred). All of these preparations, not to mention the legal fees, represented a great deal of money being spent by Salmi's backers. The musicians' salaries alone, for example, reportedly totaled $700 per week.[38] It is not surprising that Morse and his associates would be willing to try anything—even breaking the law—in the desperate conviction that, once seen, *The Passion* would overcome all opposition and be allowed its license.

It was not about to open, however, before the auditorium was finished, the sets were built and the costumes made. Thus, Salmi's repeated threat of an opening never seemed to be made good. Nevertheless, even with constant delays, rumors of an early presentation abounded. Mayor Edson sent an urgent letter to the Board of Police on February 9 informing them that he had heard Salmi would open his Shrine the following night; the Board promptly passed a resolution directing Police Superintendent George W. Walling to "issue the necessary orders to prevent the said theatre from being opened for public performances" unless a license had been obtained.[39] Walling, noted the *Tribune*, then "sent for Captain Williams and told him on no account to let Mr. Morse open his theatre."[40]

"Captain Williams" was the Police Captain Alexander S. Williams, a rather notorious figure in the New York police force for many years. Known for his brutality and his "shoot-first-ask-questions-later" approach to law enforcement, Williams was often at odds with the community and, as a result, his superiors. He had been brought before the Police Commissioners in 1879 for allegedly clubbing and kicking a citizen who, along with several others, had hissed the captain one night during his evening rounds. The charges were eventually set aside, by a vote of two to one, but afterward the unpopular Williams took to making his nightly rounds accompanied by three burly bodyguards.[41]

Williams's presence was not needed that night, however, for Morse did not present *The Passion* on February 10 as Edson feared. Instead, he and his advisors had come up with yet another ploy to get around the law.

There had still been no decision announced by Justice Ingraham concerning the mandamus to force the Mayor to grant the license. So now, in the meantime, Salmi applied to the courts for an injunction to restrain the police from interfering with any of his rehearsals. Then, as if to test the waters, when renovations were near completion a week later, he invited a small group to witness one of those "rehearsals."

On Friday evening, February 16, for an audience of approximately one hundred invited guests, the cast of *The Passion* presented the first four acts of the play. It was their first time in costume, and it took over two hours to complete the four acts. Corporate Counsel Andrews had earlier that day advised Mayor Edson that Morse would be violating the law if he gave a "full dress rehearsal," so Salmi deviously avoided that terminology, calling this instead "a rehearsal to try the costumes." Captain Williams and his police did not interfere. The *Times* reported that the small audience applauded several of the scenes, and that Salmi, emboldened by this experiment, intended to "rehearse" the entire play the following night.[42]

Even so, the next morning Salmi and his counsel were in court again, still arguing for their injunction. The Shrine, they said, was Mr. Morse's private residence and the "rehearsals" were given only before his friends. Therefore, the police had no right to enter the premises. Maddeningly, the judge postponed giving a ruling until the following week.[43]

Without such an injunction to protect them, Salmi and his lawyers wisely opted to postpone that night's announced complete "rehearsal." Sitting in the empty auditorium that evening, while disappointed "guests" were turned away from the door and the cast milled aimlessly about the

9. The Shrine of the Holy Passion

stage discussing the possible actions of the police, Salmi told a reporter that "pretty much everybody of any note had been invited, from the President and Beecher down—prominent clergymen, doctors, lawyers, city officials—everybody, in fact, except the Salvation Army. The line had to be drawn somewhere." Salmi was entirely confident that he would, in fact, obtain the injunction.[44]

Three days later, on February 20, Supreme Court Judge Ingraham upheld Mayor Edson's denial of a license for Salmi's Shrine, and refused to grant the mandamus that would compel the mayor to do so. Bitterly disappointed at yet another setback, Morse promised to appeal Ingraham's decision. He was determined to find protection in the American legal system in which he seems so strongly to have believed.

But his interpretation of the First Amendment was too outlandish for his opponents' tastes. The *Times* complained, "There are few persons who are less needed in New York than is Mr. SALMI MORSE, and the most popular thing he could possibly do would be to leave it." The *Times* had no patience with Morse's defense of his play, and categorized his arguments concerning freedom of speech and constitutional rights with "the sophistries of Socialism or the wild crazes of European anarchists."

> From Mr. MORSE's point of view, it is an outrage that a thrifty Hebrew should not be allowed to make money by blasphemy.... Mr. MORSE's idea of freedom is evidently that of the anarchist, who claims that all laws should be abolished and every man permitted to do what is right in his eyes.
> ...Mr. MORSE made the mistake of ... [claiming] that his sole motive in producing his play was to promote the interests of Christianity. This would have been sufficiently sickening had Mr. MORSE been an ordinary adventurer, but coming from a Jew, it was to the last degree revolting....
> Meanwhile, it rests with the Police to see that this fellow does not violate the law by giving unlicensed theatrical events thinly disguised as "full-dress rehearsals."[45]

VIII

These skirmishes only cemented Morse's resolve to bring *The Passion* before the public. But they also hardened the resolve of his opponents. And from this point on the battle would move mainly to the city's courtrooms. Salmi first set in motion an appeal of Judge Ingraham's ruling; pending the outcome of that, he sued again for an injunction to prevent the police from interfering with a full dress rehearsal, to which he was inviting many of the most prominent citizens of New York. "Mr. Morse, his counsel said, claimed the right to do in his home what William H. Vanderbilt or any other distinguished citizen may do in his."[46]

The announced night of this full "rehearsal" was Saturday, February 24. Then, another reversal. That very morning, Justice Donohue, in Supreme Court, denied the second application for an injunction to restrain the police from interfering. E. R. Robinson's earlier advice to Mayor Edson, that a judge would not challenge the mayor's right to refuse a license, was borne out in Donohue's ruling. As no court had ever before been asked to rule on the construction of the Theatrical Licensing Act, the judge stated, the police could interpret the law as they saw fit. If they broke any other laws in carrying out the requirements of the act, *then* the court could deal with them, but it could not restrict their actions by prior restraint. This "prior restraint" argument was essentially the same position that Salmi had taken in pleading with the mayor not to suppress *The Passion*, but now it had been used against him.

However, Judge Donohue's ruling could also be seen as an invitation, of sorts. If the courts had never before heard a challenge to the construction of the act, perhaps Salmi Morse should be the one to facilitate just such a reexamination of the limits of the statute.

Salmi gave notice that his dress rehearsal that night would go on — without Donohue's injunction, and without a proper theatre license.

IX

Long before the doors to the Shrine were opened that evening, crowds began to gather at both the main entrance on 23rd Street and the rear entrances on 24th. An unnamed "police official" had told the *Mirror* that the police feared a riot, should *The Passion* be presented. "You are aware how very bitter all religious contests are," he said. "If *The Passion* is given, I believe that a mob will ransack the place on opening night. Of course it will be the duty of the police to protect Morse and his company of actors, and this will bring on a conflict."[47] But the next morning's newspaper accounts reveal that the "curious crowd" gathered outside the Shrine this night was not there to ransack the place. Rather, onlookers were supportive of Salmi and critical of the city's efforts to suppress the play.[48]

At 7:30 p.m., the doors were opened and those with invitations were allowed inside. Among the first to enter the hall were some twenty to thirty *un*invited policemen, led by Captain Williams. Half entered from the front, taking seats in the last row, where they remained, contemptuously refusing to remove their hats. Just behind them, near the main entrance, Acting Inspector Thorne leaned against the rear wall. Williams and the rest of the patrolmen entered at the rear door on 24th Street and took up places in the wings around the perimeter of the stage itself.

The *Mirror* had asked Captain Williams whether he would prevent the rehearsal, to which he replied: "I shall not prevent any one from going inside, for the more the merrier, as each one will only add ten dollars to the total amount of fines; but I shall obey orders and do my duty."[49]

Salmi's invitation list for the evening had included "many prominent men in the professions and mercantile life," reported the *Times*,

> and the audience that rapidly filled the auditorium was, as a rule, well-dressed and well-behaved. Gentlemen whose clothes and air were clerical mingled in the throng; the Hebraic element was noticeable, and there were many actors and actresses whose successes, such as they were, were made years and years ago. Sealskins and diamonds were as plentiful as at a Wallack on Union Square matinee, and everybody seemed to expect an evening of uninterrupted pleasure. The orchestra and balcony were packed until standing-room was at a high premium, and there must have been at least 2,000 people in the house.*
>
> Meanwhile, [backstage,] the scene in the temple having been set, the Jewish mothers were putting on their warpaint and *poudre de riz* and hunting up their rubber babies; the High Priest was busily adjusting his baker's cap and straightening out the hairs in his long, white beard, and the Virgin Mary was trying to make a reporter believe that she appeared in the play "for love and not for money." Salmi was busy here and there hurrying up the laggards, chaffing the pretty girls of the chorus, and rolling and smoking cigarettes in the corridor with imperturbable equanimity. "There never was a more persecuted man than myself," he casually remarked as he blew a cloud heavenward, "except Jesus Christ."

Captain Williams now met backstage with Morse and his lawyers and told Salmi that he would be arrested as soon as the curtain rose and the first words of the play were spoken. If the cast attempted to continue with the performance they, too, would all be arrested. But Salmi, well-versed in the protocol of how to become a test case, assured Williams there would be no resistance.

As promised, the arrest was orderly. The curtain rose not long after 8 p.m. to "wild applause," and the Chorus "impressively" sang the opening invocation as the hundred mothers with their babies entered the Temple in Act One. The High Priest had no sooner begun his opening speech than Captain Williams suddenly appeared on stage to stop the show, leading Salmi Morse. The *Times* described what followed:

> A hum of excitement ran through the house, many persons rising in their seats, and murmuring disapprobation. The Priest retired, the chorus pressed forward, and stage manager [Converse L.] Graves . . . made a rush for the footlights. He informed the audience that Salmi's counsel had something to say. The hubbub ceased in an instant. . . .

---

*The *Mirror* put the number at five hundred; the *Tribune* said only that the house was "well filled."

Mr. Howe "expressed his regret" that Morse had been arrested to the accompaniment of such sacred music.

> A storm of hisses filled the house, and cries of "Shame! shame!" were heard in the balcony and orchestra.... Counsel advised the audience to remember carefully all that they had seen. This was the beginning of the end, and he believed that in this free City of New York citizens had some rights.... Wild applause greeted this sentiment....
> A gray-haired man arose at this point and shouted: "Excuse me, Sir, for this interruption, but I saw the Passion Play in California before a large audience and it contained nothing improper."
> "That is Charles R. Thorne, Sr.," shouted somebody several times and then Counsel, amid approving applause, invited Mr. Thorne to come on the stage and address the audience.

Charles R. Thorne, Sr. (1814?–1893), was a well-known American actor whose fifty-year career had taken him across the continent; he had even once managed the Baldwin Theatre in San Francisco. Even greater fame, however, had come to him as the father of Charles R. Thorne, Jr. (1840–1883), who had been a major star throughout the 1870s, and who had only recently been forced into early retirement due to illness.[50]

Now the elder Thorne was helped onto the stage of the Shrine, where he was "warmly received"; he

> declared that he saw nothing in [*The Passion*] that would offend a person of any denomination.... Loud applause followed, with calls for Salmi Morse, and to the music of salvos of applause, Salmi said that he was an outlaw, and had no right to speak.

Of course, speak he did, saying that he was condemned because he chose not to present prize fights or licentious exhibitions but rather because he wanted to present Jesus Christ. "I have dedicated this temple to that purpose," he said, "and I would rather see it burned down tonight and not get one cent of insurance than see it used for any other play. I hope you will agitate this question and see me righted." Again, his remarks were answered with loud applause. He humbly praised his company and graciously thanked his supporters. Then:

> Salmi argued that he had committed no crime, but he must say good night as he had to "go with his guard." Salmi's counsel said there was no law to prevent the staging of the "Hallelujah Chorus" in a church or on a street, and the singers broke out in a plaintive melody:
> "Christ is born,
> Man is saved.
> Christ redeems
> Man depraved."

9. The Shrine of the Holy Passion

The curtain was then rung down, and as Salmi moved off the stage in the custody of Capt. Williams the members of his company pressed around him and pathetically bade him good-bye, as if he were condemned for life.

There was no Black Maria waiting to carry Morse away to jail, as had been waiting for James O'Neill in San Francisco, but Salmi's arrest was none the less memorable. A large and noisy crowd tagged along behind Captain Williams, the patrolmen, Salmi and his lawyers, as they all trooped through the darkened streets of Manhattan to the 23rd Precinct station house. Along the way, several "handsomely dressed ladies" — this was the *Times*'s description; the *Tribune* called them "silly women" — had their escorts stop the parade in order "to tender [Morse] their sympathy."

"I am now entirely in my counsel's hands," Salmi was quoted as saying as the charges were entered against him at the police station. "Let them crucify me if they will."

Even James O'Neill had not been booked with such panache.

10
The Passion Plays New York at Last

I

Salmi was charged with presenting a theatrical performance without a license; bail was set at five hundred dollars. A friend of Morse's named Frederick A. Schilling, who owned a restaurant on Sixth Avenue near Washington Square Park, had accompanied the cortege to the station house and it was he who posted the bond. Arraignment was scheduled for 9:30 the following morning, at the Jefferson Market Police Court.[1]

There were in the end to be two preliminary hearings. The first, as scheduled, was held in the Jefferson Market Courthouse, on the southwest corner of 10th Street and Sixth Avenue (most recently, the building has housed the Jefferson Market Branch of the New York Public Library). There, Police Justice Patrick G. Duffy heard arguments in Morse's case on Sunday, February 25. Captain Williams was the only witness called to give a statement. Justice Duffy ordered a second hearing for the following Tuesday, February 27, in the Court of Special Sessions, in order to further determine whether the facts warranted a full trial.[2]

The Court of Special Sessions was held downtown in the massive granite building facing Centre Street officially known as "The Halls of Justice" and popularly nicknamed "The Tombs." Briefly, police justices in New York City had jurisdiction in minor, routine offenses, such as drunkenness, disorderly conduct, etc. As did district judges, police justices also acted as committing magistrates for the Supreme and Superior courts, which tried the more-serious civil and criminal cases. Therefore, it was the police and district judges before whom the majority of those arrested in New York first appeared, regardless of the charge. And thus, when Salmi had been arrested on Saturday night, the judge who set his bail at the 23rd Precinct station house had been a police justice, Solon B. Smith.

There were eleven police justices, each appointed to a ten-year term by the mayor with the consent of the Board of Aldermen. These eleven men

10. The Passion *Plays New York at Last*

could hold court in any of the six Police Court districts and two or more police justices together constituted a Court of Special Sessions, empowered to try cases of misdemeanor "too important" to be settled by the other Police Courts.[3] Salmi's case fell into that category.

Originally, police justices had been elected by their respective districts. But in an effort to remove the office from the arena of "politics," the appointment process had been put in the hands of the mayor and the Board of Aldermen. Inevitably, that move only drove the politicking underground. "There are no offices in this city made more the object of bargains and deals than those of the Police Justices," the *World* complained in 1884. Making the situation worse, city statutes allowed virtually anyone to be appointed a police justice — whether he knew the law or not. In fact, at the time of Salmi Morse's troubles, the eleven police justices holding office in New York City included among their number only two actually trained as lawyers. (One of these was Justice Duffy.) Of the others, one had been a butcher, one a "sash and blind manufacturer," one had sold tin cans, another coal and coke, while still another sold fertilizer. The remaining three were Tammany men who had "no other trade but politics."[4]

Salmi's second hearing before Police Justice Duffy resumed at the Court of Special Sessions in the "Tombs" on Tuesday morning, February 27. Sitting in with Duffy were Police Justices Solon B. Smith (who had first set bail for Morse on Saturday night); J. Henry Ford (a former saloon owner and Tammany appointee); and Andrew J. White (the aforementioned fertilizer dealer). Salmi was given emotional support by several of the cast members of *The Passion*, who sat as a group among the spectators.

This second preliminary hearing produced nothing new in the way of evidence; Captain Williams was again the only witness called. But, as had been the case in San Francisco, the prosecution now shied away from exploring the morality or immorality of the play, and held instead that the issue must be confined to the breaking of the Licensing Act: first, *The Passion* was a play; second, it had been presented before the public; clearly, a license was required. Salmi's lawyer, Howe (whom the *Times* sarcastically identified not by name but only as "the stout man with the well-developed lungs"[5]), continued to defend the work as a religious event for which no license was needed. He demanded that all charges be dropped on the grounds that the presentation was an act of worship and not a play. With a great show of histrionics, he dramatically proclaimed this a case "wherein the liberties of a whole city were trembling in the balance. A private place had been invaded and Mr. Morse had been arrested. Much less than this had stirred up the Revolution that had set this people free."[6] Howe even went so far as to threaten to sue the city for damages.

An unruffled Justice Duffy reserved judgment, and took a copy of *The Passion* home with him to help him in his decision.

II

The presence of cast members in the courtroom was an almost surprising show of support, for, with the increasing number of delays and postponements and the inevitable tension arising from the legal problems, reports were beginning to surface alleging dissension among Salmi's company. These accounts had begun as early as that first, brief dress rehearsal on February 16, when it had been reported that the musicians had refused to play for the rehearsal unless they were paid in advance.[7]

More ominous than the stories of grumbling performers, however, were the disturbing reports of resentments being engendered among Salmi's backers. Most of their complaints were said to be directed at Morse himself, and for good reason. It was revealed that on February 24, the day of Salmi's arrest, his lawyers had filed with the City Register a five-year lease assigning the Shrine to the stage manager, Converse L. Graves. Under the conditions of this lease, Graves was to pay Morse five hundred dollars per week (although the terminology was confusing and could have been interpreted "per year"), for "all the scenery, fixtures, and other properties contained in the structure"[8]; it was further stipulated that Graves could produce in the Shrine only moral works that met with Salmi's explicit approval.

Most of the newspapers rightly viewed this lease as just another attempt to get around the law, and they pointed to the prior-approval clause as proof. As Harrison Fiske in the *Mirror* pointed out, Morse had sworn often enough that "he will not allow any other play than the Passion to be produced."[9] Even so, Fiske allowed, the more anonymous Graves might be granted a theatre license, whereas the notorious Salmi never would. The *Tribune* agreed, but put a slightly different reading to the meaning of the lease:

> ...Mr. Morse knew that if he were absolutely refused a license for the building on the score of the Passion, he could not hope to secure it on any other representation of intention. He therefore transferred the building to Mr. Graves, who would be able to obtain a license for a house devoted to ordinary theatrical attractions. The stipulation in the lease that Mr. Graves ... should produce nothing without the consent of Mr. Morse, protects the interests, pecuniary and otherwise, of everybody concerned.[10]

Unfortunately, "everybody concerned" had evidently not been informed that such a lease was even being considered. As the *Tribune* further reported, on February 28:

> There have been some disagreements between Mr. Morse and Albert J. Eaves, one of his associates, and the transfer of the lease having been made without a conference and without the latter's entire concurrence, it was taken to be significant of a hostile purpose. There was a meeting

last evening at Mr. Morse's rooms at which Mr. Eaves and Messrs. Severance and Ferris, the other persons interested, were present, and the result of an extended conference was that these three men signed a paper stating that the lease was transferred for the purpose of a legal accommodation, and not for the purpose of defrauding them.[11]

But feelings of anger and resentment would continue to fester, with Eaves especially growing more public in his discontent. There would be strenuous objections to Salmi's desire to have the name of the Shrine changed to "Morse's Hall,"[12] and his continued claims that his own fortune was paying for *The Passion* would finally drive a disgusted Eaves to tell one New York journalist that "if it had not been for Salmi there would have been no trouble as regards the securing of a license."[13]

Salmi, of course, seemed to remain indifferent to all such rumblings, and continued to present a confident front, even when Justice Duffy ruled on March 1 that the evidence against him presented in the preliminary hearings warranted binding him over for trial on the misdemeanor charge.[14] While he awaited his next date in court, free on bail, rehearsals continued at the Shrine and Salmi welcomed any reporter who would listen to his woeful tale of continued misunderstanding and persecution.

III

At this point in the judicial process, the defendant in a case called before the Court of Special Sessions had a choice to make: to either remain in Special Sessions, in which his or her case would be presented to and decided by the presiding justices alone; or to opt for the Court of General Sessions, in which the case would be argued before a jury. For some reason Salmi's counsel, unlike his lawyers in San Francisco, elected not to have a jury trial. Presiding over the trial at the Court of Special Sessions would be Police Justice James T. Kilbreth, a former Ohio lawyer who was "the oldest Police Judge on the bench, in years of service"; the 42-year-old Kilbreth had, in fact, only recently been reappointed to another ten-year term by Mayor Edson. According to the *World*, "On account of his legal attainments [Judge Kilbreth] generally acts as presiding Justice of the Court of Special Sessions.... [His] associates on the Bench ... as a rule acquiesce in his decisions. He tempers justice with mercy and occasionally suspends sentence when an offender is brought before him for the first time." Assisting Kilbreth at Morse's trial would be Justices Ford and Smith, neither of whom had been trained in law, but both of whom had sat in on Salmi's second preliminary hearing with Justice Duffy.[15]

Morse's trial finally began at 10:30 a.m. on Tuesday, March 13, 1883.

Surprisingly, that morning the courtroom was not crowded with spectators. There were neither the expected delegations of irate ministers nor any brigades of petition-bearing society ladies. Even out of the several hundred people on the payroll of *The Passion*, only Pontius Pilate, Salome and "a few mothers of the innocents" were there. Undoubtedly, *The Passion*'s opponents were growing tired of it all, and were confident that the Court would shut Morse up once and for all.

Salmi had been suffering from "neuralgia," and he cut a pathetic figure as he entered the courtroom that day, his right cheek swollen to nearly twice its size and his right eye almost closed. He stood humbly before the bench alongside his counsel, and entered a plea of not guilty.[16]

The Corporation Counsel Andrews methodically set out, first, to prove his contention that *The Passion* was a play, and second, that it had been presented before the public. Witnesses described the theatre-like accoutrements inside the 23rd Street Shrine, and Andrews entered into evidence the "programme" handed out that Saturday night, which broke the work down into the dramatic form of "acts" and "scenes." As to the second question, Andrews refuted the defense's argument that the presentation had been intended only for "invited friends," producing several young men who testified that they had been invited "but had no acquaintance with Mr. Morse."

Salmi's counsel, the flamboyant Mr. Howe, interrupted the testimony frequently and, in the *Times*'s opinion, put on a performance of his own: "He beat the table, he stamped his feet, he threatened, implored and importuned and sank into his chair exhausted." Again, he moved for a dismissal of all the charges, arguing that *The Passion* was not a play but a privately exhibited religious production, and the police had no constitutional right to invade the home of a private citizen.

The closing arguments were finally completed late in the afternoon, and the three justices immediately conferred. The result was a surprising two-to-one split. Justice Solon Smith read the majority decision: there was no question, he said, that *The Passion* was a play. But the performance presented that Saturday night, at which Salmi Morse had been arrested, could not be held to have been a public one.

Salmi Morse was therefore discharged. He had won.

Significantly, it was the lawyer, Justice Kilbreth, who dissented. It was his lone view that "Mr. Morse had merely endeavored to evade the statute." Fortunately for Salmi, this was one instance in which Kilbreth's untutored associates on the bench did not acquiesce to his learned opinion. At the same time, however, the larger, more important issues of the case — freedom of speech, separation of church and state, the right of the Mayor to arbitrarily employ prior censorship by refusing a license — had not been settled at all by the decision. Rather, the verdict simply absolved Morse, in this specific instance, of presenting a theatrical performance before the public.

Salmi, however, chose to see it as a complete vindication of his claim that the Shrine was not a theatre and *The Passion* not a play. Joyfully, he announced to reporters that he "should inform his people at once of the court's decision, and should present another dress rehearsal within a week at his Temple. He had no doubt, he said, that he should be able to produce the play before the public in a very short time."

Harrison Grey Fiske, who had so often promised that *The Passion* would never be seen in New York City, was about to be proved wrong. It looked like smooth sailing at last.

IV

Salmi returned to the Shrine determined to fine-tune his *Passion* and to resume as soon as possible the presentations of his "rehearsals." Then, with an almost farcical inevitability, everything seemed to fall apart.

Mere days after his acquittal, the Cosmopolitan Iron Company unexpectedly showed up at the Shrine and carted away several hundred of the seats in the auditorium, claiming Morse still owed a balance of $300.[17] As Salmi over the next two weeks frantically negotiated for the return of his chairs, reports of more "defection and dissatisfaction" within his company appeared. According to the *Tribune*,

> It is understood that the twelve disciples have recently held an important indignation meeting on the situation. The usual complaints of disheartening delay and endless postponements were of course prominent, but outside of this, they accused Mr. Morse of bad faith in the matter of salaries.... If the twelve disciples withdraw from the already diminished cast, it will throw, of course, one more obstacle in the way of Mr. Morse proceeding with the dress-rehearsal. It is said that satisfactory arrangements have been made for the retaining of Mr. Wannemaker's services for the part of the Nazarene, and other defections have been remedied in the best way possible. The twenty-five members of the chorus, who, it is asserted by their friends, were the backbone of it, have refused to return.[18]

The Passion had now been in rehearsal for more than three grueling, tension-filled months, and actor dissatisfaction was certainly not surprising. Rumors of a falling out among Salmi and his backers were also being recirculated.[19]

But the indefatigable Salmi forged on. It was rumored that he had arranged with an ordained clergyman to finally have the Shrine dedicated on Easter Sunday, March 25. The next "rehearsal" was then to take place the subsequent Friday, March 30. By Saturday, the day before Easter, the $300 owed Cosmopolitan Iron had somehow been collected and paid, and the chairs had been returned, but they were still not in place by Easter morning. As with so many other promised deadlines, that one, too, passed with no dedication ceremony taking place.[20]

By sheer force of his own will, however, Salmi drove forward his plans for the first legally sanctioned dress rehearsal of *The Passion* on that next Friday. All those who had held invitations for the night that Salmi had been arrested were asked to return on March 30, and Morse dispensed new invitations with abandon. Virtually every major figure in the city of New York was invited, especially his most-hardened Protestant enemies. In addition, anyone remotely connected with the production was besieged by friends seeking invitations. Salmi told one reporter that over two thousand applications had been refused in one day, and that "at one time there was a line of messenger boys reaching from his room down stairs and out into the street. He had also employed three persons who during the day did nothing but write polite and courteous answers to those asking for tickets of admission."[21] As the Friday performance time neared, and this increased — and seemingly favorable — public attention manifested itself, any further talk of defection among the cast and crew was effectively silenced, if not completely mollified.

V

By now it had become a familiar scene. A crowd began to gather on 23rd Street by late that Friday afternoon, and the police, still claiming they feared a riot, were once again present in conspicuous numbers. As before, however, the mob was not there to protest but only to gain admittance. The house was filled to capacity by a quarter of eight and, outside, well-dressed couples brandishing invitations were being turned away. Police Captain Williams finally ordered that the doors be closed. Indignant gentlemen "threatened, pleaded, begged" to be let in, but Williams refused. The scene was appropriately chaotic. "Clothes were torn," the *Times* revealed, "watches stolen, and one woman fainted."[22] "By eight o'clock," according to the *Tribune*,

> the sidewalk, in front, was packed with people and still every stage and car that passed continued to pour out additions to the already great crowd. Again and again was the assurance given that no more persons would be admitted, and large numbers went regretfully away, but others continued to press closely around the doors until Captain Williams used force to make them disperse.[23]

10. The Passion *Plays New York at Last*

A somewhat smaller crowd received the same treatment at the 24th Street stage door.

Those who had managed to make it inside were "respectable people," in the *Tribune*'s estimation. Several well-known faces could be recognized in the crowd. "Fully a third were women in fashionable attire," said the *Times*, "and politicians, especially City officers, theatrical folk, lawyers, journalists, doctors, and gentlemen of clerical aspect were seen in the orchestra and balcony chairs." The *Times* also made note of "a large gathering of the Hebrew element" in attendance.

The performance finally began at about 8:10 p.m. The plain red curtain rose and the "mothers" with their "babies" — unfortunately no longer numbering one hundred — slowly entered the Temple, beginning Act One. This time there was no interruption from Captain Williams, and the relieved actors played the entire scene. As the curtain fell on Act One to the strains of the "Hallelujah Chorus," the audience burst into applause. Loud cries of "Morse! Morse!" were heard, and, finally, Salmi pushed the curtain aside and stepped before the footlights.

It was indeed a moment to be savored. "Ladies and Gentlemen," he said, his hands folded humbly across his chest, "I have much on my mind, but my heart is full, and I will say, therefore, only a few words to you. After all my troubles, happiness has at last come to me, and I thank you for the kindness with which you have greeted *The Passion*."[24] He then bowed himself off the stage, and the crowd settled back to await the second act.

The *Times* observed that there was

> a buzz of conversation between the acts. "I don't see anything wrong about that," and, "If that's all they made a row about they made a mistake," were typical remarks. Commissioner Hess said he did not see anything in the play to which the most fastidious could object.

During Intermission a *Herald* reporter spoke with Senator Jones of Nevada, who was quoted as saying that there had been in the East "a great deal of misrepresentation [about] the play in San Francisco. It was not objected to by the best class of people. It was only the bigoted, strictly faultfinding Christians who were against it. They would not accept anything, good or bad." It was Senator Jones's opinion, however, that in Morse's present production, he had made a "mistake by having amateurs.... The Herod is good, but you can't run a 'Passion Play' on Herod." In San Francisco, Jones added, only "the best actors were employed."[25]

It is impossible to know exactly what Salmi's staging of *The Passion* at the 23rd Street Shrine entailed. Certain observations gleaned from press reports, however, may lead one to several generalizations. First of all,

Senator Jones's criticism of the amateur acting must surely be given credence. The *Times* complimented the Baptist minister Wannemaker for a "well-modulated voice," but the *Herald*, in a bow to the more florid acting conventions of the age, dismissed the acting in *The Passion* as "too little and too feeble to excite anyone for or against any character."

But what the production lacked in thespian artistry was more than offset by the polished technical and scenic expertise. Even without a David Belasco among them, Salmi's uncredited designers were evidently able to hold the attention of an audience accustomed to grand-scale stage wizardry. The *Tribune* reporter felt that the scenery throughout was "tasteful, and faithful, it is said, to history." Even the *Mirror* had to admit, "As a series of tableaux the affair is more successful, and the spectacular features alone kept many in the audience from giving up the business ... and leaving their seats for home." The production was also highly praised for Oscar Weil's musical score and for Fred Lyster's conducting. Fiske thought the music "in places beautiful and generally characteristic." In fact, the *Mirror's* music critic would later write that Weil's score (sung in concert at the Cosmopolitan Theatre on April 8) "showed the handling of a master of the art": "Rarely have we heard anything more touchingly beautiful than the 'Pastorale,' and the 'March to Calvary' is the most melodiously plaintive we have heard of late, taking equal rank with that of Handel in Saul and of Beethoven in The Eroica."[26] At least Salmi still had the wherewithal — including, fortunately, the money — to surround himself with talented colleagues. And for that reason, again, it would seem that this production of *The Passion*, even under Salmi's sole managership and mounted at the stable-turned-Shrine, cannot be written off as a complete fiasco.

There is also evidence to suggest that new scenes were staged — including one of Jesus ministering to the little children; the raising of Lazarus from the dead; and Christ's entry into Jerusalem. As in the first San Francisco production, Salmi omitted the controversial Crucifixion and Descent from the Cross scenes. Also omitted here was the betrayal scene at the Garden of Gesthemane (which "Betsy B." had found so repulsive). However, in New York the Ascension was staged to conclude the evening. Each of these later scenes was "equally well received" by the attentive crowd. Backstage, all was "quiet and orderly, ... and every effort was made by scene-shifters to do their work as quickly as possible." Even so, the performance lasted three-and-a-half hours, the curtain finally falling at 11:40 p.m., again to prolonged applause.

After a struggle of almost three years, Salmi Morse had made good his promise. *The Passion* had been presented in New York, and from all indications it had been well-received by its audience.

Salmi was elated. He warmly received well-wishers and friends who crowded into his rooms above the Shrine after the play to noisily extend their congratulations. Likewise, members of the cast and crew stopped by to express their good wishes, as well as their "satisfaction at going entirely through the six acts of the play without molestation from the Police."

"It was a triumph," an exhausted Salmi exulted to the *Times*, "and I shall feel satisfied even if I never give another performance." Of course, he was already planning the next performances of *The Passion*, saying that he was free to prepare the other acts of the play — which he claimed now numbered twenty-four in all. He envisioned an ever-changing pageant in which scenes could be interpolated and interchanged at will, growing and metamorphosing as the decades passed. *The Passion*, he had always felt, would become an American institution; it might run forever. Even as the audience left the Shrine that Friday evening, they were apprised via printed handouts that public performances of *The Passion* for the benefit of the Salle d'Asile Francaise (French Orphan Asylum) were to begin at the "Temple of the Passion" on the following Tuesday, April 3, and would continue "Every Evening and Saturday Matinee until further notice."[27] Although the scale of prices had yet to be determined, Salmi told the *Times* that night, tickets would probably range from one to two dollars.

VI

Salmi had always protested that once those who opposed *The Passion* had seen it they would realize how wrong they had been. To a certain extent, that was indeed the case. But he did not allow for the fact that this realization might also be tinged with great disappointment; he never thought that he might be just as mistaken about *The Passion* as they. As the *Herald* politely worded it, "the work is not what fancy has painted it.... The story as presented is entirely without offensive features; [but] neither does it appear to promise to exert the great moral influence which the author has claimed for it...."[28] Harrison Grey Fiske, predictably, was more derisive:

> When the first tableau was over the audience realized that a great hue and cry had been raised about nothing at all. The game wasn't worth the powder spent in suppressing it....
> Without the advertising it has received from the Mayor, the courts and the press, the Passion Play would, in all probability, die an easy death in one week, or less.

Fiske's acknowledgement, after three years of anti–*Passion* editorializing, that the struggle had been over nothing did not, however, represent an admission that his own campaign had been a misguided one. He remained convinced that,

> Viewed as a religious matter, the Passion is blasphemous and sacrilegious. It cannot be otherwise, for the representation of a divine being [by a mortal] ... is not only repugnant, but absolutely appalling.

As for Morse's claim to protection under the First Amendment,

> Religious liberty is one thing and sacrilegious license another. The belief of every class should be protected. The belief of Christians should enjoy immunity from the exhibition of the Son of their God in character on the public stage, and for a purpose that it is foolish to deny is monetary gain. There is no article in the Constitution of the United States which says that a large class of our citizens may be shocked and insulted by such a speculation.[29]

VII

Now that the full dress "rehearsal" of *The Passion* had been presented unopposed, Salmi was absolutely convinced that the Shrine had won unanimous public approval. Moreover, with the next few performances announced as "charitable benefits" for the French Orphan Asylum, it seemed certain that no further objections to the play could possibly be raised. After all, the Licensing Act had been amended in 1875 to specifically exclude amateur productions staged for charitable purposes.

So, over the next four days, Salmi elatedly supervised the last-minute polishing in preparation for the first paying audience on Tuesday night, April 3, 1883. "It is now the correct thing," George Barnes informed his San Francisco readers, "for the ladies of his company to salute Salmi Morse with a chaste kiss when he meets them on the stage at rehearsal of the 'Passion.' They are not rehearsing the Judas kiss, we hope."[30]

That was entirely possible, for many in the ensemble, or so they would claim, had not seen a paycheck since November, and dissatisfaction was still boiling just beneath the surface. But it would not be the disaffected actors who would in the end ring down the final curtain on Salmi Morse's *Passion*.

It would be the secular legal system.

Even as Salmi and his cast were busily preparing for the April 3 opening, his tireless opponents were moving to stop him. Morse could not have known that he himself had given them the weapons with which they would defeat him. It was E. Randolph Robinson, the Counsel for the Society for the Reformation of Juvenile Delinquents, who petitioned the State Supreme Court for an injunction to stop the performance. Armed with sworn affidavits from several of his own law clerks, whom he had sent to witness the legally allowed rehearsal of March 30, Robinson now offered irrefutable proof that *The Passion* was indeed a dramatic entertainment: it included, he said, "tableaux, minstrelsy and dancing." This undeniably brought it under the jurisdiction of the 1872 statute. Furthermore, Robinson reminded the court that Salmi himself in his own testimony at his trial had admitted that his actors were being paid; thus, strictly speaking, they could not claim to be "amateurs." Finally, the unlicensed rehearsal of March 30 had not been given for any charitable purpose. Therefore, under the terms of the law, Robinson argued, his Society was claiming its right both to fine the producers for the illegal Friday night "rehearsal" of this stage drama, and to halt any further performances of *The Passion* until a proper license should be obtained.[31]

The beauty of this, of course, was that no mayor would ever grant such a license for *The Passion*. It was another legal "Catch-22."

Perversely, Robinson waited until the day of the first public performance to file his complaint. Late Tuesday afternoon, Supreme Court Justice Donohue—who had two months earlier denied Salmi's request for an injunction to stop police interference—granted the Society for the Reformation of Juvenile Delinquents a temporary injunction to stop that evening's scheduled premiere of *The Passion*. Once again, it was Captain Williams and Inspector Thorne who served the restraining order on Salmi Morse at the Shrine, only thirty minutes before the performance was to begin. "You are not under arrest now," Williams told Morse, "but I advise you not to begin the performance."[32]

Salmi claimed that he had been ignorant of the injunction until it was served. He immediately sent for William Howe, who shortly arrived at the Shrine and, after examining the documents, advised his client to obey. It was now eight o'clock and there were almost a thousand people sitting in the auditorium.[33] Once again, Salmi had the unpleasant duty of facing an expectant audience and telling them to go home. This time the announcement was doubly unpleasant, as the box office, for the first time, had actually taken in money.

"I do not wish to complain here," Salmi told those present, "but I am a persecuted man; there is only one thing left for me, and that is crucifixion and then I shall stand in the place of my Master." William Howe also addressed the disappointed crowd, denouncing the last-minute service of the injunction and branding it "an insult to the people."

"What are you going to do?" asked a reporter from the *Tribune* after the audience had gone, to which Salmi tiredly replied, "I don't know."

"Are you getting discouraged?"

"No. My cause is just. I have tendered the society the license money twice, through the Mayor, and it was each time refused. That is on the record. My company is suffering for food, and the cost to me while I have waited to produce this play has not been less than $1,200 a day. Until this case is settled [as well as] my application to the Court of Appeals to compel the Mayor to give me a license, I can do nothing."

There were several members of the chorus still waiting backstage for some bit of news, and Salmi could only look at them with pity. "I'm very sorry for these poor people," he told the reporter, "but I can't help them. Tell them to go home, and I'll let them know what we intend to do for them by [letter]."

The chorus members were not so easily dismissed, however, and took this opportunity to complain bitterly to the reporter of their treatment by Morse and his backers. "There are eighty of us," cried one of the women,

> who haven't received a cent since November 23, when we were engaged by Mr. Morse. He has promised and promised, and lied day after day, and we have trusted in him and believed him. At first we were sorry for him, but not now. We know that he has men back of him who are putting up the money for everything, and we know too that his favorites in the company got a part of their money at least, but we got nothing but words. A short time ago there was a strike, but we wouldn't go in because we didn't want to hurt him, and we kept it out of the papers. He had a singular influence over us, and would cheer us up by telling us his troubles and patting our cheeks and telling us we were good girls and boys, and all that, but that didn't help. I gave up a position in Mapleson's chorus, and that girl who is crying lost several chances . . . and now she has pawned her sealskin sacque and hasn't a decent pair of shoes to her feet. It's pretty hard for a girl who is trying to be decent, I tell you.

The frustration and rage of the past four months found voice at last, and the loss of confidence in their besieged leader was now out in the open. Salmi's skill at keeping actors on a string had been tested one time too many.

Dispiritedly, Salmi postponed further performances of *The Passion* and began to prepare for yet another day in court. His equally dispirited company was once again forced to await the decision of a high court judge. The hearing date for arguments on the S.R.J.D.'s injunction was set for Wednesday, April 11.

Even before that, however, there was another, more devastating development. As had happened in San Francisco in 1879 with the Board of Supervisors, and in New York in 1880 with the Board of Aldermen, Salmi was now dealt one final blow by pressured secular legislators seeking to formulate into law the protection of religious sentiment from any perceived insult by the stage. But this time the governing body was not some local board with limited power; this body spoke with the voice of the state. In truth, this last offensive legitimized the issue as the First Amendment versus the First Amendment—freedom of religion *versus* freedom of speech. On

Thursday, April 5, two days after the S.R.J.D.'s injunction, State Senator Boyd introduced a bill entitled "An act to prevent any attempt to personate or represent Jesus Christ, the Saviour of Mankind, in any exhibition, show, play, dramatic or other theatrical performance."[34] As had been evident in every such previous enactment attempted for the suppression of *The Passion* in San Francisco and New York City, the broad range and vague language of Boyd's bill represented a threat as well to oratorios and church-sponsored pageants throughout the state. But that didn't stop the Senate from sending the proposal for study and recommendation to its Committee on the Judiciary.

The Committee apparently viewed the situation as urgent, because the very next day they reported in favor of the bill's immediate passage, and further broadened its provisions to cover *any* biblical character — Old or New Testament — viewed as "a divinity." The text of the amended bill now read as follows:

> SECTION 1. It shall not be lawful to exhibit, produce or give, or cause to be exhibited, produced or given publicly, or in any public hall, or place used as a public hall or exhibition room, with or without admission fee, any exhibition, show, play, dramatic or other theatrical performance, or any part or parts thereof, in which any person shall attempt to assume to personate or represent any being or character mentioned in the Old or New Testament, worshipped as a divinity.
>
> SECTION 2. Any person violating the provisions of this act shall be deemed guilty of a misdemeanor, and upon conviction thereof shall be punished by imprisonment for a term of not less than six months nor more than one year or by a fine of not less than five hundred nor more than two thousand dollars, or by both such imprisonment and fine, in the discretion of the court.
>
> SECTION 3. This act shall take effect immediately.[35]

Boyd's bill then passed to the next step in the process of becoming law; it was referred to the Committee of the Whole.

The legal battle over *The Passion* had never before gone so far as a state legislative body, and the interference of the state, no matter how well-intentioned, once again threatened church/state separation by using its police power to establish the primacy of the "Christian religion" over every secular instrument of society. The *New York Herald* professed itself alarmed at this new wrinkle. "When Senator Boyd, or anyone else, proposes to regulate religious opinions by a public law," said the *Herald*, "we unhesitatingly say they mistake the public."[36] (This demonstrated a conveniently short memory, for the *Herald* itself had called for the city aldermen to pass just such a law during the more intense days of Henry Abbey's production only three years before.)

However, Boyd's proposed bill, and the Senate's eagerness to consider it, were developments that changed irrevocably Salmi's claim to constitutional protection; and even though it was not yet a law but was only being debated, the proposed legislation must have been a palpable presence at the hearing held before Judge Barrett of the Superior Court in New York City, on April 11, 1883, to decide the fate of the S.R.J.D.'s injunction against *The Passion*.

In this important hearing, as in virtually every one of Salmi's trials, the hidden agenda of protection for the church was never adequately addressed. The issue was again confined to the simple matter of an unlicensed performance; the far more troubling constitutional question that had shadowed this controversy from the beginning, the question that Salmi had long been trying to raise — of how far a nominally free society should go to institutionalize a widely held (but by no means universal) religious belief — remained unasked.

Not surprisingly, Judge Barrett, after weighing all the arguments, decided in favor of the Society. The injunction was made permanent; Salmi would have to be granted a license from the mayor before his Temple of the Passion could reopen.[37] This was not seen by the court as suppression or censorship or denial of the right of free speech, but merely the enforcement of the law.

It was ironic that it was the Society for the Reformation of Juvenile Delinquents which had brought about the successful conclusion to the *Mirror*'s long anti-*Passion* campaign. For Harrison Grey Fiske, it will be recalled, was even now awaiting the outcome of his own lobbying efforts to stop the Society from doing just this sort of thing. The point could not have been lost on Fiske, and no doubt for that reason the *Mirror* barely mentioned the trial — or its successful conclusion — at all.[38]

While Morse was discouraged, he seemed fairly optimistic and appeared fully prepared to face the mayor yet again. Then, as if to drive the final nail into the coffin, the day after Barrett's decision in New York City, Senator Boyd's bill came before the State Senate in Albany for its third and final reading. Put to a vote by the President of the Senate, the bill was passed by a margin of twenty-one to one.[39] The new Senate Bill No. 418 was then forwarded to the State Assembly for its concurrence. The Assembly that same afternoon had it read twice, and by unanimous consent referred it to its own Committee on the Judiciary.[40]

With the joint passage of the Boyd bill imminent, the full degree of state opposition to his work could no longer be denied, even by Salmi. He now knew that *The Passion* would never become an American Oberammergau; it would never be sanctioned by the church; it would never grace library shelves; it was now even conceivable that, by law, *The Passion* could be legislated out of existence forever.

His own personal fortunes were no better. He was beset by mutinous

10. The Passion *Plays New York at Last*

performers; at odds with his financial backers; still denounced by the clergy and the press throughout the nation; and enjoined by the courts from presenting his only successful play without a license.

Salmi Morse, after more than four years of almost continuous battling on behalf of his *Passion*, finally admitted defeat. The war was over. On April 13, two days after his last trial before the Superior Court and one day after the Senate's passage of the Boyd bill, Salmi quietly announced that he would abandon all attempts to stage *The Passion*.

Asked what he intended to do now, he said he thought he might go back into journalism.[41]

11

The Aftermath: "Alas, Poor Yorick!"

I

The Passion continued making headlines for some time afterward, usually in the guise of some spurious report that the play would still be produced, either in New York or in some other American city.[1] Each report met with immediate denunciations, and these occasional whispered threats only underscored how deeply the Victorian psyche had been shocked by Morse and his play. *The Passion* was not revived. In fact, Salmi Morse was entering his own dramatic final chapter. In less than a year he would be dead.

Along with the rumors of *The Passion*'s resurrection, there were also accounts of the ongoing soap opera unfolding behind the scenes. Early in May, A. H. Warren, the actor who had ended up playing both Herod and Pontius Pilate, filed suit in the State Supreme Court to recover $1,358 he claimed was owed him in back salary, naming not only Salmi Morse but, as codefendants, Roberts, Severance, Ferris and both Mr. and Mrs. Eaves. Warren's was to be the first of many lawsuits begun over the next few months by performers and backstage personnel alike.[2] But these legal hassles were minor in comparison to the infighting engaged in by Salmi's partners to decide who was to have control over the "Temple of the Passion." Both Albert J. Eaves and George D. Roberts applied for licenses on the property, each in his own name.[3]

The unexpected result of these attempted coups was that Salmi was suddenly roused from his post–*Passion* despondency and inspired to fight for control of his domain. Gone were all thoughts of journalism. In early May, he reapplied for a theatrical license, earnestly assuring Mayor Edson that he did not intend to produce *The Passion* but one of his other works, an "exalted comedy" written in the Shakespearean style and entitled *A Bustle Among the Petticoats*. The mayor and his advisors being understandably cautious, they required Salmi to sign an unusual agreement specifically stating that he would not attempt to present *The Passion*. Only then was he given a license, on May 15, 1883.[4] Advanced the sum of $1,250 by an unnamed "friend," perhaps Frederick Schilling, Salmi quickly paid the rent on the Temple for the month of May "and thus secure[d] the house against all comers."[5]

Morse was now determined to take his place among the ranks of the nation's leading dramatists. Perhaps he felt that, over time, he could gain acceptance for *The Passion* through the widespread approval of his other plays. Abandoning his company of amateurs, he set out to hire a repertory troupe of professional actors to stage an entire season of his great works, including *A Midwinter Night's Dream*, which he personally considered to be his best play, and a revived (revivified?) *Doctor of Lima*. His new company included Frederick Paulding, who, it will be recalled, had earlier opposed *The Passion* because it humanized "divine" emotions; Paulding was engaged to play the juvenile leads. Also:

> Theodore Hamilton, heavy lead; Mr. [J. B.] Eversham, character comedian; Helen Blythe, leading woman; Ida Aubrey, ingenues; Sara Goldberg, heavies; Lena Morehouse, juveniles. Fred Lyster is musical director; [Converse L.] Graves, stage manager, and Signor Baptistin, balletmaster.[6]

The Temple itself was now rechristened the 23rd Street Theatre.

A Bustle Among the Petticoats premiered on Monday evening, May 21, 1883, to a good house and uniformly bad reviews. As had been made evident by *The Doctor of Lima*, *Petticoats* reinforced the fact that Morse's ambitions as a *littérateur* were not matched by any great talent. Lacking the opportunities for spectacle, the uplifting music and the advantageous notoriety of *The Passion*, *Petticoats* had to rely upon Salmi's Achilles' heel: the actual mechanics of playwriting; that is to say, plotting and dialogue.

The play was set in Brittany during the reign of Louis XIV, and "treats of the laws of those days." Salmi promised much color and excitement — including a carriage "drawn by four horses, which will come dashing on the stage at full speed."[7] But the truth was that lack of money and time forced him to cut corners. The scenery from *The Passion* was recycled and made to fill in for seventeenth-century France, and the rush to production left the disparate elements unintegrated. As for the plot of the play, at least as capsuled by the various reviewers, it is virtually impossible to reconstruct.[8]

Critics termed it a "Dramatic Nightmare," a "wretched concoction ... absolutely without a single discernible merit," and at least one critic — from the *Times* — did not even remain for the entire six acts. Even more discouraging, some reviewers used their critiques of *Petticoats* to continue scoring personal points against Salmi. "Mr. Morse," declared Harrison

Grey Fiske, "is a literary sham whom it were charitable to call an egotistical crank."[9]

For Salmi, it was the culminating personal catastrophe. Somehow he managed to keep the play running for two weeks, although, as usual, that meant shamelessly exploiting the good faith of the actors. The stagehands demanded their first week's pay, and Salmi was able to come up with that; the poor actors had to wait until the following Monday.[10] By the end of the second week, it was obvious that *A Bustle Among the Petticoats* could not survive, and Morse's squabbling partners finally joined forces and leased the 23rd Street Theatre out from under him. The producer Max Strakosch bought the lease for five years, grandly announcing that he would present operas, melodramas, extravaganzas, "everything." On behalf of the theatre, the lease was signed by G.T. Roberts and Albert J. Eaves. The name of Salmi Morse did not appear.

For some time, Salmi had been allowing a Baptist minister, the Reverend S. Thomas Williams, and the members of his Christ's Free Church to hold their Sabbath services in the Temple. On Sunday, May 27, Morse called the Reverend Williams to his upstairs room. "His face was sad," Williams later recalled, "and he said that he had bad news to communicate. He said that he had severed his connections with the house, and our church and the Temple would have to part. I felt more sorry for Salmi Morse than for the church, for it was a bitter blow to him."[11]

Ironically, the *Tribune*, in announcing this ignominious loss, granted to Salmi what he had never really had. The headline read: "Morse's Temple Leased by Strakosch."[12]

II

Within days of the closing of *A Bustle Among the Petticoats*, more lawsuits were instigated against Morse and his backers by Fred Lyster, Converse L. Graves, and the theatre's latest business manager, a man named Chipman. "Salmi, I hear, retires from the concern with depleted pockets," noted Fiske in the *Mirror*. And yet, even now, Salmi could not drop his charade: "To carry on the unfortunate enterprise," Fiske wrote, "he heavily mortgaged his extensive plantations in the island of San Domingo."[13]

Strakosch's season not opening until August, Albert Eaves announced that he would reopen the 23rd Street Theatre with an interim season of Gilbert and Sullivan operettas.[14]

During these same months, Booth's Theatre was finally abandoned and closed its doors forever. Its interior was gutted and the building was turned into a department store.

III

"I am either eighteen hundred years behind the age or eighteen hundred years in advance of it, I don't know which," a saddened Salmi told a reporter for the *New York Clipper*. "But I do know that I am not wanted here."[15] The *Petticoats* debacle had convinced him that the continued bad press was entirely personal, and wholly unmerited. His work, he felt, would never get a fair hearing in New York City, at least not so long as his own name was attached to it. And the reason for this persecution, he knew, was *The Passion*.

"That man never got over the failure of his Passion Play," an acquaintance would say. "Why, you wouldn't know him to be the same man now he was then. He used to come to me and wring his hands and say, 'My God, man, why did I fail? Why didn't they let me go on?'"[16]

He gave up his rooms above the Temple and moved back to Mrs. Gault's boardinghouse on 21st Street, to begin all over again. He was now fifty-seven years old, destitute once more, and the object of nationwide contempt. He struggled through the next few months, reportedly revising a manuscript he had written entitled "Jew and Jesus," which was intended "to show the Christians what the Hebrew is and the Hebrews what a Christian is." He still talked about securing a production of *The Passion* somewhere, even planning a trip to Europe, where he hoped to find a willing manager in London.[17] He also continued to present himself as a man of independent means, the usual story now being that he was living on a monthly pension from the British government for his services in the Crimean War.[18] But the sad truth was that he was surviving mainly on the occasional largess of stalwart friends, such as Frederick Schilling, the restaurateur who had posted his bond the night of his arrest, and who sometimes lent him money; his trusting landlady, Mrs. Isabella Gault; and John L. O'Sullivan, formerly the United States Minister to Portugal, a friend with whom Morse often discussed the failure of *The Passion*. According to O'Sullivan Morse was "quite frequently" depressed during this period and "he often said he wished God would take him from this life. I remember once ... having a talk with him about 'hari kari' [sic], the Japanese mode of committing suicide."[19] Many of his friends also recalled that, after he lost the Temple, Salmi's drinking began to increase.

What seemed to keep him going now was his attempt to further the career of his latest protégée, a young lady from California named Mary C. Blackburn. Advancing the pretty Miss Blackburn's theatrical fortunes became Salmi Morse's new obsession.

Actually, Mary had been in New York for some months, Morse having sent for her to appear in his final production of *The Passion*. She was also in the cast of *A Bustle Among the Petticoats*. Mary claimed that she had known Salmi since she was a child in California; that he had studied law in San Francisco with her father, the well-known "Judge Blackburn"; and that her father, on his deathbed, had entrusted her to Morse's care.[20]

"Mr. Morse was more like a father to me than a mere friend," Mary would say. "He was the best friend I had in the world since my father died.... He had only my interests at heart." Whatever their relationship, Salmi thought enough of the young lady to entrust to her his will, dated August 6, 1883, in which he left to her the one thing he valued most: all rights to *The Passion*.[21]

At any rate, the 25-year-old Mary was in New York now, and trusting that Salmi would do right by her. Accordingly, he set out to find a backer for *On the Yellowstone*, a "grand spectacular" new Western play of his which he had written for Miss Blackburn. By late in the fall, he had found Thomas J. McGivney, a burly liquor retailer from Harlem, of about Morse's age, whose willingness to capitalize on this romantic extravaganza was based on the fact that he was hopelessly smitten with the beautiful leading lady.[22]

With McGivney's money behind them, Salmi and Mary took a lease on the Cosmopolitan Theater at 41st and Broadway, intending to present *On the Yellowstone* in early February 1884. The Cosmopolitan, like Booth's, had recently been plagued by one managerial failure after another, the result being that the theatre had been closed since December 1, 1883. William Winter welcomed the opening of a new show there for, he wrote, the pretty little theater had too long seemed dead.[23]

Salmi and Mary agreed that the only way for this play to succeed was to keep the name Salmi Morse out of the affair entirely. "He was hated by everyone in the theatre," was the explanation Mary gave for this duplicity. Even the backer, McGivney, was not told that Morse was the author. The early announcements credited the work to "R. M. Daggett."[24] While Salmi was often noted by the press as being present—and being a pest—at every rehearsal, it was always given out that he was there only because of his paternal interest in Miss Blackburn's fortunes. Whenever asked, both he and Mary strenuously denied that Salmi had anything whatever to do with the production itself.[25]

Naturally, however, Salmi could not remain in the background for long as he watched his play being staged. All too soon there were clashes between Morse and the stage manager, William Fleming, over changes in the script, and Salmi's usual attempts to present himself as the wealthy backer of the play inevitably led to violent arguments with the true backer, Thomas McGivney. It fell upon Mary to try to keep things on course. "I found that [Salmi] had many enemies," Mary said, "and I was often obliged to stand between him and them."[26]

With tempers short and egos warring, *On the Yellowstone* lurched toward its premiere, originally scheduled for Monday, February 11, but postponed for several days "in consequence of the immensity of the preparation."[27]

On the Yellowstone was a Western melodrama based on the true-life experiences of Mrs. Fanny Kelly, who had been abducted by a tribe of Sioux Indians and made their "veritable QUEEN" (as the advertising had it); her husband, after a lengthy search, ultimately found and rescued her. It was exciting material, to be sure, considerably enhanced by its being true. Unfortunately, the periphrastic Morse could not leave well enough alone.

He "improved" the main story with a subplot involving a pretty young "female scout," Nancy Jane (the role he wrote for Miss Blackburn), who falls in love with the distraught Mr. Kelly (played by Randolph Murray). Following him around like an adoring puppy, Nancy Jane manages to save her hero from a number of dangers, including Indian attacks and a suicide attempt over the Yellowstone Falls. It is Nancy Jane who, in Morse's version, finally brings about the successful return of Kelly's missing wife (Miss Lida Talbot, actually the former musical-comedy star Pauline Markham acting under an assumed name[28]). There was much more to Morse's plot, as one reviewer would recite,

> such as soldiers, a horse, a fort, protean performances by Nancy Jane, who exchanges costumes with a deserter, some Sioux shooting of arrows, the final killing of Jumping Bear [the Indian who abducts and then falls in love with Mrs. Kelly], the restoration of the lost and a satisfactory settlement of things generally.[29]

A plot summary was provided in the program, but that didn't seem to help. In Morse's heavy hands, the resulting script was burdened with unbelievable characters and situations, hackneyed Victorian moralizing, and poorly structured scenes. The stage manager William Fleming later complained that "all the climaxes were in the middle of the acts. Morse would not allow me to change anything. He said, 'We do not want it to be a blood and thunder piece, Fleming,' but in the first [act] he had at once on the stage two dead negroes, thunder and lightning, Indian yells and musketry-firing, to say nothing of bringing on the bloody scalp of a child just before the act closed."[30] And finally, there was Morse's usual pseudo-Shakespearean dialogue — delivered even by some of the Indian characters. This play, said the *Herald*, "introduced a Western *patois* that is certainly novel in contemporaneous elocution."[31]

However, *On the Yellowstone*, as it was presented at the Cosmopolitan beginning February 13, 1884, did give its audience what had been strongest in *The Passion*: "Sensational Effects — Immense Mechanical Illusions!" Set in one of America's most breathtaking natural wonderlands, which had been established as a National Park in 1872, *On the Yellowstone* was, in the words of one critic, "strung to some scenery which out-Bierstadts the wildest of Bierstadt's wild Western scenes." The outdoor panoramas, he applauded, were "among the most striking ever shown in this theatre, or, it is safe to say, in any other theatre." Even the *Mirror* agreed, saying "The scenery was really beautiful. The [canyon] of the Yellowstone in the first act, and the rapids and falls in the third, were realistic as well as picturesque." (As William Fleming sardonically put it, "Mr. Morse was a great stickler for realism.") For the critics, however, scenic splendor was not enough to save the evening. "It is a pity," the *Mirror* continued, that "such fine scenic achievements should be wasted on such balderdash as the play itself." The *Times* was more succinct, if no less cruel: "This play — if it is a play — ," the reviewer concluded, "is one of scenery — not of acting."[32]

IV

It was one thing to be reviled because you were the infamous Salmi Morse. But this time, the reviewers were not supposed to have known they were reviewing a Morse play.[33]

The critical failure of *On the Yellowstone* signified for Salmi that, quite simply, he had finally run out of excuses. Already unsettled by the events of the past two years, he was driven to deeper despair by this latest failure to demonstrate his "genius," even anonymously. While Mary kept the play open by somehow appeasing McGivney, Morse turned more and more to the solace of the bottle, where his dreams of glory could be kept alive. William Fleming later described one rather mad afternoon when Morse read to him his latest play, *Gustaf Adolph*, an historical potboiler which Salmi declared was better than Shakespeare's *Henry V*. Its success was guaranteed, he told Fleming, because this play contained a sure-fire gimmick: a horse with a mane and tail that would sweep the ground. True, he had not yet found such a horse, and that, said Fleming, had made him "nearly crazy." But Salmi had a plan. "He finally told me that he had an idea which would make a great success of the piece," Fleming said. "We were to have a property mane and tail made and take in the public, who would flock in [the] thousands to see a horse with a mane that swept the ground."[34]

As Salmi searched the city for the horse that would bring him his fortune, *On the Yellowstone* entered its second week with the financial and emotional crises worsening. Undoubtedly, much of the problem between Thomas McGivney and Morse came because of Mary Blackburn. "[McGivney] hated Mr. Morse," Mary claimed, "and was continually worrying me about him. He was actually jealous of that old man."[35] At the same time, it seems equally clear that McGivney, because he so desired

11. The Aftermath: "Alas, Poor Yorick!"

Mary, was taken advantage of by both the lady and her mentor. McGivney was, after all, under the confused impression that she "acted as if she would consent to become [my] wife."³⁶ As McGivney's jealousy grew, so did the threat of his sabotaging the production, to which he had already committed over five thousand dollars.

Nor were Morse's old habits helping matters. "He took $475 I had given to Miss Blackburn to pay off the company," McGivney charged, "and he, representing himself as a moneyed man, wanted to pay out the money, to which I objected. We had some words."³⁷ According to Mary, these "words" had several times lately led to blows.³⁸

As the crisis came to a head, Mary called a meeting at the theatre for Friday morning, February 22, at ten o'clock. Not only was the overdue payroll to be met at that time, but she intended to bring all of the principals—Morse, McGivney, Fleming and herself—to some sort of an amicable truce.

V

The night before the meeting, Salmi walked Mary home from the theatre after the performance, as had become their custom. Morse was a frequent visitor at Mary's West 43rd Street flat, as was Mary in his rooms at Mrs. Gault's on 21st Street. This evening, they went for a late supper to Frederick Schilling's restaurant on Sixth Avenue. Although he had lately been despondent, this night Salmi seemed as amiable as ever, happy that attendance was beginning to climb, talking of his plans for his new play, *Gustaf Adolph*, and an upcoming religious lecture tour arranged by the Reverend Williams (the preacher who had once held services in the Temple).³⁹ They finished supper and finally reached Mary's apartment sometime between one and two a.m. on Friday morning.⁴⁰

What followed then was a scene straight out of *The Wages of Sin*. Not long after they had returned to Mary's flat, Thomas McGivney, who had evidently been following them, suddenly burst into the room. McGivney claimed he caught the pair in bed together; Mary said she was lying on the bed—suffering an attack of "neuralgia of the heart"—while Salmi was "bending over me." McGivney did not wait for an explanation, but immediately attacked Morse, striking him in the face and sending him sprawling over the sofa. "You old rascal," McGivney shouted, "you have ruined this woman!" Morse struggled to his feet, said Mary, "and putting his hand to his head said, 'Oh, and this,' while a strange look came into his eyes. Mr. Morse then left the room, followed by McGivney."

No one knows where Morse went that morning, or what he did during the next several hours. But McGivney, it would later be learned, behaved

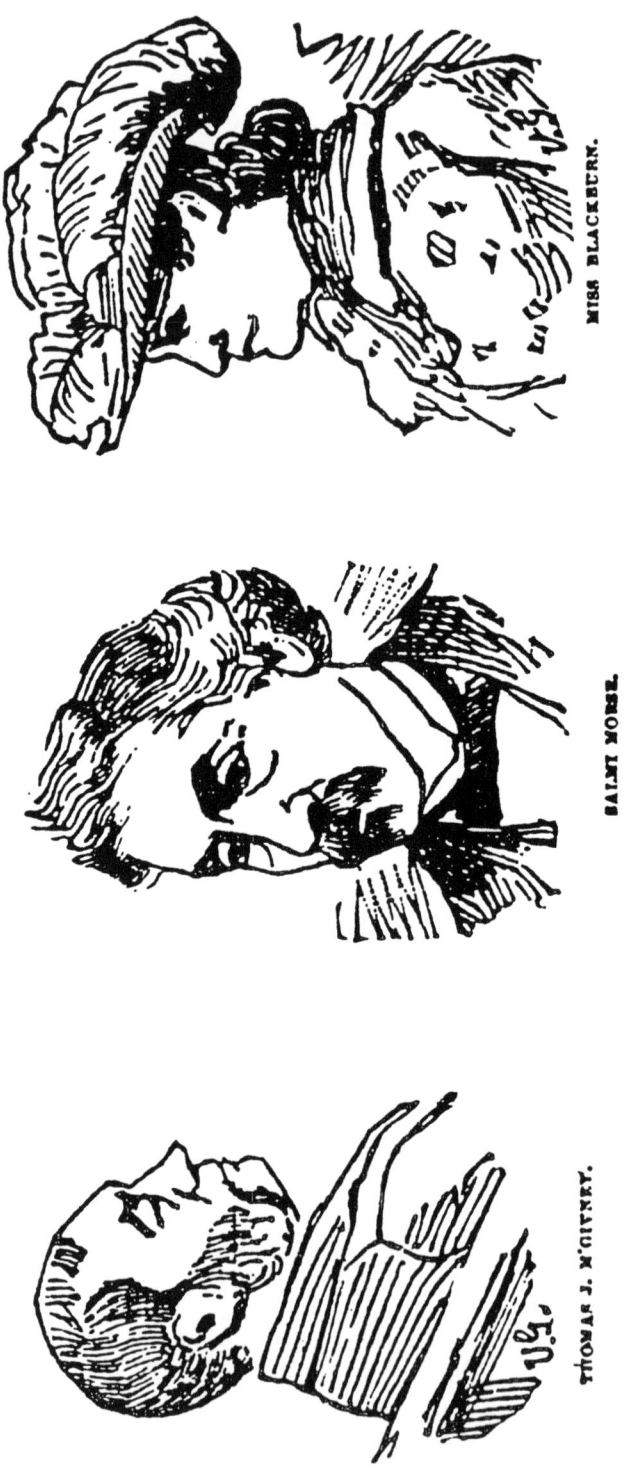

Thomas McGivney, Salmi Morse and Mary C. Blackburn, as sketched by the artist for the "New York World" during the inquest into Morse's mysterious death in 1884. Miss Blackburn, a young California actress whose career Morse had been trying to further, accused McGivney, the backer of Salmi's last play, of murdering Morse. Note that the sketch of Morse was taken from his formal portrait. ("New York World," February 29, 1884)

11. The Aftermath: "Alas, Poor Yorick!"

suspiciously indeed. He went to a hotel on Eighth Avenue and 51st Street, where for some mysterious reason he registered under the name "Thompson." He appeared "terribly nervous," said the desk clerk, and had a "wild, crazy look in his eye." After about fifteen minutes in his rented room, he returned to the lobby, where he asked for a glass of whiskey. McGivney told the clerk he was a detective and that he was "going out to look for a man." He left the hotel in great agitation, and did not return until almost sunrise. It is known that he showed up at Mary's rooms again, rapping at her window and wanting to talk. Mary said she sent him away.

The following morning, at ten o'clock, the meeting at the Cosmopolitan was to have begun, but Salmi had not showed up. After almost an hour of waiting, a frantic Mary sent a hurried message to him at his boardinghouse: "For God's sake come up at once. He is subdued." But Salmi was not there, either. In fact, Mrs. Gault said she had not seen her famous boarder for several days.

Friday, February 22, was George Washington's birthday, and a special holiday matinee performance of *On the Yellowstone* had been scheduled. So it was that Mary C. Blackburn was backstage at the Cosmopolitan Theatre when a small boy rushed in from the street with the terrible news that Salmi Morse had been found that morning, floating dead in the Hudson River. The body had been discovered by someone hunting driftwood near Riverside Park. "My God, not that!" was Mary's response. "Say that he's not that!" "Yes'm," the boy told her. "He's down at the Morgue, and all the police know about it."

"Miss Blackburn," say the news reports, "turned deadly pale and dropped to the floor without saying a word."

VI

"Salmi Morse's Life Ended!" "Salmi Morse Takes His Own Life!" "Suicide of Salmi Morse!" "Alas, Poor Yorick!" The news was reported from one end of the country to the other.[41] Journalists dredged up the highlights of his life, accurate and fictitious, and sought out those who had known him, for their reactions. In New York, virtually everyone connected with *On the Yellowstone* was questioned by the press, as were Salmi's sister, his friends and even his landlady. In San Francisco, Morse's estranged widow Harriet was tracked down by a *Chronicle* reporter, who found her running a small candy and stationery store. "I was expecting something of this sort," Harriet said bitterly, pointing to a table full of newspaper clippings, "and there are my documents. But what good will it do to show them? It is no satisfaction to me." She submitted to a lengthy interview all the same, dispassionately debunking every facet of Morse's colorful autobiography as represented by the many press clippings she had obviously saved over the years. "Oh," Harriet finally sighed, "I think he was crazy."[42]

No one received as much press attention as Mary Blackburn, especially once she began to speak of the events of early February 22. She was concerned about a "precious medallion" Salmi supposedly always wore, which had not been found on the body. Where was it?, she demanded. And then there were the bruises on his face—caused, the police said, by sharp rocks along the shore. Mary didn't believe that. "Everyone has been urging me to say nothing of what I know about this matter," she confided to a reporter, "and I hardly know what to do." Soon she was saying that she was convinced Morse had been murdered. "I shall believe it to my dying day. Why? Because he was sane as I am this minute." Accusations which had begun as vague innuendo—"The people connected with this theatre hated Morse"—soon took a more specific turn. "Have you seen Mr. McGivney?" she challenged a reporter for the *Tribune*. "Make him tell you where *he* saw Mr. Morse last. If he won't tell you, I will."[43]

Mary's emotional turmoil was not eased any by Salmi's funeral. His sister Charlotte had been given the body, and she hastily held a service at her home on 105th Street on Sunday, February 24, only two days after Salmi's death. To the outrage of Salmi's Christian friends, Charlotte, who was said to have been not particularly religious, arranged for an Orthodox Jewish service; the women were relegated to a back room while the few men present offered prayers over the unembalmed corpse in the front parlor. Morse's large body was stuffed—literally—into a small pine coffin, and, as a final affront, was buried in the Jewish cemetery at Bayside.[44] According to Jewish custom, neither Mary nor any of the other women were allowed to be present at the gravesite.

Mary found it all a "horrible scene." "I asked to be allowed to defray the expenses and give Morse a Christian burial," she complained, "for again and again he had told me that he would never be buried in the Jewish faith and with their rites. This was refused me." She went to his rooms on 21st Street, but Mrs. Gault would not let her in, on orders from Charlotte. "His relatives have locked up his effects and refused me admission to the house." As if that weren't enough, "I cannot tell you how I have suffered from the cruel slanders of the city press."[45]

Mary determined to pursue the truth of Salmi's death, both for his sake and for hers. "This matter does not end here," she promised. At her insistence, and with the influential aid of John O'Sullivan, a coroner's inquest was called, the first session of which convened on Wednesday, February 27. The long-familiar saga of Morse's life and now the intriguing questions surrounding his death brought curious crowds thronging to the courtroom each day of the inquest, and every detail was served up in the daily papers. It was, in a perverse way, Salmi's last, and most successful show.

11. The Aftermath: "Alas, Poor Yorick!"

Mary made her charges in court — and, as a result, in the pages of every city newspaper. Salmi's friends, too, had their say about the matter. "Morse did not commit suicide," O'Sullivan swore. "I know it. He had gone through thousands of worse troubles than his last one. The bruise on his cheek and one on his nose and head were made by some blunt instrument wielded with great force."[46] As the inquest progressed, even some newspapers — most notably the *World*, which had recently come under the ownership of Joseph Pulitzer and which, of all the dailies, took the greatest pleasure in serving up the more sordid aspects of the story — came to agree.[47]

In the end, the coroner's jury ruled that Salmi Morse did not intentionally take his own life; on the other hand, there was insufficient evidence to declare that he was murdered. Therefore, the official conclusion was that his death had been "accidental." "Perhaps this is all the evidence justified," concluded the editor of the *Tribune*,

> but none the less is the case a peculiar one, and it is plain that much remains to be cleared up, though there is little probability that it will be.... [There] are some unexplained mysterious circumstances which even tend to cast doubt upon the theory of accident. But the facts before the coroner's jury were too confused and indeterminate for them to reach any positive conclusion, and in expressing the opinion that Morse did not mean to commit suicide they have probably done all that was possible under the circumstances.[48]

"SALMI MORSE's life was a mystery," Pulitzer intoned in the *World*. "His plays were deeply mysterious. It is not strange that his life should have gone out in mystery."[49]

VII

The discovery of Salmi Morse's body brought him his last notoriety, as well as a wave of bathetic near-affection. Most editorial commemorations were notably forgiving, now that he was gone. "He was a strange, undisciplined mixture of the philosopher, the adventurer and the charlatan," said one editor, while another lamented the "tragi-comedy of his life." None of them apologized for their role in the suppression of *The Passion*, nor wished to reconsider the controversy in any new light. As one editor dismissed it:

> He probably passed out of life firm in the conviction that he was a great dramatist, cheated by stupid conservatism of all opportunity to show his ability.... The trouble with poor SALMI was that he was born a century too soon. A hundred years from now he would probably have been allowed to make a dismal failure without any opposition.[50]

That was all the issue represented to most of them now, a case of an untalented crackpot wishing to make a fool of himself. The religious furor he had created was forgotten.

At the same time, some editors felt compelled to deny any possible complicity of their own in Morse's professional problems. "The ministers and the newspapers never let up on Salmi," one of his friends had been saying. "They had a right to criticize the 'Passion Play,' but they had no right to blacken his character the way they tried to do."[51] Nonsense!, retorted the *San Francisco Chronicle.* "We do not think the robust conceit of the dead dramatist could be hurt by the most vitriolic criticism. What wore him out was the flat failure of everything which he touched.... All enthusiasts, all men of genius, come dangerously near the borderline of lunacy; the trouble with Morse was that he fell on the other side."[52] And Harrison Grey Fiske, recalling Salmi as "a singular crank," once again defended his anti-*Passion* crusade as a necessary, even a noble act:

> Poor Morse was *The Mirror*'s bitter opponent a few years ago, when Abbey backed his Passion Play. I must say that he fought pluckily, and it required the expenditure of a good deal of energy to defeat his project. But I knew *The Mirror* was right and that the desecration of the theatre by the production of a play which was held to be downright blasphemy by great numbers of people must be prevented at all hazards. It was not the Church but the Stage that would have sustained injury had The Passion been represented by actors at Booth's, as planned. In squelching the attempt this paper was not inspired by ill-feeling toward Morse, but by a determination to protect the profession from odium. I must say this for Morse, that throughout the controversy which ended so disastrously for his hopes he was a fair and courteous adversary.[53]

Fiske's protestations aside, the theatrical community did not seem to feel that Morse was one of their number; his passing left few of them moved, much less relieved that the threat he supposedly represented was now gone. There were no public memorials from fellow managers, no eulogies from saddened fans. In fact, one report noted that the news of his death had caused little excitement around Union Square. "This was because Mr. Morse in his lifetime did not associate with theatrical people," the writer theorized. "He was a student and writer rather than an active worker in the ranks of his profession, and few on the square knew him personally."[54]

In life, he had tried to amalgamate the Christian church and the professional stage. In death, he was claimed by neither.

One colleague who did remember him, though, was James O'Neill, interviewed in San Francisco where his *Monte Cristo* company was playing to excellent houses. Asked if he thought that Salmi Morse had committed suicide, the rising new star emphatically answered,

I do not. My theory of his death is, that, brooding over his misfortunes he sought to forget care and took a glass or two too much; after which, wandering in the vicinity of the river—a favorite walk of his—he lost his balance, fell in, and was unable to recover himself. So he drowned.

"Poor old Salmi!" said the former Jesus Christ of America's first professional Passion play. "He was not bad at heart at all; but he would spin such yarns and tell such whoppers! ... Poor, deluded old gentleman! I hope he's in Heaven!"[55]

12

The Resurrection and Redemption of *The Passion*

I

"History," Rodney A. Smolla has recently written, "reveals that, as often as not, the great First Amendment battles have been fought by our cultural rejects and misfits."[1] This description might certainly apply to Salmi Morse. Morse was not a great dramatist nor a theatrical visionary nor even a particularly good writer. He was a cultural outcast who fought a fruitless battle against a moralistic society whose most cherished institutions he had unintentionally offended. But over the course of that bitter warfare, Salmi Morse tried desperately to extend to the American theatre what society and its legal system had not yet countenanced: the idea that the stage, and especially the playwright, might be protected from the censorship of the majority by virtue of the United States Constitution's free-speech guarantees.

Today this concept is still of vital importance. As Irwin Karp, the Counsel for the Dramatists Guild, has written, "Dramatists, actors, directors, producers and even theatre owners depend on the [First] Amendment for their indispensable freedoms to create and communicate."[2] As much as playwrights and other artists would like to think such a concept is obvious, it is not. But it is essential to understanding Salmi Morse's story.

Was Morse the first to argue this crucial drama-speech connection? Such an assertion would be impossible to prove. But it can be posited that he was the first to project such a claim into the arena of national debate. Prior to 1879, no state or federal court had ever been petitioned to consider the question, and no precedential decisions would indicate that courts were willing to extend *any* Bill of Rights protections to the arts. Indeed, just the opposite was true. Many early judicial opinions upheld as constitutional state laws that actually limited, in one way or another, the perimeters of free speech and free press in America.[3] The religious opposition to *The*

12. The Resurrection and Redemption of The Passion

Passion aside, the fundamental legal and constitutional setbacks suffered in the case illustrate the long road that First Amendment law has had to march in the last one hundred years to become such an important tenet of American jurisprudence.

More important, however, the story of *The Passion* should also warn us how easily First Amendment protection for the arts can be abridged, especially by those who profess to work in the name of public morality. The outraged Americans who have recently rallied around Senator Jesse Helms's amendment to curtail government monies supporting "immoral art" clearly illustrate how volatile this subject remains one hundred years later, and how manipulative such emotional terms as "immoral" and "sacrilegious" still can be.

II

Victorian Americans believed that the First Amendment, indeed, any constitutional freedom, could be limited. What was best for society was best for everyone; the practice of democracy had, as John Morley put it, come to mean "government by public opinion."[4] The *New York Times* was expressing the general sentiment when it characterized Morse's "idea of freedom" as that of an "anarchist."[5] Certainly, most Victorian playwrights, managers and critics would have agreed with William Winter, that the drama must be a "repository of noble thought, romantic imagery, and pure influence." The moral censorship practiced in the nineteenth century, in plays as in novels, was primarily self-imposed; as a result, as Peter Gay has noted, the actual boundaries between the "permissible and the impermissible" were for most artists "uncertain and remained little explored."[6]

Thus Morse's claim to constitutional protections for a play deemed shocking had neither legal precedent nor popular support. His was predestined to be a losing battle. And, to be sure, there was a certain amount of bravado in his First Amendment defense. It must be remembered that, for all he talked about it, wrote about and believed in it, Salmi and his lawyers never actually argued the point in a court of law.[7]

Not until the twentieth century, in fact, has the Supreme Court wrestled with the difficult issues that Salmi Morse was trying to raise in 1879.

The modern judicial attitude toward the First Amendment can be traced back only to around the First World War. Beginning with the minority dissenting opinions of Justices Oliver Wendell Holmes and Louis Brandeis, the movement toward constitutional protection for speech that offends has only gradually become the accepted reading of the First Amendment. Much like those few individuals in 1879 who felt that *The Passion* was best dispensed with not by a law but by a public that refused to patronize it, Justice Holmes argued that "the ultimate good desired is better reached by a free trade in ideas — that *the best test of truth is the power of the thought to get itself accepted in the competition of the market*"[8][emphasis added].

It was during the Second World War, however, that the majority of the Court began to agree with Holmes's viewpoint. A 1943 Supreme Court decision declared the new primacy of free speech in ringing terms: "If there is any fixed star in our constitutional constellation, it is that no official, high or petty, can prescribe what shall be orthodox in politics, nationalism, religion, or other matters of opinion."[9] Holmes's "marketplace" was clearly to be an open one. Six years later, the Supreme Court further extended its proscriptions to include not only the civil authorities but the general public as well, saying that not even a mob has a right to inhibit free speech by means of a "heckler's veto" (this, in a broad sense, is what happened to *The Passion*). In the words of Justice William O. Douglas:

> A function of free speech under our system of government is to invite dispute. It may indeed best serve its high purpose when it induces a condition of unrest, creates dissatisfaction with conditions as they are, or even stirs people to anger. Speech is often provocative and challenging. It may strike at prejudices and preconceptions and have profound unsettling effects as it presses for acceptance of an idea. That is why freedom of speech ... is nevertheless protected against censorship or punishment, unless shown likely to produce a clear and present danger of a serious substantive evil that rises far above public inconvenience, annoyance, or unrest.[10]

The Passion was most certainly a "public inconvenience," an "annoyance" and a source of "unrest." But a "serious substantive evil" to the body politic it was not.

Even though these decisions had buttressed the legal standing of unpopular public and published speech, their protections did not necessarily extend to playwriting or other dramatic forms. In fact, a 1916 ruling, *Mutual Film Corp. v. Industrial Com. of Ohio*, had specifically declared motion pictures to be only a business and thus beyond the protection of the Constitution, and throughout the 1920s state and local governments had freely regulated theatrical and motion picture offerings by means of restrictive legislation.[11] It was not until 1952, in *Burstyn v. Wilson*, which involved the suppression in New York City of Roberto Rossellini's film *The Miracle* (1948), that the U.S. Supreme Court finally held that the basic principles of free speech and free press did indeed apply to motion pictures, just as they applied to books, newspapers, magazines and "other media of communication of ideas." In fact, *Burstyn* specifically overturned the earlier *Mutual Film Corp.* ruling.[12]

Moreover, Rossellini's film had been suppressed for the same reason as *The Passion*: church groups (in this case it was the Catholics who were offended and now had the requisite political clout) had declared it "sacrilegious" and "blasphemous," and, supported by the state, thus had it removed from public viewing. In his majority opinion overturning the state's suppression of the film, Justice Clark addressed at great length the issue of government censorship of the arts on behalf of religion, concluding that

> from the standpoint of freedom of speech and the press, it is enough to point out that the state has no legitimate interest in protecting any or all religions from views distasteful to them which is sufficient to justify prior restraints upon the expression of those views. It is not the business of government in our nation to suppress real or imagined attacks upon a particular religious doctrine, whether they appear in publications, speeches, or motion pictures.[13]

This Jeffersonian-influenced statement finally officially placed the writings of the screenwriter and the dramatist in the same constitutionally protected category as those of the journalist and the politician.

III

Did Morse's argument on behalf of *The Passion* have any effect at the time? Immediately very little; yet, as in any radical action, the seeds for change were planted. The fact that nationally distributed newspapers like the *Herald*, *Tribune* and *Evening Express* had come to see Morse's point — or, at least, were made uncomfortable by the inappropriate interference of the state — represented an important beginning. In California, in fact, the controversy may even have been responsible for more positive results. In 1896 — twelve years after Salmi Morse's death — a Superior Court judge in San Francisco attempted to suppress a new play because it was based on a murder case still being tried; the California State Supreme Court ruled the judge could not restrain the production, *as the play was protected by the state consitution's guarantee of freedom of speech*. "The production of a tragedy or comedy upon the theatrical stage is a publication to the world by word of mouth of the text of the author," the Court declared, and "it is immaterial whether the words be publicly spoken from the stage or upon the hustings, or go out to the world through the channels of the printing-press."[14]

This is the first instance found of any state court's ruling that a play is, in fact, a form of speech.[15] It was, to be sure, an anomaly. But while the attitude expressed in this California decision would not find wider credence in America for another half century, it nonetheless indicates that some local justices were open to expanding the limits of protected speech. At the very least, for future playwrights, favorable judicial precedents were finally being set.

This 1896 decision also reflects a change in attitude on the part of American society itself, at least where theatrical content was concerned. The increasing embracement of the drama as a forum for ideas came at the same time as the rise of our modern mass culture, the end result of urbanization. The subsequent "social rearrangements," as Benjamin MacArthur phrases it, further tolled the declining influence of both the clergy and fashionable society in dictating societal standards and attitudes for everyone.[16]

In the theatre, one important indication of this shift in moral outlook could be seen in the more daring subject matter beginning to be explored by some playwrights and producers, a phenomenon ushered in by the dramas of Henrik Ibsen. Championed in America by such leading performers as Minnie Maddern Fiske and Richard Mansfield—and vehemently opposed by some of our leading Victorian critics, especially William Winter and John Ranken Towse—the "Ibsenite movement" had begun to take hold in earnest by the turn of the century.

In less than two decades after *The Passion* had outraged the nation, the public's perception of what was permissible on the stage had been altered dramatically. But more importantly, Ibsen's new ideas of "realism" helped free native dramatists from the strictures of the old codes of moral self-censorship. In fact, one of the first American playwrights to be thus liberated was the man who had introduced Salmi Morse to the San Francisco theatre in 1877—James A. Herne.[17]

In this new atmosphere of theatrical freedom, even religious subjects and New Testament stories were more widely accepted, perhaps as a counterbalance to the new permissiveness of modern social drama. Although it would still be some time before Jesus Christ could be portrayed by an actor onstage, religious themes by the 1890s had become "regularly central" to many melodramas.[18] Henry Irving brought *Beckett* to American audiences in 1893; and seven years later both *Ben Hur* and *Quo Vadis* (in three separate versions) thrilled New Yorkers with their Christian pieties and spectacular New Testament locales.[19] Needless to say, not one of these plays, nor their many progeny, provoked the kind of religious protest that had hounded Morse's *Passion*. As George Rowell writes, church and chapel leaders increasingly pointed to these religious melodramas "as evidence of the theatre's growing responsibility."[20]

None of these biblical epics better demonstrates the depth of the change in attitude toward religious plays—especially relative to the New Testament Passion story—than *Mary of Magdala* (1902).[21] Based on a

German drama by Paul Heyse, the play centered on the events of the Crucifixion. While again the figure of Christ was never seen onstage, His Disciples were—most notably Judas (played by Tyrone Power)—and all of the sacred events of what "Betsy B." had once called "our Holy of Holies" were retold from the stage of a secular theatre. There was a familiar ring to the preparations: the director reportedly walked around with a Bible under his arm; scenic designers attempted to reconstruct ancient Jerusalem; and a London costume designer combed the museums of Europe in search of fabrics and colors that might match those worn in the time of Christ. Everything was to be reproduced in accurate historical detail. Finally, advance copies of the play were given to the New York clergy, all of whom were invited to a private dress rehearsal.

This time, though, the reactions were drastically different from those that had greeted *The Passion*. The New York clergy, the critics and the public were virtually unanimous in their praise. Typical was the Reverend Percy Stickney Grant, the Rector of the Church of the Ascension, who wrote that he was "astonished" to see that the stage was "capable of teaching Christianity in a way that no other art, not even the pulpit, could rival." The Reverend Grant bravely admitted that this production of the Passion story in a theatre was "a great moral force and vivid picture of those truths that sermons so often vaguely strive to present."[22]

Mary of Magdala enjoyed a lengthy run in New York City, then became a part of the company's permanent repertoire and was presented in cities all across America to similarly approving crowds.

What gives this story particular poignancy are the unexpectedly familiar names associated with it. The nominal star of the company and the actress who played the title role was Minnie Maddern Fiske, but the play had been undertaken at the insistence of, and was directed by, her husband, the now 42-year-old owner/editor of the *New York Dramatic Mirror*, Harrison Grey Fiske. And to whom did Harrison Fiske turn to write his English translation of this German Passion story? To none other than his close friend, the aged critic-poet-icon of the *New York Tribune*, William Winter. (Winter, perhaps sensing the irony, agreed to the project only if his participation was never made public.) One other old name also crops up, among the cast. Playing the minor role of "Rachel" was yet another of Morse's former nemeses, Miss Rose Eytinge.[23]

IV

As for Passion plays themselves, the religious objections to that ancient genre were also gradually lessened. In 1900, an American producer tried to offer the principal performers of that year's Oberammergau pageant five thousand dollars apiece to take part in a Passion play in New York City, confident that no moral backlash would result.[24] At about that same time, the Reverend Percy S. Grant—who would so praise the Fiske-Winter *Magdala*—was asking rhetorically in an issue of *The Theatre* magazine why the modern Christian should condemn the dramatic representation of the Passion story. Dismissing practically every ministerial objection to such a presentation, the Reverend Grant answered his own question with a strong endorsement for the power of the theatre to spread the Word:

> I should like to see a Passion Play on the American stage, under proper conditions. I do not believe it would cheapen the Christian religion. Christian people must not shut their eyes to anything which tends to give greater reality to the story of Christ through fear that it will shake their faith.[25]

Nowhere in the good Reverend's essay, however, was there any acknowledgment of Morse's *Passion* and its controversial suppression twenty years before.

By 1902, a more specific Passion drama was again being seen in America, and, fittingly, its starting point was again California. The fathers of the Jesuit College in Santa Clara presented a Passion-centered play by Clay M. Greene, entitled *Nazareth*, which was later that year presented at the Garrick Theatre in New York by members of the Lambs' Club. In Greene's play, as in *Mary of Magdala* and the other New Testament plays, the pivotal character of Christ was still absent from the stage, although here His holy presence was symbolically suggested: "a light prefigured Him."[26]

Finally, seven years later, the Franciscan fathers in San Francisco presented at St. Boniface's Church a more traditional Passion play, complete with Christ and Crucifixion, written and directed by Father Josaphat Kraus. The *Overland Monthly* ecstatically gushed over the "novel" experience of seeing an authentic Passion play, pronouncing it "the drama divorced from the theatre." The writer further averred that a Passion play must surely have a wholly moral effect on any viewer "with an alert mind and an open heart."[27]

It was Father Josaphat's plan, modeled after Oberammergau, to revive his Passion pageant every ten years. He was, it turned out, on the cutting edge of a trend. In the decades since, Oberammergau has been the inspiration for any number of Passion plays seen in this country, in sites as diverse as Hollywood, California; San Antonio, Texas; Bronxville, New York; Columbus, Ohio; Union City, New Jersey; Lake Wales, Florida; and Strasbourg, Virginia. As a final harbinger of the embracement of entertainment by religion, the two most famous modern-day Passion stagings in America have been offered not as acts of faith but as patent tourist attractions: the

Black Hills Passion Play in Spearfish, South Dakota; and the "Great Passion Play" of the Ozarks, in Eureka Springs, Arkansas.[28] And proving that some modern religions have in fact become theatre, one can point to the regularly scheduled Passion Play performances given daily at Jim and Tammy Bakker's fundamentalist Christian Disneyland, "Heritage Village, U.S.A."

V

There remains one final point to be made concerning the governmental, religious and societal changes that occurred in the waning years of the Victorian era, and how they might possibly have affected Salmi Morse, had he lived: No matter how much society's attitude toward religious drama had softened in the years following his death in 1884, *it made no difference in how Morse's pioneering Passion was perceived.*

In 1889, James O'Neill, using profits he had earned from *Monte Cristo*, announced that he would play Christ in a revival of *The Passion* at Omaha, Nebraska. No sooner had he applied to the city for a permit, however, than the Episcopalian Church and the Y.M.C.A. rose up in opposition and the plan had to be abandoned. Twice more O'Neill tried to get the play produced, in 1891 and again in 1896, and both times *The Passion* brought forth the wrath of America's moralists, who refused to accept it as anything but the sacrilege it had been declared in 1879.[29] *The Passion*, then, could never have benfited from the rise in permissiveness; *it* was never to be forgiven. *The Sign of the Cross, Herod, Quo Vadis* and *Ben Hur* might now be allowed to address the events surrounding the Crucifixion, but never the Great Victorian Sacrilege that was the San Francisco Passion play by Salmi Morse.

Further proof of this contention can be found in the fact that *The Passion* was, in a way, resurrected in 1898, and to unqualified praise — only no one at the time knew that it was Morse's hated pageant they were seeing. This remarkable footnote to the story of *The Passion* was just the sort of redemption for which Salmi had always hoped, and it is, therefore, the most appropriate ending to his improbable saga.

The story is told by the film historian Terry Ramsaye in his landmark chronicle of the beginnings of the cinema, *A Million and One Nights* (1926).[30] It began in 1897 — only one year after O'Neill's last futile attempt to stage *The Passion*, and less than two years after motion pictures had first been projected onto a screen. In those twenty-odd months since the projection of "flickers" had begun, public demand for the new Living Pictures had spawned an instant industry; the pioneers fought viciously over patents while grinding out crude one-reel filmic records of almost anything that moved—waterfalls, locomotives, boxing matches, Presidents and vaudeville acts. No one had as yet filmed a basic story, much less created an entirely new story specifically for the camera; the specially staged fictional narrative film would not come along in America until the advent of Edwin S. Porter, after the turn of the century.[31]

Among the early establishments showcasing this new form of show business was a rather odd museum of wax figures, lantern slides and miscellanea, called the Eden Musée, located in New York on 23rd Street near Sixth Avenue—not far from Morse's former Temple of the Passion, in fact. Its proprietor was Rich G. Hollaman. In 1897 Hollaman was approached to invest in the filming of an annual Passion play enacted at Horitz, Austria. Somehow, Hollaman was later cut out of the deal in favor of the prominent theatrical managers Marc Klaw (1858–1936) and Abe Erlanger (1860–1930). The Klaw/Erlanger-financed expedition sailed for Europe that fall of 1897 and quickly returned with a film of the Horitz performance captured by the crude black box. This had its premiere in Philadephia later that same year.

The rebuffed Hollaman traveled to Philadelphia to see what his rivals had wrought, and was perversely pleased to note that the quality of the pictures was poor. Accompanying him that night was Frank Russell, a New York actor "of some note." As fate would have it, both Hollaman and Russell were acquaintances of that prominent New York costumer and former investor in the 23rd Street Temple, Albert G. Eaves.

What followed was inevitable.

Albert Eaves still had the costumes and the script from the last ill-fated mounting of *The Passion*. Rich G. Hollaman had the capital and the burning desire to quickly outdo Klaw and Erlanger. And Frank Russell wanted to try his hand at becoming the next James O'Neill.

They all came together on the roof of the Grand Central Palace, on Lexington Avenue and 43rd Street, which Hollaman secretly leased for use as a sky-light studio. "The agent for the structure," Terry Ramsay relates, "was annoyed later when he found the freight elevator laden with camels going aloft to the new Holy Land on the roof."[32] The cast included Russell as Jesus Christ, Frank Gaylor as Judas Iscariot and Fred Strong as Pontius Pilate. L. J. (Leon John) Vincent, who had for years been the stage director for Niblo's Garden Theatre, was hired to direct.[33]

In the blustery winds of the New York winter, with the actors wearing woolen underwear beneath their Judean robes, secret filming of Morse's *Passion* was completed on the snowy rooftop of the Grand Central, December 1897–January 1898.

Deliberately advertised as the Oberammergau Passion play and not Salmi Morse's still-outlawed drama, the newly filmed version of *The Passion* opened at the Eden Musée on January 30, 1898. "I knew I had them,"

Hollaman reportedly commented, "when I saw the tears in the eyes of those Broadway sports."

"The tableaux, in their entirety, bring the Saviour's mission on earth, and his sufferings, more vividly before the spectator than any portrait by tongue or pen could possibly do," raved the *Mail and Express*. "These pieces have their own excellencies," intoned the *Tribune*, "and they are quite capable of standing on their own ... and should be allowed to do so." The *Times*, *Herald*, and *Evening Express* also praised the presentation, finding in it no burlesque, no mimicry, no sacrilege and no blasphemy. The common man's reaction was every bit as laudatory. "After the exhibition was over," claimed a New York lawyer, "I left feeling like living a better life, becoming a better man, trying to follow the teachings of the One whom I now know as I never knew before."[34] Not even the startlingly realistic Crucifixion scene raised the least moralistic ire, although the film's acceptance prompted the *Times* to reflect that, were Salmi Morse still alive, he might be prompted to try staging his own version of *The Passion* again. "Two or three times since [his death] the scheme has been discussed, but without result. Now the 'Passion Play' is on exhibition here in a modified form, and no one has expressed amazement or anger."[35]

Such widespread approval—of a play which James O'Neill *only a year before* could still not get produced—might have been vindication enough, but even more significant is the fact that, when Hollaman and Eaves began selling copies of the film (for $580 apiece), it was bought by showmen and churchmen alike. One prominent Protestant evangelist, Colonel Henry H. Hadley, immediately incorporated the film into his touring revival meetings. Hadley, if anything, was himself converted. "These pictures," he fervently predicted, "are going to be a great force." The scenes of the Passion play were, he proclaimed, "the best teachers and the best preachers in the history of the world."[36] Unbeknown to Hadley, his highly successful tours with this film over the next several years had the ironic distinction of further disseminating Salmi Morse's "blasphemous" work throughout the entire country.

"Many prints of the picture were sold when Hollaman released it to the open market," Terry Ramsaye notes. "Copies went abroad and covered the world of the motion picture. The success of the Hollaman-Eaves production resulted in many similar attempts."

Beyond the fact that this crude film had resurrected and redeemed Morse's *Passion*, however, it had an even more important distinction. Spawned as it had been by necessity, this hasty production was, says Ramsaye, an unintentional and completely unheralded milestone in the history of motion pictures: "the first construction of a dramatic event especially for the camera," the screen's "first step toward conscious art." Salmi Morse's self-proclaimed masterwork for the stage had now become "the first motion picture scenario."[37]

Some modern film historians are beginning to accept Ramsaye's claim. Tom Stempel, in *Framework: A History of Screenwriting in the American Film* (1988), repeats Ramsaye's story, and historian Edward Azlant goes so far as to suggest that the current Writer's Guild "could do worse than mark the spot where Salmi Morse threw himself into New York's North River."[38] While it is no doubt overstating the case to credit Morse himself as the first "screenwriter," this landmark film of *The Passion* must surely be acknowledged as the first narrative staged specifically for the camera (i.e., not a filmic record of a production that already existed).[39]

It was *The Passion's* last, greatest — and totally anonymous — hurrah.[40]

VI

The story of America's first professional Passion play is part farce, part tragedy, and, in the end, part cautionary morality tale. For the question with which the modern reader is left is obvious: could it ever happen today?

Anyone remotely familiar with the history of the American theatre in the twentieth century knows that the effort by concerned citizens to regulate the stage has never died.[41] Indeed, the theatre is not the only medium to feel the wrath of the church. Novels, motion pictures and videocassettes, television, radio, the recording industry, the fine arts — all have offended, at one time or another, someone's religious or moral sensitivities. The most recent examples of attempted religiously motivated censorship of the performing arts have involved nationwide protests mounted against a comic one-act play and a major Hollywood film.

In 1982, the national Catholic League for Religious and Civil Rights attempted to have Christopher Durang's 1980 satirical one-act *Sister Mary Ignatius Explains It All for You* banned in St. Louis, Boston, Detroit and other American cities. In Missouri, the Chairman of the Senate Appropriations Committee, a Catholic, actually threatened the funding of the Missouri Arts Council unless it agreed not to award any more grants to the acting company that had staged the play.[42]

In 1988, a nationwide protest organized mainly by conservative Protestant Christian groups called for the suppression of Martin Scorsese's film

Opposite: A scene from the silent film version of "The Passion" (1898). This landmark film, made secretly on a hotel rooftop in New York City, was advertised as the Oberammergau Passion play so as to avoid the controversy that surrounded Morse's pageant, which was still being banned in cities across America. This scene, Christ's entrance into Jerusalem, was not in the original San Francisco production, but was added to the play in New York. Frank Russell portrays Christ. (Courtesy The International Museum of Photography at George Eastman House, Film Stills Collection)

12. The Resurrection and Redemption of The Passion

The Last Temptation of Christ. "It cannot be released," cried one evangelical minister, who said he was not worried about "solid Christians ... who know the truth," but about the "millions of impressionistic [sic] people" who might flock to see the film merely out of curiosity.[43] Carefully staged picket lines and protests greeted the film in virtually every city in America in which it was shown. And when the film was broadcast by a premium pay-cable television service in 1989, some local cable companies, bowing to local pressure groups, blacked it out.

These were tempests that Salmi Morse could have appreciated.

Indeed, the recent resurgence of moral conservatism in the United States, which has been the cause of much comment, seems to carry the echoes of a Victorian society fighting desperately against the forces of change that would inevitably bring its influence to an end. And, like our Victorian forebears, there are many today who would willingly use the power of the state to protect the sanctity of their moral beliefs. Likewise, there are those, like the playwright Christopher Durang, smarting from his own brush with attempted censorship, who feel that, "As our country turns more and more conservative, authors should know that free speech is not something the religious right holds especially sacred. And that we *could* lose it."[44] As the pendulum makes its inevitable swing, academics and Supreme Court nominees attempt to debate the "original intent" of the Constitution's framers, and question whether we may have come too far. Allan Bloom's best-selling indictment of the American educational system, *The Closing of the American Mind* (1987), argues that public discourse, i.e., free speech, *should* be "regulated" in order to "elevate" it. Professor Bloom has this to say about the framers of the First Amendment:

> Freedom of thought and freedom of speech were proposed in theory, and in the practice of serious political reformers, in order to encourage the still voice of reason in a world that had always been dominated by fanaticisms and interests. How freedom of thought and speech came to mean the special encouragement and protection of fanaticism and interests is another of those miracles connected with the decay of the ideal of the rational political order.... They [i.e., the Constitution's framers] were not particularly concerned with protecting eccentric or mad opinions or life-styles. Such protection, which we now often regard as the Founders' central intention, is only an incidental result of the protection of reason, and it loses plausibility if reason is rejected....

Opposite: "The Crucifixion." By far the scene in the stage production that most offended moralists, this filmed version caused no outrage at all but instead was praised as climaxing a truly reverent, religious experience. Ironically, by using Morse's script and staging a new, complete production specifically for the camera, the filmmakers turned Salmi Morse's despised play into the first written "screenplay" in American film history. (Courtesy The International Museum of Photography at George Eastman House, Film Stills Collection)

> The moment of the Enlightenment's success seems to have been the beginning of its decay.⁴⁵

Obviously, Bloom would not have agreed with Salmi Morse's "eccentric" free-speech claims, either. In fact, as America now faces the very real possibility of a predominantly conservative Supreme Court sitting well into the twenty-first century, it is not beside the point to note that many of the critical First Amendment cases of the last fifteen years have been decided by five-to-four votes.⁴⁶

The struggle over free speech seems to strike at the very basis of democracy in a pluralistic, ever-changing society. Does "freedom of speech" have to mean free speech for absolutely everybody?

While one can sympathize with those outraged citizens who protest unrestricted speech, especially in the arts, we have also recently seen a very real example of what absurd and terrible consequences can result when religious outrage is conjoined to the full power of the law: the death sentence imposed on the British novelist Salman Rushdie by Iran's late religious leader, the Ayatollah Khomeini. Not that Salmi Morse's plight was as potentially lethal as Rushdie's, of course. There is a big difference between praying for God to strike down an offending writer, and ordering one's followers to do the job on His behalf! Still, as insane and outlandish as this death sentence may seem in the twentieth century, the fact remains that, as of this writing, Rushdie is still in hiding in fear of his life.⁴⁷ And, as difficult as it may be to admit, the point must be made that the recent efforts in America to restrict artistic expression by law are, at heart, born of the same motivation as Khomeini's mad act — an attempt to kill off ideas that offend. For all too often such attempts are arbitrary attacks on other, broader targets. Just as *The Passion* was suppressed in part not because it was actually sacrilegious but because it was perceived as being "Catholic," so Khomeini's attack on Rushdie was really another attack on the encroachments of the West, and Helms's arts funding bill was really an attack on homosexuality. Justice Douglas's observation in 1949 that it is a *function of free speech* — and, it might be argued, of art — to sometimes offend, to invite dispute, to challenge and to "strike at prejudices and preconceptions," is not finding much favor in the changing political climate of forty years later.

Truth? asks Pontius Pilate in Act VI of *The Passion*. "What is truth? a shield of cobweb/And a lance of straw...."

So the debate goes on. And these recent, growing restirrings of the demand that the state's police power be employed to protect religious feelings illustrate an important point made by Rodney Smolla: "The most powerful assaults on freedom of speech in America have always come not from bad people but from good people, people who would sanitize our speech to

12. The Resurrection and Redemption of The Passion

make it less sexist or sexual, less racist, less vulgar, less stinging."[48] This simple truth is, finally, the most important — and most urgent — reason for reexamining the tribulations undergone by a forgotten minor playwright named Salmi Morse who over a hundred years ago wrote an American Passion play.

"Whoever would overthrow the liberty of a nation," Benjamin Franklin once said, "must begin by subduing the freeness of speech."[49]

As Salmi Morse's four-year struggle in defense of *The Passion* ought to show us, the right of the dramatist (or any artist) to express himself in America without fear of suppression or censorship by the majority can be as ethereal as Pontius Pilate's definition of "Truth": a shield of cobweb and a lance of straw.

Notes

Part One: "The Passion" in San Francisco, 1879

Prologue

[1] Quoted in James D. McCabe, Jr., *New York by Sunlight and Gaslight* [*New York by Gaslight*] (1882; repr., New York: Greenwich House, 1984), 76. Rest of account compiled from *New York Tribune*, February 23, 1884; *The (New York) World*, February 23, 1884. The *World* gives the two men's names as "Grube" and "Navin."

[2] David Belasco, "My Life's Story," *Hearst's Magazine* 26 (November 1914): 611. Herne quoted in Doris Alexander, *The Tempering of Eugene O'Neill* (New York: Harcourt, Brace & World, 1962), 55. Jefferson De Angelis and Alvin F. Harlow, *A Vagabond Trouper* (New York: Harcourt, Brace & Co., 1931), 109. Other quotes: "fiasco" — "Hostility of City Prevented Continuance of 'The Passion,'" *San Francisco Chronicle*, April 14, 1929; "disastrous" — Arthur & Barbara Gelb, *O'Neill* (New York: Harper & Bros., 1962), 46; "catastrophe" — John Perry, *James A. Herne: The American Ibsen* (Chicago: Nelson-Hall, 1978), 45.

[3] Morse was not the only playwright to face moral censure. Dumas *fils* was excoriated for *La Dame aux camelias* (1848), while some twenty years after Morse, Clyde Fitch was called immoral for writing *Sapho* (1900). But here again, the majority of ministerial condemnations and legal proceedings were directed against the actresses who played these roles. Thus, it was Olga Nethersole who took most of the heat for *Sapho*, not Fitch. Granted, her higher degree of public visibility made her a better target; but Fitch's long track record as a successful dramatist no doubt helped give him a kind of immunity that a lesser writer like Morse could never have. The same observation might be made of those other two "morally degenerate" playwrights of the late nineteenth century, Ibsen and Shaw, both of whom enjoyed high literary reputations despite the frequent condemnations of moralists.

[4] "How to Judge Judge Bork," *The New York Times*, July 7, 1987, A26.

Chapter One

[1] Leigh Eric Schmidt, "Church-State Relations in the Colonial South," in John F. Wilson, ed., *Church and State in America: A Bibliographical Guide, The Colonial and Early National Periods* (New York: Greenwood Press, 1986), 75.

[2] Mark Valeri, "Puritanism and the Civil Order in New England from the First Settlement to the Great Awakening," in *Church and State*, 48.

[3] Thomas Jefferson, *Notes on Virginia*, Query XVII, reprinted in full in Perry Deane Young, *God's Bullies: Native Reflections on Preachers and Politics* (New

York: Holt, Rinehart & Winston, 1982), 337. Jefferson notes that, fortunately, no Quaker was ever executed in Virginia. Such was not the case in Puritan New England, however; there, at least four Quakers are known to have been hanged for their faith (184).

[4]J. T. Jable, "Pennsylvania's Early Blue Laws: A Quaker Experiment in the Suppression of Sport and Amusements, 1682-1740," *Journal of Sport History*, I (Fall 1974): 109-11.

[5]Young, 183.

[6]Young, 184.

[7]Jerry Falwell, *Listen America!* (Garden City: Doubleday & Co., 1980), 208.

[8]Young, 182-83.

[9]David H. Flaherty, Univ. of California Press, 1985). "Law and the Enforcement of Morals in Early America," *Perspectives in American History*, 5 (1971): 206, 208.

[10]Quoted in Jonas Barish, *The Antitheatrical Prejudice* (1981; paperback edition, Berkeley: of California, 1985). Prynne quote, 85; Barish's description, 83.

[11]Barish, 86-87.

[12]Barish, 87. For an interesting argument that the English stage itself actually supported and actively promoted the Puritan cause, see Martin Butler, *Theatre and Crisis 1632-1642* (Cambridge: Cambridge Univ. Press, 1984).

[13]Flaherty, 213.

[14]Paul Slocumb-Rolley, "Ye Beare and Ye Cubb," *Equity Magazine*, July-August 1965, 9. The three defendants were acquitted, and Martin ordered to pay court costs.

[15]William Dunlap, *History of the American Theatre* (1832; repr., New York: Burt Franklin, 1963), 125.

[16]Jable, 109.

[17]See James H. Dorman, Jr., *Theater in the Ante Bellum South 1815-1861* (Chapel Hill: Univ. of North Carolina Press, 1967), and Hugh F. Rankin, *The Theater in Colonial America* (Chapel Hill: Univ. of North Carolina Press, 1965). See also Dunlap.

[18]Dunlap, Rankin and Dorman all note evidence of earlier theatrical offerings, perhaps even organized companies, but documentation is sparse. The Murray-Kean Company, led by Walter Murray and Thomas Kean, is known to have appeared in Philadelphia in 1749, three years before Hallam's arrival. A year later the records place the company in New York. Not much else is known about it, however, except that it was at one time known as the Virginia Company of Comedians. According to Gerald Bordman, in *The Oxford Companion to American Theatre* (New York: Oxford Univ. Press, 1984): "Their repertory consisted entirely of the English plays then most popular in London" (494; see also 394).

[19]Daniel R. Ernst, "Church-State Issues and the Law: 1607-1870," in *Church and State*, 334.

[20]Leigh Eric Schmidt, in *Church and State*, 80. For more on George Whitefield and the Great Awakening in America, see William Howland Kenney III, "George Whitefield, Dissenter Priest of the Great Awakening, 1739-1741," *William and Mary Quarterly*, 3rd ser., 26 (January 1969).

[21]Elizabeth B. Clarke, in "Church-State Relations in the Constitution-Making Period," in *Church and State*, notes that, "In part disestablishment in New England was a contest between Puritan and pietistic forces and signaled not a reordering of civil power but a sharing of power within Protestantism itself" (159).

[22]See Rankin, 61, 78, 81-83, 96, 109-11, 115, 136, 170; Dunlap, 19-21; Dorman, 14.

²³Thomas Jefferson, *Notes*, reprinted in Young, 339. These last two lines caused no end of trouble for Jefferson. According to his biographer, Fawn M. Brodie (Thomas Jefferson: *An Intimate History* [1974; paperback edition, Toronto: Bantam Books, 1975], 60-61), these were "the two lines which would be quoted against him for the rest of his life as proof that he was an atheist."

²⁴Jefferson, "An Act for Establishing Religious Freedom," reprinted in full in Young, 335-36.

²⁵Ironically for the subject at hand, this amendment also established both freedom of speech and of the press. The full text reads:

> Congress shall make no law respecting an establishment of religion or prohibiting the free exercise thereof; or abridging the freedom of speech, or of the press; or the right of the people peaceably to assemble, and to petition the Government for a redress of grievances.

²⁶Ernst, in *Church and State*, 335. Other New England states that continued supporting Congregationalism into the nineteenth century included Connecticut (which ceased support in 1818) and New Hampshire (1819).

²⁷Chapel Street Riot: Rankin, 109-10; Grand Jury quote: Rankin, 185. Curiously, this Charleston meeting and its resultant resolution (voted down) are not mentioned by Dorman. The problem of expenditure leads to the question of just how much the colonial theatre did, in fact, cost. Julian Mates, in *The American Musical Stage Before 1800* (New Brunswick: Rutgers Univ. Press, 1962), documents ticket prices and concludes, "Eight, six and four shillings (or one dollar, seventy-five cents, and fifty cents) were the standard fees for box, pit, and gallery respectively. These figures, with some negligible variation, held all over the colonies" (47). Ignoring the fact that Mates fails to tell us whether his conversions are current-day or colonial equivalents, these prices indicate that going to the theatre was no more expensive than other entertainments that were *not* condemned, such as concerts—one dollar per ticket (p. 15)—and circuses—one-dollar box seats, fifty-cent pit (p. 24). This would lead one to imagine, then, that mere "extravagance" was not solely the issue.

²⁸Rankin, 53; Dunlap also notes the chaotic conditions in colonial theatre auditoriums (p. 32); and Mates goes so far as to say that "riots were almost expected" (see 65-66).

²⁹Quoted in Page Smith, *The Shaping of America: A People's History of the Young Republic*, III (New York: McGraw-Hill, 1980), 386.

³⁰H. P. Phelps, *Players of a Century: A Record of the Albany Stage* (1880; repr., New York: Benjamin Blom, 1972), 16-17.

³¹According to Bordman, "The name, prompted to some extent by growing anti-British sentiments of the day, seems to have been used first in 1763 while the company was touring Virginia and the Carolinas" (22).

³²"No. 44. The Association," reprinted in full in William MacDonald, ed., *Documentary Source Book of American History 1606-1913* (New York: Macmillan, 1916), 166-71.

³³Flaherty, 216.

³⁴Quoted in Smith, 394.

³⁵Timothy Dwight, *An Essay on the Stage: In Which the Arguments in Its Behalf, and Those Against It, Are Considered: and Its Morality, Character, and Effects Illustrated*, (n.d.; repr., London: Sharp, Jones & Co., 1824), 101.

³⁶Nat Hentoff, *The First Freedom: The Tumultuous History of Free Speech in America* (New York: Delacorte Press, 1980), 61.

[37]Hentoff, 73.

[38]Hentoff, 74.

[39]While few cases concerning theatrical censorship *per se* have been argued before the U.S. Supreme Court, decisions on novels and motion pictures have been accepted as applying to the stage. However, those cases have most often concerned obscenity, an issue that goes beyond the circumstances under which the theatre was suppressed in the first two centuries in America, nor does that apply to Salmi Morse's troubles. While "immorality," including profanity, was surely one reason for the church's condemnations of the stage, more important was the fact that the very *principle* of theatre was damned by the church. For a discussion of twentieth-century Supreme Court decisions concerning literature and obscenity, see Hentoff, 283-99.

[40]Norman Philbrick, ed., *Trumpets Sounding: Propaganda Plays of the American Revolution* (New York: Benjamin Blom, 1972), 1. For the following discussion, I have also drawn extensively from Richard Moody's list of Revolutionary War-era plays in Moody, ed., *Dramas from the American Theatre 1762-1909* (Cleveland: World Publishing, 1966), 67-69, as well as individual entries in Bordman.

[41]Bordman, 244.

[42]Hallam and Douglass, in fact, both argued the theatre's merits only on the moralists' own terms. Evidence indicates that neither they nor any of their numerous champions ever questioned the church's equation of "sin" with "crime," or, far worse, the teaching that branded theatre a sin in the first place. Thus, Hallam loudly (and often) proclaimed both a didactic *and* a moral intent for his performances, asserting that

> the principal Business of the Stage is, or should be to satyrize *Vice*, and represent her in her true Colours, that Youth, and the Unexperienced, may receive instructions, and be the better able to guard against, and avoid her enchanting Deceptions (Quoted in Rankin, 70).

Douglass went so far as to announce, in a 1758 Epilogue, that

> ...wise men own, a play well chose may teach
> Such useful moral truths as churchmen preach.
> (see Dunlap, 20).

By claiming for itself a moral purpose equal to that of the pulpit, the theatre made rebuttal by the church that much easier. For an excellent example of this, see Timothy Dwight's sarcastic remarks in his *Essay*, 21-22.

[43]Brodie, 60-61. The inclusion of Greek plays in Jefferson's list makes one wonder even more why the colonial theorists should have ignored the importance of the theatre, for they were surely conversant with the fact that in ancient Greece—so admired and emulated by the Founding Fathers in the structuring of our own democratic republic—the theatre occupied a place of honor, and fulfilled both a religious and a political function in society. In fact, the comic theatre of Athens in the fifth century B.C. was, as I.F. Stone has put it, "the equivalent of a crusading newspaper." In their attitude toward the stage, our Founding Fathers seem to have followed more the ancient Romans (who distrusted the theatre) than the free speech-loving Greeks. For an excellent example of the important free-speech role theatre played in ancient Athens, see Stone's *The Trial of Socrates* (1988; paperback edition, New York: Anchor Books, 1989) 134-37; 219-24; 265n.

[44]Introduction to "College Dialogues," in Moody, 1-4; see also Rankin, 5.

⁴⁵Quoted in Moody, 2.

⁴⁶Quoted in Dunlap, 64. Quincy also wrote in his diary: "The stage is the nursery of vice, and disseminates the seeds far and wide with an amazing and baneful effect."

⁴⁷Washington was an avid theatregoer all of his life (see Paul Leicester Ford, *Washington and the Theatre* [1899; repr., New York: Benjamin Blom, 1967]). It is even recorded that a play staged by Continental soldiers at Valley Forge—in defiance of this very ban—was attended by "His excellency and Lady" (Colonel William Bradford, letter to his sister, quoted in Moody, 67-68). So that the point was not lost on even "His excellency's" troops, Congress's third antitheatre resolution (see note 48, following) made it illegal "for any officeholder in the United States government to promote, attend, or act in stage plays." Failure to comply would result in dismissal from office (see J. Thomas Jable, "The Pennsylvania Sunday Blue Laws of 1779: A View of Pennsylvania Society and Politics During the American Revolution," *Pennsylvania History*, 40 [October 1973]: 422).

⁴⁸The first of these, on October 12, 1778, encouraged each individual state to "take the most effectual measures . . . for the suppressing of theatrical entertainments . . . and such other diversions as are productive of idleness and dissipation." The last resolution, addressed to the Continental Army and previously noted, was passed four days later (both quoted in Jable, "Blue Laws of 1779," 422). Most colonies did indeed pass such individual legislation.

⁴⁹For a concise discussion of music in colonial society, see W. Thomas Marrocco and Harold Gleason, eds., *Music in America: An Anthology From the Landing of the Pilgrims to the Close of the Civil War, 1620-1865* (New York: W. W. Norton & Co., 1964).

⁵⁰Marrocco and Gleason, 98.

⁵¹Marrocco and Gleason, 177-78; Mates, 6-19.

⁵²Mates, 16-17.

⁵³Smith, 399.

⁵⁴Dorman, 21.

⁵⁵See Dunlap for extensive summaries of the various postwar antitheatre campaigns: e.g., Pennsylvania Assembly debate, 56-58; New York Council, 58-64; and so on. For Albany's opposition, see Phelps, 23-29.

⁵⁶Dunlap, 130.

⁵⁷Oscar G. Brockett, *History of the Theatre*, 4th ed. (Boston: Allyn and Bacon, 1982), 470.

⁵⁸Robert C. Toll, *On with the Show: The First Century of Show Business in America* (New York: Oxford Univ. Press, 1976), 4-5.

⁵⁹Ann Douglas, *The Feminization of American Culture* (1977; paperback edition, New York: Avon Books, 1978), 23-24. By way of contrast, the 1988 Gallup Poll finds that two-thirds of the adults in the United States today (67 percent) claim membership in a church or synagogue. Yet only four out of ten (42 percent) say they actually attended during the year. Fifty-four percent of the Americans in the poll said they "consider religion very important in their lives" ("Trends in Religious Life Changed Little Since '69," Minneapolis *Star Tribune*, December 18, 1988, 30A).

Interestingly, Douglas argues that the powerlessnes of the nineteenth-century Protestant clergyman brought on by disestablishment drove him to align himself with the equally powerless Victorian housewife, whose traditional, active role in the home had been displaced by the Industrial Revolution, and that together they created a new, "sentimentalized" ideal of Victorian femininity, which in turn "feminized" the entire culture. Within her exploration, Douglas makes some very pertinent observations about the changing social role of religion and the clergy in the nineteenth century, which also help explain the church's role in the *Passion* controversy. "By 1875," she writes,

> American Protestants were much more likely to define their faith in terms of family morals, civic responsibility, and above all, in terms of the social function of churchgoing.... In an analogous way, Protestant churches over the same period shifted their emphasis from a primary concern with the doctrinal beliefs of their members to a preoccupation with numbers. In ecclesiastical and religious circles, attendance came to count for more than genuine adherence (6).

[60]Douglas, 24. In 1800, according to Smith, the Congregationalists had numbered some 600,000, while there were 40,000 Baptists and only 5,000 Methodists. There were far fewer Jews, of course—only around 2,000 (313). The great rise in the number of Jewish immigrants, which was to have such a profound impact on the American theatre, would not begin until later in the nineteenth century, after *The Passion* controversy.

[61]Young, 169.

[62]*Daily Alta California*, February 18, 1884.

[63]Douglas, 33-34.

[64]See Peter Gay, *The Bourgeoise Experience: Victoria to Freud, Vol. II: The Tender Passion* (New York: Oxford Univ. Press, 1986), 153, for remarks on self-censorship by some of the novelists of the time. Even those authors whose explorations of the human condition might have exceeded propriety found themselves corrected by the blue pencils of their editors. Leslie Stephen, editor of *Cornhill Magazine* in 1874, deleted several lines from the final proofs of Thomas Hardy's *Far From the Madding Crowd*, admitting to the author that he had done so "from an excessive prudery of wh. I am ashamed; but one is forced to be absurdly particular" (quoted in Gay, *The Bourgeoise Experience, Vol. I: Education of the Senses* [New York: Oxford Univ. Press, 1984], 412).

Chapter Two

[1]J. S. Holliday, *The World Rushed In: The California Gold Rush Experience* (New York: Simon & Schuster, 1981), 34. For an excellent and accessible overview of the Gold Rush, see William Weber Johnson, *The Forty-Niners*, a volume of the Old West Series (New York: Time-Life Books, 1974).

[2]See William Issel and Robert W. Cherny, *San Francisco 1865-1932: Politics, Power, and Urban Development* (Berkeley: Univ. of California Press, 1986), 9-10. For a more standard, general history of the city, in addition to any cited below, see, among others, Lewis Francis Byington and Oscar Lewis, eds., *The History of San Francisco*, 3 vols. (Chicago: S. J. Clarke, 1931).

[3]Quoted in Issel and Cherny, 13. Rest of description of San Francisco in Johnson, 163-73.

[4]Constance Rourke, *Troupers of the Gold Coast* (New York: Harcourt, Brace, 1928), 22.

[5]Walter M. Leman, *Memories of an Old Actor* (1886; repr., New York: Benjamin Blom, 1969), 238-39; see also Johnson, 182; Rourke, 23-24.

⁶Rourke, 25-27; Leman, 231-32.

⁷Rourke, 28-31; Johnson, 182.

⁸Rourke, 31-33. This theatre and saloon burned to the ground seven months later, on May 4, 1851; Maguire promptly built a second, even larger Jenny Lind, seating several thousand. Nine days later, it, too, burned down. Maguire finally got wise and built his third Jenny Lind out of brick (Rourke, 34; Johnson, 185). For descriptions of the Jenny Linds I and II, see William C. Young, *Documents of American Theater History, Volume I: Famous American Playhouses 1716-1899* (Chicago: American Library Association, 1973), 160-61. Young gives the seating capacity as 800; Rourke (p. 32) says it was 2,000. As the article reprinted by Young, from the *Alta California*, October 27, 1850, reports "probably five hundred persons with ease," Young's figure is undoubtedly the more accurate.

For an excellent biography of Tom Maguire, see Lois Foster Rodecape, "Tom Maguire, Napoleon of the Stage," *California Historical Society Quarterly*, XX-XXI (December 1941 et seq.).

⁹Joseph Gaer, ed., *The Theatre of the Gold Rush Decade in San Francisco* (1935, repr., New York: Burt Franklin, 1970), 5.

¹⁰Leman, 234.

¹¹David Dempsey, with Raymond P. Baldwin, *The Triumphs and Trials of Lotta Crabtree* (New York: William Morrow & Co., 1968), 101.

¹²San Francisco *Daily Examiner*, February 23, 1884; San Francisco *Daily Morning Call*, March 2, 1884.

¹³*San Francisco Chronicle*, March 3, 1884.

¹⁴*New York Mirror*, November 12, 1881. The *Mirror* later added the word "Dramatic" to its name, and it is under the title *Dramatic Mirror* that it is usually known.

¹⁵G. E. Barnes, "Pallida Mors," *Daily Morning Call*, March 2, 1884; hereafter referred to as *Barnes's Eulogy*.

¹⁶*New York World* interview, quoted in *San Francisco Chronicle*, February 26, 1884.

¹⁷Date of birth: *New York Clipper*, March 1, 1884; Morse/Moss: "Deposition of Salmi Morse on behalf of Defendants, in the action of Harriet Jay Elliott Morse—*Pltff.*, vs. Annie E. Wright and Joseph J. Wright—*Defds.*," p. 9, in "Salmi Morse Papers 1857-1880," California Historical Society, San Francisco; hereafter referred to as *Morse Deposition I*.

Even after his death, the papers couldn't get his biography right. The *New York World*, February 23, 1884:

> Salmi Morse's right name was Solomon Moses. He ... was born in Russia of Jewish parents, who educated him for a rabbi. He went to Palestine and attracted the attention of Sir Moses Montefiore, who took him to London. There he changed his name to Salmi Moss, which, on his arrival in this country, he again changed to Morse. Acquiring a large fortune he travelled all over the world.

¹⁸*New York Tribune*, February 23, 1884; see also the Second Morse Deposition, "on behalf of Plaintiff," 43, hereafter referred to as *Morse Deposition II*, in "Salmi Morse Papers."

¹⁹*New York City Directory*, various editions, 1850-1884.

²⁰Mrs. Meyer: "Salmi Morse Estate File 1885-86," Surrogates Court of the City of New York; the third brother: *San Francisco Chronicle*, February 26, 1884. This

last-cited source was Salmi Morse's estranged wife, whose understandable bitterness toward Morse naturally makes her own testimony somewhat suspect. For example, she also claimed that Lewis Moss was, in 1884, "in a madhouse." But Charlotte said Lewis had died several years before (*Tribune*, February 23, 1884).

[21]*New York World* interview, quoted in *San Francisco Chronicle*.

[22]George R. MacMinn, *The Theater of the Golden Era in California* (Caldwell, ID: Caxton Printers, 1941), 43.

[23]William Kelly, *Life in Victoria; or, Victoria in 1853, and Victoria in 1858* (London: Chapman & Hall, 1859), I: 39. The Australian rush began when Edward Hargreaves discovered gold at Summerhill Creek on February 12, 1851. Ironically, Hargreaves had just returned home after having failed to strike it rich in the California gold fields. Gold had actually been found in Australia as early as 1823, but the government had suppressed the news, "or," as one Governor said in 1841, "we shall all have our throats cut" (David Wallechinsky and Irving Wallace, *The People's Almanac #2* [New York: William Morrow & Co., 1978], 419).

[24]William Westgarth, *Personal Recollections of Early Melbourne and Victoria* (Melbourne: George Robertson & Co., 1888), 132.

[25]Kelly, 329.

[26]W. H. Newnham, *Melbourne, Biography of a City*, Revised Edition (Melbourne: Hill of Content, 1985), 48, 49. Newnham seems to have used Kelly's remembrances as his primary source material, and this could explain why he gives the date of Morse's lesseeship as beginning in 1853. But Kelly makes it clear that Morse's lesseeship lasted for several years, so even though Kelly was writing about Melbourne in 1853, it does not necessarily follow that that was the year in which Morse took over the hotel.

[27]Kelly, 334.

[28]Morse's account of the meeting is in Morse Deposition II, 10; Harriet's account: *Chronicle*, February 26, 1884, hereafter referred to as *Harriet Morse Interview*. It is not known what became of Harriet's first husband; perhaps he was still living in 1852 when she met Morse, but presumably she was a widow by 1858, when she and Salmi became engaged.

[29]*San Francisco Daily Examiner*, February 23, 1884.

[30]Kelly, 336.

[31]Morse Deposition II, 11.

[32]This entire account of Robert Jay and the California ranch is taken from the Morse Depositions and the Harriet Morse Interview. Morse was called as a witness in an unsuccessful suit brought by Harriet in 1879 to get the ranch back. Curiously, over the course of his four separate court appearances, Morse placed the location of their ranch as both Sonoma and Mendocino counties. According to the deed in question, however, the ranch was in the Feliz, or Sanel, Valley in upper Mendocino County.

[33]The marriage was announced in the *San Francisco Daily Evening Bulletin*, July 12, 1859; other details from Morse Depositions and Harriet Morse Interview.

[34]Synagogue E-manuel and Sherith Israel had both been built in 1854. The first Jewish service recorded in San Francisco was held on the Day of Atonement, 1849. See K. M. Nesfield, "The Jew from a Gentile Standpoint," *Overland Monthly* XXV, Second ser. (April 1895): 44.

[35]Petaluma, California, *Argus*, March 1, 1884, quoted in full in *An Illustrated History of Sonoma County, California* (Chicago: Lewis Publishing, 1889), 199–200. The *Argus* editor also recalls first seeing Morse at a "Methodist camp-meeting" in either 1856 or '57. However, Morse was in the Middle East during those years, and

the physical description the *Argus* editor gives for "Brother Morse" — "a man small in stature and bald-headed" — does not in any way fit Salmi. The rest of his remembrance, however, concerning Morse the Rancher, is supported by other corroborative evidence.

[36]Issel and Cherny, 16; for political developments in the 1860s, see William F. Heintz, *San Francisco's Mayors from the Gold Rush Through the Silver Bonanza, 1850-1880* (Woodside, CA: Gilbert Richards Publications, 1975).

[37]Quoted in Issel and Cherny, 18; Hunt quote, 20.

[38]Issel and Cherny, 14.

[39]Maguire's sale of the Jenny Lind for a City Hall resulted in a public scandal; see MacMinn, 43-45. For a description of Maguire's Opera House, see MacMinn, 53-54; also, Johnson, 185.

[40]See Monographs III ("Tom Maguire") and XIII ("Adah Isaacs Menken") in the "San Francisco Theatre Research Series" (San Francisco: Works Progress Administration, 1938). Maguire reportedly paid Menken the then-unheard-of salary of five hundred dollars per performance; the production played for sixty nights (Monograph XIII, 62). See also Bernard Falk, *The Naked Lady, or Storm Over Adah: A Biography of Adah Isaacs Menken* (London: Hutchinson & Co., 1934). Menken, like Morse, claimed to have changed faiths, although she went the reverse route: after marrying a Jew, she became fanatically Jewish. Falk doubts her story of conversion, and contends that she was Jewish by birth.

[41]*The Daily Dramatic Chronicle*, January 31, 1865; see also Richard Rapaport, "The Chronicle Clan: Part 1," *San Francisco Magazine*, I (November 1987): 40.

[42]"Sabbath-keepers" quote: MacMinn, 272; for a full account of these early moral efforts, see MacMinn, 269-74. Tom Maguire's trial: Lois Foster Rodecape, "Tom Maguire, Part II," *California Historical Society Quarterly*, XXI (March 1942): 66.

[43]In his second "Deposition" (p. 5), Morse testified that, after leaving the ranch, he and Harriet lived "at San Francisco and at San Buneventura [sic]," but unfortunately he gives no dates. Later on in his testimony (II: 32), Morse was shown a letter sent him by his brother, Lewis, dated October 15, 1868, and testified that at that time he was "in Santo Domingo, I think." A second letter, dated December 2, sent by Morse from New York to his wife in Monte Cristo two months later, was also introduced. These two letters definitely place the couple in the Dominican Republic by late Fall 1868.

[44]"Geological Survey Contract," Exhibit XII of the "Report of the Commission of Inquiry to Santo Domingo," in *The Executive Documents of the Senate of the United States: First Session Forty-Second Congress [1871]* (Washington: Government Printing Office, 1871), 185-87; hereafter referred to as *Commission Report*. For a detailed recounting of the annexation saga, see William S. McFeely, *Grant: A Biography* (New York: W. W. Norton & Co., 1981), 332-50. McFeely traces the various ways in which the Santo Domingo Company, which funded Gabb's expedition, was connected to one of Grant's close advisors, who then persuaded Grant to work for passage of the annexation treaty. After several years of intense politicking, the move failed. In the end, the entire episode only worsened Grant's reputation for poor judgment as President, and wound up being, in McFeely's words, "a cheap effort to buy a bit of Caribbean real estate" (332).

[45]At least two were from California: Benjamin Holliday, who ran a "line of steamers," and his vice-president, Mr. Norris. See Professor Gabb's interview, Commission Report, 238. Among the other investors named by Gabb was "Mr. McCormick, the reaper man."

[46] William M. Gabb, *Geology*, 2 Vols. (Philadelphia: Caxton Press of Sherman & Co, 1865).

[47] It is also important to note that Gabb, in describing his surveying party, never mentions any assistant or employee who might resemble Morse. He says he had seven assistants ("six foreigners"), and all of them "are professional men" (see Commission Report, 235–36). Morse may have worked as a record-keeper or in a secretarial capacity.

[48] Monte Cristo is the only address Morse names in his Second Deposition (see 32, 37, 39); it is also the only city given by Harriet in her testimony (in "Salmi Morse Papers").

[49] Source unknown, quoted in Harriet Morse Interview.

[50] *San Francisco Chronicle*, March 21, 1899.

[51] Morse Deposition II, 25. When asked what happened to the money, Morse answered, "I used it all for expenses."

[52] Samuel Williams, "The City of the Golden Gate," *Scribner's Monthly* 10 (July 1875): 276.

[53] *Langley's San Francisco City Directory*, 1876 and 1877 editions (San Francisco: Henry G. Langley, various dates). In 1876 his listing is "Samuel Morse"; in 1877, "Samuel Moss." In the 1878 edition, he is not listed at all. It is not until 1879, the year of the *Passion*, that he is finally listed as "Salmi Morse."

[54] *Barnes's Eulogy*. Unfortunately, Barnes does not give the name of this "leading lawyer." This claim was to become important for Morse in 1884, as will be seen later, and therefore Barnes's confirmation of the episode is noteworthy. However, it should also be noted that in Morse's Deposition II, given January 13, 1880, he testified that he had never studied law anywhere (44).

[55] See John Perry, *James A. Herne*, 40–45, for information on Herne at the Baldwin. Of course, there are any number of biographies of Belasco. I have drawn extensively from his own "My Life's Story," serialized in *Hearst's Magazine*, as well as from William Winter's *The Life of David Belasco* (New York: Moffat, Yard & Co., 1918), and Craig Timberlake, *The Bishop of Broadway: The Life and Work of David Belasco* (New York: Library Publishers, 1954).

[56] Baldwin: Lucius Beebe and Charles Clegg, *San Francisco's Golden Era: A Picture Story of San Francisco Before the Fire* (Berkeley: Howell-North, 1960), 177; Baldwin Stock Company: San Francisco newspapers; the arrival of the Morrisons and O'Neill: Joan Bennett and Lois Kibbee, *The Bennett Playbill* (New York: Holt, Rinehart & Winston, 1970), 161–62. Beebe and Clegg imply that the gloriously opulent Baldwin Hotel, which he erected around his theatre in 1878, was also built to enhance Baldwin's public image, as well as to rival the older Palace Hotel, down the street. However, they note that Baldwin's gamble was never entirely successful: "the character of its owner prevented it from enjoying the cachet of social approval which The Palace claimed from the beginning" (177). Luckily, such social snobbery does not seem to have prevented Maguire from turning the Baldwin into one of the most influential theatres in town.

[57] The *San Francisco Daily Examiner*, February 23, 1884, gives the date of Morse's first managerial effort as 1875, not 1877; but the Grand Opera House was not opened until 1876, and Charles Wheatleigh managed the house until May '77 (see "History of Opera in San Francisco, Part I," Monograph XVII, in "San Francisco Theatre Research").

[58] Bennett and Kibbee, 161. Rodecape, in "Tom Maguire, Part IV," 249, writes that "losses in three of the local establishments were estimated to total between $120,000 and $150,000."

⁵⁹*Barnes's Eulogy*. The "young lady" in question may well have been Mary C. Blackburn, about whom more will be heard later. If it was not, then this was the first of several young female "protégées" mentioned in connection with Morse the Playwright.
⁶⁰*San Francisco Chronicle*, March 3, 1884.
⁶¹*Barnes's Eulogy*. Although everyone seemed to know that Morse got his tobacco from a local tobacconist, he insisted that it came from Santo Domingo. The way he told the story to the *New York World:*

> [S]o profoundly was I venerated in Santo Domingo that my birthday was declared a national holiday. It remains so even now. On my birthday all the little children in Santo Domingo get together in the various towns and villages and contribute handfuls of tobacco. All this tobacco is made up into a bale and the bale is forwarded to me as a birthday present. I keep myself and my friends in smoking material all the year round.

⁶²*Barnes's Eulogy;* "my Pawssion": *San Francisco Chronicle*, March 3, 1884.
⁶³Arthur Wallace Peach and George Floyd Newbrough, eds., *Four Plays by Royall Tyler* (1940), reissued as Volume XV of *America's Lost Plays*, Barrett H. Clark, gen. ed. (Bloomington: Indiana Univ. Press, 1965). There is no evidence that any of Tyler's three extant sacred plays was ever produced.

Chapter Three

¹"Letter from Salmi Morse, to the Public of San Francisco," *The Illustrated Wasp*, May 15, 1880.
²The Archbishop's revisions were included as an Appendix to the version of *The Passion* which Morse had printed in San Francisco in 1879, the only known extant version of which is in the Library of Congress. Salmi Morse, *The Passion: A Miracle Play in Ten Acts* (San Francisco: Edward Bosqui & Co., 1879), 67-69.
³Although Morse first applied in 1878, the actual date of copyright was 1879. Library of Congress Number PN6120.R4M6.
⁴This is not to say that only American dramatists were guilty of such "borrowing." English playwrights such as Dion Boucicault and Tom Taylor freely lifted characters, sensation scenes and even whole plots from the French; so did Charles Reade, although he was conscientious enough to pay the French authors for the rights. See Frank Rahill, *The World of Melodrama* (University Park, PA: The Pennsylvania State Univ. Press, 1967), 193-200, for a discussion of "The Fine Art of Plagiarism" in Victorian theatre.
⁵"Letter from Salmi Morse." Coincidentally—or perhaps not—Rondo reportedly was the Archbishop's native city. According to Morse, Alemany told him, "The only Passion Play I ever beheld was at Rondo . . . and to this is due my being a priest today."
⁶Winter, 116. Winter's account of Morse and *The Passion*, including his prejudices and inaccuracies, has been used as the basis for most of the better-known subsequent retellings, especially the accounts in Craig Timberlake, and in Arthur and Barbara Gelb.
⁷Even such a standardbearer of Victorian values as the famous explorer Richard F. Burton, in *A Glance at the Passion-Play* (London: W. H. Harrison, 1881), felt that, "At Oberammergau there is no idea of fair play" (135), and that "we have been shown the chief priests and Pharisees, the flower of their nation, in the

basest light, bloodthirstiness, insane violence, and wicked treachery. But is there nothing to be said on their side?" (157–158). For a turn-of-the-century rabbi's reactions, see Rabbi Joseph Krauskopf, *A Rabbi's Impressions of the Oberammergau Passion Play* (Philadelphia: Edward Stern & Co., 1901). Jewish protests against the Oberammergau *Passion Play* continue today.

[8]Winter, 120.

[9]Harriet Morse interview.

[10]See Edinburgh *Review*, 141 (April 1875), 482–521. Intriguingly, this same issue includes a lengthy article on the history of the Crimean War.

[11]Some historians argue that Passion dramas may have been staged in Oberammergau three hundred years earlier. See Saul S. Friedman, *The Oberammergau Passion Play, A Lance Against Civilization* (Carbondale, IL: Southern Illinois Univ. Press, 1984), 24–26, for a discussion of some of these theories.

[12]Friedman, 36, discusses Devrient, the *MacMillan* article and the Andersen book; Franz Schoebel, *The Passion-Play at Ober-Ammergau*, trans. Catherine Thompson (Stuttgart: Verlag der Kruell'schen Buchhandlung, 1871); Burton, 13. Friedman notes (206) that Oberammergau was even made a part of an "abysmally dull" romantic novel of the period, Baroness Jemima Tautphoeus's *Quits* (New York: G. P. Putnam's, 1863).

[13]Burton, 75.

[14]"Letter from Salmi Morse."

[15]*Daily Alta California*, January 23, 1879.

[16]*Alta*, January 23, 1879.

[17]"A Passion Play," *The Argonaut*, February 22, 1879.

[18]"San Francisco Passion Play," *New York Sun*, March 13, 1879.

[19]Winter, 118.

[20]*Barnes's Eulogy*.

[21]"Amusement Notes," *The Morning Call*, March 14, 1879.

[22]Ada Patterson, "James O'Neill—the Actor and the Man," *The Theatre Magazine* (April 1908), ix.

[23]Unidentified article in "O'Neill, James," *Robinson Locke Collection*, Billy Rose Theatre Collection, New York Public Library/Lincoln Center. Hereafter referred to as *Locke Collection*.

[24]Winter, 115.

[25]Belasco, "My Life's Story," 610.

It is interesting to note that the *Daily Alta*, on January 26, 1879 (before anyone had agreed to do *The Passion*), reports that "the contracts with the Baldwin company terminate in May"; that same column also reports that O'Neill, "at the close of the present season, though remaining in San Francisco, will probably transfer his services to another theatre." O'Neill was certainly not the first actor to use a newspaper column to bluff his way into a better contract. At any rate, it is obvious that the plum role of Jesus Christ in *The Passion*—a role O'Neill clearly wanted very much to do—came along at just the right time for everyone involved.

[26]Morse's negotiations: *Alta*, February 2, 1879; Baldwin and Maguire's tears: *The Argonaut*, March 1, 1879; Lyster's tears: *Call*, February 23, 1879.

[27]See "History of Opera in San Francisco, Part I" (Monograph XVII), "San Francisco Theatre Research Series," 99, 102–03, for the story of the Grand Opera House. The writers note that the Grand "never paid steadily except for a period toward the end of its days when sensation melodrama was shown by Manager [Walter] Morosco at very popular prices." The Grand Opera House was destroyed in the earthquake of 1906.

²⁸These are the cast members as listed in the review in the *Chronicle*, March 4, 1879. The *Alta* (February 23, 1879) had speculated that the role of Salome would be played by Rose Wood, but Miss Wood did not, in fact, appear in the play (see Bennett and Kibbee, 163). Another report published in New York asserted that "a difficulty was experienced ... in getting women to appear in it, and several withdrew after attending rehearsals" (*New York Sun*, March 12, 1879).

²⁹Jerome A. Hart, *In Our Second Century, From an Editor's Note-Book* (San Francisco: Pioneer Press, 1931), 445. Widmer later achieved minor notoriety when he assaulted Ambrose Bierce for calling his wife, Miss Mayhew, a "charming blackguard."

³⁰Arthur Hornblow, *A History of the Theatre in America from Its Beginnings to the Present Time*, II (1919; repr., New York: Benjamin Blom, 1965), 315; Belasco; Winter, 115; Hart, 445; Monograph III ("Tom Maguire"), 54; Timberlake, 72; "Betsy B.", *The Argonaut*, March 8, 1879.

³¹The advertising says "A Full Choir of Eighty Singers."

³²Belasco, like Morse, was born a Jew but converted to Christianity; reared by Catholics, in later years Belasco took to wearing his collar reversed.

³³"My Life's Story"; also quoted in Winter, 124; Hornblow, 316; Timberlake, 72.

³⁴Lise-Lone Marker, *David Belasco: Naturalism in the American Theatre* (Princeton: Princeton Univ. Press, 1975), 27.

³⁵*Alta*, February 16, 1879; "A Passion Play," *Argonaut*, February 22, 1879; *Call*, February 23, 1879; *Chronicle* February 23, 1879.

Chapter Four

¹*Call*, February 26, 1879.

²M. B. Leavitt, *Fifty Years of Theatrical Management, 1859–1909* (New York: Broadway Publishing, 1912), 247. Ironically, Leavitt was having his own legal troubles at the same time that Morse's *Passion* was facing suppression. As manager and proprietor of the Standard Theatre, he had been featuring "Mdme. Rentz and her Female Minstrel Troupe"; on March 14, 1879, Leavitt and the entire company were arrested and charged with giving lewd and indecent performances (*Call*, March 15, 1879). Earlier, the *Call* (March 12) had stopped accepting advertising for the presentation and called for *its* suppression, on the grounds that, "for obscenity it surpasses any performance we have ever witnessed, and the police authorities of the city should see that it is stopped." The dancer in question, Mabel Santley, was tried and found guilty on March 27. Her crime: dancing the can-can (*Call*, March 27 and 28).

³Timberlake, 66.

⁴See Heintz, 102; Issel and Cherny, 24, 125. Heintz gives the population as 300,000 and the unemployment rate as ten percent, which roughly works out to be the same figure of unemployed: over 30,000 citizens.

⁵*Chronicle*, various issues, February–April 1879; Heintz, 104–08; Issel and Cherny, 125–30. The California constitution of 1879 also called for "such socialistic reforms as free schools and free textbooks, regulation of railroad fares and freight rates, and regulation of the stock exchange" (Rapaport, 42).

⁶"As Others See Us," *Alta*, February 14, 1879.

⁷*New York Sun*, November 28, 1880; "Religion Is Dead," *Sun*, December 20, 1880.

⁸Presbyterian resolution: *Sun*, May 17, 1879; Methodist ban: Benjamin

McArthur, *Actors and American Culture, 1880-1920* (Philadelphia: Temple Univ. Press, 1984), 130. Baptist quote: "The Religious Press," *Call*, December 12, 1880. Beecher: "Actors, Preachers and Monkeys," *New York Daily Mirror*, May 27, 1882. Montana expulsion: *Sun*, February 26, 1879.

[9]McArthur, 128.

[10]Quoted in "The Passion Play," *Call*, March 3, 1879.

[11]William Ingraham Kip, "Miracle Plays," *Argonaut*, March 8, 1879. See also "The Clergy," *Chronicle*, March 4, 1879. It is noteworthy that neither a March 3 statement from the Protestant Ministerial Union of San Francisco, nor one from the Protestant Epsicopal Church of the Diocese of San Francisco, under Bishop Kip, adopted March 1, 1879, called for outright suppression by the legal authorities, but only urged "all good citizens who have reverence for sacred things" to "absent themselves" from the performances. Evidently, not all ministers were agreed that the church ought to play censor for the entire community. Nevertheless, both the Reverend Smith, of the former organization, and Bishop Kip, of the latter, actively took part in the legal proceedings that led to suppression of the play.

[12]"Another Criticism," *Call*, March 3, 1879; Kip, "Miracle Plays."

[13]See the *Alta*, February 16, 19, and March 25, 1879, for advertisements of the three events. On March 31, 1879, the Handel and Haydn Society presented Felix Mendelssohn's Old Testament oratorio *Athalie* at Platt's Hall, also to no objections (*Alta*, April 1, 1879).

[14]Peter Shaffer, "Preface" to *Amadeus* (New York: Harper & Row, 1981), viii.

[15]"Betsy B.," "Drama," *Argonaut*, March 8, 1879; Hemphill: "A Sermon Disturbed," *Call*, March 31, 1879; Smith: "The Passion Play," *Call*, March 3, 1879.

[16]"The Clergy," *Chronicle*, March 4, 1879.

[17]Winter, 121.

[18]"Another Criticism," *Call*; "Spirit of the Religious Press," *Chronicle*, March 9, 1879.

[19]Issel and Cherny, 17. Jewish objection to O'Neill: "A Jew," Letter to the Editor, *Argonaut*, March 8, 1879; also quoted in Timberlake, 76. The following week, March 15, a second *Argonaut* reader replied:

> If your correspondent will read ancient Irish history he will be apt to find that Uriah's beauteous wife, which made David seek his life, was a Hoy Nial on the mother's side. Therefore, as the O'Neills were once the Hoy Nials, and as Uriah's wife was King Solomon's mother, and as Solomon was the distinguished ancestor of Jesus, it stands to reason that James O'Neill is anthropologically a proper person to play that character. Let "A Jew" read history.

[20]Quoted in "Spirit of the Religious Press," *Chronicle*, March 16, 1879.

[21]"Letter from Salmi Morse."

[22]"The Archbishop Non-Committal," *Chronicle*, March 4, 1879.

[23]Perhaps for a similar reason, John Bernard McGloin, in his biography of Alemany, makes no mention whatsoever of *The Passion* controversy, (*California's First Archbishop: The Life of Joseph Sadoc Alemany, O.P., 1814–1888* [New York: Herder & Herder, 1968]). As for Denis Kearney, McGloin downplays completely his connection with the Catholic Church:

> Since this Irishman, who had deserted his faith, recruited his supporters in large part from the ... Irish Catholic laborers of San Francisco ... it

was only to be expected that his rabble-rousing tactics and incendiary commands would become an object of grave concern to Alemany (293).

Whether or not Kearney had "deserted his faith," it is clear that San Franciscans accepted the Workingmen's Party as a predominantly Catholic movement. After Alemany issued a public plea for Catholics not to engage in violent disorders, one Protestant newspaper, the *California Christian Advocate* (August 23, 1877), sarcastically asked its readers:

> Do you wish proof that Romanism has trained a most violent and dangerous group in our population? ... I refer you to Archbishop Alemany's recent letter of admonition and entreaty to his people ... to abstain from violence, incendiarism and murder.... [Did] anybody think it unfit or untimely for the Archbishop publicly to advise his people in that way? No, for the reason that every man knows that the Papists of our cities are the fiercest, least self-governed, most unreasoning and furious mob element.

[24]See Note 34, Chapter Two, above.

[25]Danziger, 399; also, 390-95.

[26]Morse, however, did ask the "chief Jewish Rabbi here," the Rev. Dr. Henry Vidaver, his opinion on the subject. The Rabbi's reply, dated "April 12, [1879]," was included in Morse's rambling "Letter," published in the *Wasp*, May 15, 1880:

> In reply to your query regarding the propriety of your "Passion Play" on the stage, I beg to state that as a Jewish Rabbi, and as a man of plain, common sense, I consider no work of art as a sacrilege unless it shocks our sense of decency; unless it be calculated to sow the seeds of impurity in the hearts of the young and thus tend to pollute our firesides — and certainly the "Passion Play" is none of the works of art of that nature. The question may be asked, why should there be more objection made to the presentation of the life of Jesus on the Stage than to that of Moses or Elijah?
> If Christian ministers fear that a 'Play' could batter the fortress of Christianity, then they seem to think very little of its intrinsic power. The Jew has no fear in his belief.

Danziger, writing in 1895, singled out Dr. Vidaver as one of the four most important Jewish leaders in the city's history. "He excelled in learning all the rabbis that have ever been in San Francisco, past or present," Danziger wrote, "and as an orator, he had no peer in any pulpit, Christian or Jewish. Most persuasvie, logical, forcible, he was at the same time learned and everyone [sic] of his sermons or lectures was a masterpiece of erudition and rhetoric" (395). One might, then, accept Morse's assertion that Vidaver spoke for many in the Jewish community.

[27]See M. M. Marberry, *The Golden Voice: A Biography of Isaac Kalloch* (New York: Farrar, Straus, 1947). Also, Timberlake, 66-70.

[28]"Pulpit and Politics," *Call*, April 7, 1879.

[29]Even some members of Hemphill's own congregation protested his denunciatory preachments against *The Passion*. See "A Sermon Disturbed," *Call*, March 31, 1879, as well as the followup article, "Pulpit and Politics," noted above.

[30]*History of Journalism in the United States* (New York: D. Appleton & Co., 1928), 372.

³¹John P. Young, *Journalism in California* (San Francisco: Chronicle Publishing Co., 1915), 122; *Illustrated Wasp*, August 5, 1876; Young, 73–74.
³²Payne, 375.
³³John Bruce, *Gaudy Century: The Story of San Francisco's Hundred Years of Robust Journalism* (New York: Random House, 1948), 152; Rapaport, 42.
³⁴"Betsy B.", "Drama," *Argonaut*, March 1, 1879.
³⁵See J. P. Young, 100, for his comments on the *Call* and the *Bulletin*.
³⁶J. P. Young, 73.
³⁷Editorial, *Alta*, February 27, 1879.
³⁸Editorial, March 8, 1879.
³⁹"Betsy B.", "Drama," *Argonaut*, March 8, 1879.
⁴⁰Rapaport, 39. Rapaport adds that M. H. de Young's scheme succeeded "far beyond his expectation":

> A generation after his death in 1925, the family was so firmly established that its members could not conceive of a world in which they were not the bloom of Northern California's social garden. De Young succeeded in replacing a largely Protestant turn-of-the-century *beau monde* with his own French Catholic milieu. Moreover, he succeeded in moving the locus of the "smart set" from San Rafael to the family preserve in Burlingame, where it remains today.

⁴¹Rapaport, 40. This slur on their mother's good name was the cause of more than one gunfight and lawsuit. When Ben Napthaly, of the rival *San Francisco Sun*, prepared to publish the charge, Charles de Young got the San Francisco police to storm the offices of the *Sun* and destroy the offending plates. Napthaly and de Young, meanwhile, were shooting it out in the city streets (42).
⁴²"A Threatened Sacrilege," *Chronicle*, February 26, 1879.
⁴³"The Passion Play," and "Footlights," March 2, 1879.
⁴⁴See J. P. Young, 68; "Tom Maguire" (Monograph III), 37; Rodecape, Part III, 143–44.
⁴⁵J. P. Young, 68.
⁴⁶"Tom Maguire" (Monograph III), 37. Also Rodecape, Part III, 143–44.
⁴⁷"The Passion Play. A Card," *Chronicle*, February 27, 1879. See also the *Call*, February 28, and the *Alta*, March 1, 1879.
⁴⁸Editorial, *Argonaut*, March 8, 1879.
⁴⁹See, among others, *Chicago Tribune*, March 2, 4 and 5, 1879; *Atlanta Daily Constitution*, March 11, 1879 (the *Constitution* erroneously places Miss Rose Eytinge among the cast); and "A Miracle Play in America," *The Theatre* (London), II (New Series, May 1, 1879), 213–16. An attempt to produce a Passion play in London had recently been abandoned, and *The Theatre*'s editors discouraged any other manager from trying. "The devout would regard a Miracle play as a profanation," they felt, "and would be alienated from the theatre at the very moment when they are rising superior to unfounded prejudices respecting it" (216). As will be seen, this was also Harrison Grey Fiske's argument one year hence.
⁵⁰"A Bit of Blasphemy," *New York Daily Mirror*, March 8, 1879; *Boston Times* quoted in *Mirror*, March 15, 1879.
⁵¹*New York Sun*, March 14, 1879.
⁵²"Betsy B.," in *The Argonaut*, March 8, 1879, wrote of Morse's supporters, some of whom were Protestants:

You will be surprised to know that Mr. Salmi Morse has advocates even among Christian, God-fearing people, and that none of these uphold him more warmly than those who object to the theatrical pomp and display of the Roman Catholic Church. They advance arguments innumerable, as it is always possible to do in religious discussion; but it may be they are animated rather by a desire to be eccentric, and to appear to have overcome the prejudices of their early training, than by a genuine approval.

[53]Timberlake asserts that the production had originally been scheduled to open on Saturday, March 8, but was moved ahead a week in order to avoid "adverse action by the aroused Board of Supervisors" (73). However, all of the earliest newspaper accounts of *The Passion* simply state that the production would open after the run of *Within an Inch of His Life*; the first formal advertising lists March 3, not March 8; and in subsequent contemporary reports, there is no mention that the opening had been moved ahead in order to thwart the opposition. At the same time, scheduling for the San Francisco theatres of this period was casual, at best, and new plays were at the mercy of the popularity of the current attraction; cf., the account of Rose Eytinge's opening after *The Passion*'s initial run, in Chapter Five, following.

[54]"The Supervisors Discuss It," *Chronicle*, March 4, 1879; *Sun*, March 13, 1879.

[55]Issel and Cherny, 123–24.

[56]List of Board of Supervisors 1878–79, in *Municipal Reports 1878–79* (San Francisco: P. J. Thomas, 1879), n.pag.; descriptions of wards: Issel and Cherny, 120. See also their map of ward boundaries, 121.

[57]Morse mentions this, in his "Letter From Salmi Morse"; he characterizes Rountree as "a not over creditable member of a not over ornamental Board of Supervisors."

[58]Maguire, letter to the *Call*, March 5, 1879; "The Passion," *Chronicle*, March 4, 1879.

[59]"The Supervisors," *Chronicle*, March 4, 1879.

[60]*A Worthy Tradition: Freedom of Speech in America* (New York: Harper & Row, 1988), 7.

[61]"The Supervisors," *Chronicle*, March 4, 1879.

[62]"The Passion," *Chronicle*, March 4, 1879.

[63]"The Passion," *Chronicle*, March 4, 1879; "San Francisco Passion Play," *Sun*, March 13, 1879; "Betsy B.," "Drama," *Argonaut*, March 8, 1879.

[64]Quoted in Perry, 45.

Chapter Five

[1]"The Passion Play," *Chronicle*, March 7, 1879.

[2]Programme for *The Passion*, in San Francisco Archives, San Francisco Room, San Francisco Public Library. The other three pages are given to advertisements.

[3]"The Passion," *Chronicle*, March 4, 1879. Hereafter referred to as *Chronicle Review*.

[4]The Gelbs, for example, inexplicably label the entire production "disastrous" (46).

[5]"The Passion Play," *Chronicle*, March 7, 1879. This curious article was so out of character for the *Chronicle* that its publication prompted the *Pacific Methodist* to charge that it had actually been written by a Catholic priest (see Note 18, Chapter Four, above).

[6]"San Francisco Passion Play," *New York Sun*, March 12, 1879; "Off the Stage," *Sunday Chronicle*, August 3, 1879. Alexander quotes several other stories about O'Neill in *The Passion*, including the touching remembrance of Lewis Morrison, who recalled:

> The first night of the Passion play ... he [O'Neill] came into the dressing room after his first scene and sat down. For a few minutes he did not speak. Then mechanically, from sheer force of habit, he reached for his pipe. When his hand touched it, he seemed to awake. He started and looked at me. I said, "Don't, Jim; not now"—and he didn't (54-55).

[7]Belasco, 611; also quoted in Winter, 124-25. Herne would say the same thing: "I have never heard or read anything anywhere which so ennobled and dignified religion as did that play and that actor" (quoted in Alexander, 55).

[8]*Chronicle* Review.

[9]*Chronicle* Review.

[10]"San Francisco Passion Play," *New York Sun*, March 12, 1879.

[11]See Timberlake, 74; Bennett and Kibbee, 46; the Gelbs, 46; Hornblow, 315.

[12]Winter, 117.

[13]"The 'Passion' Ordinance," *Call*, April 22, 1879.

[14]*Chronicle* Review.

[15]"Betsy B.", "Drama," *Argonaut*, March 8, 1879.

[16]"Pulpit Precepts," *Chronicle*, March 10, 1879.

[17]"The Theatres," *Call*, March 9, 1879.

[18]New York rumor: *Call*, March 9, 1879. *Midwinter Night's Dream:* "The Stage," *Alta*, March 16, 1879.

[19]California editors were uncomfortably aware of the national attention. See the comment in "Footlight Flashes," *Chronicle*, March 23, 1879.

[20]See "Biblical Characters in Court," *Sun*, March 1, 1879, and "Passion Play in New York," *Sun*, March 16, 1879. In February (before Morse's *Passion* opened in San Francisco) two of the New York actresses had had to sue the manager for their back salaries; but after Morse's play had made national headlines, the New York *tableaux* were revived to much higher profits.

[21]"The Passion Play," *Chronicle*, March 7, 1879. The Keller Troupe, led by Polish immigrants Lewis Keller and his wife, had toured America in the late 1850s, presenting living statues posed as famous art works—including at one time Rubens' "Descent From the Cross." George C. Odell places the troupe in New York in 1858 (see *Annals of the New York Stage, VII [1857-65]* [rprt., New York: AMS Press, 1970], 152). According to the *New York Sun* (March 16, 1879), Keller had "travelled through[out] the United States, Mexico, the West Indies, South America and Brazil, and is believed to have realized at least $1,000,000 by his enterprise." See also T. Allston Brown, *History of the American Stage, Containing Biographical Sketches of Nearly Every Member of the Profession That Has Appeared on the American Stage, from 1733 to 1870* (1870; rprt., New York: Burt Franklin, 1969), 202.

It is also possible that San Francisco newspapers in 1879 were confusing the famous Keller Troupe with the Collyer Troupe of "Model Artists," evidently a far-less-genteel living statue troupe, which had appeared in San Francisco in 1850 (see MacMinn, 253-58, for a description of the Collyer Troupe and its offerings).

22"The Passion Play," *Alta*, March 8, 1879.
23"The Passion Play Order Legal," *Call*, March 11, 1879.
24This is the wording as it went into the city statute books. See "Order No. 1,587," Section 62, *General Orders of the Board of Supervisors Providing Regulations for the Government of the City and County of San Francisco* (San Francisco: P. J. Thomas Printer, 1884), 34.
25"The 'Passion Play' Order," *Call*, March 13, 1879.
26"The Passion Play Ordinance," *Call*, March 19, 1879.
27Belasco, 614.
28The Gelbs, 46; see also Bennett and Kibbee, 166.
29"The Theatre," *Call*, February 23, 1879; *Alta*, March 2, 1879.
30Announcement in *Chronicle*, March 10, 1879. See also the comment in the *Call*, March 11, 1879, noting that Miss Eytinge's opening might be delayed for as long as another week.
31"Amusement Notes," *Call*, March 14, 1879.
32"Amusement Notes," March 14, 1879.
33*New York Mirror*, March 29, 1879.
34"Amusement Notes," March 14, 1879.
35"The Passion Play Ordinance," *Call*, March 19, 1879.
36"Footlight Flashes," *Chronicle*, March 23, 1879.
37Public interest: "Footlight Flashes," *Chronicle*, April 13, 1879. Fortune quote: "Personal," *New York Dramatic News*, January 29, 1881.
38"Footlight Flashes,"*Chronicle*, April 13, 1879; see also *Chronicle*, April 11, 1879.
39"Footlight Flashes," April 13, 1879.
40"Footlight Flashes," April 13, 1879.
41*Argonaut*, March 15, 1879.
42"Amusement Notes," *Call*, April 16 and April 18, 1879. By contrast, the Religious Plastic Art Company in New York depicted the Ascension by having the posed actor remain stagebound and lowering the scenery around him (see *Sun*, March 16, 1879).
43"Amusement Notes," *Chronicle*, April 20, 1879. Of the major papers, only the *Alta* and the *Bulletin* maintained their silence toward the production.
44*Chronicle*, April 17 and April 19, 1879; *Call* April 16; *Alta*, April 16. Timberlake (79), as well as those who seem to base their accounts on his, such as Bennett and Kibbee (166–67), confuses two separate arrests (see Chapter Six, below); also, a more careful reading of the newspaper accounts shows that O'Neill was arrested by Bradford at the *end* of the performance, not "before the final tableau, depicting the removal of the Saviour's body from the Cross," as Timberlake writes.

Chapter Six

1Quote: James O'Neill, "Personal Reminiscences," *Theatre Magazine* (December 1917), 388; two hours: Patterson, ix; one hundred dollars bail: "The Passion Play," *Call*, April 16, 1879. See also the *Alta*, April 16, 1879, and the *Evening Bulletin*, April 16, 1879.
2*Call*, April 17, 1879. Except where otherwise noted, the ensuing account of the first trial is compiled from the *Chronicle*, April 17 and 18, 1879, and the *Call*, April 17, 18 and 19, 1879.

³*Chronicle*, April 17, 1879.

⁴Winter, 118; the Gelbs, 46; the *Chronicle*, April 18, 1879; *Call*, April 17, 1879; *Alta*, April 17, 1879. According to the *Alta*, their bail was set at ten dollars apiece; the *Call* gives the sum as fifty dollars apiece. In his account of the story for *Hearst's Magazine*, Belasco never mentions any of these arrests—neither O'Neill's, nor his own.

⁵*Call*, April 18, 1879.

⁶"Card from Salmi Morse," *Chronicle*, April 18, 1879. Also published in the *Call*, April 18, 1879.

⁷"Card from Salmi Morse."

⁸"Card from Salmi Morse." See also the advertisement in the *Chronicle* of April 18.

⁹"The Passion Play," *Chronicle*, April 19, 1879. The ensuing account of the District Court proceedings is taken from the *Chronicle* of April 19 and 22, 1879, and the *Call*, April 19 and 22, 1879. See also the *Alta*, April 19, 20, and 22, 1879.

¹⁰*Alta*, April 21, 1879; see also *Alta*, April 20.

¹¹*Argonaut*, April 19, 1879. Also quoted in Timberlake, 80.

¹²Quoted in Timberlake, 80.

¹³"The Passion Play," *Chronicle*, April 22, 1879. See also "The 'Passion' Ordinance," *Call*, April 22, 1879.

¹⁴"The 'Passion' Ordinance," *Call*, April 22, 1879.

¹⁵"The 'Passion' Ordinance," April 22, 1879.

¹⁶"The 'Passion' Ordinance," *Alta*, April 22, 1879; see note in the *Chronicle*, April 22, 1879.

¹⁷*Chronicle*, April 22, 1879.

¹⁸*Dramatic News*, September 18, 1880.

¹⁹M. B. Leavitt, 248.

²⁰"History of Opera in San Francisco, Part I," Monograph XVII.

²¹*Mirror*, July 12, 1879; *Call*, September 25, 1880; see also *Dramatic News*, October 2, 1880.

²²"The Doomed Passion Play," *Alta*, April 24, 1879.

²³"The Passion Play," *Call*, April 25, 1879; also, "Footlight Flashes," *Chronicle*, April 25, 1879; Bennett and Kibbee, 167. There is no way of corroborating this last story, of course, but—considering everything uncomplimentary written about O'Neill as an older actor—if Miss Bennett heard this from her grandfather, one almost hopes that it was true. She further writes:

> Grandfather was somewhat cautious in his opinion of the experience, and asked for his impressions of *The Passion Play*, he replied with customary reserve, "It was a most enlightening experience." ... There was no nonsense in Grandmother's [i.e., Rose Wood's] view. She called it "The Holy Circus" (168).

²⁴*Sun*, March 20, 1879.

²⁵"Letter from Salmi Morse," 676.

²⁶*Wasp*, January 24, 1880. George Barnes quote and information on Korbels: Barnes's Eulogy.

²⁷*Wasp*, September 13, 1879; see also any number of issues, March through December 1879, for Morse's jabs at his various enemies.

²⁸*Wasp*, July 26, 1879.

²⁹*Wasp*, November 1, 1879.

30Salmi Morse, "The Bell of the Cross," *Wasp*, December 24, 1879.
31All comments were reprinted in the *Wasp*, January 24, 1880.
32"Amusement Notes," *Call*, June 25, 1879.
33See, among other accounts, Rapaport, 42–44. An indication of de Young's lack of public favor can be seen in the fact that the younger Kalloch was quickly acquitted at his trial.
34"The Passion Play," *Call*, April 10, 1880.
35"The Passion Play," *Call*, April 12, 1880.
36"The Passion Play," *Call*, April 14, 1880.
37"Letter from Salmi Morse."
38See comment in "Footlight Flashes," *Chronicle*, September 5, 1880.
39*Dramatic News*, August 14, 1880.
40*Mirror*, August 21, 1880.
41Rodecape, Part IV, 252.
42"Theatrical Notes," *Call*, September 3, 1880.
43*Dramatic News*, September 18, 1880.
44"Theatrical Notes," *Call*, September 9, 1880.
45Rodecape, Part IV, 257.

Part Two: "The Passion" in New York, 1880–1884

Chapter Seven

1*Compendium of the Tenth Census (June 1, 1880)* (Washington: Government Printing Office, 1883), I: 396. Also McCabe, 33. Of the official census number, 727,629 were native-born Americans, 478,670 were immigrants (459). When one included the citizens in the boroughs, the population of the entire metropolis was 2,061,191. George E. Waring, Jr., comp., *Report on the Social Statistics of Cities: Part I. The New England and the Middle States* (Washington: Government Printing Office, 1886), 531.

2McCabe, 35, 36.

3Lloyd Lewis and Henry Justin Smith, *Oscar Wilde Discovers America (1882)* (New York: Harcourt, Brace, 1936), 42–43.

4McCabe, 269. Elevated railroads: 186.

5New York City *Directory*, 1880–81 edition.

6McCabe, 62–63.

7David J. Pivar, *Purity Crusade: Sexual Morality and Social Control, 1868–1900* (Westport, CT: Greenwood Press, 1973), 163–64. For an abbreviated discussion, see Joel H. Wiener, "Social Purity and Freedom of Expression," in *Censorship: 500 Years of Conflict* (New York: Oxford Univ. Press, 1984).

8See the *Sun*, December 1, 1880, for a report on the convention.

9McCabe, 620. These estimates, totaling over forty million dollars, almost equaled the total value of *city-owned* property—$46,821,180 (Waring, 566).

10"Our Pulpit Teachers," *World*, March 2, 1882.

11Lewis and Smith, 132.

12Lewis and Smith, 132; "Our Pulpit Teachers," *World*. Anachronism quote: "Abbey and Talmage," *World*, November 28, 1880. For reports on Talmage's 1879 trial before the so-called "Court of Jesus Christ," see *Sun*, various issues, March–May 1879. This was, it will be noted, the same period during which *The Passion* was being restaged in San Francisco. After charges against Talmage had been dismissed and he had resumed his pulpit fulminations against the stage, Charles A. Dana was prompted to write in the *Sun* (May 17, 1879):

> One thing is certain: All the plays in all the well-reputed playhouses of New York and Brooklyn during the past two months have not done a tithe of the harm to public morals, religion, or Presbyterianism, that has been inflicted upon all three by the remarkable spectacle just withdrawn from the boards of the Brooklyn Presbytery.
> So long as TALMAGE is allowed to perform every Sunday in a Presbyterian pulpit, the less a Presbyterian General Assembly has to say about legitimate week-day drama the better.

[13]McCabe, 629.

[14]Virtually any New York newspaper of the time will present the reader with varying views on the election. See especially the *Herald*, November 1, 1880, for a six-column-long summary of Protestant/Catholic arguments.

[15]"Human organism": *Herald*, November 1, 1880. Newman quote: "Religious Intelligence," *World*, October 30, 1880. Rev. Newman was known as the "Political Preacher" because of his connections to the Grant administration. Grant reportedly created the office of Inspector of Consulates for Newman, who had earlier served as chaplain of the U.S. Senate ("Our Pulpit Teachers," *World*).

[16]"Chap. 836. An Act to regulate places of amusement in the city of New York," *Laws of the State of New York Passed at the Ninety-Fifth Session of the Legislature* (New York: Banks & Bros., 1872), II: 1,989. The Act was amended in 1875 to exclude religious and charitable presentations given by amateurs, and further amended the following year to exclude entertainments in the New York Masonic Temple.

[17]"The $500 Tax on Theatres," *Mirror*, May 20, 1882; "Theatre License-Money," *Mirror*, September 23, 1882. The *Mirror* in 1882 did not call for an end to the theatre tax, but wanted the money given over instead to the Actor's Fund, the pet project of its editor, Harrison Grey Fiske, for which he began campaigning in 1881.

[18]"A Very Mysterious Society," *Dramatic News*, December 25, 1880. Byrne, unlike Fiske, wanted the tax abolished.

[19]See any number of examples in the Police Department Files ("Concerning Licensing of Theatres, Concert Halls") of the Mayor's Papers of both William R. Grace, 1881–1882, and Franklin Edson, 1883–1884, Municipal Archives, Department of Records and Information Services, City of New York.

[20]Elsie Janis, in *So Far So Good! An Autobiography* (New York: E. P. Dutton & Co., 1932), gives an account of her childhood run-ins with the Gerry Society. Her reminiscences, plus those of Buster Keaton and others, can also be found in Charles W. Stein, ed., *American Vaudeville as Seen by Its Contemporaries* (New York: Alfred A. Knopf, 1984). The Gerry Society's influence was to last far longer than any other's; it still oversees working conditions of child actors today (Bordman, 287–88).

[21]McCabe, 571; "The Prosperity of the Theatres and the Mirror's Victory," *Mirror*, December 4, 1880. Waring makes no distinction between "first-" and "second-class" houses, but lists 29 licensed theatres, plus 51 "halls" and 15 concert- and beer-gardens (568).

[22]McCabe, 427. See also McArthur, 16–17. The theatre season in New York ran from early fall until late spring.

[23]See Waring, 568. McCabe (134–56) describes a trip up Broadway in 1882, including capsule descriptions of most of the city's theatres.

²⁴Bordman, 151.
²⁵*Dramatic News*, September 11, 1880. Blackguard quote: McArthur, 149.
²⁶Bordman, 259, 209. See also the references to Fiske in the biography of Fiske's wife, by Archie Binns, with Olive Kooken, *Mrs. Fiske and the American Theatre* (New York: Crown Publishers, 1955), 32-42; and in Louis M. Simon, *A History of the Actors' Fund of America* (New York: Theatre Arts, 1972).
²⁷See Jack Poggi, *Theatre in America: The Impact of Economic Forces, 1870-1967* (Ithaca: Cornell Univ. Press, 1968), 5-6.
²⁸McArthur, 8-9.
²⁹McArthur, 19.
³⁰See Dempsey and Baldwin, 194-96; also, Claudia D. Johnson, *American Actress: Perspective on the Nineteenth Century* (Chicago: Nelson-Hall, 1984), 167-68.
³¹Stephen Fiske, *Off-Hand Portraits of Prominent New Yorkers* (New York: Geo. R. Lockwood & Son, 1884), 5-6.
³²"Two Representative Managers," *Mirror*, April 12, 1879. The other manager singled out for praise with Abbey was John H. Haverly (1838-1901), of Mastadon Minstrels fame.
³³For the story of Edwin Booth's problems with his theatre, see Eleanor Ruggles, *Prince of Players* (New York: W. W. Norton & Co., 1953), 219-46.
³⁴"Our Managers," *Mirror*, July 30, 1881.
³⁵Dempsey and Baldwin, 206.
³⁶Abbey: "No 'Passion Play,'" *Herald*, November 28, 1880. Morse quote: "The Passion Play," *Dramatic News*, October 2, 1880.
³⁷"Sacred Scenes on a New York Stage," *Tribune*, September 10, 1880.
³⁸"A Message from the East," San Francisco *Call*, September 19, 1880; *Dramatic News*, October 16, 1880. Barnes had earlier mentioned, in his column of September 12, 1880, Palmer's alleged willingness to produce *The Passion* in New York. Palmer, upon his return East later that month, and seeing which way the wind was blowing, denied to New York reporters that he ever "had any intention of producing a Passion Play, and indeed, I would be afraid to undertake such a thing." At the same time, he would say nothing against the play itself: "It may be good in every particular, and, in fact, I do not doubt that it is." He also offered the opinion that James O'Neill should play Christ, "for [he] showed me his makeup while I was in San Francisco, and it resembles the pictures of Jesus very much" (interview in *Dramatic News*, October 9, 1880).
³⁹"Sacred Scenes on a New York Stage."
⁴⁰See Barnes's comment on Morse's many interviews, in "A Message from the East."
⁴¹Morse interview in "The Passion Play," *Dramatic News*, October 2, 1880.
⁴²Reprinted in "Footlight Flashes," *Chronicle*, October 24, 1880.
⁴³Abbey interview in "The Passion Play," *Dramatic News*, October 9, 1880.
⁴⁴"Theatrical Notes," *Call*, October 18, 1880.
⁴⁵Abbey interview. Details on the copartnership: "No 'Passion Play,'" *Herald*.
⁴⁶Winter, while ridiculing Morse as a playwright, conceded that his play, as a stage spectacle, would "possess two qualities which are meritorious. One of these is accuracy of historic illustration; the other is picturesqueness of tableau" ("The Drama," *Tribune*, October 18, 1880).
⁴⁷"The Passion Play," *Dramatic News*, October 2, 1880.
⁴⁸Maguire arrived in California in early October, "looking younger than ever," in the opinion of the *Call* (October 10, 1880). Among others offered contracts from

Abbey were Olive West (*Call*, October 18, 1880); and Kate Denin and John Wilson, both of whom refused (*Call*, October 31, 1880).

[49]"The Drama," *Tribune*, October 18, 1880. Boucicault had lowered the proscenium arch by some fifteen feet, in order to make the huge auditorium appear "more cozy." As a result, the rear of the 55-foot-deep stage was cut off to viewers in the balcony (*Dramatic News*, October 30, 1880). For a description of Booth's, see William C. Young, 195–99. Description of statue: "Edwin Booth's Theatre," *Tribune*, November 18, 1868, reprinted in Young, 197.

[50]"Footlight Flashes," *Chronicle*, October 24, 1880. Abbey interview, *Dramatic News*; "The Drama," *Tribune*, October 18, 1880.

[51]"The Drama," *Tribune*, October 18, 1880; "Theatrical Notes," *Call*, October 18, 1880; "Brief Notes," *Call*, October 10, 1880; "The Passion," *Dramatic News*, November 20, 1880.

[52]Abbey interview, *Dramatic News*.

[53]"Sacred Scenes on the Stage," *Tribune*, November 15, 1880.

[54]"The Proposed Passion Play," *Mirror*, October 30, 1880; "The Proposed Passion Play," *New York Evening Post*, September 25, 1880; "Warned Against the Theatre," *Sun*, November 22, 1880; "The Jews and the Passion Play," *Times*, November 26, 1880.

There were, of course, many who did take to their pulpits. For other interviews or quoted sermons, see, among many others, "The Proposed Passion Play," *Mirror*, November 6 and November 20, 1880; "Sacred Scenes on the Stage," *Tribune*, November 15, 1880; "The 'Passion Play,'" *Herald*, November 22, 1880; "Preaching Against the 'Passion Play,'" *New York World*, November 22, 1880.

Furthermore, New York was treated to a letter from the ubiquitous Reverend Smith of San Francisco, advising New Yorkers on how *The Passion* had been exorcised from California. Painting in the darkest possible hues both the production and Salmi Morse ("this Israelite, in whom there is very much guile indeed"), Reverend Smith — of "thunders-of-Sinai" fame — claimed that a "part of the staging fell" at the last performance, injuring two actresses, one of whom "has never fully recovered, and has since sued the management for damages" ("Letters from the People," *Tribune*, November 8, 1880).

Needless to say, there was no mention of such an accident in any of the San Francisco newspapers at the time. However, this demonstrates how such apocryphal stories get their start. The tale was repeated in a 1929 article about *The Passion* ("Hostility of City Prevented Continuance of 'The Passion,'" *Chronicle*, April 14, 1929).

[55]Both quoted in "The Proposed Passion Play," *Mirror*, October 30, 1880. It is possible that, as the reporter was from the *Mirror*, the pastors were tempering their remarks to fit the medium.

[56]"The Proposed Passion Play," *Mirror*, October 30, 1880; "Warned Against the Theatre," *New York Sun*; "The Proposed Passion Play," *Mirror*, November 6, 1880.

[57]Editorial, *Celtic Monthly* (October 1880), quoted in "The Proposed Passion Play," *Mirror*, October 9, 1880.

[58]"The Proposed Passion Play," *Mirror*, November 6, 1880. For some other comments by Catholic clergy, see "Sacred Scenes on the Stage," *Tribune*, November 15, 1880.

[59]*Mirror*, November 6, 1880.

[60]Morse interview in "The Passion Play," *Dramatic News*, October 2, 1880.

[61]McCabe, 592.

⁶²Payne, 325.
⁶³For the story of the *Tribune*, see, among others, Richard Kluger, *The Paper: The Life and Death of the New York Herald Tribune* (New York: Alfred A. Knopf, 1986). See also Payne, 269-81.
⁶⁴"The Passion Play in New York," *Tribune*, October 3, 1880.
⁶⁵Kluger's book, of course, is also the story of the early *Herald*. See also Payne, 255-68.
⁶⁶Editorial, *Herald*, reprinted in *Mirror*, September 25, 1880.
⁶⁷There are any number of books on the *New York Times*, both favorable and unfavorable. See, among others, Meyer Berger, *The Story of the New York Times, 1851-1951* (New York: Simon and Schuster, 1951); Gay Talese, *The Kingdom and the Power* (New York: World Publishing, 1969); and Harrison E. Salisbury, *Without Fear or Favor: The New York Times and Its Times* (New York: Times Books, 1980); also Payne, 282-94.
⁶⁸Editorial, *New York Daily Times*, September 18, 1851. This was the paper's inaugural issue.
⁶⁹"After the Passion Play," *New York Times*, November 26, 1880.
⁷⁰See the editorial reprinted in the *Mirror*, September 25, 1880. For information on Dana and the *Sun*, see Payne, 240-54, 336.
⁷¹See Tice L. Miller, "John Ranken Towse: Last of the Victorian Critics," *Educational Theatre Journal* 22 (May 1970): 161-78.
⁷²See Bordman, 720.
⁷³"The Drama," *Tribune*, October 18, 1880; also Winter, 116-17.
⁷⁴McArthur, 146.
⁷⁵Winter, *The Wallet of Time* (New York: Moffat, Yard, 1913), 336, 596. See similar attitudes in Winter's *The Actor* (New York: Burt Frankel, 1891). This moralistic outlook would harden over the following decades; William Winter would, in fact, be one of the most outspoken enemies of the modern theatre, especially the plays of Henrik Ibsen.
⁷⁶"The Drama," *Tribune*, October 18, 1880. This article, slightly adapted, forms the basis for Winter's telling of *The Passion* story in his *Life of Belasco*, 116-117. It is interesting to compare the more moderate tone of the young Winter with that of the older critic, rewriting this column some thirty-eight years later.
⁷⁷Editorial, *Herald*, reprinted in the *Mirror*, November 27, 1880.

Chapter Eight

¹"Footlight Flashes," *Sunday Chronicle*, October 24, 1880.
²"The 'Passion Play,'" *Herald*, November 25, 1880; "The Proposed Passion Play," *Mirror*, November 6, 1880; "The Passion Play," *Mirror*, November 27, 1880.
³"A Plea for the 'Passion Play,'" *Herald*, November 27, 1880; Letter to the Editor, under "The 'Passion Play,'" *Herald*, November 25, 1880.
⁴Letter to the Editor, under "The 'Passion Play,'" *Herald*, November 23, 1880. The Editor, in this same issue, dismissed Campbell's arguments as "ingenious," and reiterated his contention that the play was "an offence to religion." Again, the *Herald* called for the authorities "to declare it a crime." Information on Campbell: Napier Wilt, ed., *The White Slave and Other Plays by Bartley Campbell* (1940),

reissued as Volume XIX of *America's Lost Plays* (Bloomington: Indiana Univ. Press, 1965), ix–xiv; Bordman, 122.

⁵See Lewis and Smith, 90–94.

⁶"The Passion," *Dramatic News*, November 20, 1880. The *Dramatic News* had defended the production after the very first broadside from the *Sun*, in September. At that early date, Byrne had presciently predicted:

> The other dailies will see in this a good chance at sensational writing, and will take a hand in. Would it not be well, before taking up the cudgels for religion, faith, respect, and all that sort of thing, that the exact motive and effect of this play be inquired into?
>
> The press, in place of following the course of the *Sun*, should frown down that bigotry and intolerance which would seek to interfere with the production of this remarkable spectacle [editorial, September 25, 1880].

Byrne's advice, of course, was ignored.

⁷It was on the basis of Byrne's editorials that the *Chronicle* (see Note 1, above) described the New York press as "about equally divided."

⁸See, for example, Byrne's unflattering description of Winter in the *Dramatic News*, September 4, 1880.

⁹By November 1880, the *Mirror* was alerting advertisers that Ernest Harvier was no longer connected with the paper. The third partner was a Colonel Lewis (Binns, 41). Other biographical information: Simon; Bordman, 259.

¹⁰Binns, 37.

¹¹*Mirror*, October 7, 1882.

¹²"Brought About by Progress," *Mirror*, December 16, 1882.

¹³Binns, p. 40, puts Fiske's age at seventeen when he bought into the *Mirror*. But if Bordman's birth date for Fiske—1861—is correct, then he was nineteen at the time.

¹⁴"The Passion Play at Booth's," *Mirror*, September 25, 1880.

¹⁵"Passion Play or No Passion Play?," *Mirror*, November 6, 1880.

¹⁶"Abbey's Attempt to Bulldoze the Mirror," *Mirror*, November 13, 1880.

¹⁷"The Proposed Passion Play," *Mirror*, October 30, 1880; "Abbey's Attempt to Bulldoze the Mirror"; "Passion Play or No Passion Play?"

¹⁸"Passion Play or No Passion Play?"

¹⁹Abbey's Attempt to Bulldoze the Mirror."

²⁰*Mirror*, November 6, 1880.

²¹"The Danger We Predicted," *Mirror*, November 27, 1880.

²²"Abbey's Attempt to Bulldoze the Mirror"; "The Proposed Passion Play," *Mirror*, November 20, 1880.

²³"The Proposed Passion Play," *Mirror*, November 20, 1880.

²⁴*Mirror*, November 27, 1880. Among the signers of the petition, in addition to the expected number of ministers, are found G. W. T. Lord, of Lord & Taylor; Samuel Ward, socialite and brother of Julia Ward Howe; publisher A. D. Harper of Harper Bros.; and Henry Bergh, President of the S.P.C.A. The only well-known theatrical name published in the list is Abbey's rival manager James McVicker.

²⁵"Manager Abbey's Sickness and Our Remedy," *Mirror*, November 20, 1880.

²⁶"A Dangerous Fool," *Mirror*, January 8, 1881.

²⁷See "The Passion Play," *Mirror*, November 27, 1880.

²⁸"The Passion Play," *Mirror*, November 27, 1880.

²⁹"The Danger We Predicted."

Chapter Notes — Chapter 8

³⁰See the letters and editorials reprinted in the *Mirror*, November 27 and December 18, 1880; January 1 and 15, 1881. Circulation: "Manager Abbey's Sickness." Fiske proudly announced that he had just received an "urgent order" from his distributor, the American News Company, for 350 extra copies of the *Mirror*, "all of the previous large supplies having been sold out." There is, of course, no way to corroborate this.

³¹Small clique: "Manager Abbey's Sickness." Tool of California schemers: "The 'Crime' of the Passion Play," *Mirror*, November 27, 1880.

³²"The 'Crime' of the Passion Play."

³³"Theatrical Notes," *Call*, October 19, 1880. The benefit performance was Bartley Campbell's *Fairfax*, starring James O'Neill and featuring little Maude Adams.

³⁴"The Theatres," *Call*, October 24, 1880.

³⁵See comments in *Dramatic News*, October 9 and 23, 1880.

³⁶"The Passion Play," *Call*, November 28, 1880.

³⁷"In the Theatres," *Call*, October 31, 1880; *Dramatic News*, November 20, 1880.

³⁸"Collecting a Rabble for the Passion Play," *New York World*, November 12, 1880.

³⁹Quoted in Alexander, 55. See also James O'Neill's remarks in *Dramatic News*, December 4, 1880.

⁴⁰"The Stage," *Examiner*, December 12, 1880; *Dramatic News*, December 4, 1880; "The Theatres," *Call*, November 21, 1880.

⁴¹"The Theatres," *Call*, November 21, 1880.

⁴²Abbey interview, *Dramatic News*.

⁴³McCabe, 118, 120.

⁴⁴Quoted in "The Passion Play," *Herald*, November 24, 1880, also in "An Argument for the Passion Play," *World*, November 24, 1880; "Aldermanic Virtue Aroused," *Times*, November 24, 1880; "The Passion Play," *Mirror*, November 27, 1880. This account of the arguments presented at the meeting is compiled from all of these articles.

⁴⁵"The 'Passion Play,'" *Herald*, November 27, 1880.

⁴⁶Both editorials quoted in "No 'Passion Play,'" *Herald*, November 28, 1880. The *Herald* pooh-poohed the *Evening Express* as being one of "John Kelly's organs."

⁴⁷"The 'Passion Play,'" November 24, 1880.

⁴⁸"The Passion Play," *Mirror*, November 27, 1880; see also the interview with Booth, then appearing in London, published under "The 'Passion Play,'" *Herald*, November 25, 1880. For references to still other letters from Booth on the subject, see Daniel J. Watermeier, ed., *Between Actor and Critic: Selected Letters of Edwin Booth and William Winter* (Princeton: Princeton Univ. Press, 1971), 167. Charles Byrne termed Booth's opinion "disgustingly caddish" (*Dramatic News*, December 4, 1880).

⁴⁹"Mr. Abbey's Decision," *Times*, November 28, 1880. Abbey's card can also be found in the *Herald*, the *World*, the *Tribune* and the *Sun*, all on the same date.

⁵⁰*Dramatic News*, December 4, 1880.

⁵¹"No 'Passion Play,'" *Herald*, November 28, 1880.

⁵²*Dramatic News*, December 4, 1880; see also the comment in "More of the Passion Play," *Chronicle*, December 12, 1880. Bernhardt did not, in fact, appear in San Francisco on this first tour.

⁵³"The 'Passion Play,'" *Herald*, November 29, 1880. Noting that the other ministers had all rewritten their sermons in time for Sunday services, the *Sun*

(November 30, 1880) joked that Abbey had inadvertently helped show that New York's clergy all read the Sunday papers.

[54]"The 'Passion Play,'" *Herald*, November 29, 1880. See also the transcription of Talmage's sermon in the *World*, and the *Tribune*, same date.

[55]"The 'Passion Play' Withdrawn," *Herald*, November 28, 1880; "Abbey and Talmage," *World*, November 28, 1880.

[56]"The Passion Play and 'Salathiel,'" *Evening Post*, November 29, 1880. Croly's novel, reissued in 1901 as *Tarry Thou Till I Come*, recounted the events in Palestine following the Crucifixion, delineating the conflict between early Judaism and Christianity. General Lew Wallace, the author of *Ben Hur*, considered it one of the six greatest English novels. See George Croly, *Tarry Thou Till I Come; or, Salathiel, the Wandering Jew* (New York: Grosset & Dunlap, 1901).

[57]"The Prosperity of the Theatres and the Mirror's Victory," *Mirror*, December 4, 1880.

[58]See Fiske's comments in the *Mirror*, September 24, 1881.

[59]"The White Feather," *Dramatic News*, December 4, 1880.

[60]*Dramatic News*, December 4, 1880.

[61]Maguire: "No 'Passion Play,'" *Herald*. O'Neill: *Dramatic News*, December 4, 1880. Interestingly, at least one newspaper, the *Tarrytown Press*, made the accusation that the *Mirror* was "Haverly's sheet," and that Fiske "puffed" Haverly at Abbey's expense (see Fiske's denial in the *Mirror*, March 19, 1881).

[62]*Examiner*, December 12, 1880. The *Chronicle* gives the name of the stage manager as J. H. Vinson ("More of the Passion Play," December 12, 1880).

[63]Interview with Salmi Morse, *Dramatic News*, December 4, 1880.

[64]"The 'Passion Play,'" *Herald*, November 29, 1880.

[65]Morse interview, *Dramatic News*.

[66]Salmi Morse, letter to the Editor of the *New York Tribune*, dated November 30, 1880, in William Winter Papers, Rare Books and Manuscripts Division, New York Public Library. This letter is erroneously filed in the year 1886.

[67]"The Passion Play Read," *Times*, December 4, 1880. The *Times* reporter may have found nothing blasphemous in Morse's reading, but his editor—who quite clearly did not attend—painted a different picture in his editorial that same day:

> The dramatic monstrosity of MR. MORSE'S Passion Play is redeemed by no trace of literary merit.... Last night about a hundred persons seem to have sat patiently through what must have been to any intelligent auditor a grievous infliction. Apart altogether from the painful burlesque of sacred mysteries which such a presentation would have involved, it is inconceivable that any adjuncts of scenic effect or dramatic interpretation would have redeemed the play from the stigma of insufferable dullness....

[68]"Reading the Passion Play," *Sun*, December 4, 1880; "Reading the Passion Play," *Tribune*, December 4, 1880; "The Passion," *World*, December 4, 1880.

[69]*Mirror*, December 11, 1880.

[70]"More Passion Play," *Tribune*, December 6, 1880. The Messiah: *Sun*, December 26, 1880.

[71]*Mirror*, December 25, 1880. For more of Fiske's criticisms, see, for example: December 18, 1880; May 7, 1881; September 24, 1881.

[72]Fiske, 8.

[73]Bordman, 3. The outcome of the *Passion* controversy also did little to raise

Abbey's opinion of the clergy. On tour with Sarah Bernhardt, he sometimes exhibited an almost malicious contempt for the outraged preachers, at one point sending $200 to the Episcopal Bishop of Chicago "for the poor of your parish," explaining that he had been able to cut his advertising budget by that amount because of the "free" advertising the Bishop's scurrilous attacks had given Miss Bernhardt (Simon, 24).

[74]See Rodecape, "Tom Maguire, Part V," 261–68; also, Miriam Allen deFord, *They Were San Franciscans* (Caldwell, ID: Caxton Printers, 1947), 119–21.

[75]For the rest of the Morrisons' story, see Bennett and Kibbee. Widmer: *Mirror*, September 17, 1881. Fiske, in fact, pronounced Widmer "the best theatrical musician in America."

[76]O'Neill, 388.

[77]*Dramatic News*, February 5, 1881.

Chapter Nine

[1]Twenty years: *Mirror*, February 5, 1881. Approached other managers: "Salmi Morse's Holy Shrine," *Mirror*, October 21, 1882.

[2]"Personal," *Dramatic News*, January 29, 1881.

[3]*Mirror*, February 12, 1881.

[4]Elocution lessons: San Francisco *Call*, February 4, 1883. Articles: see Fiske's comment, "At the Theatres," *Mirror*, November 12, 1881.

[5]Program notes, *The Doctor of Lima* programme for November 7, 1881, 2; in "Nineteenth Century Programmes" Scrapbook, Billy Rose Collection.

[6]*Sixty Years of the Theater: An Old Critic's Memories* (New York: Funk & Wagnalls, 1916), 209. See also Bordman, 378.

[7]Odell, *Annals*, XI (1879–82): 437.

[8]*Times*, November 8, 1881; Towse, 213; *Mirror*, September 24, and November 12, 1881.

[9]*Mirror*, May 13, 1882.

[10]*Call*, March 18, 1883; *Tribune*, February 28, 1883. Information on Eaves Costumes: New York *City Directory*, 1880–81; Bordman, 222.

[11]Eaves purchasing copyright: *Call*, March 18, 1883. Morse to Barnes: *Call*, February 4, 1883.

[12]Details on the old armory: "Salmi Morse's Holy Shrine," *Mirror*, October 21, 1882; *Call*, February 4, 1883; Mary C. Henderson, *The City and the Theatre: New York Playhouses from Bowling Green to Times Square* (Clifton, NJ: James T. White, 1973), 147–48. Official address: advertisement for *The Passion*, *Tribune*, April 4, 1883.

[13]"Salmi Morse's Holy Shrine"; "Morse's Little Racket," *Mirror*, October 21, 1882. Stage depth: "The Passion Play," *Evening Post*, December 28, 1882. Weil & Lyster: *Mirror*, November 11, 1882.

[14]"Morse's Little Racket." O'Neill stays on tour: *Mirror*, October 28, 1880; Alexander, 56.

[15]*Call*, March 18, 1883.

[16]*Call*, March 18, 1883; "The Passion Play," *Tribune*, February 28, 1883. Severance and Ferris are also listed among the defendants in a suit brought against the backers by A. H. Warren, one of their actors, who sued them all for back pay in 1883 ("City Summary," *Clipper*, May 26, 1883). The *Tribune* reported that Ferris had first approached Morse, then enlisted Severance. Both men, according to the

Tribune, "were some years ago men of enormous wealth and substantial business position in San Francisco, but they have of late years been unfortunate in their ventures."

[17]*Barnes's Eulogy;* also, *Call*, March 18, 1883; "The Passion Play," *Tribune*, February 28, 1883. Roberts listed himself in the New York *City Directory* for 1880-81 as a "capitalist," and in the 1883-84 edition, his entry simply reads "mining."

[18]$60,000: *Call*, March 18, 1883. $100,000: *Tribune*, February 28, 1883.

[19]*Mirror*, October 7, 1882.

[20]Lyster: *Mirror*, November 11, 1882. Jesus and Mary: "For and Against the Passion Play," *Tribune*, December 24, 1882; also, "The Passion Play," *Times*, December 24, 1882. Wannemaker: "The Passion Play," *Tribune*, February 28, 1883. Warren was the plaintiff in the aforementioned suit (Note 16, above).

[21]"Morse and the Passion Play," *Mirror*, November 4, 1882.

[22]*Mirror*, December 16, 1882.

[23]"Morse's Little Racket."

[24]"The Passion Play," *New York Evening Post*, December 23, 1882. The following account, including quoted speeches, is taken from this article, as well as "For and Against the Passion Play," *Tribune*; "The Passion Play," *Times*, December 24, 1882; and "Fighting the Passion Play," *Mirror*, December 30, 1882.

[25]"Doing Good," *Times*, December 25, 1882.

[26]Quoted in "The Passion Play," *Evening Post*, December 28, 1882. The following is taken from this account, as well as those in the *Tribune* and *Times* for December 29, 1882.

[27]See Miss Eytinge's letter in the *Herald*, December 28, 1882.

[28]"Salmi Morse Determined," *Times*, December 30, 1882.

[29]"Salmi Morse Determined," December 30, 1882.

[30]Report, dated January 3, 1883, in "Department of Police, 1883" File. In Franklin Edson, Mayor's Papers, 1883-1884, Municipal Archives, Department of Records and Information Services, City of New York. Hereafter referred to as "Edson Papers." Howe and Hummel: New York *City Directory*, 1883-84.

[31]*Tribune*, January 6, 1883; "Salmi Morse's Backset," *Mirror*, January 6, 1883.

[32]"In re 'Passion Play,'" Report to U. Hartwell, Assistant Corporation Counsel, from E. R. Robinson, dated January 10, 1883. In "Mayor's Correspondence, Jan.-Dec. 1883" File, Edson Papers.

[33]*Mirror*, January 20, 1883; *Herald*, January 25, 1883.

[34]Belasco, 612. Langtry and Belasco in New York: Lewis and Smith, 423.

[35]*Mirror*, February 3, 1883. Other background information: Bordman, 168, 248-49, 526.

[36]This summary is taken from "Mr. Salmi Morse's Theatre," *Times*, February 4, 1883.

[37]"License or No License?," *Mirror*, February 3, 1883.

[38]See reports in the *Mirror*, January 27 and February 17, 1883.

[39]William Kipp [?; signature is unclear], First Deputy Clerk, Letter to Mayor Edson, dated February 10, 1883. In "Department of Police, 1883" File, Edson Papers.

[40]"Rehearsing the Passion Play," *Tribune*, February 11, 1883.

[41]See the reports on Williams's trial in the *Sun*, various issues, April-May 1879. Ironically, Williams's trial was being held at the same time that Talmage was on trial before his Brooklyn Presbytery. In both cases, Charles Dana, editor of the *Sun*, favored conviction. For another account of Captain Williams in action, see McCabe, 381-83.

Chapter Notes — Chapters 9, 10   269

⁴²"Dresses in the Passion Play," *Times*, February 17, 1883.
⁴³"The Passion Play," *Times*, February 18, 1883.
⁴⁴"The Passion Play," *Times*, February 18, 1883.
⁴⁵"A Martyr," *Times*, February 21, 1883.
⁴⁶"Persistent Mr. Morse," *Times*, February 24, 1883.
⁴⁷"The Police and the Passion," *Mirror*, February 24, 1883.
⁴⁸"Salmi Morse Arrested," *Times*, February 25, 1883. The bulk of my account is taken from this article, as well as "The Passion Play Stopped," *Tribune*, February 25, 1883. See also the reports in the *Herald* and other New York dailies for the same date.
⁴⁹"Salmi Morse's Discomfiture," *Mirror*, March 3, 1883.
⁵⁰Bordman, 666.

Chapter Ten

¹"The Passion Play Stopped"; "Salmi Morse's Discomfiture"; "Salmi Morse Arrested."
²"Salmi Morse in Court," *Times*, February 26, 1883.
³McCabe, 417. Other information on the Police Court system can be found in McCabe, 409, 412, 416.
⁴"Judicial Bosses," *World*, February 24, 1884.
⁵"Salmi Morse as a Martyr," *Times*, Feburary 28, 1883.
⁶"Salmi Morse in a Police Court," *Tribune*, February 28, 1883.
⁷"Dresses in the Passion Play," *Times*, February 17, 1883.
⁸"Salmi Morse Arrested."
⁹"Salmi Morse's Discomfiture."
¹⁰"The Passion Play," *Tribune*, February 28, 1883.
¹¹See also reports in the *Herald*, March 2, 1883; and the *Mirror*, March 3, 1883.
¹²"The Troubles of Salmi Morse," *Tribune*, March 26, 1883.
¹³*New York Music and Drama*, quoted in the San Francisco *Call*, March 18, 1883.
¹⁴"Mr. Morse Held for Trial," *Times*, March 2, 1883.
¹⁵George P. Andrews, Letter to Mayor Edson, dated March 1, 1883, in "Law Dept., Counsel to the Corporation, 1883-1884" File, Edson Papers. On Kilbreth: "Judicial Bosses," *World*.
¹⁶"Salmi Morse Discharged," *Tribune*, March 14, 1883; "Salmi Morse Discharged," *Times*, March 14, 1883. See also the reports in other dailies for the same date.
¹⁷"A Powerful Play," *Tribune*, March 18, 1883.
¹⁸"The Troubles of Salmi Morse."
¹⁹There is a curious letter in Mayor Edson's Papers, dated March 19, 1883, and signed by Albert J. Eaves. Eaves requested a license for "my theatre . . . to be known as the '23rd St. Theatre.'" The letter continues:

> The play to be produced at this house is *not* the so-called "Passion Play" (that having been by me entirely modified, by the removal of the objectionable features) but, a Moral Scenic Drama unobjectionable to any person of whatever belief.
> I herewith send a copy of the manuscript to be enacted, and shall not appeal from your decision if adverse to my place. I shall be glad if you

will yourself peruse it, or cause it to be perused by any Committee of gentlemen, in whom you have confidence, and upon whose opinion—as to the effect of the Drama—you might rely. I propose for their benefit a rehearsal—and to them alone—as invited guests.

Mayor Edson's notes on the back of the letter indicate that he suspected the request really came from Salmi Morse; Edson denied the request the very day he received it.

It is obvious that the play in question was *The Passion*, but whether the disgruntled Eaves was acting in concert with Morse or on his own is less clear.

See "Mayor's Correspondence, Jan.–Dec. 1883" File, in Edson Papers.

[20]"The Troubles of Salmi Morse."

[21]"The Passion Play Given," *Times*, March 31, 1883.

[22]"The Passion Play Given," *Times*, March 31, 1883; The *Clipper* ("Introductory," April 7, 1883) also mentions the many pickpockets plying their trade that night.

[23]"The Passion Play Produced," *Tribune*, March 31, 1883.

[24]"The Passion Play Produced," *Tribune*, March 31, 1883.

[25]"The Passion Play," *Herald*, March 31, 1883. See also "The 'Passion Play,'" *Call*, April 1, 1883.

[26]*Mirror*, April 14, 1883. *Saul* (1739) was a Biblical oratorio by Handel; the "Eroica" (1803) was Beethoven's Third Symphony in E-flat. Odell also mentions the concert of music from *The Passion*, in *Annals*, Vol. XII (1882–1885): 62.

[27]This printed circular for *The Passion*, distributed that night, was entered as Schedule B in "Society for the Reformation of Juvenile Delinquents vs. Salmi Morse," 1883, Supreme Court of the City and County of New York, filed in New York County Clerk's Office, New York City. Hereafter referred to as *S.R.J.D. v. Morse*.

[28]*Herald*, March 31, 1883.

[29]"Morse's Play," *Mirror*, April 7, 1883.

[30]"The Theatres," *Call*, April 1, 1883.

[31]Complaint, *S.R.J.D. v. Morse*. The affidavits were given by Richard Keef and Charles R. Groth, both employed in Robinson's law firm, and by John J. Fitzgerald, an Examiner in the Office of the New York City Corporation Counsel. A fourth affidavit was offered by Edwin A. Tuomey, whose identity is unknown.

[32]"Closing Mr. Morse's Temple," *Tribune*, April 4, 1883.

[33]"City Summary," *Clipper*, April 14, 1883.

[34]*Journal of the Senate of the State of New York: at Their One Hundred and Sixth Session* (Albany: Weed, Parsons & Co., 1883), 569.

[35]Senate Bill No. 418, *Bills of the Senate of the State of New York, Numbers 1 to 488 Inclusive, Printed During the One Hundred and Sixth Session of the Legislature* (Albany: Weed, Parsons & Co., 1883), I: 418.

[36]*Herald*, April 6, 1883.

[37]*Tribune*, April 12, 1883. See also other dailies for the same date, as well as the *Clipper*, April 21, 1883.

[38]As for Fiske's legislative drive against the Society for the Reformation of Juvenile Delinquents, it was not until 1886 that the New York State Legislature finally allowed the Actors' Fund to receive monies form theatre licensing fees—and then only fifty percent, the other half still being allocated to the S.R.J.D. Unfortunately, in 1900, New York Mayor Van Wyck, the first Mayor to serve under the new Charter of Greater New York (which amalgamated all five boroughs into one entity), exercised his power of "home rule" and ended the Actors' Fund share of the

revenues. The S.R.J.D., however, continued receiving monies from theatre licenses for some years after the turn of the century (Simon, 53–54, 72–73).

[39]*Journal of the Senate*, 651.

[40]*Journal of the Assembly of the State of New York: at Their One Hundred and Sixth Session* (Albany: Weed, Parsons & Co., 1883), II: 1018.

[41]*Call*, April 15, 1883. See also the *Mirror*, April 14, 1883. Morse thought briefly of publishing a New York version of *The Illustrated Wasp*.

With Morse's withdrawal of his production of *The Passion*, the urgency for the Boyd bill's passage quickly waned and it seems to have died in committee. Without the Assembly's concurrence, the Senate Bill did not become law.

Chapter Eleven

[1]See, for example, the *Clipper*, March 31 and May 26, 1883; the *Mirror*, May 19 and June 16, 1883.

[2]"City Summary," *Clipper*, May 26, 1883. Warren's contract with Morse had been signed on December 10, 1882, and called for Warren to receive $100 per week. For mentions of other lawsuits instituted against Morse and his backers, see: "City Summary" *Clipper*, May 19, 1883; and the *Mirror*, June 9 and 16, 1883, and February 16, 1884.

[3]*Mirror*, May 19, 1883; "City Summary," *Clipper*, May 26, 1883. As early as March 3, the *Mirror* had reported that several legitimate New York theatrical managers were interested in assuming Morse's lease on the 23rd Street "Temple," and urged Salmi to accept one of these offers, as that was "the best way out of the difficulty" ("A Way Out of It," *Mirror*, March 3, 1883).

[4]"Salmi Morse Happy," *Mirror*, May 19, 1883.

[5]"Salmi Morse Happy," *Mirror*, May 19, 1883.

[6]"Salmi Morse's Stock Company," *Mirror*, May 12, 1883.

[7]"Salmi Morse Happy."

[8]William Winter, for example, was able to ridicule the play's absurdities simply by describing what he saw:

> It was amid the tropical foliage and Judean architecture of the French town of Namur—where palm trees abundantly flourish and the streets are as the streets of Jerusalem—that Mr. Salmi Morse's ... hysterical audience beheld a juvenile linen-draper who studied Oliendorf's Italian grammar and gently murmured of "the brazen sunflower." There ... Mr. Frederick Paulding met Miss Ida Aubrey, and, clasping her to his bosom, touchingly remarked: "My caprice for art culminates at music."

And so on ("Bustle Among Petticoats," *Tribune*, May 22, 1883).

[9]"At the Theatres," *Mirror*, May 26, 1883; *Clipper*, May 26, 1883; "Bustle Among Petticoats," *Times*, May 22, 1883. See also the *World* and the *Herald* reviews for May 22, 1883.

[10]*Mirror*, June 2, 1883.

[11]Quoted in "In Memory of Salmi Morse," *World*, March 3, 1883.

[12]*Tribune*, June 1, 1883.

[13]*Tribune*, June 9, 1883.

[14]*Mirror*, February 16, 1884.

[15]"Introductory," *Clipper*, June 9, 1883.

[16]T. J. McGivney, quoted in "Our Own Country," *Chronicle*, February 23, 1884.

[17]"Salmi Morse's Funeral," *World*, February 24, 1884.

[18]"Mystery of Salmi Morse," *World*, February 29, 1884.

[19]Quoted in "Cause of Salmi's Death," *World*, March 1, 1884.

[20]See Miss Blackburn's comments in "Suicide of Salmi Morse," *World*, February 23, 1884; and in "Cause of Salmi's Death."

The mysterious Miss Blackburn seems to have been almost as much a fabulist as old Salmi himself. To begin with, there was a famous "Judge" Blackburn in California—William Blackburn, an early pioneer who had earned his nickname by serving as a Mexican-appointed alcalde from 1847 to 1849. But the records show that Judge Blackburn, who died in 1867, had only one child, a boy (see the Santa Cruz, California, *Riptide*, Centennial Issue, October 19, 1950; also J. M. Guinn, *History of the State of California and Biographical Record of Coast Counties, California* [Chicago: Chapman Publishing, 1904], 152).

Mary may have been distantly related to the Judge, but her actual father was an English-born carpenter named Charles Blackburn, who had emigrated with his wife to California from the Midwest in the early 1850s, during the Gold Rush; they settled in Sonoma County, north of San Francisco, in a tiny gold camp near Petaluma City. There Mary was born in 1858, the youngest of four children, and the only girl (1860 California Census for Sonoma County [Petaluma City]; in California Historical Society, San Francisco).

It will be recalled that Salmi and his wife Harriet were ranching near Sonoma County between 1859 and 1865, and, if Salmi did, in fact, know Mary's family, it was surely during this period that they met. But when Mary's father died, he did not entrust her to Salmi's care. In 1870, the California census records show, Mary, then 12, and her older brother Hiram, 14, were living with Oscar Ash and his family at Antelope Dish, a far-away mining community in Mono County, on the eastern slope of the Sierra Nevadas near the California-Nevada border (1870 California Census for Mono County [Bridgeport]). In 1870, Morse and Harriet were living in Santo Domingo. It should also be noted that Harriet claimed not to know who "this Mary Blackburn" was (Harriet Morse Interview).

In 1875, at the age of seventeen, Mary married a newspaperman from Bodie, California, named Harry J. Norton, in Virginia City, Nevada. Four years later, Norton died. By this time, the 21-year-old widow was back in San Francisco, and, as Salmi had by that time returned from the Dominican Republic (without his wife), their old acquaintanceship—again, if there had been one—may have been renewed at that time. It is possible that Mary was the "young married lady," mentioned by George Barnes, whose dramatic career Salmi had hoped to launch with his very first attempted play, *Anno Domini 1900*, in 1877.

However, the first time the name Mary C. Blackburn actually enters the story is in New York, listed among the cast of *A Bustle Among the Petticoats*.

[21]"Did Mr. Morse Commit Suicide?," *Tribune*, February 24, 1884.

[22]See McGivney's testimony, in "Mystery of Salmi Morse."

[23]"The Dramatic Week," *Tribune*, February 18, 1884. Closed since December 1: Odell, XII (1882–85): 305. The Cosmopolitan was primarily a musical house; it had begun its existence as the Metropolitan Concert Garden (*Tribune*, February 11, 1883).

[24]"Salmi Morse," *Call*, February 23, 1884.

[25]See the comment in the *Clipper*, February 16, 1884.

26"Suicide of Salmi Morse," *World*, February 23, 1884. See also "Mystery of Salmi Morse"; "Salmi Morse's Life Ended."
27Notice in *Tribune*, February 11, 1884.
28Odell, XII: 305.
29"On the Yellowstone," *World*, February 14, 1884.
30Quoted in "Clamoring for Coin," *Chronicle*, February 27, 1884.
31Quoted in Odell, XII: 305. It is not known who designed the scenery; music was composed by G. Operti.
32"On the Yellowstone," *World*; "At the Theatres," *Mirror*, February 23, 1884; "On the Yellowstone," *Times*, February 16, 1884. See also the critiques in the *Herald* and other dailies. William Winter did not review the play in the *Tribune*.

33While most journals expressed surprise that Morse was the true author of the play, the *Times*'s opening-night review had speculated: "We are fully led to the conclusion that 'On the Yellowstone' was evolved from chaos by that great and crushed genius, Salmi Morse." Anyone familiar with the rumor mill that operates within the theatrical community — and was active even in 1884 — would find it hard to believe that rumors of Morse's possible involvement had not been bandied about.
34Quoted in "Salmi Morse's Life Ended."
35"Did Mr. Morse Commit Suicide?"
36See "Mystery of Salmi Morse."
37"Mystery of Salmi Morse."
38"Who Last Saw Mr. Morse?"
39See "Salmi Morse to Rest in Peace," *World*, February 26, 1884.
40The following account of the events taking place on that Thursday evening and early Friday morning is taken from: "Suicide of Salmi Morse," *World*; "Salmi Morse's Life Ended," *Tribune*; "Our Own Country," *Chronicle*, February 23, 1884; "Did Mr. Morse Commit Suicide?," *Tribune*; "Sequels to Salmi Morse's Death," *Tribune*, February 27, 1884; "Who Last Saw Mr. Morse?," *World*; "Mystery of Salmi Morse"; "Cause of Salmi's Death."
41*New York Tribune, San Francisco Chronicle, New York World, San Francisco Daily Examiner*, all for February 23, 1884.
42Harriet Morse Interview.
43See Mary's comments in "Did Mr. Morse Commit Suicide?"; and in "Funeral of Salmi Morse," *Tribune*, February 25, 1884.
44"Funeral of Salmi Morse." Others at the funeral included the Rev. J. W. Henry Carroll, Dean of the New York College of Archeology and Esthetics; John O'Sullivan; Mrs. Gault; Mrs. Fanny Kelly, upon whose life *On the Yellowstone* was based, and who had come to New York to help pull in an audience; Signor Operti, the composer; and, surprisingly, T. J. McGivney (*Chronicle*, February 26, 1884).

Even in death, Salmi evoked controversy. Many Jews strongly protested his being allowed burial in Bayside ("Salmi Morse to Rest in Peace," *World*, February 26, 1884).
45"Salmi Morse," *Alta*, February 26, 1884. Morse's Christian friends did hold a memorial service for him, officiated by Rev. Williams, at the new quarters of Christ's Free Church, on March 2, 1884. Comparing Salmi to "Saul of old," Williams called him "a soldier" and "a man who in his day was wise." "I sat as a student at the feet of a master," the pastor told the gathering.
46Quoted in "Salmi Morse," *Alta*, February 26, 1884. O'Sullivan even tried to answer the mystery of Salmi's death by asking Morse himself, in a bizarre seance held via a "well-known Spiritual medium," in late February or early March. O'Sullivan wrote out the following message:

> MY DEAR FRIEND MORSE: Will you kindly inform me how and by what means you met your death?

The medium, in a trance, wrote out the following reply:

> MY DEAR O'SULLIVAN: Do you call me back so soon? When I was an infidel I was petted, feted and honored, but when I came out as a Christian I was spat upon and made to suffer many indignities. Do not blame me for lying down as I did. Take care of my poor child. SALMI.

The last reference was taken to refer to Miss Blackburn ("The Salmi Morse Inquest," *World*, March 3, 1884).
[47]See *World* editorial for February 29, 1884.
[48]*Tribune*, March 2, 1884. The jury's verdict was reached in thirty minutes. It read:

> We, the jury, find that Salmi Morse came to his death by drowning, but the evidence does not enable us to say whether it was intentional, and we therefore believe it was accidental.

(Reprinted in "Morse's Death an Accident," *Tribune*, March 1, 1884).
    Several newspapers pointed out that suicide had played a part in both of Morse's last plays, *Petticoats* and *Yellowstone*. The latter, in fact, had two suicide attempts (one successful, one not). But *A Bustle Among the Petticoats* had been written some years ago; George Barnes recalls in *Eulogy* that Salmi had asked him to help revise it before Morse left San Francisco in 1880. On the other hand, *Yellowstone* was a recent work, probably written after the closing of *The Passion*, and the ghoulish coincidence is striking.
    Drowning oneself was not the method of choice for suicides in 1880s New York (although the newspapers record several drownings and attempted drownings at around the same time as Morse's death). Of the 83 suicides recorded in New York City in 1880, only five—the least number—were by drowning. Eight cut their own throats; fourteen hanged themselves; twenty used guns; and twenty-three—the highest number—took poison. The remaining thirteen were listed as "other modes." See John S. Billings, *Report on the Mortality and Vital Statistics of the United States as Returned at the Tenth Census (June 1, 1880)* (Washington: Government Printing Office, 1886), II: cvi.
[49]*World*, March 1, 1884.
    On the Yellowstone closed after Morse's death, having run 15 performances. Total receipts were reportedly only $1,600; McGivney had invested almost $7,000. The closing resulted in still more lawsuits ("Clamoring for Coin"; "The Salmi Morse Inquest," *World*).
[50]*Chronicle*, February 23, 1884. Charlatan quote: *World*, February 23, 1884.
[51]"Salmi Morse's Funeral," *World*.
[52]*Chronicle*, February 25, 1884.
[53]*Mirror*, March 1, 1884.
[54]"Salmi Morse's Funeral."
[55]"James O'Neill," *Call*, June 15, 1884.

Chapter Twelve

[1] Rodney A. Smolla, *Jerry Falwell v. Larry Flynt: The First Amendment on Trial* (New York: St. Martin's Press, 1988), 302.

[2] Irwin Karp, "The Critic and the Law: Honor the First Amendment," *The Dramatists Guild Quarterly*, XV (Spring 1978): 7.

[3] See the judicial decisions listed under Paragraph 172, "Freedom of speech and of the press," *Century Edition of The American Digest: A Complete Digest of All Reported American Cases from the Earliest Times to 1896* (St. Paul: West Publishing Co., 1904) X: 1500–1504.

[4] Quoted in Payne, ix.

[5] It should be noted that the *Times*'s comment had a very specific meaning for readers of the day. Anarchism as a political movement, one that argued for the abolition of the state as an intrinsic evil, was being espoused by Emma Goldman, among others, and was of growing concern in America. In fact, one of the most infamous acts credited to the American anarchist movement—the Haymarket Square bombing in Chicago—was only a few years away (1886) when the *Times* contemptuously placed Salmi Morse among the anarchists' number.

[6] Gay, 410.

[7] It should also be remembered that in the nineteenth century it was still widely held that the restrictions placed on the federal government by the U.S. Constitution, including any proscriptions on free speech, *did not necessarily apply to the individual states*. For this reason, many state constitutions—including those of California and New York—contained their own versions of the Bill of Rights. The cherished tradition of "States' Rights," the notion that each state could operate independently of the federal system, had, in fact, been one of the South's legal justifications for the Civil War, and remained an emotionally charged issue throughout the late 1800s, despite the fact that the Fourteenth Amendment, ratified in 1868, had in effect made every state answerable to the laws of the nation at large. Like the lengthy demise of the established churches, it took until 1925 for the Fourteenth Amendment to become a nationwide legal reality.

Even had Morse in 1880 been able to argue his case on the basis of his First Amendment rights as a *United States citizen*, California or New York authorities could well have claimed their own right to treat those freedoms as they pleased.

[8] *Abrams v. U.S.* (250 U.S. 616 [1919]). More information on this and the other cases cited below can be found in Smolla, Hentoff, and Kalven; and in Fred W. Friendly and Martha J. H. Elliott, *The Constitution—That Delicate Balance: Landmark Cases That Shaped the Constitution* (New York: Random House, 1984). Readers interested in conflicting interpretations of the First Amendment can consult, as just two examples, Leonard W. Levy, *The Establishment Clause: Religion and the First Amendment* (New York: Macmillan, 1986), which argues for complete separation of church and state; and Walter Berns, *The First Amendment and the Future of American Democracy* (New York: Basic Books, 1976), which argues for government support of all religions.

[9] *West Virginia State Board of Education v. Barnett* (319 U.S. 624 [1943]).

[10] *Terminello v. Chicago* (377 U.S. 1 [1949]).

[11] *Mutual Film Corp. v. Industrial Com. of Ohio* (236 U.S. 230 [1916]). For an overview from the perspective of the 1920s, see James N. Rosenberg, *Censorship in the United States, an Address Delivered at the Association of the Bar of the City of New York, March 15, 1928* (New York: Court Press, 1928). Speaking at a time when the Wales Padlock Law—under which theatre *owners* were punished if plays

deemed "immoral" were presented in their theatres — was in force in New York City, Rosenberg decried all forms of modern societal censorship, which he characterized as "this power to prevent, as distinguished from the power to punish, this power to suppress as opposed to the immemorial American practice of punishing after fair and open trial" (4). Arguing fervently for an unrestrained freedom of speech, Rosenberg concluded his address by reminding his colleagues that "there is little to choose between dictatorship of monarch, moralist or mob" (28).

[12]*Burstyn v. Wilson* (343 U.S. 495 [1952]).

[13]*Burstyn*, at 505. However, this decision ruled only on censorship for reasons of "sacrilege," leaving open entirely the question of whether motion pictures — like books or magazines — could be censored for other reasons, such as obscenity.

[14]*Dailey v. Superior Court of the City and County of San Francisco* (112 Cal. 94 [1896]). The Court's decision was based on the argument that speech could not be stopped by prior restraint. (Once the play had opened, if it broke a law it could be closed.)

[15]Once again California was generations ahead of New York in its tolerance of the theatre. A New York Supreme Court decision in 1890, *People v. Grant* (58 Hun 455; 12 NY Supp 879), had decided exactly the opposite, that is, that a play was not protected speech. In deciding still another challenge to a New York mayor's granting of theatre licenses, the court upheld the Mayor's discretionary right to refuse a license — that is, to practice prior restraint — simply because he feared that the play to be produced *might* offend. In yet another irony to this story, one of the cases cited in defense of the Mayor's discretionary rights was *Morse v. Edson* (Super. Ct. MS. Opinion [1890]).

[16]McArthur, 141.

[17]John Perry titled his biography of the dramatist *James A. Herne: The American Ibsen.*

[18]George Rowell, *The Victorian Theatre, 1792-1914*, Second Edition (Cambridge: Cambridge Univ. Press, 1978), 162.

[19]Dates of these productions and those that follow are primarily from Bordman and Rowell; also, Daniel Blum, *A Pictorial History of the American Theatre: 100 Years — 1860 to 1960* (New York: Bonanza Books, 1960). Blum's listings for the early periods, however, are not always reliable.

Other religion-centered plays of this period include *Herod* (1900), a staging of *Everyman* (1902), and *Judith of Bethulia* (1904).

[20]Rowell, 162.

[21]The production was presented in Milwaukee and in Chicago before it was brought to New York in 1903.

[22]Quoted in Binns, 131.

[23]For the entire story of this play, see Binns, 128–135.

[24]The Bavarians turned him down (Janet H. M. Swift, *The Passion Play of Oberammergau: Its History and Significance* [New York: Fleming H. Revell, 1930], 90). A delegation of Oberammergau craftsmen/performers did come to New York in 1923, not to perform but to sell their work to American buyers (96).

[25]The Rev. Percy Stickney Grant, "The Passion Play on the American Stage," *The Theatre*, II (May 1902): 12.

[26]Grant, 12. See also Bordman, 308.

[27]Will Scarlet, "San Francisco Passion Play," *Overland Monthly*, LIV (November 1909): 507. It is interesting to ponder the fact that rowdy San Francisco was the site of so many Passion dramas.

[28]See Friedman, 157–60, 238.

[29]Alexander, 56.

[30]*A Million and One Nights: A History of the Motion Picture Through 1925* (paperback ed., New York: Touchstone Books, 1986), 366–78.

[31]See Ephraim Katz, *The Film Encyclopedia* (1979; paperback edition, New York: Perigree Books, 1982), 923–25. Porter's *The Great Train Robbery* (1903), writes Katz, "remains one of the most important milestones in screen history" (924).

[32]Ramsaye, 370. This is a cute story; however, there are no camels in the film, only one donkey.

[33]Ramsaye, 370. Vincent's connections with Niblo's Garden went back many years; he was reportedly there when the first acknowledged musical comedy, *The Black Crook*, was presented (1866), and was still there when Niblo's finally closed its doors in 1895 ("Theatres," *Times*, May 9, 1897).

It is possible that this was the same Vincent—listed as "J. H." Vincent in the *Examiner*—who served as stage manager for Henry Abbey's proposed production of *The Passion* in 1880 (see Chap. 8, Note 62, above). If, in fact, it was, then it is understandable why Hollaman and Eaves should have hired the aged Vincent to stage their film.

Even more intriguing, however, is the speculation that, as Vincent would have been familiar with Abbey's production, the final film might represent not only a very rough idea of Morse's work but a hint of how Abbey's staging would have looked as well.

[34]*Tribune* review, "Scenes on Bible Subjects," January 29, 1898; other papers' reviews and lawyer quoted in an advertisement for *The Passion Play* (film), *Herald*, February 6, 1898. The *Tribune* observed that the scenes could not have been shot at Oberammergau, as the "cinematograph" ("that marvelous machine") had not yet been invented in 1890, the last date on which the Bavarians offered their play. But the possibility of its being Morse's *Passion* was never entertained.

[35]*Times*, February 6, 1898.

[36]Quoted in Ramsaye, 375.

[37]Ramsaye, 370, 366.

[38]Quoted in Tom Stempel, *Framework: A History of Screenwriting in the American Film* (New York: Continuum, 1988), 4. My thanks to Stanley Kauffmann for first informing me of this work.

[39]Naturally, the "first" story film is a matter of much interest to film historians, and several candidates for that honor have been championed by different writers. The French pioneering filmmaker Georges Méliès (1861–1938) is most reasonably credited with telling the first complete "story" via film (see Katz, 796–98). From 1896 through 1899, he made several hundred little films, lasting a minute or two, most of them created specifically for the camera and many employing crude "special effects." But the Méliès film most often mentioned as the first complete "story" was *Cinderella*, which was shown in 1899. The Hollaman-Eaves film of Morse's *Passion* predates that by one year. *Cinderella* consisted of 20 scenes; *The Passion* was constructed of 24 scenes, and lasted more than 20 minutes. Employing a large cast of actors, it began with the Birth of Christ and unfolded, in chronological sequence, to the Ascension into Heaven. It, too, of course, was staged specifically for the camera. Thus, the case might be made that this was not only the first story film in American film history, but in world film history as well.

[40]Incredibly, the film has survived. It was found in Huntsville, Alabama, in 1965, by Charles Nicks. His wife's grandfather, Charles E. Huston, a Pennsylvania showman, had bought a print of the film and toured with it until 1905. He packed the three reels of film and the special projector into a trunk and kept them with him

until the mid-1960s, when he gave them to Nicks. Nicks, in '65, took the miraculously preserved nitrate print to New York and had it reproduced on 16mm film (Alan Moore, "Huntsvillian Finds Historic 1897 Movie," *Huntsville [Alabama] Times*, March ?, 1965, in "Passion Play [Cinema 1898]," Clipping Files, Billy Rose Collection). Copies of this historic film are now in the collections of both the George Eastman House and the Museum of Modern Art.

Viewing it today, one can easily understand the reason for Hollaman's satisfaction. As primitive and "artless" as is the film's technique — as distracting as it is to see set pieces flapping in the winter wind — the film's images nonetheless still have the cumulative power to convey a strong emotional impact. By the time the film reaches the stark brutality of the Crucifixion, it has also reached a kind of poetry; the Descent from the Cross ("after Rubens," as Morse had dictated) and the unexpected literalness of the Ascension are truly beautiful to behold. One can sense the force these scenes must have carried on the stage, and can appreciate why the Victorian mind must rebel. No wonder men cried. Reduced to the relative unreality and distancing effect of the early stationary camera, moreover, it is also easy to understand why the impact of the film should be less psychologically disturbing than that of seeing live actors in a play.

The film contains scenes not in the published 1879 script, lending credence to Morse's claim of having written at least 24 "acts." But the scenes in the film that do parallel those in the published script — the Presentation of the Infants at the Temple, Salome's dance, the Last Supper, etc. — all have moments that identify them definitely as Morse's work.

The film begins with several shepherds viewing the Star of Bethlehem, then leaving to find the Christ Child (although no nativity scene follows, but rather the Presentation at the Temple — with only seven mothers). Also included are new scenes of Jesus raising Lazarus from the dead; of Jesus ministering to little children; and a scene of His triumphal entry into Jerusalem. And while there is some attempt at scenic specificity, far more visually impressive are the costumes. The groupings of the actors are also surprisingly sophisticated — in the trial before Pontius Pilate, for example, women look on from the second story of a house, Stage Left (the sort of stage detail one would not expect from a hasty enterprise such as this) — again, indicating that Vincent may have been recreating what he recalled from an earlier production. The final scenes, from Crucifixion through Ascension, as previously noted, are also effectively staged.

One rather confusing element in the surviving film is the inclusion of a lengthy opening sequence, showing a small Bavarian village; visitors arriving at the train station; crowds walking through town to the theatre; a shot of the exterior of the theatre building itself — all of this before the staged portion of the film begins. It is obvious that the shots of the German town (an early example of establishing shots?) are authentic. But where did they come from? Hollaman could not have staged them on the roof of the Grand Central. The only plausible explanation seems to be that they were interpolated onto the *Passion* film at some later date. Perhaps they are even remnants of the Klaw-Erlanger film, which is not known to have survived.

[41]See Laufe, *The Wicked Stage*, for rather chatty discussions of censorship cases in American theatre. For censorship of films in America, see Richard S. Randall, *Censorship of the Movies: The Social and Political Control of a Mass Medium* (Madison, WI: Univ. of Wisconsin Press, 1968).

[42]The theatre in St. Louis in which the play was originally to have been staged suddenly became "unavailable" to the acting company; two local colleges then

stepped in to offer their facilities. Later, both of these colleges (one of which was privately funded) were also threatened by the aforementioned Senator.

See Christopher Durang, "Threats on *Sister Mary Ignatius* Threaten Freedom of Speech," *The Dramatists Guild Quarterly*, XXI (Winter 1985): 36–45, for the entire story. For two opposing critical views, see Pamela Schaeffer, "St. Louis Brouhaha over 'Sister Mary,'" *The Christian Century* (March 9, 1983): 219–20 (for suppressing the play); and Katha Pollit, "Bookends" column, *The Nation* (July 2, 1983): 23–24 (against suppression).

[43]John Dart, "Christian Group Attacks Film About Jesus," *Los Angeles Times*, July 17, 1988.

[44]Durang. 36. In 1986, the lobbying group People for the American Way reported that censorship of books and public school curriculums had, within one year, increased by 35 percent and doubled within the preceding four years. These incidents had come primarily — but not, the report stressed, exclusively — from the religious right (Fred M. Hechinger, "Censorship Found on the Increase," *Times*, September 16, 1986). As of this writing, television advertisers are being pressured (successfully) both by individuals and by such religious groups as Christian Leaders for Responsible Television (led by the Rev. Donald Wildmon), to pull television spots on shows unacceptable to these censorious groups. And in an eerie echo of that Victorian convention mentioned in Chapter Seven, Arizona moralists in January 1989 managed to persuade the Arizona State Republican Party to persuade the Arizona State Republican Party to pass a controversial resolution declaring that the United States is "a Christian nation."

[45](New York: Simon & Schuster, 1987), 261.

[46]Smolla, 251.

[47]"London Journal: Rushdie 'Pretty Cheerful' and Writing Defiantly," *Times*, November 7, 1989.

[48]Smolla, 302.

[49]Quoted in Hentoff, 57.

Bibliography

I. Manuscripts, Collections and Primary Sources.

Edson, Franklin. Mayor's Papers, 1883–1884. Municipal Archives, Department of Records and Information Services, City of New York.
Grace, William R. Mayor's Papers, 1881–1882. Municipal Archives, Department of Records and Information Services, City of New York.
Mason, Edward T. Scrapbook and Journal, 1880. Billy Rose Theatre Collection, New York Public Library at Lincoln Center, New York.
Morse, Salmi. Estate File, 1885–86. Surrogate's Court of the City of New York, New York.
Nineteenth Century Programmes Scrapbook. Billy Rose Theatre Collection, New York Public Library at Lincoln Center.
The Passion. Produced by Tom Maguire, San Francisco, 1879. Programme. San Francisco Archives, San Francisco Room, San Francisco Public Library, San Francisco.
"Passion Play (Cinema 1898)." Clipping Files. Billy Rose Theatre Collection, New York Public Library at Lincoln Center, New York.
The Passion Play. Produced by Richard G. Hollaman and Albert Eaves. Photographed by William Paley. 22 min. B & W. Silent. 1898. George Eastman House Film Archive, The Museum of Modern Art Film Study Center, New York.
Robinson Locke Collection. Billy Rose Theatre Collection, New York Public Library at Lincoln Center, New York.
Salmi Morse Papers, 1857–1880. California Historical Society, San Francisco.
San Francisco Theatre Research Series. MSS. San Francisco: Works Progress Administration, 1938.
Society for the Reformation of Juvenile Delinquents v. Salmi Morse (1883). Supreme Court of the City and County of New York. New York County Clerk's Office, New York City.
William Winter Papers. Rare Books and Manuscripts Division. New York Public Library, New York.

II. Newspapers, Periodical Indexes.

Houghton, Walter E., ed. *The Wellesley Index to Victorian Periodicals 1824–1900*. 3 vols. Toronto: Univ. of Toronto Press, 1966–1979.
New York Clipper. Various issues, 1883–1884.
New York Dramatic News. Various issues, 1880–1881.

New York Evening Post. Various issues, 1879–1884.
New York Herald. Various issues, 1879–1899.
New York Mirror. Various issues, 1879–1884.
New York Sun. Various issues, 1879–1884.
New York Times. Various issues, 1879–1899, 1986–1989.
New York Tribune. Various issues, 1879–1899.
New York World. Various issues, 1879–1884.
San Francisco. *The Argonaut.* Various issues, 1879–1884.
San Francisco Chronicle. Various issues, 1879–1929.
San Francisco. *Daily Alta California.* Various issues, 1879–1884.
San Francisco Daily Evening Bulletin. Various issues, 1879–1884.
San Francisco Daily Examiner. Various issues, 1883–1884.
San Francisco. *Daily Morning Call.* Various issues, 1879–1884.
San Francisco. *The Illustrated Wasp.* Various issues, 1879–1880.
Santa Cruz Riptide. October 19, 1950.

III. Public Documents, City Directories, Guidebooks.

Bills of the Senate of the State of New York, Printed During the One Hundred and Sixth Session of the Legislature. 2 vols. Albany: Weed, Parsons & Co., 1883.
Brooks, James Wilton. *History of the Court of Common Pleas of the City of New York with Full Reports of All Important Proceedings.* New York: Published by Subscription, 1896.
Century Edition of the American Digest: A Complete Digest of All Reported American Cases from the Earliest Times to 1896. St. Paul: West, 1904.
Compendium of the Tenth Census (June 1, 1880). Washington: Government Printing Office, 1883.
General Orders of the Board of Supervisors of San Francisco. San Francisco: P.J. Thomas, 1884.
Journal of the Assembly of the State of New York: at Their One Hundred and Sixth Session. Albany: Weed, Parsons & Co., 1883.
Journal of the Senate of the State of New York: at Their One Hundred and Sixth Session. Albany: Weed, Parsons & Co., 1883.
Laws of the State of New York Passed at the Ninety-Fifth Session of the Legislature. New York: Banks & Brothers, 1872.
McCabe, James D., Jr. *New York by Sunlight and Gaslight* [*New York by Gaslight*]. 1882; reprint, New York: Greenwich House, 1984.
MacDonald, William, ed. *Documentary Source Book of American History 1606–1913.* New York: Macmillan, 1916.
New York City Directories. 1850–1884. Various titles and publishers.
Pomeroy, C. P. *Reports of Cases Determined in the Supreme Court of the State of California.* Vol. 112. San Francisco: Bancroft-Whitney, 1896.
"Report of the Commission of Inquiry to Santo Domingo." In *The Executive Documents of the Senate of the United States: First Session, Forty-Second Congress.* Washington: Government Printing Office, 1871.
San Francisco City Directories. 1875–1880. Various titles and publishers.
San Francisco. *Municipal Reports 1878–79.* San Francisco: P. J. Thomas, 1879.
U.S. Census Office. California Census for Sonoma County. 1860. Microfilm. California State Historical Society, San Francisco.

———. California Census for Mono County. 1870. Microfilm. California State Historical Society, San Francisco.
Waring, George E., Jr. *Report on the Social Statistics of Cities: Part I. The New England and the Middle States.* Washington: Government Printing Office, 1886.

IV. Books and Articles.

Alexander, Doris. *The Tempering of Eugene O'Neill.* New York: Harcourt, Brace & World, 1962.
Barish, Jonas. *The Antitheatrical Prejudice.* 1981; reprint, Berkeley: Univ. of California Press, 1985.
Beebe, Lucius, and Charles Clegg. *San Francisco's Golden Era: A Picture Story of San Francisco Before the Fire.* Berkeley: Howell-North, 1960.
Belasco, David. "My Life's Story." *Hearst's Magazine* 26 (November 1914): 610-612.
"Belasco, Magician of the Stage, Is 75." *New York Times Magazine,* July 21, 1929.
Bennett, Joan, and Lois Kibbee. *The Bennett Playbill.* New York: Holt, Rinehart & Winston, 1970.
Berger, Meyer. *The Story of the New York Times, 1851-1951.* New York: Simon & Schuster, 1951.
Binns, Archie, with Olive Kooken. *Mrs. Fiske and the American Theatre.* New York: Crown, 1955.
Bloom, Allan. *The Closing of the American Mind.* New York: Simon & Schuster, 1987.
Blum, Daniel. *A Pictorial History of the American Theatre: 100 Years — 1860 to 1960.* New York: Bonanza, 1960.
Bordman, Gerald. *The Oxford Companion to American Theatre.* New York: Oxford Univ. Press, 1984.
Brockett, Oscar G. *History of the Theatre.* 4th ed. Boston: Allyn & Bacon, 1982.
Brodie, Fawn M. *Thomas Jefferson: An Intimate History.* 1974; reprint, Toronto: Bantam, 1975.
Brown, T. Allston. *History of the American Stage, Containing Biographical Sketches of Nearly Every Member of the Profession That Has Appeared on the American Stage, from 1733 to 1870.* 1870; reprint, New York: Burt Franklin, 1969.
Bruce, John. *Gaudy Century: The Story of San Francisco's Hundred Years of Robust Journalism.* New York: Random House, 1948.
Burton, Richard F. *A Glance at the Passion-Play.* London: W. H. Harrison, 1881.
Butler, Martin. *Theatre and Crisis 1632-1642.* Cambridge: Cambridge Univ. Press, 1984.
Byington, Lewis Francis, and Oscar Lewis, eds. *The History of San Francisco.* 3 vols. Chicago: S. J. Clarke, 1931.
Clark, Barrett H., gen. ed. *America's Lost Plays.* 20 vols. Princeton: Princeton Univ. Press, 1940; reissue, Bloomington: Indiana, 1965.
Clarke, Elizabeth B. "Church-State Relations in the Constitution-Making Period." In *Church and State in America: A Bibliographical Guide, The Colonial and Early National Periods.* Edited by John F. Wilson, pp. 151-163. New York: Greenwood, 1986.
Danziger, Gustav Adolph. "The Jew in San Francisco the Last Half Century." *Overland Monthly* XXV (April 1895): 281-410.

Dart, John. "Christian Group Attacks Film About Jesus." *Los Angeles Times*, July 17, 1988.
De Angelis, Jefferson, and Alvin F. Harlow. *A Vagabond Trouper.* New York: Harcourt, Brace & Co., 1931.
deFord, Miriam Allen. *They Were San Franciscans.* Caldwell, ID: Caxton, 1947.
Dempsey, David, with Raymond P. Baldwin. *The Triumphs and Trials of Lotta Crabtree.* New York: William Morrow & Co., 1968.
Dorman, James H., Jr. *Theatre in the Ante Bellum South 1815–1861.* Chapel Hill: Univ. of North Carolina Press, 1967.
Douglas, Ann. *The Feminization of American Culture.* 1977; reprint, New York: Avon, 1978.
Dunlap, William. *History of the American Theatre.* 1832; reprint, New York: Burt Franklin, 1963.
Durang, Christopher. "Threats on *Sister Mary Ignatius* Threaten Freedom of Speech." *The Dramatists Guild Quarterly* XXI (Winter 1985): 36–45.
Dwight, Timothy. *An Essay on the Stage: In Which the Arguments in Its Behalf, and Those Against It, Are Considered: and Its Morality, Character, and Effects Illustrated.* n.d.; reprint, London: Sharp, Jones & Co., 1824.
Ernst, Daniel R. "Church-State Issues and the Law: 1607–1870." In *Church and State in America: A Bibliographical Guide, The Colonial and Early National Periods.* Edited by John F. Wilson, pp. 331–346. New York: Greenwood, 1986.
Eytinge, Rose. *The Memories of Rose Eytinge.* New York: Frederick A. Stokes, 1905.
Falk, Bernard. *The Naked Lady, or Storm Over Adah: A Biography of Adah Isaacs Menken.* London: Hutchinson & Co., 1934.
Falwell, Jerry. *Listen, America!* Garden City: Doubleday & Co., 1980.
Fiske, Stephen. *Off-Hand Portraits of Prominent New Yorkers.* New York: Geo. R. Lockwood & Son, 1884.
Flaherty, David H. "Law and the Enforcement of Morals in Early America." *Perspectives in American History* 5 (1971): 203–253.
Ford, Paul Leicester. *Washington and the Theatre.* 1899; reprint, Benjamin Blom, 1967.
Friedman, Saul S. *The Oberammergau Passion Play, A Lance Against Civilization.* Carbondale: Southern Illinois Univ. Press, 1984.
Friendly, Fred, and Martha J. H. Elliott. *The Constitution — That Delicate Balance: Landmark Cases That Shaped the Constitution.* New York: Random House, 1984.
Gaer, Joseph, ed. *The Theatre of the Gold Rush Decade in San Francisco.* 1935; reprint, New York: Burt Franklin, 1970.
Gagey, Edmond M. *The San Francisco Stage, A History.* New York: Columbia Univ. Press, 1950.
Gay, Peter. *The Bourgeois Experience: Victoria to Freud, Volume I: Education of the Senses.* New York: Oxford Univ. Press, 1984.
_____. *The Bourgeois Experience: Victoria to Freud, Volume II: The Tender Passion.* New York: Oxford Univ. Press, 1986.
Gelb, Arthur and Barbara. *O'Neill.* New York: Harper & Brothers, 1962.
Grant, The Reverend Percy Stickney. "The Passion Play on the American Stage." *The Theatre* II (May 1902): 10–12.
Guinn, J.M. *History of the State of California and Biographical Record of Coast Counties, California.* Chicago: Chapman, 1904.

Hart, Jerome A. *In Our Second Century, from an Editor's Note-Book.* San Francisco: Pioneer, 1931.
Hazard, Samuel. *Santo Domingo, Past and Present; with a Glance at Hayti.* New York: Harper & Brothers, 1873.
Hechinger, Fred M. "Censorship Found on the Increase." *New York Times,* September 16, 1986.
Heintz, William F. *San Francisco's Mayors from the Gold Rush Through the Silver Bonanza, 1850–1880.* Woodside, CA: Gilbert Richards, 1975.
Henderson, Mary C. *The City and the Theatre: New York Playhouses from Bowling Green to Times Square.* Clifton, NJ: James T. White, 1973.
Hentoff, Nat. *The First Freedom: The Tumultuous History of Free Speech in America.* New York: Delacorte, 1980.
Holliday, J.S. *The World Rushed In: The California Gold Rush Experience.* New York: Simon & Schuster, 1981.
Hornblow, Arthur. *A History of the Theatre in America from Its Beginnings to the Present Time.* 2 vols. 1919; reprint, New York: Benjamin Blom, 1965.
"Hostility of City Prevented Continuance of 'The Passion.'" *San Francisco Chronicle,* April 14, 1929.
"How to Judge Judge Bork." *New York Times,* July 7, 1987.
An Illustrated History of Sonoma County, California. Chicago: Lewis, 1889.
Issel, William, and Robert W. Cherny. *San Francisco 1865–1932: Politics, Power, and Urban Development.* Berkeley: Univ. of California Press, 1986.
Jable, J. T[homas]. "Pennsylvania's Early Blue Laws: A Quaker Experiment in the Suppression of Sport and Amusements, 1682–1740." *Journal of Sport History* I (Fall 1974): 107–122.
―――――. "The Pennsylvania Sunday Blue Laws of 1779: A View of Pennsylvania Society and Politics During the American Revolution." *Pennsylvania History* 40 (October 1973): 413–426.
Johnson, Claudia D. *American Actress: Perspective on the Nineteenth Century.* Chicago: Nelson-Hall, 1984.
Johnson, William Weber. *The Forty-Niners.* A volume of *The Old West Series.* New York: Time-Life Books, 1974.
Kalven, Harry, Jr. *A Worthy Tradition: Freedom of Speech in America.* New York: Harper & Row, 1988.
Karp, Irwin. "The Critic and the Law: Honor the First Amendment." *The Dramatists Guild Quarterly* XV (Spring 1978): 6–8.
Katz, Ephraim. *The Film Encyclopedia.* 1979; reprint, New York: Pedigree, 1982.
Kelly, William. *Life in Victoria; or, Victoria in 1853, and Victoria in 1858.* 2 vols. London: Chapman & Hall, 1859.
Kenney, William Howland, III. "George Whitefield, Dissenter Priest of the Great Awakening, 1739–1741." *William & Mary Quarterly,* 26 (January 1969): 75–93.
Kluger, Richard. *The Paper: The Life and Death of the New York Herald Tribune.* New York: Alfred A. Knopf, 1986.
Krauskopf, Rabbi Joseph. *A Rabbi's Impressions of the Oberammergau Passion Play.* Philadelphia: Edward Stern & Co., 1901.
Leavitt, M. B. *Fifty Years of Theatrical Management 1859–1909.* New York: Broadway, 1912.
Leman, Walter M. *Memories of an Old Actor.* 1886; reprint, New York: Benjamin Blom, 1969.

Lewis, Lloyd, and Henry Justin Smith. *Oscar Wilde Discovers America (1882)*. New York: Harcourt, Brace, 1936.
McArthur, Benjamin. *Actors and American Culture, 1880-1920*. Philadelphia: Temple Univ. Press, 1984.
McFeely, William S. *Grant: A Biography*. New York: W. W. Norton & Co., 1981.
McGloin, John Bernard. *California's First Archbishop: The Life of Joseph Sadoc Alemany, O.P., 1814-1888*. New York: Herder & Herder, 1968.
MacMinn, George R. *The Theater of the Golden Era in California*. Caldwell, ID: Caxton, 1941.
Marberry, M. M. *The Golden Voice: A Biography of Isaac Kalloch*. New York: Farrar, Straus, 1947.
Marker, Lise-Lone. *David Belasco: Naturalism in the American Theatre*. Princeton: Princeton Univ. Press, 1975.
Marrocco, W. Thomas, and Harold Gleason, eds. *Music in America: An Anthology from the Landing of the Pilgrims to the Close of the Civil War, 1620-1865*. New York: W. W. Norton & Co., 1964.
Mates, Julian. *The American Musical Stage Before 1800*. New Brunswick: Rutgers Univ. Press, 1962.
Miller, Tice L. "John Ranken Towse: Last of the Victorian Critics." *Educational Theatre Journal* 22 (May 1970): 161-178.
"A Miracle Play in America." *The Theatre* (London) II, New Series (May 1879): 213-216.
Moody, Richard, ed. *Dramas from the American Theatre 1762-1909*. Cleveland: World, 1966.
Morse, Salmi. *The Passion: A Miracle Play in Ten Acts*. San Francisco: Edward Bosqui & Co., 1879.
Nesfield, K. M. "The Jew from a Gentile Standpoint." *Overland Monthly* XXV (April 1895): 410-420.
Newnham, W. H. *Melbourne, Biography of a City*. Rev. ed. Melbourne: Hill of Content, 1985.
O'Brien, Robert. "RIPTIDES: The Story of Salmi Morse." Parts 1-6. *San Francisco Chronicle*, September 17-28, 1951.
Odell, George C. *Annals of the New York Stage*. Various volumes, 1880-1884. Reprint, New York: AMS, 1970.
O'Neill, James. "Personal Reminiscences." *Theatre Magazine* (December 1917): 338.
Patterson, Ada. "James O'Neill – The Actor and the Man." *Theatre Magazine* (April 1908): 101-04, ix.
Payne, George Henry. *History of Journalism in the United States*. New York: D. Appleton & Co., 1928.
Perry, John. *James A. Herne: The American Ibsen*. Chicago: Nelson-Hall, 1978.
Phelps, H. P. *Players of a Century: A Record of the Albany Stage*. 1880; reprint, New York: Benjamin Blom, 1972.
Philbrick, Norman, ed. *Trumpets Sounding: Propaganda Plays of the American Revolution*. New York: Benjamin Blom, 1972.
Pivar, James J. *Purity Crusade: Sexual Morality and Social Control, 1868-1900*. Westport, CT: Greenwood, 1973.
Poggi, Jack. *Theatre in America: The Impact of Economic Forces, 1870-1967*. Ithaca: Cornell Univ. Press, 1968.
Rahill, Frank. *The World of Melodrama*. University Park, PA: Penn State Univ. Press, 1967.

Ramsaye, Terry. *A Million and One Nights: A History of the Motion Picture Through 1925.* 1926; reprint, New York: Touchstone, 1986.
Randall, Richard S. *Censorship of the Movies: The Social and Political Control of a Mass Medium.* Madison: Univ. of Wisconsin Press, 1968.
Rankin, Hugh F. *The Theater in Colonial America.* Chapel Hill: Univ. of North Carolina Press, 1965.
Rapaport, Richard. "The Chronicle Clan: Part I." *San Francisco Magazine* I (November 1987): 39.
Robbins, Millie. "The Character's Brainchild." *San Francisco Chronicle,* January 29, 1964.
―――――. "Salmi Morse — Hero or Humbug?" *San Francisco Chronicle,* March 30, 1970.
Rodecape, Lois Foster. "Tom Maguire, Napoleon of the Stage." *California Historical Society Quarterly* XX–XXI (December 1941 *et seq.*).
Rosenberg, James N. *Censorship in the United States: An Address Delivered at the Association of the Bar of the City of New York, March 15, 1928.* New York: Court, 1928.
Rourke, Constance. *Troupers of the Gold Coast.* New York: Harcourt, Brace, 1928.
Rowell, George. *The Victorian Theatre, 1792–1914.* 2nd ed. Cambridge: Cambridge Univ. Press, 1978.
Ruggles, Eleanor. *Prince of Players.* New York: W. W. Norton & Co., 1953.
Salisbury, Harrison E. *Without Fear or Favor: The New York Times and Its Times.* New York: Times Books, 1980.
Scarlet, Will. "San Francisco Passion Play." *Overland Monthly* LIV (November 1909): 497–507.
Schmidt, Leigh Eric. "Church-State Relations in the Colonial South." In *Church and State in America: A Bibliographical Guide, The Colonial and Early National Periods.* Edited by John F. Wilson, pp. 75–92. New York: Greenwood, 1986.
Schoebel, Franz. *The Passion-Play at Ober-Ammergau.* Translated by Catherine Thompson. Stuttgart: Verlag der Kruell'schen Buchhandlung, 1871.
Shaffer, Peter. *Amadeus.* New York: Harper & Row, 1981.
Sheaffer, Louis. *O'Neill, Son and Playwright.* Boston: Little, Brown & Co., 1968.
Simon, Louis M. *A History of The Actors' Fund of America.* New York: Theatre Arts, 1972.
Slocumb-Rolley, Paul. "Ye Beare and Ye Cubb." *Equity Magazine* (July–August 1965): 9–10.
Smith, Page. *The Shaping of America: A People's History of the Young Republic.* 3 vols. New York: McGraw-Hill, 1980.
Smolla, Rodney A. *Jerry Falwell v. Larry Flint: The First Amendment on Trial.* New York: St. Martin's, 1988.
Stein, Charles W., ed. *American Vaudeville as Seen by Its Contemporaries.* New York: Alfred A. Knopf, 1984.
Stempel, Tom. *Framework: A History of Screenwriting in the American Film.* New York: Continuum, 1988.
Stone, I. F. *The Trial of Socrates.* 1988; reprint, New York: Anchor, 1989.
Swift, Janet H. M. *The Passion Play of Oberammergau: Its History and Significance.* New York: Fleming H. Revell, 1930.
Talese, Gay. *The Kingdom and the Power.* New York: World, 1969.
Timberlake, Craig. *The Bishop of Broadway: The Life and Work of David Belasco.* New York: Library, 1954.

Toll, Robert C. *On With the Show: The First Century of Show Business in America.* New York: Oxford Univ. Press, 1976.
Towse, John Ranken. *Sixty Years of the Theater: An Old Critic's Memories.* New York: Funk & Wagnalls, 1916.
"Trends in Religious Life Changed Little Since '69." *Minneapolis Star Tribune,* December 18, 1988.
Valeri, Mark. "Puritanism and the Civil Order in New England from the First Settlement to the Great Awakening." In *Church and State in America: A Bibliographical Guide, the Colonial and Early National Periods.* Edited by John F. Wilson, pp. 43–56. New York: Greenwood, 1986.
Wallechinsky, David, and Irving Wallace, eds. *The People's Almanac.* New York: Doubleday, 1975.
———. *The People's Almanac #2.* New York: Doubleday, 1978.
Watermeier, Daniel J., ed. *Between Actor and Critic: Selected Letters of Edwin Booth and William Winter.* Princeton: Princeton Univ. Press, 1971.
Westgarth, William. *Personal Recollections of Early Melbourne and Victoria.* Melbourne: George Robertson & Co., 1888.
Wiener, Joel H. "Social Purity and Freedom of Expression." In *Censorship, 500 Years of Conflict,* pp. 91–102. New York: Oxford Univ. Press, 1984.
Williams, Samuel. "The City of the Golden Gate." *Scribner's Monthly* 10 (July 1875): 266–285.
Wilson, John, ed. *Church and State in America: A Bibliographical Guide, the Colonial and Early National Periods.* New York: Greenwood, 1986.
Winter, William. *The Actor.* New York: Burt Frankel, 1891.
———. *The Life of David Belasco.* New York: Moffat, Yard & Co., 1918.
———. *The Wallet of Time.* New York: Moffat, Yard & Co., 1913.
Young, John P. *Journalism in California.* San Francisco: Chronicle, 1915.
Young, Perry Deane. *God's Bullies: Native Reflections on Preachers and Politics.* New York: Holt, Rinehart & Winston, 1982.
Young, William C. *Documents of American Theater History, Volume I: Famous American Playhouses 1716–1899.* Chicago: American Library Association, 1973.

Index

Numbers in **boldface** refer to pages with illustrations.

Abbey, Henry E. 144, 148, 158, 160–162, 172, 174, 177, 184, 205, 220, 266nn.61,73, 277n.33; early career 133–134; options *The Passion* 134–135, 151; contract with Morse 136, 162, 163; losses on *Passion* 138; attacked by *Mirror* 146–156, 168, **169**; withdraws production 162–165; after *The Passion* 168–170; death of 170
The Actor's Fund 150, 170, 176, 184, 270n.38
Alemany, Joseph Sadoc (Archbishop of San Francisco) 50–52, 56, 59, 81, 118, 178, 252n.23; responds to production 77
Ambrose, E. A. (actor) 107, 114
Andersen, Hans Christian 54
Andrews, George P. (New York Corporate Counsel) 185–186, 196
Anno Domini 1900 (1877) 47–48, 272n.20
Anti-*Passion* Legislation: in San Francisco 89, 92, 100, 103–104, 105, 106–107, 110–111, 113–114, 117–118, 136; in New York 154, 159–160, 205–207; Senate Bill No. 418 (Boyd Bill) 206, 271n.41
The Argonaut (San Francisco) 68, 75, 82–83, 86–87, 104; *see also* "Betsy B."
Art in America: during Revolution 23–24
Aubrey, Ida (actress) 209, 271n.8

Bach, Johann Sebastian 23, 90; music in *The Passion* 67, 94
Bakker, Jim and Tammy 229
Baldwin, E. J. "Lucky" 46, 47, 64, 65, 68, 84, 85–86, 94, 103, 106, 112, 117, 121, 170, 248n.56; losses on *The Passion* 99, 112–113, 121
The Baldwin Stock Company 46, 64, 66, 94, 101–102, 114, 118, 132–133, 156
Baldwin's Theatre (San Francisco) 46, 47, 64, 101–102, 103, 157, 170, 175, 184, 190
Barlow, Wilson, Primrose and West Minstrel Troupe 64, 101
Barnes, George 34, 36, 37, 39, 44, 46–49, 50, 55, 56, 61, 63, 81, 105, 109, 115, 117, 121, 135, 137, 156, 157, 158, 171, 174, 176, 202, 274n.48
Barrett, Judge (New York) 206
Barrett, Lewis (actor) 158
Bassett, Russell (actor) 158
Becket (Tennyson) 226
Beecher, The Rev. Henry Ward 129, 141, 149, 187
Beecher, The Rev. Thomas K. 73
"Beecher Town" 129
Behrend, Charlotte (nee Moss) 35, 126, 217, 218
Belasco, David 4, 46, 64, **65**, 66, 67–68, 83, 92, 94, 95–96, 100–101, 105, 133, 184, 200; arrest and trial 107, 114
"The Bell of the Cross" (poem) 116
Bellows, The Rev. Dr. Henry W. 72, 138, 177–179
Ben Hur (Young) 226, 229
Bennett, James Gordon 80
Bennett, James Gordon, Jr. 142
Bennett, Joan 114
Bernhardt, Sarah 134, 139, 142, 153, 158, 163, **165**, 168, 265n.52, 266n.73

"Betsy B." (critic, San Francisco) 75, 81, 83, 86, 91, 98, 142, 200, 227; see also *The Argonaut*
Bevan, The Rev. Dr. Llewellyn 139
Bierstadt, Albert 214
Blackburn, Mary C. 211-214, 215-217, 216, 218, 248n.59, 272n.20
Blackburn, "Judge" William 212, 272n.20
Bloom, Allan 235-236
Blythe, Helen (actress) 209
Booth, Edwin 134, 161, 265n.48
Booth's Theatre (New York) 121, 132, 137-138, 144, 153, 155, 184, 210, 212, 220; history of 134
Boucicault, Dion 136, 137-138, 249n.4; 262n.49
Bowles, The Rev. Dr. B. F. 98
Boyd, Senator 205, 206; see also Anti-*Passion* Legislation
Bradford, A. E. C., Jr. (San Francisco Police) 105, 107-108
Bradley, A. D. (actor) 107, 114
Brandeis, Justice Louis 223
Brooks, Forrest (actor) 107, 114
Brown, Henry (actor) 67
Bryant, Andrew J. (Mayor, San Francisco) 91, 100, 102, 103
Burnett (San Francisco City and County Attorney) 91, 99, 100
Burstyn v. Wilson (343 U.S. 495 [1952]) 224
Burton, Charles (actor) 158
Burton, Sir Richard F.: on Oberammergau 54-55, 74, 249n.7
Bush Street Theatre (San Francisco) 46
A Bustle Among the Petticoats (1883) 119, 208-210, 211, 271n.8, 272n.20, 274n.48
Byrne, Charles 131, 132, 149-150, 164-165, 264nn.6,7, 265n.48; see also *Dramatic News*

California Theatre (San Francisco) 46, 117, 181
Campbell, Bartley 148-149
Cartwright, The Rev. Peter 28
Catholic League for Religious and Civil Rights 233
Censorship: in Victorian America 28, 127, 223, 244n.64; of plays, 111, 152, 160, 206, 225, 243nn.47,48, 251n.2, 275n.11; of books, 279n.44; see also Anti-*Passion* Legislation; First Amendment; Freedom of Speech; Laws
Chapel Street Theatre Riot 16-17
Chatham Street Theatre (New York) 72
Clarke, Alfred (actor) 111
"College Dialogues" 21-22
Comstock, Anthony 127, 131; Comstock Act of 1873 127
Consolidation Act of 1856 88, 110
Constitution, U.S. 16, 19-20, 28, 90, 127, 149, 177, 202, 222, 275n.7; see also First Amendment; Freedom of Speech; Laws
Continental Congress: ban on theatres 9, 17-18, 19, 21, 22, 28; further resolutions 23, 243nn.47,48
Cooper Institute (New York) 166, 168
Copyright Laws 52
Corcoran, Katherine (actress) 46
Cosmopolitan Theatre (New York) 200, 212, 213, 217, 272n.23
Crabtree, Charlotte ("Lotta") 133, 134-135
Criterion Hotel (Melbourne) 36-37, 55
Crosby, The Rev. Howard 128, 138, 177-179
Crucifixion Scene 81; cut from S. F. prod. 96-97, 98; reinstated 105; cut from N. Y. perf. 178, 200; in film version 231, **234**, 235, 278n.40
Curr, The Rev. Allen 71-72

"Daggett, R. M." (pseud., Salmi Morse) 212
Daily Alta California 82, 83
Daly, Augustin 161
Daly's Theatre (New York) 132
La Dame aux camillias (Dumas fils) 66, 85, 174, 239n.3
Dana, Charles 87, 143, 260n.12; see also *New York Sun*
Danforth, E. (San Francisco City Supervisor) 89, 91, 101
Danziger, Gustav Adolf 78, 253n.26
De Angelis, Jefferson vii, 5, 63
Delafield, Lewis L. 177-179, 180-181
Denin, Kate (actress) 46, 67, 262n.48
The Deputy (Hochhuth) 6
Devrient, Eduard 54
de Young, Charles 42, 80-81, 83, 117,

Index

254n.41; and Tom Maguire, 85–86; see also *San Francisco Chronicle*
de Young, Michael ("M. H.") 83–84, 254n.40
Dickens, Charles 39–40, 48, 172
Dix, The Rev. Morgan 129
The Doctor of Lima (1881) 48, 172–173, 174, 209
Donohue, Justice 188, 203
Douglas, Justice William O. 224, 236
Dramatic News (New York) 132, 149, 171, 172; see also Byrne, Charles
Duffy, Patrick G. (Police Justice, New York) 192–193, 195
Duignan, W. J. (actor) 107, 114
Durang, Christopher 233, 235
Dwight, The Rev. Timothy 19

Eaves, Albert J. 174, 175–176, 177, 180, 194–195, 208, 210, 230, 231, 269n.19, 277n.39
Eaves Costumes 174
Eden Musee (New York) 230
Edson, Franklin (Mayor, New York) 181, 182–184, 186, 187, 188, 208, 269–270n.19
Edwards, Henry (actor) 117
Erlanger, Abe see Klaw, (Marc) and (Abe) Erlanger
Eversham, J. B. (actor) 209
Eytinge, Rose 101–102, 103, 104, 180–181, 227, 254n.49, 257n.30

Falwell, The Rev. Jerry 10
Federal Street Theatre (Boston) 25
Ferris, John 176, 180, 195, 208
First Amendment 6–7, 19, 28, 90, 187, 204, 222–223, 235, 241n.25, 275n.7; ratified 16; first argued 19–20; and *The Passion* 104, 107, 159–160, 202, 223; Supreme Court decisions on vii, 223–225, 236; see also Censorship; Constitution, U.S.; Freedom of Speech; Laws
Fiske, Harrison Grey 132, 145, 146–156, **147**, 161, 164, 167, 168, 170, 172, 173, 176, 177, 184, 194, 197, 200, 201–202, 206, 210, 220, 227, 266n.61, 270n.38; early career 150–151; see also *New York Dramatic Mirror*

Fiske, Minnie Maddern 226, 227
Fitch, George K. 82
Flanagan, John F. 140
Fleming, William (stage manager) 212, 213, 214, 215
Fontaine, Felix Gregory de (critic, New York) 143
Ford, J. Henry (Police Justice, New York) 193, 195
Franklin, Benjamin 19, 24, 237
Freedom of Speech 19–20, 28, 115, 149, 160, 187, 235; applied to stage 21, 107, 150, 206, 222–223, 224–225, 276nn.13,15; see also Anti-*Passion* Legislation; Censorship; Constitution, U.S.; First Amendment; Laws
Frohman, Charles and Daniel 133

Gabb, William M. 43–44; 247nn.44,47
Gardner, Frank (theatrical manager) 172
Garrick Theatre (New York) 228
Gault, Mrs. Isabella 135, 211, 215, 217, 273n.44
Gaylor, Frank (actor) 230
Gerry, Elbridge T. (Gerry Society) 131, 155, 177–179, 260n.20
Gilmore, E. G. (theatrical manager) 161
Goldberg, Sara (actress) 209
Goodwin, Nat 135
Grace, William R. (Mayor, New York) 130, 141, 160, 177–179, 180–181
Grand Opera House (New York) 161
Grand Opera House (San Francisco) 47, 64–66, **66**, 69, 73, 74, 89, 91, 92, 99, 101–102, 103, 104, 107, 112, 134, 137, 250n.27
Grant, The Rev. Percy Stickney 227, 228
Grant, Ulysses S. 43, 247n.44, 260n.15
Granville-Barker, Harley 68
Graves, Converse L. (stage manager) 189, 194, 209, 210
Greeley, Horace 80, 142, 143
Green Pastures (Connelly) 6
"Gustaf Adolph" (unfinished play, 1884) 214, 215

Hadley, Col. Henry H. 231
Haley, John J. 44–45, 53

Hallam-Douglass Troupe 13, 17, 19, 22, 242n.42; productions 22; during Revolution 23; return to America 24–25; *see also* Theatre in America
Hamilton, Theodore (actor) 209
Handel, George Frederick 90, 103, 168; music in *The Passion* 67, 190
Harriott, Fred 48
Hart, Jerome 67
Haverly, J. H. 165, 261n.32, 266n.61
Hedly, King (actor) 67
Helms, Senator Jesse viii, 223, 236
Hemphill, The Rev. John 75, 79, 89, 117–118
Herne, James A. 4, 46–47, 226, 256n.7
Heron, Matilda 32, 85
Hill, J. M. (theatrical manager) 174
Hollaman, Rich G. 230–233, 277n.33, 277–278n.40
Holmes, Oliver Wendell vii, 223–224
Howe, William F. (lawyer) 182, 185, 189–191, 193, 196, 203

Ibsen, Henrik 226, 239n.3, 263n.75
The Illustrated Wasp (San Francisco) 80, 115–116, 118–119, 137, 271n.41
Ingersoll, Robert 148, 149, 166
Ingraham, Judge 184–185, 186, 187
Irving, Henry 226

Jackson, Thomas (actor) 158
Janauschek, Fanny (actress) 172–173
Jay, Robert 38, 45
Jefferson, Thomas 15, 19, 21, 22, 25, 90; "Act for Establishing Religious Freedom" 15–16
Jesus Christ Superstar (Rice/Webber) 6
Jews: in San Francisco 39, 74, 76, 78, 91, 97, 246n.34, 252n.19; responses to *Passion* 76, 78, 139, 179, 199, 253n.26; in New York 139, 164, 273n.44
Johns, Tremenhere 85
Joint Committee on Health and Police and Licenses and Orders (San Francisco) 117–118
Jones, Senator 199
Jones, George 142
Jordon, George (actor) 158

Kalloch, The Rev. Isaac Smith 78–79, 117, 129
Karp, Irwin 222
Kearney, Denis 71, 77, 115, 166, 252n.23; *see also* Workingman's Party of California
Keller Troupe 99, 256n.21
Kelly, Mrs. Fanny 213, 273n.44
Khomeini, The Ayatollah 236
Kilbreth, James T. (Police Justice, New York) 195–196
King of William, James 80
King Rene's Daughter (1882) 174
Kip, Bishop William Ingraham 74, 251–252n.11
Klaw, (Marc) and (Abe) Erlanger 230, 278n.40
Korbel Brothers 115
Kraus, Father Josaphat 228

Lambs' Club 228
Langtry, Lillie 170, 184
The Last Temptation of Christ (Scorsese) 6, 233–235
Laws: moral laws 11–12, 18, 25, 28, 111, 126, 149, 160, 179, 181, 225; antitheatre laws 13, 24–25, 103, 155, 222–223, 243nn.47,48
Leavitt, M. B. (theatrical manager) 70, 112, 251n.2
Leonardo da Vinci 167
Lloyd, The Rev. William 139
Long, John N. (actor) 67, 102, 181; arrest and trial 107, 114
Louderback, Judge Davis 106, 107–108, 115
Lyster, Fred (conductor) 48–49, 64, 175, 176, 200, 209, 210

McConnell, J. (actor) 107, 114
McGivney, Thomas J. 212, 214–217, 216, 218, 273n.44; losses on *The Passion* 274n.49
Mackaye, Steele 161
Madison, James 15, 20, 25
Madison Square Theatre (New York) 132, 184
Maguire, Tom 31, 74, 76, 89, 92, 117, 122, 133, 137, 157, 165, 174, 181; early career 32–33, 41–43, 46; meets Salmi Morse 48–49; and *The Passion* 64–69,

Index

94, 100–102; Charles de Young feud 85–86; and Henry Abbey 134–135, 156, 163; after *The Passion* 170; death of 170; see also *The Passion*
Mansfield, Richard 226
Mapplethorpe, Robert viii, 6
Markham, Pauline 213
Marshall, Edward C. (lawyer) 106–109
Mary of Magdala (Heyse) 226–227, 228
Mayhew, Katie 67, 250n.29
Melbourne, Australia: during Gold Rush 36–37, 246n.23
Melies, Georges 277n.39
Mendes, Rabbi F. de Sola 139
Menken, Adah Isaacs 42, 247n.40
Metropolitan Opera House (New York) 170
A Midwinter Night's Dream (1883) 99, 209
Montgomery, George E. (critic, New York) 143
Morehouse, Lena (actress) 209
Morris, Clara (actress) 135
Morrison, Lewis (actor) 46, 61, 63, 67, 103, 137, 157, 158, 165, 170; arrest and trial 107, 114
Morrison, Judge Robert F. 109, 110, 113–114, 115, 136
Morse, Harriet Jay 37–38, 43–45, 55, 217–218, 272n.20; marriage to Salmi 38–39; views on *The Passion* 53
Morse, Salmi (Samuel Moss): 5, 216; 74, 77, 84, 103, 119–122, 156, 163, 171, 172–74, 236–37, 245n.17, 271n.41, 272n.20; death of 3–4, 33, 217–219; abilities as playwright 6, 56, 95, 173, 209–210; early life 29, 33–35, 36–37, 37–38, 38–40, 43–45, 45–49, 211; descriptions of 34, 137, 167, 219–221; marriage 38–39; conversion to Christianity 38–39, 83, 166, 218; in Holy Land 39–40, 50, 136, 166; Jewish background 76–77, 83, 157, 174, 218; First Amendment claims 104, 106, 108, 115–116, 177, 180–181, 187, 206, 223; as editor of *Wasp* 115–116, 119; arrest and trials in N.Y. 189–191, 192, 193, 195, 197, 206, 223; withdraws *Passion* 207; will 212; inquest 218– 219, 274n.48; funeral 218, 273n.44; seance for 273–274n.46; see also *Anno Domini 1900*; "The Bell of the Cross"; *A Bustle Among the Petticoats*; *The Doctor of Lima*; "Gustaf Adolph"; *King Rene's Daughter*; *A Midwinter Night's Dream*; *On the Yellowstone*; *The Passion*
Moss, Charlotte see Behrend, Charlotte (nee Moss)
Moss, Lewis 35, 44, 126
Moss, Samuel see Morse, Salmi
Motion Pictures in America: early history of 229–230; first "story" film 230, 277n.39; and *The Passion* 231–233, 277nn.39,40
Murphy (District Attorney, San Francisco) 111
Murray, Randolph (actor) 213
Music in America 23
Mutual Film Corp. v. Industrial Com. of Ohio (236 U.S. 230 [1916]) 224

Nash, The Rev. Stephen P. 177–179
National Reform Association 127
Nazareth (Greene) 228
New York City: growth of 3, 125–127; colonial antitheatre protests in 15, 24–25, 130; theatre in 1870s 47, 121, 133; description of (1880) 125–127, 274n.48; religion in 127–130, 139, 178; newspapers in 141–144, 159; court system 192–193
New York City Board of Aldermen 154, 155, 159–160, 192–193, 204; description of 159
New York Clipper 132
New York Dramatic Mirror 87, 131, 145, 146–156, 168, 206; founding of 132; see also Fiske, Harrison Grey
New York Evening Express 160, 225
New York Evening Post 143, 177, 181
New York Herald 141, 142, 144, 148, 149, 151, 155, 161, 163, 180–181, 184, 205, 225
New York Sun 141, 143, 151
The New York Times 141, 142–143, 187, 189, 223; anti-Semitism of 142–143, 180, 187
New York Tribune 141, 142, 149, 151, 155, 160, 225
Newman, The Rev. John P. 128, 129, 130, 138, 260n.15
Niblo's Garden Theatre (New York) 161, 230
Noble, The Rev. T. K. 74, 76

Oberammergau Passion Play 52, 53, 159-160, 168, 206, 227-228, 230, 249n.7, 276n.24, 277n.34; history of 54-55; as viewed by Americans 55, 74, 84; compared to *Passion* 57-59; see also Passion Plays
On the Yellowstone (1884) 212-215, 217, 274n.49
O'Neill, James 46, 48-49, 63, 65, 74, 76, 103, 118, 121, 137, 156-158, 165, 175-176, 181, 184, 191, 220-221, 230, 231, 250n.25, 257n.44, 265n.33; in role of Christ 64, 67, 73, 84, 91, 94-96, 102, **120**, 255-256n.6, 261n.38; arrest and trial 105, 106-111, 114; after *The Passion* 170-172; attempts to restage *Passion* 172, 229
O'Sullivan, John L. 211, 218-219, 273-274n.46

Palmer, A. M. (theatrical manager) 121, 135, 161, 261n.38
Park Theatre (New York) 132, 133, 143, 153, 165; burning of 170, 184
The Passion: **51, 93**; first proposed 49; published 50; anti-Semitism in 53, 58-59; analysis of 53-55, 57-63; first reading 55-56; Protestant response to 56, 73-78; rehearsals 67-69; public debate on 70; ticket prices 74; as "Catholic tainted" 76-77; newspaper response to 80-87, 98, 105; opening night 91-97; closing 100-102; reopening 102, 104-105, 107-109; other productions proposed 103, 114, 117, 118, 119-120, 135, 172, 208, 211, 229, 231; closes in San Francisco 112; Abbey's N.Y. prod. 136-137, 144, 157-158; historical accuracy of 137, 178; N.Y. clergy's reponse to 138-141, 163; newspaper response to 141-145, 164-165, 201-202; theatre community response to 145-150; Abbey withdraws 162; Cooper Inst. reading 166-167; in the 23rd St. Temple 176, 186-187, 188-191; cost of 181, 185, 203; actor dissatisfaction 197-198, 202, 204, 208, 210; only N.Y. perf. 197-201; injunction against 203, 206; closes in N.Y. 206; after Morse's death 229-233
The Passion Play (film, 1898) 232, **234**;

229-233, 277nn.33,34,39, 277-278n.40; filming of 230; reactions to 231; importance of 231-233; rediscovery of 277n.40
Passion Plays 52, 53, 84, 87, 99, 118, 136, 227-229, 254n.49; see also Oberammergau Passion Play
Paulding, Frederick (actor) 146, 209, 271n.8
Pickering, Loring 83, 157
Piercy, Samuel (actor) 46, 67, 103
Platt, The Rev. Dr. 88, 115, 117
Players' Club 151
Polk, James K. 30
Porter, Edwin S. 230
Potter, The Rev. Henry C. **128**, 138, 177-179
Power, Tyrone 227
Prynne, William 11-12
Pulitzer, Joseph 219
Puritans: attacks on theatre 11-12; Great Migration of 12; and music 23; see also Religion in America

Quincy, Josiah 22, 242n.46
Quo Vadis? (Stange) 226, 229

Raymond, Henry Jarvis 142
Reform Societies 126-127, 131, 155; see also Society for the Reformation of Juvenile Delinquents; Gerry, Elbridge T.; Comstock, Anthony
Reid, Whitelaw 142, 160, 182; see also *New York Tribune*
Reinhardt, Max 68
Religion in America 9-16, 26-28, 244n.60; Protestant/Catholic friction 8, 11, 27, 72-73; colonial establishment 9-11; Great Awakening 14; church/state separation 14-15, 16, 26-28, 90, 243-244n.59, 275n.7
Religious Drama in America 49, 163, 226-229
Religious Plastic Art Company 99, 256n.20, 257n.42
Rieman, George B. 119, **120**
Roberts, George 176, 180, 208, 210
Robinson, Dr. David "Yankee" 30-31
Robinson, Edward R. 131, 177-179, 182-184, 188, 202-203; see also

Society for the Reformation of Juvenile Delinquents
Robinson, Forrest (actor) 157, 158, 165
Rossellini, Roberto 224
"The Round Table" 48–49, 172, 175
Rountree, James O. (City Supervisor, San Francisco) 89–90, 91, 101, 255n.57; anti-Passion resolution 89, 92, 100
Rushdie, Salman viii, 236; see also *The Satanic Verses*
Russell, Frank (actor) 230
Russell, Sol Smith 135–136

Salathiel, the Wandering Jew (Croly) 164, 266n.56
Salle d'Asile Francaise (French Orphan Asylum) 201, 202
Salvation Army 187
San Francisco: history of 29–33, 40–43, 45, 47–48, 70–71; theatre in 30, 32–33, 41–43, 46–49, 66, 112–113, 122; Protestant influence on 40–41; Catholic immigrants in 41, 71; theatre in 1870s 47–48, 70–71; Protestant/Catholic tensions in 56, 71, 76, 254n.52; newspapers in 80, 115
San Francisco Board of Supervisors 79, 88–91, 99–100, 103, 104, 108, 110, 114, 115, 117, 159, 204; description of 88
San Francisco Chronicle 33, 42, 71, 80, 83–86, 110, 112, 142, 146, 157, 220; opposition to *The Passion* 83–86; see also de Young, Charles; de Young, Michael ("M. H.")
Sapho (Fitch) 239n.3
The Satanic Verses (Rushdie) 6; see also Rushdie, Salman
Schilling, Frederick A. 192, 209, 211, 215
Schwab, Frederick (critic, New York) 143
Searle, Cyril 101
Severence, M. 176, 180, 195, 208
Seymour, William (actor) 67; arrest and trial 107, 114
Shakespeare, William 11, 21, 22, 33, 48, 119, 137, 208, 213, 214
Shaw, George Bernard 127, 239n.3
The Sign of the Cross (Barrett) 229
Sister Mary Ignatius Explains It All For You (Durang) 6, 233
Smith, Solon B. (Police Justice, New York) 192, 193, 195–196
Smith, The Rev. W. J. 73–74, 75, 92, 252n.11, 262n.54
Society for the Reformation of Juvenile Delinquents 126, 131, 155, 176, 177, 182, 184, 202, 206, 270nn.27,31,38; injunction against *The Passion* 203, 206; see also Reform Societies; Robinson, Edward R.
Standard Theatre (New York) 132
Standard Theatre (San Francisco) 49
Strakosch, Max 210
Strauss, Levi 78
Strong, Fred (actor) 230
Stuart, Alexander H. (actor) 173
Stuart, Everard (business manager) 175, 177
Sutliffe, Albert (critic, San Francisco) 98, 105

Talmage, The Rev. T. De Witt 28, 72, 128, 129, 138, 154–155, 163, 164, 259–260n.12; "falsehood" trial 129
Tammany Hall 130, 140–141
Taylor, James H. (actor) 173
Theatre in America: first acting companies 8–9, 13, 240n.18; banned by Continental Cong. 9, 17–18, 19; and the church 9–16, 26–28, 72–73, 241–242n.39; colonial protests 13, 15, 16–17; and the law 16–24, 28, 222, 225–226; Revolutionary War-era plays 20–21; "drama" v. "stage" 21–22, 56, 82, 104; after Revolution 25–26; rise in 1800s 73, 131–133, 153; see also Chapel Street Theatre Riot; Hallam-Douglass Troupe; Freedom of Speech; Laws; "Ye Beare and Ye Cubb"
Theatre Licensing Act of 1872 ("$500 Theatre Tax") 131, 150, 155, 176, 183, 185, 188, 193, 202, 260n.16
Thorne, Charles R., Sr. 190
Towse, John Ranken (critic, New York) 143, 173, 226
23rd Street Temple (New York) 175–181, 182, 185, 188, 194–195, 196–197, 208–210, 230, 269n.19, 271n.3; description of 175; cost of renovation 176

Tyler, Royall 49
Tyng, The Rev. Stephen H., Jr. 129

Union Square Theatre (New York) 121

Vincent, J. H. (stage manager) 165, 277n.33
Vincent, L. J. (Leon John) 230, 277n.33
Voegtlin, William T. (designer) 158

Wade's Opera House *see* Grand Opera House (San Francisco)
Wallack, Lester 132, 161
Walling, George W. (Police Superintendent, New York) 186
"Mr. Walton" (actor) 103
Wannemaker, The Rev. (actor) 176, 197, 200
Warren, A. H. (actor) 176, 208, 267n.16, 271n.2
Washington, George 21, 22, 243n.47
Weil, Oscar (composer) 175, 200
West, Olive (actress) 46, 67, 262n.48
Wetherell, Nellie (actress) 158
White, Andrew J. (Police Justice, New York) 193
Whitecar, W. C. (actor) 158
Whitefield, The Rev. George 14
Whitney, W. C. (Corporation Counsel, New York) 159–160
Widmer, Henry E. (composer) 67, 94, 137, 156, 165, 166, 170, 250n.29, 267n.75
Wilkes, May (actress) 67
Williams, Captain Alexander S. (New York Police) 186, 188–191, 192–193, 198–199, 203, 268n.41
Williams, The Rev. S. Thomas 210, 215, 273n.45
Wilson, Percy 48
Winter, William vii, 53, 58–59, 60, 64, 75–76, 94, 97, 107, 137, 143–144, 149, 161, 166, 168, 212, 227; views on theatre 143, 223, 226; views on *The Passion* 144
Wood, Rose (actress) 46, 170, 250n.28, 258n.23
Wooland, J. H. (actor) 107, 114
The Workingman's Party of California 71, 77, 78–79, 84, 88, 117, 252–253n.23; *see also* Kalloch, The Rev. Isaac Smith; Kearney, Denis

"Ye Beare and Ye Cubb" 12

www.ingramcontent.com/pod-product-compliance
Ingram Content Group UK Ltd.
Pitfield, Milton Keynes, MK11 3LW, UK
UKHW041926140426
5217IPUK00014B/333